# Transactions
## of the
# Royal
# Historical
# Society

SIXTH SERIES

VI

Published by the Press Syndicate of the University of Cambridge
The Pitt Building, Trumpington Street, Cambridge CB2 1RP
40 West 20th Street, New York, NY 10011 –4211, USA
10 Stamford Road, Oakleigh, Melbourne 3166, Australia

First published 1996

*A catalogue record for this book is available from the British Library*

*Library of Congress cataloguing in publication data applied for*

ISBN 0 521 58330 6 hardback

SUBSCRIPTIONS. The serial publications of the Royal Historical Society,
*Royal Historical Society Transactions* (ISSN 0080-4401), Camden Fifth Series (ISSN
0960-1163) volumes and volumes of the Guides and Handbooks (ISSN 0080-
4398) may be purchased together on annual subscription. The 1995 subscription
price (which includes postage but not VAT) is £35 (US$56 in the USA, Canada
and Mexico) and includes Camden Fifth Series, volumes 5 and 6 (published in
July and December) and Transactions Sixth Series, volume 5 (published in
December). There is no volume in the Guides and Handbooks series in
1995. Japanese prices (including ASP delivery) are available from Kinokuniya
Company Ltd, P.O. Box 55, Chitose, Tokyo 156, Japan. EU subscribers (outside
the UK) who are not registered for VAT should add VAT at their country's
rate. VAT registered subscribers should provide their VAT registration number.
　　Subscription orders, which must be accompanied by payment, may be
sent to a bookseller, subscription agent or direct to the publisher: Cambridge
University Press, The Edinburgh Building, Shaftesbury Road, Cambridge CB2
2RU, UK; or in the USA, Canada and Mexico: Cambridge University Press,
40 West 20th Street, New York, NY 10011-4211, USA. Copies of the publications
for subscribers in the USA, Canada and Mexico are sent by air to New York
to arrive with minimum delay.

SINGLE VOLUMES AND BACK VOLUMES. A list of Royal Historical
Society volumes available from Cambridge University Press may be obtained
from the Humanities Marketing Department at the address above.

*Printed and bound in the United Kingdom by Butler & Tanner Ltd, Frome and London*

# CONTENTS

TRANSACTIONS OF THE
# ROYAL HISTORICAL SOCIETY
## PRESIDENTIAL ADDRESS

By R.R. Davies

## THE PEOPLES OF BRITAIN
## AND IRELAND 1100–1400
## III. LAWS AND CUSTOMS

READ 24 NOVEMBER 1995

EDWARD I and his judges delivered some of the most resounding *obiter dicta* on the nature of law and justice in the medieval period; but on occasion they found themselves at the receiving end of such pontificating practices. One such occasion took place at Oswestry in January 1279. Walter de Hopton and his fellow justices were ambling their way through the interminable dispute between Llywelyn ap Gruffudd, prince of Wales, and Gruffudd ap Gwenwynwyn, lord of Powys and client of the English king. In rotund phrases, at once deeply flattering and profoundly challenging to Edward I, Llywelyn delivered himself of a grand declaration about the relationship of law, people and political power:

> Each province under the empire of the lord King has its own laws and customs according to the habit and usage of the parts in which it is situated—for example, the Gascons in Gascony, the Scots in Scotland, the Irish in Ireland and the English in England. This indeed exalts rather than diminishes the crown of the lord King. The Prince accordingly requests that he likewise should have his Welsh law and should proceed according to it. He has all the more reason for making this request since the King, of his own free will, in the recent peace treaty concluded between them, granted to Llywelyn and all Welshmen the right to have their own law. By natural justice (*de jure communi*) he ought to have Welsh law and custom, just as other peoples (*naciones*) under the empire of the lord

King have their laws and customs according to their language, or ethnic affiliation (*secundum linguam suam*).[1]

Llywelyn's statement, resonant as it may have been, was in fact as *parti pris* as many of Edward I's own self-confident declarations; but his viewpoint was by no means personal to him. His words were directly echoed by those of his ambitious brother, Dafydd ap Gruffudd;[2] and they were even more pointedly and bitterly echoed by Maredudd ab Owain, one of the native rulers of south-west Wales:

All Christians have their laws in their own lands. Even the Jews have their laws among the English. They (i.e. the Welsh of northern Ceredigion) and their ancestors had their own immutable laws and customs until the English deprived them of their laws after the recent war (i.e. of 1276–7).[3]

In what turned out to be the last desperate struggle to retain a measure of political independence, the Welsh had clearly decided to use the identity of their own laws and customs as an issue around which they could unite and as an ideological platform on which to base their case.[4] The Scots would certainly have accepted the validity of the Welsh argument. When it came to be their turn to try to resist the suffocating demands of the English king's claim to superior lordship over them, they likewise based their case in part—though never, it is true, as exclusively as did the Welsh, for they had other strings to their bow— on the defence of their 'rights, laws, liberties and customs', whether it be in the relatively trusting days of the treaty of Birgham in summer 1290 or, in the aftermath of the long struggle for independence, during the peace negotiations of 1323.[5]

There was, of course, nothing insular, or peninsular, about the arguments advanced by the Welsh and the Scots. The assumptions that laws and customs helped to define a people and that the right to enjoy their own laws and customs was an universal privilege of all peoples,

[1] *Welsh Assize Roll 1277–84*, ed. J. Conway Davies (Cardiff, 1940), 266.
[2] *Calendar of Ancient Correspondence concerning Wales*, ed. J.G. Edwards (Cardiff, 1935), 73 (1281–2).
[3] *Registrum Epistolarum fratris Johannis Peckham*, ed. C.T. Martin (Rolls Series, 1882–5), II, 454.
[4] R.R. Davies, 'Law and National Identity in Thirteenth Century Wales', in *Welsh Society and Nationhood. Historical Essays Presented to Glanmor Williams*, ed. R.R. Davies *et al.* (Cardiff, 1984), 51–69.
[5] *Documents Illustrative of the History of Scotland 1286–1306*, ed. J. Stevenson (Edinburgh, 1870), I, 162–73; G.W.S. Barrow, 'A Kingdom in Crisis: Scotland and the Maid of Norway', *Scottish Historical Review*, LXIX (1990), 120–41 (Treaty of Birgham); *Anglo-Scottish Relations 1174–1328: Some Select Documents*, ed. E.L.G. Stones (Oxford, 1965), 155 (1323). For another example: G.W.S. Barrow, *Robert Bruce and the Community of the Realm of Scotland* (3rd edn, Edinburgh, 1988), 130.

or at least of all Christian peoples, were among the commonplaces of medieval thought. Indeed law was commonly defined in the early middle ages in terms of peoples (such as Lombards or Visigoths) rather than of rulers, kingdoms or territories. A territorial concept of law, it is true, came to establish itself alongside, and perhaps increasingly instead of, such an ethnic view of law; but in the borderlands of Europe in particular, in societies where two or more peoples co-existed and intermingled, a strong sense that each people had its own distinctive laws persisted, and with it the conviction that within such mixed societies each individual and each ethnic group should enjoy his or its own laws and customs.[6] Wales and Ireland remained throughout the medieval period such societies; law and customs defined in good measure what it meant to be Welsh or Irish in what were otherwise politically fragmented and partially, or completely, conquered societies.

Such views were not the prerogative of peripheral or archaic societies; they would have been regarded as unexceptionable in the highest scholarly circles of medieval England and Europe. 'Different peoples differ from one another', so Regino of Prüm observed around the year 900, 'in descent, manners, language, and laws'; more than two centuries later Bernard, the first Norman bishop of St Davids, concurred entirely and concluded that by such a definition the Welsh were certainly a distinct people.[7] Much at the same time William of Malmesbury was composing his history of the English and revealing that he likewise subscribed, at least historically, to the same assumption. When he described how Egbert of Wessex forged the kingdoms of England into one empire under a single lord, he also added that each constituent part of Egbert's empire was allowed to retain its own laws.[8] It was precisely the same point as the one which Llywelyn ap Gruffudd's spokesman made in January 1279.

Nor did more hard-headed politicians and lawyers necessarily challenge such a view. The English may have found the laws of the Irish, Scots and Welsh bizarre and sometimes utterly objectionable; but they did not in general challenge the right of these peoples to enjoy their own laws, even under English rule. In Wales, for example, in the thirteenth century over-zealous royal officials were recurrently reminded to treat the Welsh 'according to Welsh law and custom' or 'according to the laws and custom of those parts'; it was only mischief-making *provocateurs* who put about the false rumour that the king wished to

[6] Cf. Robert Bartlett, *The Making of Europe. Conquest, Colonization and Cultural Change* (1993), 204–11.
[7] Regino of Prüm quoted in S. Reynolds, *Kingdoms and Communities in Western Europe 900–1300* (Oxford, 1984), 259; Bishop Bernard: Giraldus Cambrensis, 'De Invectionibus', ed. W.S. Davies, *Y Cymmrodor*, XXX (1920), 141–2.
[8] William of Malmesbury, *Gesta Regum*, ed. W. Stubbs (Rolls Series, 1887–9), I, 101–2.

abolish Welsh law.[9] Lords and chroniclers sometimes boasted how the Normans and the English had imposed their rule and laws on the Welsh; but even such braggarts were sensitive enough to concede that ethnic divisions and sensibilities had been respected. The earl of Warwick, for example, claimed in 1358 that his ancestor, Roger, had conquered Gower and established the law there at his will; but he was prudent enough to add 'one (law) for the Welsh, and one for the English'.[10] He could hardly do otherwise for in the Gower of his day, as indeed in almost every part of Wales, the existence of two separate peoples with two distinct laws was fully recognised in a pattern of English courts on the one hand and Welsh courts of the other, each with its own distinctive procedures and substantive laws.[11] And much the same was true of Ireland, or such parts of Ireland as were within the ambit of English rule. There could be no more practical recognition of the fact that law defined a people and that a people was defined by law.

The English likewise subscribed to the view that law was the property and one of the characteristics of a people. We are so used to defining the English common law in territorial terms as the law of England, *lex Anglie* or *consuetudo regni*—and indeed are encouraged to do so by the regnal and territorial language of contemporary law books[12]—that we forget that such a view of law is actually constricting. The common law was the law of the English rather than the law of England.[13] The large English communities in Wales and Ireland were adamant on that point; they, as much as the people who lived in England, were among the beneficiaries of English law. The kings of England and the English lords in Wales fully endorsed their claim. Nor was this more rhetoric. Some of the most distinctive procedures and devices of English law— such as possessory assizes or the final concord—were freely available to the English communities in south Wales soon after they were introduced in England.[14] By the fourteenth century, and probably well

---

[9] *Cal. Patent Rolls 1232–47*, 430; *Close Rolls 1247–51*, 113, 236, 408, 541, 555; *1251–3*, 185, 419, 465, 467, 483, 511; *Welsh Assize Roll*, 286.

[10] C.A. Seyler, 'The Early Charters of Swansea and Gower', *Archaeologia Cambrensis*, 7th series, IV (1924), 77.

[11] R.R. Davies, *Lordship and Society in the March of Wales 1282–1400* (Oxford, 1978), 310–12.

[12] A. Harding, 'Legislators, Lawyers and Law-Books', in *Lawyers and Laymen. Studies Presented to Dafydd Jenkins*, ed. T.M. Charles Edwards *et al.* (Cardiff, 1986), 237–8.

[13] Cf. the comment in Roger Howden's chronicle: 'by his [Glanvill's] wisdom the laws which we call English were established' in *Tractatus de Legibus et Consuetudinibus Regni Anglie qui Glanvilla vocatur*, ed. G.D.G. Hall (Oxford, 1965), xxxi.

[14] R.R. Davies, 'The Law of the March', *Welsh History Review*, V (1970–1), 1–30, esp. 19–23. For examples of final concords and possessory assizes in Glamorgan *c.* 1200, *Cartae ... de Glamorgancia*, ed. G.T. Clark (6 vols., Cardiff, 1910), II, nos. 225 (1197), 291 (1205).

before then, the general assumption was that English settlers in Wales and indeed even Welshmen who came to hold by English tenure or secured a grant of English liberty would normally plead by English law.[15] English communities in Wales could indeed demand that they be prosecuted by 'the common law, as enjoyed by all (the king's) liege subjects'.[16] They were Englishmen living in Wales; the privilege of using English law was part of their identity and ethnic birthright.

What was true of English settlers in Wales was even more true of their colleagues in Ireland. The English settlement of Ireland was at its peak in the fifty or so years after 1170, in the very period when the English laws were being codified by 'Glanvill' and 'Bracton' and when the practice of the king's court came to be equated with the common law of England. The orthodoxy in Ireland, or rather in English Ireland, from an early date, was that 'the laws and customs of the realm of England be kept in that land'.[17] It was an orthodoxy to which the English settlers in Ireland readily subscribed; for them indeed it was a triumphant affirmation of their own Englishness, of their sense of belonging to a greater English community. As Edward III put it in 1357, what bound the English born in Ireland and the English born in England and dwelling in Ireland together as 'true English' was that they shared 'the same laws, rights and customs'.[18] True Englishness and the common law already went hand in hand in a way which would have warmed the cockles of Sir Edward Coke's heart.

Such ethnic and legal triumphalism can, of course, have a negative dimension. It can easily beget a mentality of exclusiveness, especially in societies where one ethnic group is militarily and politically a dominant minority. So it was in medieval Wales and Ireland. Respect for the laws and customs of the Welsh and Irish may be said to reveal an attitude of magnanimous pluralism on the part of the English rulers; but it could be accompanied by a mean-minded exclusiveness and a tendency to regard the tolerated different as the culturally and ethnically inferior. Thus in Wales the attempts of the Welsh community to share in some of the benefits of English law, especially on the vexed questions of the succession to and the alienation of land, were regularly met by the pious but disingenuous response that 'the king is not minded to abolish the ancient customs of Wales'.[19] But it was in Ireland that an

---

[15] Davies, *Lordship and Society*, 449–56.

[16] *Calendar of Ancient Petitions relating to Wales*, ed. W. Rees (Cardiff, 1975), no. 1092.

[17] Roger of Wendover, *Flores Historiarum*, ed. H.O. Coxe (English Historical Society, 1841–4), III, 233–4; *Statutes and Ordinances and Acts of the Parliament of Ireland, King John to Henry V*, ed. H.F. Berry (Dublin, 1907), 23–4. For comment see esp. Paul Brand, 'Ireland and the Literature of the early Common Law', *Irish Jurist*, XVI (1981), 95–113.

[18] *Statutes ... of Ireland*, ed. Berry, 417–18.

[19] For example *Calendar of Ancient Petitions*, ed. Rees, no. 3179. For comment: J.B. Smith, 'Crown and Community in the Principality of North Wales in the Reign of Henry

increasingly intolerant legal exclusiveness[20] on the part of the English did most to harm the relationship between peoples, be it in the appearance of the notorious 'exception of Irishry' (which in effect discriminated in favour of the English in their disputes with the Irish), in the recurrent failure of the attempts from the 1270s to make English law available to the Irish, and in the insistence that no Englishman should use the laws and customs of the Irish.[21] Nowhere in short was a people more clearly, and sometimes offensively, defined by its law than in ethnically composite societies, such as medieval Ireland and Wales.

To acknowledge as much is to recognise that law occupies a crucial role in the mythology and ideology of a people. Scholars of early medieval written law-collections have reminded us of late that such collections are 'ideological rather than practical in origin'; they are, as Alan Harding has put it, works of political theology.[22] Part of their function also is surely to create and promote collective solidarity, to underwrite, as it were, the notion that a people's identity may be expressed in, and fortified by, its laws. Law continued to occupy this function, at least to a measure, among the peoples of the British Isles throughout the medieval period.

One way in which law could play its part in the ideology of collective identity was by emphasising the antiquity of people's law and the role of a Solon-like figure in codifying it. England provides the classic, but by no means unique, example. The notion of the immemorial law of England is no invention of the legal polemicists of the seventeenth century; men such as Andrew Horn in the early fourteenth century or Chief Justice Fortescue in the fifteenth had already veiled the origins

---

Tudor', *Welsh History Review*, III (1966–7), esp. 146–9; idem, 'Edward II and the Allegiance of Wales', ibid., VIII (1976–7), esp. 144, 150–1; R.R. Davies, *The Age of Conquest. Wales 1063–1415* (Oxford, 1991), 433.

[20] Matters may have been different in the early thirteenth century, as suggested by K. Nicholls, 'Anglo-French Ireland and After', *Peritia*, I (1992), esp. 375; cf. Robin Frame, ' "Les Engleys née en Irlande": The English Political Identity in Medieval Ireland', *ante*, 6th ser., 3 (1993), esp. 87–9.

[21] See generally G.J. Hand, *English Law in Ireland 1290–1324* (Cambridge, 1967), and Robin Frame, *Colonial Ireland 1169–1369* (Dublin, 1981), esp. 105–10 and the references given there.

[22] P. Wormald, '*Lex Scripta* and *Verbum Regis*: Legislation and Germanic Kingship, from Euric to Cnut', in *Early Medieval Kingship*, ed. P.H. Sawyer and I.N. Wood (Leeds, 1977), at 125; Alan Harding, 'Regiam Majestatem amongst Medieval Law-Books', *The Juridical Review*, XXIX (1984), at 110. On this issue see most recently Robin C. Stacey, 'Law and Order in the Very Old West: England and Ireland in the Early Middle Ages' in *Crossed Paths. Methodological Approaches to the Celtic Aspect of the European Middle Ages*, ed. Benjamin Hudson and Vickie Ziegler (1991), 39–61.

of the English law in a venerable, even aboriginal, antiquity.[23] For those whose chronological register in this respect was more modest there remained, nevertheless, a determination to emphasise the pre-Conquest foundations of English law and to convert Edward the Confessor into a Solon-like figure. The *laga Edwardi* became a central feature of the Normans' determination to repair their bridges with England's pre-Conquest legacy. Already in the opening decades of the twelfth century when—as Sir Richard Southern showed in a memorable presidential address to this Society—a remarkable group of historians evoked the sense of the Anglo-Saxon past, other scholars were busy at work, familiarising themselves with, and putting order on, the corpus of Anglo-Saxon legal lore.[24] Of course, with the passage of the generations and with the momentous changes in the character and administration of the law from the twelfth century onwards, pride in law assumed a variety of new forms; but what that pride emphasised, ever more defiantly and stridently, was the distinctively English quality and the venerable antiquity of the laws of the English.

Nor were the Scots and the Welsh slow in following suit. Scottish chroniclers in their more immodest moments, and provoked no doubt by some of the extravagances spawned by Geoffrey of Monmouth, might be tempted to claim that their laws were derived from those given by Gaythelos, Scota's husband, to their ancestors in Spain;[25] but on the whole they, like their English confrères, preferred to find their law-givers in the historic period. Three in particular were given this status: the first was the ninth-century Kenneth MacAlpin, of whom it was later remarked that 'he was called the first king, not because he was the first, but because he first established the Scottish laws, which they call the Laws of Mac-Alpin'; the second was Malcolm Mackenneth, an early eleventh-century king whose 'laws' in their present form were assembled more than three centuries later; the third was good King

---

[23] Jeremy Catto, 'Law and History in Fourteenth-Century England', in *The Writings of History in the Middle Ages: Essays Presented to R.W Southern*, ed. R.H.C. Davis and J.M. Wallace-Hadrill (Oxford, 1981), 367–93; Sir John Fortescue, *De Laudibus Legum Anglie*, ed. S.B. Chrimes (Cambridge, 1942), 38–41.

[24] R.W. Southern, 'Aspects of the European Tradition of Historical Writing: 4. The Sense of the Past', *ante*, 5th ser., 23 (1973), 243–65; J.C. Holt, *Magna Carta and Medieval Government* (1985), esp. chap. 1; P. Wormald, 'Quadripartitus', in *Law and Government in Medieval England and Normandy: Essqays in Honour of Sir James Holt*, ed. G. Garnett and J. Hudson (Cambridge, 1994), 111–72, esp. 140–7; idem, '*Laga Edwardi*: The *Textus Roffensis* and its Context', *Anglo-Norman Studies*, XVII (1995), 243–66. For respect for the laws of Cnut see John Hudson, 'Administration, Family and Perceptions of the Past in Late-Twelfth-Century England: Richard FitzNigel and the Dialogue of the Exchequer', in *The Perception of the Past in Twelfth-Century Europe*, ed. Paul Magdalino (1992), 75–98, esp. 94–8.

[25] John of Fordun, *Chronica Gentis Scotorum*, ed. W. F. Skene (Edinburgh, 1871–2), I, 18; II, 17.

David, David I, whose laws came to be regarded, both within Scotland and beyond, as the base-line of the Scottish legal tradition in the middle ages.[26] If the Welsh were to compete in this world they must likewise find a monarchical law-giver to whom the shaping of their distinctive legal tradition could be ascribed. They found him, but possibly not before the thirteenth century, in Hywel Dda, the Good (d. 949/50); henceforth Welsh law would frequently be known as the law of Hywel, *cyfraith Hywel*. The prologues to the Welsh law-texts provide a further insight into the role of law, and specifically written law, in the ideology of peoples. They explain how Hywel summoned six men from each *cantref* of Wales to an assembly to review and amend the laws; king and people are thereby linked as sources of authority for law.[27] Law was one of the crucial bonding agents between them; it was the law of a people but issued by a king. Law thereby sanctioned both monarchical authority *and* the corporate individuality of a people.

It also performed a second, if associated, key function: it was, both ideologically and practically, one of the most potent instruments for bonding diverse peoples into a single nation. A people, as was observed in the first of these addresses, is a most evanescent and elusive concept; it lacks fixed form and geographical definition. This is precisely where law could be helpful: it helped to establish the identity of a people in its own eyes and those of others. The English arguably stood less in need of this stiffening quality of law than did other peoples, since their unity had been substantially forged already in pre-Conquest days from a whole variety of directions. Nevertheless, as Patrick Wormald has observed, 'Anglo-Saxon law was an essential ingredient in the personality of the English state',[28] and pride in the legal unity and singularity of England and in the essential Englishness of English law became an increasingly and raucously evident feature of English political postures and practice as the middle ages progressed. The English may have come early to the knowledge and practice of the fact that they were, in spite of differences in regional and local customs, a single

---

[26] *Early Sources of Scottish History A.D. 500 to 1286*, ed. A.O. Anderson (Edinburgh, 1922), I, 270; A. A. M. Duncan, 'The "Laws of Malcolm Mackenneth"', in *Medieval Scotland, Crown, Lordship and Community. Essays Presented to G.W.S. Barrow*, ed. A. Grant and K.J. Stringer (Edinburgh, 1993), 239–74; Hector MacQueen, 'Scots Law under Alexander III', in *Scotland in the Reign of Alexander III 1249–1286*, ed. N.H. Reid (Edinburgh, 1990), esp. 84–5, 87–8; idem., *Common Law and Feudal Society in Medieval Scotland, (Edinburgh, 1993), esp. 85–8*.
[27] J.G. Edwards, *Hywel Dda and the Welsh Lawbooks* (Bangor, 1929); H. Pryce, 'The Prologues to the Welsh Lawbooks', *Bulletin of the Board of Celtic Studies*, XXXIII (1986), 151–87. I am not aware of any clear pre-thirteenth-century evidence which ascribes the law to Hywel Dda, though this may, of course, reflect the lateness of the manuscript tradition of Welsh law.
[28] Wormald, 'Quadripartitus', at 147.

people in terms of law; the Scots had a much longer road to travel. The Scots were, after all, a fairly recent amalgam of four or five different peoples, each of which doubtless had its own laws and customs. The Gallovidians, for example, defended their 'liberties' and their 'law of Galloway' well into the fourteenth century;[29] while Scottish legal historians have of late emphasised anew the powerful, but often under-rated, contribution that Celtic law may have made substantively to later Scottish law and practice.[30] Yet if the Scottish people were to be welded into one people under one king, it was important that such legal pluralism be modestly concealed beneath a facade of unity. And so it was. References to 'the common law of Scotland' and to 'usage throughout our kingdom of Scotland according to ancient approved custom and by the common law' multiply from the mid-thirteenth century onwards;[31] by the time of the political crises of the 1290s 'the laws and customs of Scotland' were one of the crucial elements which defined the identity of Scotland.[32] In reality, and particularly at the local level, matters are very unlikely to have been that simple; but one of the crucial functions of law was to manufacture the image of the unity of a realm and a people in the service of its independence.

If that was true of England how much more true was it of Wales and Ireland? Both of them were countries which lacked the structure and institutions of political unity; in both English domination and settlement introduced a further fissure into the country and posed an extra challenge to the sense of the unity of the native peoples. In such a context it was crucial to cling on to, and if need be to manufacture, an ideology of legal unity as a practical basis to its claim to be, and to be treated as, a single people. The Welsh applied themselves to the task with enthusiasm: their legal texts proclaimed that the great law-giver, Hywel Dda, was 'prince of the whole of Wales' and that the curse of 'the whole of Wales' was to be visited on anyone who failed to observe those laws 'in Wales'.[33] Thirteenth-century princes took up

[29] See, for example, the reference to 'the ancient laws of Galloway', *Registrum Magni Sigilli Regum Scottorum* (Edinburgh, 1882–1914), I, Appendix 1, no. 59. For the whole subject Hector MacQueen in *Galloway, Land and Lordship*, ed. R.D. Oram and G.P. Stell (Edinburgh, 1991), 131–43. Cf. A.A.M. Duncan, *Scotland. The Making of the Kingdom* (Edinburgh, 1975), 546.
[30] W.D.H. Sellar, 'Celtic Law and Scots Law. Survival and Integration', *Scottish Studies*, XXIX (1989), 1–27. Cf. the comments of R. Nicholson, *Scotland. The Later Middle Ages* (Edinburgh, 1974), 24.
[31] References are conveniently assembled in W. David H. Sellar, 'The Common Law of Scotland and the Common Law of England', in *The British Isles 1100–1500. Comparisons, Contrasts and Connections*, ed. R.R. Davies (Edinburgh, 1988), 86–7.
[32] Treaty of Birgham as above, n. 5; *Edward I and the Throne of Scotland 1290–1296*, ed. E.L.G. Stones and G.G. Simpson (Oxford, 1978), II, 140.
[33] *Llyfr Iorwerth*, ed. A.R. Wiliam (Cardiff, 1960), §1.

the campaign declaring that Welsh law was the birthright of all Welshmen, while a jury in 1278 echoed the same refrain in proclaiming that Welsh law 'prevailed throughout Wales and the Marches, as far as the power of the Welsh extends'.[34] Such protestations clearly protest far too much; but their frequent reiteration manifested how central their law, or rather their appeal to their law, was to the identity and the unity of the Welsh as a people. The same was doubtless true of the Irish, for in spite of the fissiparousness and intense and murderous competitiveness of Irish political life, the assumption that 'Irish law ... regards itself as valid for all the Irish' was one of the features which helped to sustain and foster a sense of ethnic and cultural Irish unity, aided as it was both by the deliberate exclusion of the native Irish from the benefits and privileges of English law and by the role of the brehons, as a hereditary class of jurists, in teaching and preserving Irish law.[35]

Law not only helped to give a people a sense of unity; it also served as one of the crucial bulwarks of its national identity. The English were not short of such bulwarks, but even for them their law remained a potent and cherished symbol of their identity. It was as Gaimar said in the mid-twelfth century 'the law of us English' and it was as a corpus of English laws (*leges anglicanas*) that 'Glanvill' set about to impose order upon it, or at least the royal practice of it.[36] Thereafter the patriotic chorus rang out in repeated refrains such as 'We refuse to change the laws of England'; or 'the magnates are unwilling to be judged by examples used in foreign countries'; it reached its magnificent coda in Fortescue's famous assertion that 'the customs of the English are not only good but the best'.[37] It is difficult to compete with John Bull when he is in such an expansively self-confident mood; but for the other peoples of the British Isles likewise the defence of their laws was a crucial aspect of their credibility and identity as distinctive peoples. Much of Scottish law derived its content and form from the custom and writs of Angevin England; but this made Scots not one whit less proud of it as their law. That is why they insisted in 1290 that their 'laws, liberties and customs ... (should) be preserved' in every respect, and asserted in 1320 that Robert I's title to the Scottish throne was grounded in 'our laws and customs which we shall maintain to the

---

[34] *Welsh Assize Roll*, 255, 266, 269; *Cal. of Inquisitions Miscellaneous 1219–1307*, no. 1109.

[35] D.Ó. Corráin, 'Nationality and Kingship in Pre-Norman Ireland', *Historical Studies* (Dublin), XI (1978), at 7; K. Simms, 'The Brehons of Later Medieval Ireland', in *Brehons, Serjeants and Attorneys*, ed. D. Hogan and W.N. Osborough (Dublin, 1990), 51–76.

[36] Geoffrei Gaimar, *L'Estoire des Engleis*, ed. A. Bell (Anglo-Norman Text Society, 1960), l. 4991; *Glanvill, Tractatus*, 2 (leges autem anglicanas ...).

[37] F. Pollock and F.W. Maitland, *History of English Law before the Time of Edward I* (1968 edn), I, 184, 188–9; Fortescue, *De Laudibus Legum Anglie*, 41.

death'.[38] Old-fashioned Scottish law may have appeared by then to English eyes; that was all the more reason why the Scots defended it as their own. It was probably as a conscious act of political propaganda and national ideology that *Regiam Maiestatem*, the key law-book of medieval Scotland, was composed in the 1320s.[39]

For the Welsh, law, as we have seen, was even more crucial; without it their claim to be a separate people appeared increasingly flimsy. Domesday Book had already implicitly recognised that law might help to define Welshness; in King John's reign the definition was, at least in territorial terms, acknowledged in solemn documents, be it in the treaty of 1201 with Llywelyn ab Iorwerth of Gwynedd or in Magna Carta itself.[40] But it was in the final struggle between Llywelyn ap Gruffudd and Edward I that law came fully into its own as the irreducible touchstone of Welsh identity. Llywelyn did all in his power to convert the struggle from one about the hegemony of Gwynedd or the proprieties of feudal subjection to the English crown into a fundamental struggle about the survival of Wales itself as a political concept (as opposed to a mere geographical expression) and of its inhabitants as a people. In that propaganda war, the defence of Welsh law became the defining issue. Never was its centrality more eloquently or poignantly articulated than in the declaration—already quoted in these lectures—which was made in the name of the people of Snowdon in the traumatic winter months of 1282 that 'even if their prince should give seisin of them to the king, they themselves would refuse to do homage to any foreigner, of whose language, customs and laws they were thoroughly ignorant'.[41]

There may be something almost pathetically melodramatic in such a defiant statement, yet it would be a sentiment which would have been respected and understood by even the most bitter opponents of the Welsh. People and law were like weft and warp; to attack the one was to call the other in question. That is why contemporary chroniclers revealingly, if mistakenly, assumed that it was the imposition of alien law which was among the most natural triggers of revolt. That, for example, is how the revolts of the Welsh in the thirteenth century were explained by English observers; it was in similar terms that Walter Guisborough accounted for the support for Robert Bruce in 1306 7,

[38] *Documents*, ed. Stevenson, I, 165; A.A.M. Duncan, *The Nation of Scots and the Declaration of Arbroath* (1320) (Historical Association, 1970), 35.

[39] A.A.M. Duncan, 'Regiam Majestatem: A Reconsideration', *Juridical Review*, VI (1961), 199–217; Harding, 'Regiam Majestatem' (as in n. 22); MacQueen, *Common Law*, 90–1; idem, '*Regiam Majestatem*, Scots Law, and National Identity', *Scottish Historical Review*, LXXIV (1995), 1–25.

[40] *Domesday Book, I, 185b; Rotuli Litterarum Patentium* (Record Comm. 1835), I, i, 8b; Magna Carta cap. 56–7.

[41] *Reg. Johannis Peckham*, II, 471; Davies, 'Law and National Identity' (as in n. 4).

since the Scots 'preferred to die than to be judged by English laws';
and as to the Irish, one of the charges that they paradoxically levelled
at the English in the famous Remonstrance of 1316–17 was that they
had deprived them of their written laws.[42] Nor should the English have
been surprised by such a backlash, however unfounded it may have
been, for they themselves came to regard the adoption of Irish law by
English settlers in Ireland as one of the most deplorable manifestations
of what they termed 'degeneracy'.[43] That one word, degeneracy, in a
way said it all: it was unnatural for people of one *gens* to adopt the law
of another, for law made a people.

Degeneracy was a pathological condition which applied not only to
law but likewise to customs. Law and customs were indeed almost
always twinned in the medieval period, nor is that surprising for law
was but the customs which regulated those social relationships which
had been brought within the ambit of judicial procedures and regulations. For us 'customs' is a flabby word and any talk of national
characteristics is considered to be unscholarly at best, vicious at worst.
Sociologists and anthropologists may beg to differ from such a view;[44]
medieval men certainly did so. Let us return to the statement of the
Irish in 1316–17. The English settlers in Ireland, so they declared, 'are
so dissimilar (to us Irish) in way of life and speech ... that there is no
hope whatever of our having peace with them'. The statement is, of
course, deliberately inflammatory; but in its essence it surely represented
what was the orthodox medieval view of these matters.

All peoples had distinctive customs and were proud of them. This
was a truism not only about the extraordinary peoples on the peripheries
of Europe, peoples so splendidly analysed in the ethnographic studies
of men such as Helmold of Bosau or Gerald of Wales, but of neighbours
nearer home. When in the mid-twelfth century French monks were
dispatched to Herefordshire to found the priory of Wigmore, they soon
requested to be replaced by others 'who speak and understand English

---

[42] Matthew Paris, *Chronica Majora*, ed. H.R. Luard (Rolls Series, 1872–7), V, 639; *Annales Monastici*, ed. H. R. Luard (Rolls Series, 1864–9), II, 89; III, 200, 291 (Wales); *Chronicle of Walter of Guisborough*, ed. H. Rothwell (Camden Society, 1957), 263 (Scotland); *Irish Historical Documents 1172–1922*, ed. E. Curtis and R.B. McDowell (1943), 41 (Ireland).

[43] See for example the letter of Edward III to his officials in Kilkenny, *Historical Manuscripts Commission, Tenth Report*, Appendix, part V, 260–1.

[44] Cf. the comments of A.D. Smith, *The Ethnic Origins of Nations* (Oxford, 1986), 44–6, on customs as 'border guards' of ethnic groups.

and comprehend the English character'.[45] Of course such comments can degenerate easily into ethnic abuse; but they also have an objective, almost neutral, force. A people's character and customs were grounded, like its law, in the distant past; like law, they were almost immemorial and thereby congenital. Wace, for example, explained that the Saxons had brought their ancestral customs and laws with them from Germany to Britain, thereby ensuring continuity with their past.[46] Bishop Stubbs could not have put it better. This did not mean that customs did not change over time: William of Malmesbury had observed, for example, how the customs of the English—in such basic matters as diet and dress—had evolved over the centuries, while the contemporary behaviour of Scottish kings prompted chroniclers to note how foreign influences could shape the manners, language and culture of royalty and aristocracy.[47] Nevertheless differences in customs and manners between peoples remained profound and profoundly important. We may dismiss the clearly pre-packaged lists of the characteristics of different peoples which are such a commonplace feature of medieval treatises as stock literary images. But not only do stock images acquire a life of their own, as we know only too well in our own day; they also reflect basic assumptions about the divisions of human society. As Edmund Spenser put it pithily, in a comment which could well serve as the peg on which to hang these observations, 'the difference of manners and customs doth follow the difference of nations and people'.[48]

'Manners and customs' is, of course, an extraordinarily open-ended phrase, ranging from what we might regard as the superficial and the frivolous to profound differences in social organisation, economic practices and codes of moral values. We should certainly not underrate the superficial and the frivolous, as we might view them. The Statutes of Kilkenny of 1366, which reaffirmed the distinction between the English and the Irish in Ireland, addressed themselves in their prologue to mode of riding and dress as badges of ethnic identity. Indeed the physical or even the facial aspect of a person might be the first item in a catalogue of ethnic identities. Gerald of Wales had devoted a whole chapter to describing Welsh customs with regard to

---

[45] 'The Anglo-Norman Chronicle of Wigmore Abbey', ed. J.C. Dickinson and P.T. Ricketts, *Trans. Woolhope Naturalists Field Club*, XXXIX (1964) at 425. Cf. the observation of the abbot of La Croix Saint Leuffroi on English monks as 'men whose strange customs and barbarous speech are unknown to me', Orderic Vitalis, *Historia Ecclesiastica*, ed. M. Chibnall (Oxford, 1969–80), II, 272.

[46] *Le Roman de Brut de Wace*, ed. Ivor Arnold (Paris, 1940), II, 772.

[47] William of Malmesbury, *Gesta Regum*, II, 304–5; *Scottish Annals from English Chronicles*, ed. A.O. Anderson (London, 1908), 330 n. 6.

[48] Edmund Spenser, *A View of the Present State of Ireland* (1596), ed. W.L. Renwick (Oxford, 1970), 48. For Spenser's *View* see esp. C. Brady, 'Spenser's Irish Crisis: Humanism and Experience in the 1590s', *Past and Present*, no. 111 (1986), 17–50.

hair styles and moustaches, just as Bartholomew Anglicus explained how Frisians, especially noble Frisians, could be distinguished from Germans by the cut of their hair.[49] But it was in Ireland, significantly, that ethnic differences were statutorily defined by hair style. Already in 1297 it was decreed that anyone who wore the *cúlán* (the Irish hair style) could forfeit his English status.[50] Nor was this an empty threat: when a Gaelic lord came to terms with the English in 1333 he 'had the hair of his *cúlán* cut in order to hold English law', while more than a century later it was agreed that any man who wished to be considered English must 'have no hair upon his upper lip so that the said lip be shaven at least once within two weeks'.[51] What such legislators might have made of a designer stubble is an interesting question; but such regulations are a reminder to us that what we might regard as a matter of individual taste was, or could be, a serious aspect of ethnic identity in the middle ages.

So was dress, or the lack of it. Much of the comment on dress, it is true, was descriptive rather than part of an ethnic classification. External observers were astonished by how few clothes the Welsh, Irish and Scots wore.[52] Surprise begins to turn to pity and thence to contempt when mention was made that they were also bare-legged and bare-foot, especially since such behaviour seemed to the shoed and stockinged English to be coupled with inconstancy, if not depravity. Hence the stock description, verbally and visually, of the Welsh as 'bare-footed rascals' or the Scots as a 'kilted rabble ... raising their spears under their rags'.[53] Dress was, literally and metaphorically, more than a matter of habit; in composite societies it was an ethnic identifier. It was so in medieval Wales where the English could be distinguished from the Welsh by their dress; it was even more so in Ireland where those to be admitted to the franchise of the city of Waterford had to be of English 'array, habit and apparel'.[54] Later social theoreticians were clearly of

---

[49] Giraldus Cambrensis, *Opera*, ed. J. S. Brewer *et al.* (Rolls Series, 1861–91), VI, 185–6 (*Descriptio Kambrie* bk I, c. xi), *On the Properties of Things. John Trevisa's Translation of Bartholomew Anglicus De Proprietatibus Rerum* (Oxford, 1975–88), 761.

[50] *Statutes ... of Ireland*, ed. Berry, 210–11.

[51] *Parliaments and Councils of Medieval Ireland*, ed. H.G. Richardson and G.O. Sayles (Dublin, 1947), 17, quoted in Robin Frame, *ante*, 6th ser., 3 (1993), 95; *Statute Rolls of the Parliament of Ireland: Henry VI*, ed. H.F. Berry (Dublin, 1910), 88–9.

[52] See, respectively, R.R. Davies, 'Buchedd a moes y Cymry', *Welsh History Review*, XII (1984–5) at 160; *A New History of Ireland II. Medieval Ireland*, ed. A. Cosgrove (1987), 309; A.A.M. Duncan, 'The Dress of the Scots', *Scottish Historical Review*, XXIX (1950), 210–12.

[53] *Eulogium Historiarum*, ed. F.S. Haydon (Rolls Series, 1858–63), III, 388; *Littere Wallie*, ed. J.G. Edwards (Cardiff, 1940), xxviii–xxix (Welsh); *The Political Songs of England from the Reign of John to that of Edward II*, ed. Thomas Wright (Camden Society, 1839), 164, 166 (Scots).

[54] Giraldus Cambrensis, *Speculum Duorum*, ed. M. Richter *et al.* (Cardiff, 1974); *Hist. MSS Commission, 10th Report*, App. V, 292.

the opinion that uniformity in dress was a necessary precondition of ethnic assimilation and the acceptance of Englishness in governance and in life. Edmund Spenser preached a sort of sartorial determinism: 'men's apparel is commonly made according to their conditions, and their conditions are oftentimes governed by their garments, for the person that is gowned is by his gown put in mind of gravity, and also restrained from lightness by the very inaptness of his weed'; but it was Richard Stanyhurst, as so often, who took the argument to its frightening, almost Maoist, conclusion in declaring that uniformity in dress was one of the three necessary preconditions for a complete conquest.[55]

I have deliberately dwelt on hair, moustaches and dress precisely because they might appear to us as the most external and least important of the customs that defined a people. Other external features could certainly be added to the list. Thus, according to the Statutes of Kilkenny, the manner of riding was another way in which the Irish could and should be distinguished from the English in Ireland. Dietary habits were also the target of ethnic labelling, be it in the contrast between the enforced abstemiousness of the Welsh and the Irish and the gluttony of the English (which Higden, with remarkable chronological precision, dated to the reign of Harthacnut) or in the fact that bread and wine featured so little in the diets of the Welsh and the Irish.[56] Much of this was commonplace, and often grossly oversimplified, characterisation; but such differences are, of course, among the material from which ethnic prejudices are manufactured in our own day. If dress, habits and food could excite such comment, how much more might this be true of more profound aspects of society—be it social practices (such as fosterage or inheritance customs), attitudes towards sex, marriage, divorce and legitimacy, methods of economic exploitation, and assumptions about the nature of authority? Sometimes indeed ethnic stereotypes bundled different aspects of a people's customs into a single formula, as in Ralph Glaber's revealing comment about the Bretons that their wealth consisted in 'freedom from taxes and abundance of milk'; while from the Celtic side the contempt of the Highlanders for the Lowlanders of Scotland as 'mere tillers of the soil' speaks volumes to us of the chasm in custom, attitudes and value-judgments that could divide a pastoral from an arable society within the same country.[57]

[55] Spenser, *A View*, 69; Richard Stanyhurst quoted in J.F. Lydon, *The Lordship of Ireland in the Middle Ages* (1972), 281.
[56] Ranulf Higden, *Polychronicon*, ed. C. Babington and R. Lumby (Rolls Series, 1865–86), II, 166; Davies, 'Buchedd a Moes', 159–60; *New History of Ireland*, II, 331–2.
[57] See, respectively, Robert Bartlett, *Gerald of Wales 1146–1223* (Oxford, 1982), 160–1; A. Grant, 'Scotland's "Celtic Fringe" in the Late Middle Ages', in *The British Isles 1100–1500*, ed. Davies, 120; and G.W.S. Barrow, *The Kingdom of the Scots* (1973), 368.

What these examples clearly demonstrate is that customs (*consuetudines*) and manners (*mores*) were extraordinarily vague, unstructured and elastic concepts, catch-all phrases into which a whole jumble of unrelated observations and practices could be poured. That is the weakness of these terms for purposes of analysis; but that is also precisely their strength, be it in defence of a people's identity or as the basis for a self-righteous attack on its life-style. So it was, for example, that the Irish of Ulster could claim that they had nothing to learn from the peoples of western Europe since their own customs were 'the best and most perfect in the world'.[58] There was no need to enter into detail and indeed it was better not to do so, for customs referred to the seamless web of practices which governed the life of society. Customs could also be a convenient smokescreen behind which a people and its rulers might retreat if a political or constitutional position became tricky. Thus when Eadmer, the bishop-elect of St Andrews, in 1120 failed to persuade Alexander I of Scotland to allow him to profess obedience to Canterbury, Alexander gave short shrift to Eadmer's stand by declaring that he (Eadmer) would not comply with 'the customs of the land and the manners of the people'.[59] Land and customs, manners and people were bound tightly together. That is why a people's identity seemed to reside very considerably in its laws and customs, especially so in the case of peoples such as the Welsh and the Irish who had no unitary political framework, institutions or office which could serve as a focus for their identity. And that is why so much of the rhetoric of their defence of their identity as a people is couched, especially in the thirteenth and fourteenth centuries, in that vague but crucial phrase, 'the laws, customs and usages of those parts'. It was the very elusiveness and elasticity of the phrase which was its best defence against the gimlets of the feudal lawyers and uniformist theorcticians of the day.

How far laws and customs served to define a people becomes clear, paradoxically, in the attempts that dominant peoples and political authorities made to modify the laws and customs of other peoples and to bring them into line with what were considered to be acceptable norms of social behaviour and juristic values. Let us begin with customs. The very vagueness of the concept and the fact that customs were woven into the life of a people in all its aspects did not make them an easy target for the reformer's zeal and administrative tidy-mindedness. Customs were unwritten and therefore, unlike laws, were not normally available for the critical scrutiny of the afficionados of *ius scriptum*.

[58] *New History of Ireland*, II, 348.
[59] *Scottish Annals*, ed. Anderson, 145.

Furthermore diversity and plurality of customs were seen as inevitable to the human condition as was plurality of languages after the fall of the Tower of Babel. Some customs, it is true, might be more extra-ordinary than others but even they could be assembled in ethnographic show-cases, metaphorically speaking, for the entertainment of the curious. Furthermore, medieval writers often subscribed to a theory of social evolution which admitted that customs could and did change over the generations. Thus William of Malmesbury, who has been credited as one of the spokesmen of a new attitude of cultural superiority towards the Celtic peoples, was of the opinion that the customs and manners of the English had improved over the centuries, with some regrettable regressions, since the initial Anglo-Saxon invasions until they reached a standard of civility in life, letters and the exercise of arms, which put them on a par with the French.[60]

Diversity of customs was, therefore, part of the human condition, and customs could change over time. As such they could be neutrally observed and tolerated. But observation was, in fact, rarely value-free; more often than not it was tinged with censure and a sense of superiority. Customs, so it was implied, could be placed in a league table; the purpose of such a league table, as of all league tables, was to persuade, and if need be to compel, those at the foot of the table to adopt the customs and manners of those who believed themselves to be at the head of the table. Three reasons in particular were advanced to support such an approach. The first was that it was culturally desirable; in other words all societies in Christian Europe should be persuaded to adopt the enlightened norms and habits of the most advanced societies. One rather touching example of this cultural mission comes at the end of our period when Richard II in 1394 proposed to confer the honour of knighthood on four Irish kings, provided they registered for a crash course in cultural orientation. Their tutor was to be a Gaelic-speaker, Sir Henry Cristall, who was charged to persuade them 'to adopt the habits, the appearance and the dress of England'.[61] A second reason, and a much more sinister one, for insisting on the reform of customs was that of imposing a moral and ethical norm on all peoples. It was the church, especially from the twelfth century, which was inevitably in the forefront of this crusade. For reforming churchmen the moral habits and marital and sexual practices of peoples such as the Irish and the Welsh were not just unusual or variant customs, but rather as Pope Alexander III called them, 'shocking abuses' to be extirpated; how that

---

[60] *Gesta Regum*, I, 13, 97, 105–6, 227; II, 304–5. For discussion of William of Malmesbury's attitude, John Gillingham, 'The Beginnings of English Imperialism', *Journal of Historical Sociology*, V (1991–2), 392–410.

[61] Jean Froisart, *Chronicles*, selected & trans. G. Brereton (1968), 411–12.

might be done was indicated, for example, by the measures later
outlined by Archbishop Pecham of Canterbury after the conquest of
Wales in 1282–3.[62] Ideologues are always among the most passionate
proponents of uniformity; but there was another group with a vested
interest in ironing out the differences between peoples. Political uniformity was the third reason for pressing for a closer alignment of
customs between peoples under the same governance. Phrases such as
'the unity of the king's lands' began to appear in the rhetoric of the
English government from at least the thirteenth century; they may be
said to reach a deafening crescendo in the resounding declaration of
Henry VIII's intention in the so-called Act of Union of Wales in 1536
'to extirpate all and singular the sinister usages and customs (of Wales)
differing from (the laws of this Realm)'.[63]

There is, perhaps, rather more to such ambitions than is normally
allowed for in the works of political and constitutional historians.
Administrative and legal uniformity were no doubt desirable ends in
themselves; but beyond them lay a more ambitious goal, to remove
what the Act of Union called 'the distinction and diversity' between
peoples, notably peoples under the rule of a single monarch. In the
political pamphleteering of the sixteenth and seventeenth centuries, and
particularly in the flurry of theorising prompted by the union of the
crowns in 1603, much the same arguments would be rehearsed with
respect to Scotland and the Scots.[64] Shrewd political observers were
not in doubt about what was at stake. Had not Machiavelli remarked
that political unions worked best when there were marked similarities
in 'language, customs and institutions' between peoples under a single
ruler?[65] Edmund Spenser likewise was of the opinion that the only
prospect for an eventual solution to the problem that was Ireland was
'by an union of manners and conformity of minds to bring them to be
one people'.[66] That was it: manners and customs to a considerable
degree made a people; to change its customs, be it gradually through
acculturation or persuasion or arbitrarily through ordinance and legislation, was in effect to mount a campaign to erode its identity as a
people and to swallow it into another, greater people. Ranulf Higden
and his translator John Trevisa were not given to philosophical musings;

---

[62] *Irish Historical Documents*, ed. Curtis and McDowell, 19–20; *Reg. Johannis Peckham*, II,
741; III, 776–8. Peckham urged the bishop of St Asaph 'ut ad unitatis studium cum
domino et populo Anglicano velitis per vos et alios vestros subditos informare'.
[63] *Cal. Patent Rolls 1232–47*, 488; 27 Henry VII c. 26.
[64] Jenny Wormald, 'The Creation of Britain: Multiple Kingdoms or Core and Col-
onies?', *ante*, 6th ser., 2 (1992), 175–95, esp. 177–8; B. Galloway, *The Union of England and
Scotland 1603–1608* (Edinburgh, 1986), esp. chap. 3.
[65] *The Prince*, ed. Q. Skinner and R. Price (Cambridge, 1988), 8.
[66] *A View*, 153.

but when, from the vantage point of Chester, they saw the Welsh adopting English customs—a veritable catalogue of suburban values, such as tilling gardens and fields, inhabiting towns, riding armed, wearing stockings and shoes, and even sleeping under sheets—they had no doubt that a profound shift was afoot

> So they semeth now in mynde
> More Englischemen than Walsche kynd.[67]

The erosion of its distinctive customs and habits would lead eventually to a crisis of identity, even of survival, for a people.


Nevertheless, customs, *mores*, change slowly; in spite of Henry VIII's bragging, they cannot be extirpated overnight. Laws in that respect present a much easier target. They are written and so can be scrutinised. Diversity between them appears particularly incongruous in a world which sees law increasingly as an emanation of a single royal will: *le roy le veult*. Distinction between laws, especially within a single country, based on ethnicity is a sure recipe for endless delays, appeals and charges of discrimination; and though lawyers have never been averse to profit from such opportunities, they quickly try the patience of administrators and statesmen. Diversity of laws was particularly anomalous in a world in which the judicial powers of popes, kings and princes were being more clearly articulated and their scope greatly extended and in which the benefits of a single 'common law', a clear hierarchy of jurisdiction and a professional class of lawyers seemed ever more obvious. Such was Europe increasingly in the generations after the mid-twelfth century, a world now shaped by Gratian and Glanvill and their successors.

This did not mean that respect for the individuality of each people's laws disappeared. Not only was such respect, as I have emphasised, a major dimension of the propaganda of peoples such as the Irish, Scots and Welsh in defence of their identity and independence, it was also an axiom which was rarely directly challenged by the English themselves. Nevertheless, it was an axiom which was increasingly supplemented by other considerations. One such related to one of the most vexed issues concerning the nature of political authority in the middle ages, that of the relationship of the prince to the law. No tags were bandied about more freely in the medieval period than those which declared that the prince was *solutus legibus* and that his word had the force of law. Particularly did this apply to kings and princes for whom the divine sanction of victory in battle was an adequate justification for them to

[67] Higden, *Polychronicon*, I, 411.

flex their legislative muscles. This, after all, was precisely what, according to contemporary views, the Normans had done to the English after the Norman Conquest. 'We and our fathers', so Walter Espec is alleged to have boasted in 1138, 'quickly mastered this island, placed it under our own laws and subjugated it to our customs.'[68] Richard Fitz Neal, echoing Justinian, was much more specifically royalist in his interpretation: 'William the Conqueror refounded the law of England, renewed the laws of the past, accepted some, rejected others, supplemented the whole body with French law, and reduced  everything to writing.'[69] If the Norman king could act so masterfully towards his subjects, how much more might he and his barons be justified in displaying the same legislative zeal towards the backward and barbarous peoples and their laws in the darker corners of the British Isles? And so indeed they allegedly did. We have heard already how the forebears of the earls of Warwick established their laws at their will in Gower; at a more general level the author of the *Gesta Stephani* informs us that the Normans imposed law and statutes on the Welsh; while one of Gerald's compliments to Hugh de Lacy in Ireland was that he compelled the Irish to obey and observe laws.[70] We need not, of course, necessarily take such comments at face value, nor have any such laws and statutes survived. But it is the assumption which is important: law, one of the crucial identifying badges of a people, could be amended, even abolished, by the fiat of a conquering incomer; thereby a people's personality, as it were, could be altered. It was Edward I, of course, who exercised this right most imperiously and comprehensively, in Wales in 1284 and in Scotland in 1305. 'We caused the laws and customs of those parts hitherto in use to be rehearsed before us and the nobles of our realm ... We have abolished some of them; we have allowed others; we have corrected some and likewise commanded certain others to be ordained and added thereto.'[71]

Edward I would have found no difficulty in justifying his actions. His justification brings us to a second substantial qualification to the respect to be accorded to the laws of a people. The memorandum which the king sent to the prince of Wales in May 1280 lays out the argument clearly.[72] Edward agreed that the Welsh should have their

---

[68] Aelred of Rievaulx, 'Relatio de Standardo', *Chronicles of the Reigns of Stephen, Henry II and Richard I* (Rolls Series, 1884–9), III, 186.

[69] Richard Fitz Neal, *Dialogus de Scaccario*, ed. C. Johnson (1950), 63.

[70] Cf. above, n. 10; *Gesta Stephani*, ed. K.R. Potter and R.H.C. Davis (Oxford, 1976), 14–15; Gerald of Wales, *Expugnatio Hibernica*, ed. A.B. Scott and F.X. Martin (Dublin, 1978), 190–1.

[71] Preamble to the Statute of Wales, 1284; cf. the Ordinance on the Governance of Scotland in *Anglo-Scottish Relations 1174–1328*, ed. Stones, 125.

[72] Public Record Office Chancery Miscellanea (C47) 27/2 (19), summarised in *Welsh Assize Roll*, 59–60.

own laws but only so long as they were deemed to be just and reasonable and did not derogate from the rights of his crown. He repeated the point and added his normal quota of unctuousness: Welsh laws must not deviate from the baseline of justice; if they were unjust or frivolous or evil the king was bound by his coronation oath to root them out. It was a line of argument which he consistently pursued in these years, invoking justice (*jus*, *justitita*), reason (*ratio*) and God as the benchmarks for his approval.[73] The Welsh could indeed count themselves to have emerged quite well from this rigorous test, since many of their legal practices and principles were at least tolerated after 1284. The Irish had come in for more of a drubbing, their laws being dismissed famously in 1277 as 'detestable to God and so contrary to all law that they ought not to be deemed laws'.[74] The Scots came off much more lightly, hardly surprising so since so many of their recent legal practices were derived from those of England. Yet contemporary opinion in England was in no doubt that even in Scotland legal revision was a necessary and justified consequence of political victory. As one contemporary song put it: 'The Scottish nobles submit to the English; judges are appointed; the laws are revised; for the laws themselves need to be regulated by right (*jus*)'.[75] There is no need to doubt the good faith or noble intentions of Edward I and his advisors; it is their political imagination which may be questioned, for to tamper officiously with a people's laws was to challenge one of the most valued emblems of its self-identity as a people.

Edward I had called the godhead and the abstract concepts of reason and justice to his aid in his reviews of the laws of Wales and Scotland; but there was a less elevated and more practical argument that could be used, that of political convenience and regnal solidarity. The view had once been common that the dominions of a king or an emperor were an aggregation of peoples; their very diversity in laws, customs and languages was indeed part of their strength and glory. It was precisely this argument which Llywelyn ap Gruffudd and his Welsh allies had put to Edward I in the statements with which I opened this address. But such a pluralist view had rarely enjoyed a monopoly position. A king might issue decrees which were to apply to all his subjects regardless of their ethnic affiliations and legal customs. So it was, for example, that Edgar issued an edict 'which shall be common to all the nation whether Englishmen, Danes and Britons in every province of my dominion'.[76] It was, at least in part, by the gradual

[73] *Cal. Ancient Correspondence*, ed. J.G. Edwards, 60; *Welsh Assize Roll*, 286; *Anglo-Scottish Relations*, ed. Stones, 125.

[74] *Foedera* etc., ed. T. Rymer (revised edn, 1816–69), I, ii, 540.

[75] *Political Songs*, ed. Wright, 168.

[76] IV Edgar 22: *English Historical Documents c. 500–1042*, ed. D. Whitelock (2nd edn, 1979), 435.

application of some such principle that the law in England came to be regarded as a unitary law which, notwithstanding local customs, was the property of all English people, including (as we saw earlier) English settlers in Wales and Ireland.

But the impact of such a development was unlikely to be confined to England or the English, for the English were also very much in the ascendancy in Wales and Ireland and, briefly, Scotland. It was inevitable that sooner or later the question would be raised whether political control and domination should not be accompanied by legal uniformity. It was in an Irish context that the philosophical basis of the equation was perhaps most clearly expressed. 'Where there is diversity of law', said a petition of the mid-fourteenth century, 'the people cannot be of one law or one community.'[77] The implication was clear: political cohesion depended on legal uniformity. It was a sentiment which was officially sanctioned in the preamble to the Statutes of Kilkenny. 'Diversity of government and diverse laws in one land', so they proclaimed as a self-evident truth, 'cause diversity of allegiance and disputes.'[78] It was, one might say, a statist concept of law. Nor was it, of course, peculiarly English. Thus the Scottish parliament in 1502 proclaimed the same orthodoxy in ringing terms à propos the Lordship of the Isles: 'all our soverane ordis lieges beand under hes obeysance And in speciale the Ilis be reulit be our soverane lordes aune lawes and the commoune lawis of the Realme and be nain other lawis'.[79]

It was in Ireland and Wales, of course, that the consequences of such a policy and assumption were most dramatically endorsed by statute. The so-called Act of Union of Wales of 1536 was in fact entitled 'an act for laws and justice to be ministered in Wales in like fourme as it is in this realm'. It prescribed that inheritance of land was henceforth to be 'after the forme of the lawes of this Realme of Englande and not after any tenure or after any Welshe lawes or customes' and it insisted that hereafter 'the lawes ordnances and statutes of this realme of Englande forever and none other lawes ... shal be ... used in ... Wales'. Likewise when Henry VIII adopted the title king of Ireland in 1541 he affirmed that the Irish were henceforth 'true subjects, obedient

---

[77] The petition, from the cities of Ireland, as quoted by G.J. Hand in 'English Law in Ireland, 1172–1351', *Northern Ireland Legal Quarterly*, XXIII (1972), 413, and in Robin Frame, *English Lordship in Ireland 1318–61* (Oxford, 1982), 4.

[78] *Irish Historical Documents*, ed. Curtis and McDowell, 53. Cf. the view of the commons in parliament in 1402, during the Welsh uprising, that 'the laws of England' be totally used in all royal lordships in Wales and that no custom contrary to 'the common law of England' was to be tolerated: *Rotuli Parliamentorum*, III, 509.

[79] *Acts of the Parliament of Scotland*, II, 252. Cf. the clause in the Treaty of Perth (1266) requiring the inhabitants of the Western Isles to 'be subject to the laws and customs of the Kingdom of Scotland', ibid., I, 78.

to his laws, forsaking their Irish laws, habits and customs'.[80] So was formally and statutorily buried the concept, which Llywelyn ap Gruffudd's spokesman had so eloquently articulated in 1279, of a dominion or empire of composite peoples, each with its own laws and customs duly recognised and respected. In its stead was ensconced a view of a uniform corpus of laws and customs throughout the king's dominions. It was as it were the legal and social equivalent of the doctrine *cuius regio, eius religio*. Law had become the property of a unitary state and crown; to that extent it was less the law of people, much less so the several laws of several peoples.[81] Law in the fullest sense of the term cannot be changed overnight, whatever legislators may think; and customs are clearly not at the bidding of statutes or monarchs. Nevertheless, if laws and customs were among the most cherished and potent identifiers of a people, and if both were being eroded by social and cultural change as well as by governmental fiat, how could a people—more especially a people without the institutional framework of political power and governmental institutions—preserve its identity? That is a question which I hope to address in the final of these lectures.

[80] 27 Henry VIII c. 26. It is worth quoting here the instructions (spelling modernised) that Henry VIII gave to the earl of Surrey with regard to the Irish in 1520: 'to ensearch of them under what manner and by what laws they will be ordered and governed, to the intent that if their laws be good and reasonable they may be approved, and the rigour of our laws, if they shall think them too hard, be mitigated and brought to such moderation as they may conveniently live under the same'. Quoted in Nerys Patterson, 'Gaelic Law and the Tudor Conquest of Ireland: The Social Background of the Sixteenth-Century Recensions of the Pseudo-Historical Prologue to the *Senchas már*', *Irish Historical Studies*, XXVII (1980–1), at 201.

[81] Cf. the note cited by Jenny Wormald, *ante*, 6th ser., 2 (1992), 185: 'The Kings desire to have one Crowne, and one lawe so far as maye be, and one government. But tyme must work yt. Nota for Wales how yt did grow.'

# THE MAKING OF *ANGELCYNN*: ENGLISH
# IDENTITY BEFORE THE NORMAN CONQUEST[1]

## By Sarah Foot

READ 20 JANUARY 1995

THERE are grounds for seeing an increasing sophistication in the development of a self-conscious perception of 'English' cultural uniqueness and individuality towards the end of the ninth century, at least in some quarters, and for crediting King Alfred's court circle with its expression. King Alfred was not, as Orderic Vitalis described him, 'the first king to hold sway over the whole of England', which tribute might rather be paid to his grandson Æthelstan.[2] He was, however, as his obituary in the Anglo-Saxon Chronicle described him, 'king over the whole English people except for that part which was under Danish rule'.[3] Through his promotion of the term *Angelcynn* to reflect the common identity of his people in a variety of texts dating from the latter part of his reign, and his efforts in cultivating the shared memory of his West Mercian and West Saxon subjects, King Alfred might be credited with the invention of the English as a political community.

This paper will consider why it was that Alfred, and after him the tenth-century West Saxon kings who created an English realm, chose to invent an *Angelcynn* and not the Saxonkind that might seem more obvious considering their own ethnic origins.[4] In exploring the pro-

---

[1] I owe a particular debt of gratitude to Michael Bentley, Julia Crick, David Dumville, Simon Loseby and Janet Nelson all of whom read the text of this paper in draft and made numerous suggestions for its improvement

[2] *The Ecclesiastical History of Orderic Vitalis*, ed. M. Chibnall (6 vols., Oxford, 1968–80), II.241; quoted by S. Keynes and M. Lapidge, *Alfred the Great: Asser's 'Life of King Alfred' and Other Contemporary Sources* (Harmondsworth, 1983), 46. For King Æthelstan (whose extended realm was a temporary creation, not surviving his death) see D.N. Dumville, *Wessex and England from Alfred to Edgar* (Woodbridge, 1992), ch. 4. It was a foreign conqueror, the Danish king, Cnut, who described himself as *ealles Engla landes cyning*: I Cnut, prologue, ed. F. Liebermann, *Die Gesetze der Angelsachsen* (3 vols., Halle, 1903–16), I.278–307, at 278; transl. *English Historical Documents, I, c.500–1042*, ed. D. Whitelock (2nd edn, London, 1979) [hereafter *EHD*], no. 49, 454. See P. Wormald, '*Engla lond*: The Making of an Allegiance', *Journal of Historical Sociology*, VII (1994), 1–24, at 10.

[3] Anglo-Saxon Chronicle, *s.a.* 900: *MS A*, ed. J. Bately (*The Anglo-Saxon Chronicle: A Collaborative Edition*, ed. D. Dumville and S. Keynes, III (Cambridge, 1986) [hereafter ASC], 61; *EHD*, no. 1, 207.

[4] On the adoption of collective names see A.D. Smith, *The Ethnic Origins of Nations* (Oxford, 1986), 22–4. See also P. Wormald, 'Bede, the *Bretwaldas* and the Origins of the *gens Anglorum*', in *Ideal and Reality in Frankish and Anglo-Saxon Society*, ed. P. Wormald *et al.* (Oxford, 1983), 99–129, at 103–4.

motion of this collective name for the politically united Anglo-Saxon peoples, I start from the premise that language is more than an important reflection of the thought of an age; it is essentially constitutive of that thought. Such ideas are only open to a people as they have the language available to express them; in other words, ideas are conditioned by the language in which they can be thought.[5]

For the year 886 the Anglo-Saxon Chronicle reported that King Alfred had occupied London and that 'all the English people (*all Angelcyn*) who were not under subjection to the Danes, submitted to him'.[6] It now seems probable that London had in fact been recovered from the Danes a few years earlier, perhaps in 883 when the Chronicle reports Alfred laying siege to the city, and that what occurred in 886 was either a retaking of the city or a ceremonial statement of the significance of London's restoration to 'English' rule.[7] Earlier in the ninth century Mercia had forcibly been brought under West Saxon rule by King Ecgberht, and in mid-century there is evidence for some co-operation between the two kingdoms.[8] But while the events of 886 may represent only a formalisation of this pre-existing alliance, the rhetoric by which they are described serves to construe this as a formative moment in the creation of a united West Saxon/Mercian realm. The ceremony is coupled with the submission of the Mercian

[5] For discussion in an Anglo-Saxon context of the relationship between a culture's ideas and the language in which they are expressed see M. Godden, 'Anglo-Saxons on the Mind', in *Learning and Literature in Anglo-Saxon England*, ed. M. Lapidge and H. Gneuss (Cambridge, 1985), 271–98, at 286. A helpful introduction to the wider issue of the role of language in the making of history is N. Partner, 'The New Cornificius: Medieval History and the Artifice of Words', in *Classical Rhetoric and Medieval Historiography*, ed. E. Breisach (Kalamazoo, Mich., 1985), 5–59, especially 25–40; also N. Partner, 'Making up Lost Time: Writing on the Writing of History', *Speculum*, LXI (1986), 90–117, at 94–8.

[6] ASC, *s.a.* 886, ed. Bately, 53: 'Þy ilcan geare gesette ælfred cyning Lundenburg, 7 him all Angelcyn to cirde, þæt buton Deniscra monna hæftniede was, 7 hie þa befæste þa burge æþerede aldormen to haldonne'. Transl. *EHD*, 199.

[7] That London was recovered before 886 is suggested by the numismatic evidence, which has been interpreted to mean that Alfred was minting his London-monogram pennies earlier in the 880s than 886: M.A.S. Blackburn, 'The London Mint in the Reign of Alfred', in *Kings, Currency and Alliances: The History and Coinage of Southern England, AD 840–900*, ed. M.A.S. Blackburn and D.N. Dumville (Woodbridge, forthcoming). For the significance of the ceremonies of 886 see J. Nelson, 'The Political Ideas of Alfred of Wessex', in *Kings and Kingship in Medieval Europe*, ed. A. Duggan (London, 1993), 125–58, at 154–5.

[8] The Chronicle reported for 825 that Ecgberht had defeated the Mercians at Wroughton, and for 829 that he conquered the kingdom of the Mercians and everything south of the Humber: ASC, *s.a.* 823, ed. Bately, 41; *s.a.* 827, ed. Bately, 42; transl. *EHD*, 185–6. Evidence for increased understanding between the two kingdoms is apparent in the reign of Æthelwulf (who married his daughter to the Mercian king, Burgred, and assisted him in an expedition against the Welsh in 853) and during the 840s when the West Saxon and Mercian coinages were closely related: Keynes and Lapidge, *Alfred the Great*, 12.

ruler Æthelred (to whom charge of the city was entrusted) and his acceptance of an ealdordom, and may also have coincided with his marriage to Alfred's daughter Æthelflæd.[9] According to Asser the joining of Wessex and Mercia was a new union, voluntarily entered into: 'all the Anglo-Saxons—those who had formerly been scattered everywhere and were not in captivity with the Danes—turned willingly to King Alfred and submitted themselves to his lordship'.[10]

The adoption of a new political terminology to reflect the new hegemony of Wessex over the western Mercians is, as Janet Nelson has recently argued, particularly apposite.[11] It was from this time that Alfred was styled in charters *rex Angul-Saxonum*, rather than the more usual West Saxon title of *rex Saxonum*, and from this point in his narrative that Asser adopted the same style to describe the king.[12] Alfred clearly now considered himself licensed to act on behalf of more than his West Saxon subjects; in making an agreement with the Viking ruler of East Anglia, Guthrum, he spoke of himself as acting on behalf of all the counsellors of the English: *ealles Angelcynnes witan*.[13] The discourse here is not, however, simply such as that used by any ruler consolidating a new political realm. Certainly Alfred's record of military success demonstrated the wisdom of Mercian acceptance of his rule, but he could have continued to ensure the physical safety of his subject peoples without compromising their separateness. What the Alfredian rhetoric does is to advance the notion

[9] Keynes and Lapidge (*Alfred the Great*, 228 n. 1) have argued that Æthelred accepted Alfred as his lord as early as 883, on the evidence of a Worcester charter S 218 [S = P.H. Sawyer, *Anglo-Saxon Charters: An Annotated List and Bibliography* (London, 1968)], but this could now be fitted into the new chronology for the taking of London in that year.

[10] Asser, *Life of King Alfred*, c. 80, ed. W.H. Stevenson, *Asser's Life of King Alfred* (Oxford, 1904; new impression, 1959), 69; transl. Keynes and Lapidge, *Alfred the Great*, 98.

[11] Nelson, 'The Political Ideas', 134–5.

[12] As Nelson has pointed out, although Asser described Alfred as 'ruler of all the Christians of the island of Britain, king of the Anglo-Saxons' in the preface to his Life of the king, he did not use that style again until describing events after the formal submission of 886: Nelson, 'The Political Ideas', 155. For the adoption of the royal-title *rex Angul-Saxonum* in Alfred's charters see Stevenson, *Asser*, 149–52 ; Whitelock, 'Some Charters in the Name of King Alfred', in *Saints, Scholars and Heroes*, ed. M.H. King and W.M. Stevens (2 vols., Collegeville, Minn., 1979), I.77–98; Keynes and Lapidge, *Alfred the Great*, 227–8 n. 1; Nelson, 'The Political Ideas', 134 n. 42.

[13] Alfred–Guthrum treaty; ed. Liebermann, *Die Gesetze*, I.126–9; transl. in Keynes and Lapidge, *Alfred the Great*, 171–2. Alfred might alternatively have here been asserting his right to act on behalf of the Angles (namely the Mercians), not just the West Saxons for whom he already spoke as king, which message could have had a similar propaganda value. But the text of the treaty goes on to distinguish Danishmen (*Deniscne*) from Englishmen (*Engliscne*), and I understand the *Angelcynn* mentioned here to incorporate all those in Kent and Wessex as well as the Mercian Angles. The treaty is customarily dated to 886 (capture of London) x 890 (death of Guthrum): Keynes and Lapidge, *Alfred the Great*, 171. Dumville has, however, challenged this view and argued that the treaty should rather be dated to 878: *Wessex*, ch. 1.

that all the Germanic subjects of the West Saxon king were essentially one 'Englishkind'. The common identity of the West Saxons, Mercians and the men of Kent as the *Angelcynn* was defined by the West Saxon court machine specifically with reference to their otherness from those subject to Danish rule (and from the Welsh from whom Alfred had also received submission),[14] and their common cause under one leader in opposition to the Danes, but also more generally in the sense of one people with a common heritage, one faith, and a shared history.[15]

The role of King Alfred in the development of a sense of English individuality will be examined by exploring the ways in which the Germanic inhabitants of pre-Conquest Britain described themselves and were described by outsiders.[16] The separate and individual identity of the different kingdoms of pre-Conquest Britain was clearly important to their rulers, and it is important to recognise that the apparent use of a consistent vocabulary for the English people does not prefigure any sense of political unity among the Anglo-Saxons before the late ninth century.[17] However, examination of contemporary linguistic usage can be a valuable key to concepts of the past, particularly in the sphere of naming. Not only are the words chosen by one culture to express its ideas one sign of its own distinctive and individual thought, but the collective names adopted by communities play a significant part in the process of the formation of their identity.[18]

Robert Bartlett has argued that medieval ethnicity was a social construct rather than a biological datum, being determined primarily by cultural distinctions which have the potential to evolve differently in changing circumstances.[19] He cites the example of Regino of Prüm who, writing *c.* 900, offered four categories for classifying ethnic variation: 'the various nations differ in descent, customs, language and law'.[20] Although Regino placed *genus* not *lingua* as the first of his

[14] Asser, Life of Alfred, ch. 80, ed. Stevenson, 66; transl. Keynes and Lapidge, *Alfred the Great*, 96.

[15] Keynes and Lapidge, *Alfred the Great*, 38–41.

[16] Important in shaping my ideas has been S. Reynolds, 'What do we Mean by Anglo-Saxon and the Anglo-Saxons?', *Journal of British Studies*, XXIV (1985), 395–414.

[17] The development before the Conquest of the notion of an English (as opposed to a Saxon, or Anglo-Saxon identiy) has been examined by Patrick Wormald in various articles: 'Bede, the *Bretwaldas*'; 'The Venerable Bede and the "Church of the English"', in *The English Religious Tradition and the Genius of Anglicanism*, ed. G. Rowell (1992), 13–32; '*Engla Lond*: The Making of an Allegiance', *Journal of Historical Sociology*, VII (1994), 1–24; 'The Making of England', *History Today* (February 1995), 26–32.

[18] Godden, 'Anglo-Saxons on the Mind', 286; Smith, *Ethnic Origins*, 23.

[19] R. Bartlett, *The Making of Europe* (London, 1993), 197. See also P. Geary, 'Ethnic Identity as a Situational Construct in the Early Middle Ages', *Mitteilungen der Anthropologischen Gesellschaft in Wien*, CXIII (1983), 15–26, at 18–20.

[20] Regino, letter to Archbishop Hatto of Mainz (ed. F. Kurze, *Regionis Prumiensis Chronicon*, MGH, SRG (Hanover, 1890), xix-xx): 'sicut diuersae nationes populorum inter

categories, racial differences were generally considered less relevant in the formation of concepts of nationhood in the middle ages than cultural qualities such as customs, language and law. The importance of linguistic bonds in forging collective identity was recognised by many medieval writers.[21] In an insular context, Bede distinguished the peoples of Britain (Britons, Picts, Irish and English) by the languages which they spoke.[22] Following Bede in part, Alcuin drew attention to the role of language together with lineage: 'famed Britain holds within her bounds peoples divided by language and separated by race according to their ancestors' names'.[23] In accentuating the potential of the written language—*Englisc*—to bind together his subjects as the *Angelcynn*, Alfred showed how the promotion of the common tongue they shared might be useful in overriding the inheritance of political and ancestral separateness in the creation of a new identity.[24]

The word *Angelcynn* is first found in one Mercian charter of the 850s from Worcester, where it was used to distinguish those of English origin from foreigners and was apparently synonymous with the Latin *Angli*.[25]

---

se discrepant genere, moribus, lingua, legibus'. W. Kienast (*Die frankische Vasallität* (Frankfurt, 1990), 270–1 n. 900) has noted that Regino's definition of national characteristics is similar to the famous opening sentence of Caesar's Gallic War: 'Gallia est omnis diuisa in partes tres ... Hi omnes lingua, institutis, legibus inter se differunt' (Gaul is a whole divided into three parts ... All these differ from one another in language, institutions and laws): Caesar, The Gallic War, I.1 (ed. and transl. H.J. Edwards (London, 1917)). I am grateful to Professor J.L. Nelson for drawing this reference to my attention.

[21] Bartlett, *The Making of Europe*, 198–204.

[22] *Bede's Ecclesiastical History of the English People*, ed. and transl. B. Colgrave and R.A.B. Mynors (Oxford, 1969) [hereafter *HE*], I.1, at 16–17. John Hines has commented on the significance of Bede's recognition of the existence of a single English language: 'The Becoming of the English: Identity, Material Culture and Language in Early Anglo-Saxon England', *Anglo-Saxon Studies in Archaeology and History*, VII (1994), 49–59, at 51. The extent to which Bede's language was at variance from that of other writers of his time is explored further below, see also Wormald, 'Bede, the *Bretwaldas*', 120–3.

[23] *Alcuin: The Bishops, Kings and Saints of York*, ed. and transl. P. Godman (Oxford, 1982), lines 501–2: 'in se quod retinet famosa Britannia gentes / diuisas linguis, populis per nomina patrum'. Alcuin's statement owes something to *HE*, III.6 (ed. and transl. Colgrave and Mynors, 230–1): 'omnes nationes et prouincias Brittaniae, quae in quattuor linguas, id est Brettonum Pictorum Scottorum et Anglorum diuisae sunt'.

[24] Alfred preface to the Old English *Regula pastoralis*, ed. D. Whitelock, *Sweet's Anglo-Saxon Reader in Prose and Verse* (rev. edn, Oxford, 1967), 4–7, at 5; transl. Keynes and Lapidge, *Alfred the Great*, 124–6, at 125: 'So completely had learning decayed among the *Angelcynn*, that there were very few on this side of the Humber who could comprehend their services in *Englisc*.'

[25] S 207, a charter of Burgred of Mercia dated 855 by which he granted the minster at Blockley to the church of Worcester, freeing it from various obligations including that of lodging all mounted men of the English race (& *ealra angelcynnes monna*) and foreigners, whether of noble or humble birth, which freedom was to be given for ever, as long as the Christian faith might last among the English (*apud Anglos*). That the term *Angelcynn* had been coined before Alfred's time (possibly long before its first recorded written usage) does not detract from my central argument that Alfred harnessed the word to his own particular ends.

But it becomes common only in the last two decades of the ninth century when it appears in a variety of texts associated with the Alfredian court, notably in works which were part of the king's programme of educational reform and revival. This implies that it was not chosen unwittingly but, together with the subject matter of the texts themselves, it was part of an attempt to promote a nascent conception of one people. It was as the *Angelcynn* that Alfred described his subjects in the letter which he circulated to his bishops with his translation of Pope Gregory's *Regula pastoralis*. Recalling how formerly 'there were happy times then throughout the *Angelcynn*', Alfred appealed to the collective memory of his people, reminding them of their shared past and of the consequences of their failure to abstract themselves from worldly affairs to apply the wisdom given by God: 'Remember what punishments befell us in this world when we ourselves did not cherish learning or transmit it to other men.'[26] His solution was to urge his bishops to assist him in teaching 'all the free-born young men now among the *Angelcynn*' to read English, for which project he was trans-lating, or arranging to have translated 'into the language that all can understand, certain books which are the most necessary for all men to know'.[27] These texts, as has long been recognised, were not chosen randomly, but together constituted a programme of study which if mastered would serve to restore Christianity among the English aris-tocracy, which in the king's opinion had declined so far, notably through their loss of understanding of Latin, that God had sent the Danes as divine punishment.[28]

[26] Alfred, prose preface, ed. Whitelock, 5; transl. Keynes and Lapidge, *Alfred the Great*, 125. Compare also Alfred's preface to his translation of Psalm xiii, ed. J.W. Bright and R.L. Ramsay, *Liber Psalmorum: The West Saxon Psalms* (Boston and London, 1907), 24; transl. Keynes and Lapidge, *Alfred the Great*, 158: 'When David sang this thirteenth psalm, he lamented to the Lord in the psalm that in his time there should be so little faith, and so little wisdom should be found in the world. And so does every just man who sings it now: he laments the same thing in his own time.' See also T.A. Shippey, 'Wealth and Wisdom in King Alfred's *Preface* to the Old English Pastoral Care', *EHR*, XCIV (1979), 346–55; for the interest taken in Alfred's prefatory letter by Anglican reformers and other scholars in the second half of the sixteenth century see R.I. Page, 'The Sixteenth-Century Reception of Alfred the Great's Letter to his Bishops', *Anglia*, CX (1992), 36–64, at 37–41.

[27] Alfred, prose preface, ed. Whitelock, 6; transl. Keynes and Lapidge, *Alfred the Great*, 126.

[28] Compare Alfred's translation of Psalm ii:12, ed. Bright and Ramsay, 3, transl. Keynes and Lapidge, *Alfred the Great*, 154: 'Embrace learning lest you incur God's anger and lest you stray from the right path.' Although in his Life of the king Asser depicted Alfred's thirst for learning as driven primarily by personal aspiration (for example Life of Alfred, chs. 76–8, ed. Stevenson, *Asser*, 59–63; transl. Keynes and Lapidge, *Alfred the Great*, 91–3), the final chapter of Asser's Life makes explicit the broader application Alfred envisaged: ch. 106, ed. Stevenson, *Asser*, 92–5; transl. Keynes and Lapidge, *Alfred the Great*, 109–110. S. Keynes, 'Royal Government and the Written Word in Late Anglo-Saxon England',

In this prefatory letter to the *Regula pastoralis* the king showed his sensitivity to the power of language and its potential for conveying wisdom, as well as an awareness of the benefits which earlier societies had drawn from the use of their own vernaculars: 'then I recalled how the Law was first composed in the Hebrew language, and thereafter, when the Greeks learned it, they translated it into their own language and other books as well'.[29] Language offers understanding, and understanding gives knowledge of the Law, and hence knowledge of God. The text above all others which gave Alfred's officials knowledge of the kind of wisdom they needed to fulfil their duties was, as Simon Keynes has noted, the king's law-code.[30] Here Alfred portrayed himself as a law-giver firmly rooted within an historical tradition;[31] quoting the law of Moses and earlier laws from each of the kingdoms over whom he now had lordship, he claimed not to be making new law, but to be restoring to his newly united peoples the law that they had lost. This is made explicit in the historical introduction which the king appended to his own law-book, where he begins with a collection of passages of Mosaic law, mostly taken from Exodus and beginning with the Ten Commandments, before moving on to consider how Old Testament law for the Jews was modified for Christian nations, and then the earlier medieval history of law-giving.[32]

Afterwards when it came about that many peoples had received the faith of Christ, many synods of holy bishops and also of other distinguished counsellors were assembled throughout all the earth, and also throughout all the *Angelcynn* (after they had received the faith of Christ) ... Then in many synods they fixed the compensations for many human misdeeds, and they wrote them in many synod-books, here one law, there another. Then I, King Alfred, collected these together and ordered to be written many of them which our forefathers observed, those which I liked; and those which I did not like I rejected with the advice of my counsellors and ordered them

in *The Uses of Literacy in Early Medieval Europe*, ed. R. McKitterick (Cambridge, 1990), 228–57, at 230–1.

[29] Alfred, prose preface, ed. Whitelock, 6; transl. Keynes and Lapidge, *Alfred the Great*, 125.

[30] Keynes, 'Royal Government', 231–2.

[31] Wallace-Hadrill ('The Franks and the English: Some Common Historical Interests', in his *Early Medieval History* (Oxford, 1975), 201–16, at 216) noted the relevance to Alfred of Bede's statement (*HE*, II.5) that Æthelberht of Kent had established with the advice of his counsellors a code of laws after the Roman manner, which had been written down in English to be preserved, and drew attention also to the example of ninth-century Frankish law collections.

[32] Alfred, Laws, introduction §49.7–9; ed. Liebermann, *Die Gesetze*, I.44–6; transl. Keynes and Lapidge, *Alfred the Great*, 163–4.

to be differently observed. For I dared not presume to set in writing at all many of my own, because it was unknown to me what would please those who should come after us. But those which I found, which seemed to me most just, either in the time of my kinsman King Ine, or of Offa, king of the Mercians, or of Æthelberht (who first among the *Angelcynn* received baptism), I collected herein and omitted the others.

Alfred was appropriating his subject peoples' separate—Christian—pasts to his own ends. The law he now gave to the *Angelcynn* was not one of his own creation but an amalgam of the collected laws of previous kings of Kent, Mercia and Wessex. Alfred was legislating here overtly in the tradition of a Christian king, against an historical background of Old Testament law-giving (and in the light of a contemporary Frankish commitment to written laws and to the collection of law-codes).[33] He was showing the Anglo-Saxons how similar their laws were to those of Ancient Israel and also inviting them to remodel themselves as a new Chosen People.[34] Bede had conceived of the *gens Anglorum* as the new Israel, but Alfred went further: he purported to restore a state that had formerly existed, equivalent to the state of Israel restored after the Babylonian captivity, not to create a new unitary structure of diverse peoples brought together under one Christian law.[35] Previous Anglo-Saxon kings had extended their realms by military force in order to encompass people from different *gentes*, but had not thereby either made themselves into 'emperors' or indeed defined their own kingship other than by reference to their own *gens*: although he had taken control of the previously independent kingoms of the Hwicce, the South Saxons and of Kent, removing or demoting their own kings, and he had some authority in Surrey, Essex and East Anglia, Offa was never described in contemporary documents as other than *rex Mer-*

[33] J.L. Nelson, 'Literacy in Carolingian Government', in *The Uses of Literacy*, ed. McKitterick, 258–96, at 263.
[34] Wormald, 'The Venerable Bede', 25. For the Franks' perception of themselves as a chosen people, a new Israel, see J.L. Nelson, 'Kingship and Empire in the Carolingian World', in *Carolingian Culture: Emulation and Innovation*, ed. R. McKitterick (Cambridge, 1994), 52–87, at 55–6; for ninth-century Frankish use of the exemplary world of the Old Testament see J.M. Wallace-Hadrill, 'History in the Mind of Archbishop Hincmar', in *The Writing of History in the Middle Ages*, ed. R.H.C. Davis and J.M. Wallace-Hadrill (Oxford, 1981), 43–70, at 49–51.
[35] For Bede's conception see Wormald, 'The Venerable Bede', 23–4. Alcuin had drawn a parallel between the sack of Lindisfarne in 793 and the sack of Jerusalem and destruction of the Temple by the Chaldeans, which led to the Israelites' Babylonian captivity: *Epistola* 20, ed. Dümmler, *MGH, Epistolae Karolini Aevi*, II.57 transl. *EHD*, no. 194. I am grateful to Dr Judith Maltby for suggesting the parallel with the Babylonian captivity to me.

*ciorum.*[36] Where Alfred was innovative was in his attempt to make his West Saxon and Mercian peoples into one *gens* (the *gens Anglorum* or *Angelcynn*) using his programme of educational revival and reform to encourage among his subjects an idea of their single past history. Appealing to their memory of shared experience and common law he sought to persuade them that he was restoring the English, whereas, albeit following a model provided by Bede, he was inventing them.[37]

The creation of a newly named people subject to one lord, loyalty to whom was forcibly imposed by oath,[38] might be understood in the narrow sense of the imposition of a politically defined nationhood by a cultural elite, in this case the royal court, over a wider population, an identity which could never have been exclusive nor taken priority over pre-existing, more local, allegiances. One might therefore dismiss Alfred's notion of Englishness as representative only of a restricted kind of political identity with no broader relevance beyond the rarefied circles of Alfred's immediate entourage. It might, nevertheless, at least within that confined group surrounding the king, resemble a primitive attempt at creating a single *gens*. Alfred's primitive 'nation', created out of political necessity, would to some extent conform to Gellner's definition of nationalism (articulated exclusively in relation to modern states) as 'primarily a principle which holds that the political and national unit should be congruent'.[39] But the Alfredian 'nation' was also defined in terms of its difference from the other (here clearly

[36] S. Keynes, 'Changing Faces: Offa, King of Mercia', *History Today*, XL (November 1990), 14–19. A small group of Worcester charters does give more grandiose titles to Æthelbald of Mercia: S 94, 101, 103, and S 89 (transl. *EHD*, no. 67) in which Æthelbald is called *rex sutangli* and in the witness list, *rex Britanniae*. Although this charter might be compared with the statement Bede made about the extent of Æthelbald's power south of the Humber (*HE*, V.23), these titles are not adopted by other scriptoria of the period and may reveal more of the aspirations of Worcester draftsmen than the Mercian king's own perceptions of his rule.

[37] This point was noted by Gaimar, who in his *Estoire des Engleis* (written *c.* 1140) attributed to King Alfred the responsibility for making the Anglo-Saxon Chronicle as a history of the English: *L'estoire des Engleis by Geffrei Gaimar* (Anglo-Norman Text Society, 1960), vv. 3443–50. I am grateful to John Gillingham for drawing this point to my attention and for allowing me to see his forthcoming paper 'Gaimar, the Prose *Brut* and the Making of English History'.

[38] Alfred, Laws, §1.2, ed. Liebermann, *Die Gesetze*, I.46. Carolingian parallels are particularly apt here, for example Charlemagne's imposition of a general fidelity oath in 789 after the revolt of Hardrad (*Duplex legationis edictum*, c. 18, *MGH, Capitularia*, I, no. 23, 63) and his insistence in 802 that all over the age of twelve should promise to him as emperor the fidelity which they had previously promised to him as king: *MGH, Capitularia*, I, no. 33, ch. 2, 92. See now M. Becher, *Eid und Herrschaft: Untersuchungen zum Herrscherethos Karls des Großen* (Sigmaringen, 1993), especially chs. ii and iv.

[39] E. Gellner, *Nations and Nationalism* (Oxford, 1983), at 1, and 53–62. More sympathetic to the idea that national sentiment might exist in pre-modern nations is A.D. Smith, *National Identity* (Harmondsworth, 1991).

understood to be both the Christian Welsh and, more significantly, the pagan Danes) in which context Peter Sahlin's comments, although again made in a modern context, seem pertinent: 'national identity like ethnic or communal identity is contingent and relational: it is defined by the social or territorial boundaries drawn to distinguish the collective self and its implicit negation, the other'.[40] However, while there are clearly some echoes, in placing loyalty to the primitive state too high up the agenda and apparently minimising the importance of other possible communities or identities any modern nationalist model is too exclusive for ninth-century circumstances. The creation of one political unit at this period was hindered by the fissiparous nature of the early Anglo-Saxon state, and the vigour of regional separatism—the distinctiveness of Mercia and, later, in the tenth century, of Northumbria continued to be articulated far beyond the establishment of unified rule from Wessex. There was, as Wormald has shown, no Alfredian England.[41] But, in agreeing that there was no potential for uniting the polities, must we also accept that there was no putative conception of Englishness?

Alfred's educational programme could be interpreted as a conscious effort to shape an English imagination by disseminating beyond the court his ideas about the nature of 'Englishness' and his fictive interpretation of history through the works he determined the English should read. Drawing attention to Asser's account of the king's learning of 'Saxon songs' (*carmina Saxonica*) in his childhood and his urging their memorisation on his entourage, Janet Nelson has stressed the distinctively Saxon vernacular and aristocratic cultural inheritance which Alfred wished to emphasise.[42] While this might suggest a specifically (West) Saxon focus to Alfred's endeavours, other aspects of his programme demonstrate the wider transmission of his ideas to his Kentish and Anglian (Mercian) subjects as well, through the use of the vernacular, which breadth is encompassed by Keynes and Lapidge's translation of Asser's *libri Saxonici* as English books.[43] Alfred was not

[40] P. Sahlins, *Boundaries: The Making of France and Spain in the Pyrenees* (Berkeley and Los Angeles, 1989), 271. Compare also E. Hobsbawm (*Nations and Nationalism since 1780* (Cambridge, 1990), 91): 'there is no more effective way of bonding together the disparate sections of restless peoples than to unite them against outsiders'. And L. Colley, 'Britishness and Otherness: An Argument', *Journal of British Studies*, XXXI (1992), 309–29.

[41] Wormald, 'The Making of England'.

[42] Asser, Life of King Alfred, ch. 76 (ed. Stevenson, 59); J.L. Nelson, 'Wealth and Wisdom: The Politics of Alfred the Great', in *Kings and Kingship*, ed. J. Rosenthal, *Acta* XI 1984 (Binghampton, N.Y., 1986), 31–52, at 44.

[43] Keynes and Lapidge, *Alfred the Great*, 91. Compare Asser, Life of Alfred, ch. 75 (ed. Stevenson, *Asser*, 58, transl. Keynes and Lapidge, *Alfred the Great*, 90) which refers to the school established by the king where books were carefully read in both languages, in Latin and English: *utriusque linguae libri, Latinae scilicet et Saxonicae*. Nelson was also referring

only reminding all of his aristocracy that they shared a cultural tradition (in which they might more actively participate if they reacquired the wisdom they had lost)[44] but asserting that their common cultural ethic arose from their common origins and a shared history.[45]

The historical element of the curriculum Alfred devised is striking: not only were Orosius's Histories against the Pagans and Bede's Ecclesiastical History translated into Old English at this time, but it must be in the context of this wider programme that the compilation of the Anglo-Saxon Chronicle was commissioned.[46] The Chronicle and the Old English Bede could both be seen as instruction for the English, the *Angelcynn*, in their shared inheritance of a common history. One of the themes of Bede's History, as I shall suggest further below, was the promotion of a sense of unity and common cause among the Germanic Christian peoples of Britain; where Bede wrote of a Christian *gens Anglorum*, his Mercian translator spoke of *Ongelcynn* or *Ongelþeode*.[47] Together this historical literature gave the English a myth—a story with a veiled meaning—of their common origins; the Anglo-Saxon Chronicle in particular is a history with an inner hermeneutic. It is not propaganda for one dynasty;[48] the Chronicle does

to the relevance to Kentishmen and Mercians of the wisdom which Alfred sought to foster: 'Wealth', 45.

[44] Nelson, 'Wealth', 45.

[45] One is reminded here of Anthony Smith's definition of ethnic communities as 'named populations with shared ancestry myths, histories and cultures, having an association with specific territory and a sense of solidarity': *The Ethnic Origins of Nations* (Oxford, 1986), 32. Also Colley, 'Britishness', p. 317.

[46] That the translation of Bede's Ecclesiastical History into Old English, although not made by the king himself, might be datable to Alfred's reign was argued by D. Whitelock, 'The Old English Bede', *Proceedings of the British Academy*, XLVIII (1962), 57–90; reprinted in her collected papers *From Bede to Alfred* (Aldershot, 1980), no. viii. Her opinion is shared by Keynes and Lapidge, *Alfred the Great*, 33. While I would argue that the compilation of the Anglo-Saxon Chronicle was part of King Alfred's wider scheme for the invention of a sense of shared identity among his subjects, others have sought to separate the compilation of annals from the late ninth-century West Saxon royal court both chronologically: A. Thorogood, 'The Anglo-Saxon Chronicle in the Reign of Ecgberht', *EHR*, XLVIII (1933), 353–63, and geographically: F. Stenton, 'The South-Western Element in the Old English Chronicle', *Preparatory to Anglo-Saxon England*, ed. D. M. Stenton (Oxford, 1970), 106–15; J. Bately, 'The Compilation of the Anglo-Saxon Chronicle, 60 BC to AD 890: Vocabulary as Evidence', *Proceedings of the British Academy*, LXIV (1978), 93–129.

[47] *The Old English Version of Bede's Ecclesiastical History of the English People*, at, for example, I.xiii, IV.ii, V.xxiii (ed. T. Miller, 4 vols., Early English Text Society, original series XCV–XCVI and CX–CXI (London, 1890–8), part i, 54, 258, 478–80). The word *Angelcynn* occurs in a number of annals in the A manuscript of Anglo-Saxon Chronicle before 886, used in relation to the English people as a whole (*s.a.* 443, 597, 787 and 836, ed. Bately, 17, 25, 39, 43) and of the English school in Rome (*s.a.* 874, ed. Bately, 49).

[48] *Contra* R.H.C. Davis, 'Alfred the Great: Propaganda and Truth', *History*, LVI (1971), 169–82; and J.M. Wallace-Hadrill, who saw the Chronicle as 'a reflection of urgent political need not of a people, but a dynasty': 'The Franks and the English in the Ninth Century: Some Common Historical Interests', in *Early Medieval History* (Oxford, 1975), 201–16, at 210–11.

not present, in the way that Bede did, the history of one people in a linear progression with a beginning, a middle and an end: there are indeed too many beginnings in the Chronicle. But, despite its annalistic form, it is a continuing and developing narrative.[49] The separate beginnings of Alfred's subject peoples are brought to one end: that of unitary rule from Wessex. It hard not to see the chronicler's statement about the general submission of 886 as the climactic moment of the achievement of this end to which the whole was directed, although the story continues thereafter: the *Angelcynn* have had multiple early histories, but will have one future, together. The inclusion of the different origin-myths for the separate early kingdoms illustrates the distinctiveness of each people; their ethnic diversity and the particular circumstances in which each group arrived in Britain gives each people its own traditions and culture; the genealogies for each royal line provide a record of each separate ruling dynasty.[50] Yet despite the differences in each kingdom's past history, they all share certain common features and ultimately theirs is a collective history.

In anthropological terms this might be called an instrumental ethnicity, a group identity based on the political circumstances of the moment, a subjective process for defining a collective group.[51] In this case one useful model, despite its failure to consider pre-modern societies, is that of Benedict Anderson's *Imagined Communities*.[52] Alfred was indeed trying to shape the English imagination; by collating and presenting a coherent historical whole he invented an English community, implanting into the minds of his people a personal and cultural feeling of belonging to the *Angelcynn*, the English kind. Alfred presented his subjects with an idea partly shaped by Bede, partly of his own devising, and he adopted a self-conscious way of promoting it through the educational reform-programme. Despite the differences in scale, this is similar to Anderson's argument about the importance of the mass production of print as a formative process in the creation of

[49] I differ here from H. White in his analysis of early medieval annals: *The Content and the Form: Narrative Discourse and Historical Representation* (Baltimore, Md., and London, 1987), ch. 1. On medieval writers' use of linear narrative see also Partner, 'The New Cornificius', 42–3. I am grateful to Michael Bentley for discussing these ideas with me at length; I intend to pursue some of these thoughts about the Chronicle in a forthcoming paper.

[50] For consideration of the use of genealogy in the assertion of political unity in the early middle ages see D.N. Dumville, 'Kingship, Genealogies and Regnal Lists', in *Early Medieval Kingship*, ed. P.H. Sawyer and I.N. Wood (Leeds, 1977), 72–104 (reprinted in Dumville's collected papers: *Histories and Pseudo-Histories of the Insular Middle Ages* (Aldershot, 1990), no. xv).

[51] P. Amory, 'Ethnographic Culture and the Construction of Community in Ostrogothic Italy, 489–554' (Ph.D. thesis, University of Cambridge, 1994), 8–11; Geary, 'Ethnic Identity', 24–6.

[52] B. Anderson, *Imagined Communities: Reflections on the Origin and Spread of Nationalism* (2nd edn, London, 1991), especially chs. 2–3.

imagined nations. It is significant that Alfred used the vernacular in order that his ideas might be most accessible.[53] While the texts he thought 'most necessary for all men to know' would not have been accessible to as wide an audience as that theoretically possible in a print culture, Alfred was aiming at a socially and geographically wide readership—'all free-born young men now among the English'—who were to be reached through the participation of all of the king's bishops in his extended realm. The notion of a common English identity was certainly dreamt up in the rarefied, scholarly atmosphere of Alfred's court, but it was from the outset intended for a wider audience. One might wish to question the likelihood of the notion penetrating to the wider mass of the semi-free peasantry, but the obligation of general oath-taking suggested by the first chapter of Alfred's law-code might indicate that it was to the broader group of those subjects who swore the oath that the rhetoric of Englishness was directed.

Alfred was thus manipulating the history of the Anglo-Saxon peoples to create among his own subjects a sense of cultural and spiritual identity, by invoking a concept of Englishness particularly dependent on the Christian faith. It was the loss of faith (notably through the loss of that knowledge which had given previous generations access to the wisdom of Christian writings) which had led the English to the brink of collapse and brought so many of their ethnic as well as spiritual compatriots into captivity under a foreign, and pagan, people. For all the obvious (and patently far from coincidental) advantages for the new regime, this was more than simply a rationale for the political domination of Wessex over Mercia. How original was it?

That divine vengeance might be anticipated if sin were not corrected was scarcely a novel idea; divine displeasure was indeed the most frequently adduced explanation for any disaster.[54] Nor was Alfred the only writer to make direct association between Viking raids and divine displeasure:[55] in 839 his father Æthelwulf had written to the Frankish

---

[53] In an East Frankish context one might compare here the promotion of the German vernacular by Louis the German: J.M. Wallace-Hadrill, *The Frankish Church* (Oxford, 1983), 333–4.

[54] Gildas had laboured this point in portraying the pagan attacks of Germanic peoples on Britain as a reflection of God's anger with the Christian British: *Gildas: The Ruin of Britain and Other Works*, ed. and transl. M. Winterbottom (London and Chichester, 1978). See R.W. Hanning, *The Vision of History in Early Britain* (London, 1966), chs. 2–3. For consideration of the same themes in the Second Viking Age see M. Godden, 'Apocalypse and Invasion in Late Anglo-Saxon England', in *From Anglo-Saxon to Early Middle English: Studies Presented to E.G. Stanley* (Oxford, 1994), 130–62.

[55] For example the letters written by Alcuin following the first Viking raid on Lindisfarne in June 793: *Epistolae*, 16 21, ed. E. Dümmler, *Epistolae Karolini Aevi* II, MGII, Epistolae, IV (Berlin, 1895); and see D.A. Bullough, 'What Has Ingeld to do with Lindisfarne',

emperor, Louis the Pious, warning that if men did not quickly repent and return to Christian observance pagan men would lay waste their land with fire and sword.[56] While other writers of this period looked to spiritual renewal, and improvement in individual religious observance,[57] Alfred's perception that the root of the evil lay in his subjects' ignorance, rather than in their lack of faith, led to his adoption of the innovative remedy of vernacular education.

In apparently including Bede's Ecclesiastical History among those Latin works translated as part of his vernacular programme, Alfred acknowledged the debt which he owed to Bede for the invention of a concept of the English.[58] For Bede, the Anglo-Saxon peoples, though separated by the diversity of their political arrangements, were united by their shared Christian faith into one *gens Anglorum* in the sight of God: it was as English Christians that the faithful should identify themselves to St Peter. As Patrick Wormald has argued, it was Bede who gave the idea of Englishness its particular power; Bede demonstrated that the Church not only created but named this new communal identity and made the *gens Anglorum* a people with a covenant, like Israel.[59]

For Bede, the semblance of unity was created by the existence of one language distinguishing the Germanic settlers of Anglo-Saxon

---

*Anglo-Saxon England*, XXII (1993), 93–125, especially 95–101. Among ninth-century texts see the Synod of Meaux and Paris, 845–6 (ed. W. Hartmann, MGH, *Concilia*, III (Hanover, 1984), 60–132 at 82); quoted by S. Coupland, 'The Rod of God's Wrath or the People of God's Wrath? The Carolingian Theology of the Viking Invasions', *Journal of Ecclesiastical History*, XLII (1991), 535–54, at 537 n. 6; and the *Translatio et miracula S. Germani*, chs. 2–4 (ed. G. Waitz, *MGH, SS*, xv.1 (Hanover, 1887), at 10–11). I owe this last reference to Janet Nelson.

[56] *Les Annales de Saint-Bertin*, s.a. 839, ed. F. Grat *et al.* (Paris, 1964), 29; transl. Nelson, 43. The danger which Viking attacks presented to the continuance of the Christian faith in England was noted by various outsiders in the ninth century; see my 'Violence against Christians? The Vikings and the Church in Ninth-Century England', *Medieval History*, I.3 (1991), 3–16, especially 9–10.

[57] The capitulary of Pîtres, 862 (ed. A. Boretius and V. Krause, *MGH Capitularia* II, no. 272), for example describes how 'tumults have arisen, wretchedly stirred up both by pagans and by those calling themselves Christians, and ... terrible calamities have spread through this land'. Attention is drawn to the individual sins of the Franks for which reason 'we have been exiled from the land of the living'. The remedy proposed is clear: 'in the destruction around us God has revealed to us what we should understand about the devastation within us, so that, having understood, we should return to him and believe'. I am grateful to Dr Simon Coupland for allowing me to quote from his translation of this capitulary.

[58] For the attribution of the Old English Bede to Alfred's reign see above n. 46 and D. Whitelock,'The Prose of Alfred's Reign', in *Continuations and Beginnings: Studies in Old English Literature*, ed. E.G. Stanley (London, 1966), 67–103, at 77–9 (reprinted in her collected papers *From Bede to Alfred*, no. vi).

[59] Wormald, 'The Venerable Bede', 21, 24. Compare also N. Howe, *Migration and Mythmaking in Anglo-Saxon England* (New Haven and London, 1989), 49–71.

England from their British, Irish and Pictish neighbours. His sensitivity to the role of language in defining ethnic groups was stressed at the beginning of his history, where he also introduced the idea that the Latin of the Bible had the potential to unite these differences.[60]

> At the present time there are five languages in Britain, just as the divine law is written in five books, all devoted to seeking out and setting forth one and the same kind of wisdom, namely the knowledge of sublime truth and of true sublimity. These are the English, British, Irish, Pictish as well as the Latin languages; through the study of the scriptures, Latin is in general use among them all.

One of Bede's intentions in writing his History was to demonstrate that, despite their separate ethnic and political origins, the Anglo-Saxons had been brought together into one *gens* by the unifying power of the Christian faith, transmitted to them by Rome. His summary of the state of Britain at the time when he was writing reinforces this view that religion could act as a binding force: it is as one united, Christian people that the relationship of the English with their non-Germanic neighbours (Picts, Irish and Britons) is defined.[61]

Part of what Bede had aimed to illustrate was the process by which a 'national' Church was created; as he traced the establishment of separate sees in each individual kingdom—the framework around which the History was structured—he stressed not a series of distinct institutions for each individual people but the making of a single Church, subject to Rome. The high point of his narrative was the primacy of Archbishop Theodore, 'the first of the archbishops whom the whole English Church consented to obey'.[62] Not only was this the first time when the separate churches of the individual kingdoms were united under one authority, but Theodore was the first person to whom all of the English offered any sort of authority. Although Bede's was an argument about spiritual authority not about political power, there was a potential political dimension to his historical vision, as is demonstrable from his list of kings who held *imperium*, or wide-ranging power.[63]

> In the year 616 Æthelberht of Kent entered upon the eternal joys of the heavenly kingdom. He was the third English king to rule over all the southern kingdoms which are divided from the north by the

[60] Bede, *HE*, I.1, 16–17. For the significance of dialectal variants within Old English as markers for the separate identites of different Anglo-Saxon kingdoms see Hines, 'Identity', 55–7.

[61] Bede, *HE*, V.23, 558–61.

[62] Bede, *HE*, IV.2, 332–3. The making of a single *ecclesia Anglorum* had clearly been Pope Gregory's original intention; see for example his advice to Augustine about the consecration of new bishops: *HE*, I.27, 86.

[63] Bede, *HE*, II.5, 148–51.

river Humber and the surrounding territory; but he was the first to enter the kingdom of heaven. The first king to hold the like sovereignty—*imperium*—was Ælle, king of the South Saxons; the second was Ceawlin, king of the West Saxons; the third, as we have said, was Æthelberht, king of Kent; the fourth was Rædwald, king of the East Angles, who while Æthelberht was still alive acted as military leader of his own people. The fifth was Edwin, king of the Northumbrians, the nation inhabiting the district north of the Humber. Edwin had still greater power and ruled over all the inhabitants of Britain, English and Britons alike, except for Kent only. He even brought under English rule the isles of Angelsey and Man which lie between England and Ireland and belong to the Britons. The sixth to rule within the same bounds was Oswald, the most Christian king of the Northumbrians, while the seventh was his brother Oswiu, who for a time held almost the same territory.

The context of this celebrated passage is Bede's obituary for Æthelberht of Kent, and the chapter includes material from a variety of sources, much of it probably deriving from Canterbury. It is not, however, necessary to presume that the list itself derives from Canterbury,[64] and there may be a case for attributing its construction to Bede himself, bearing in mind the importance to him of the unity of the *gens Anglorum*. This is not to argue either that there was, or that Bede was claiming that there was, one quasi-imperial office, ranking above the kingship of an individual kingdom, held by certain figures between the late fifth and seventh century, which passed from one king to another depending on their relative superiority.[65] Bede seems merely to have been hinting

[64] That Bede obtained this list second-hand has been argued by, among others, B. Yorke, 'The Vocabulary of Anglo-Saxon Overlordship', *Anglo-Saxon Studies in Archaeology and History*, II (British Archaeological Reports, British series XCII, Oxford, 1981), 171–200, at 195–6, and S. Fanning, 'Bede, Imperium and the Bretwaldas', *Speculum*, LXVI (1991), 1–26, at 25. For other arguments that Bede himself compiled this list see S. Keynes, 'Rædwald the bretwalda', in *Voyage to the Other World: The Legacy of Sutton Hoo* (Minneapolis, Minn., 1992), 103–23, at 109–10 (and for a fuller survey of other secondary opinion ibid. nn. 44–7, pp. 119–20), and N. Higham, *An English Empire: Bede and the Early Anglo-Saxon Kings* (Manchester, 1995), 49.

[65] Bede's intent here has been somewhat obscured by the use of the word *bretwalda* in the Anglo-Saxon Chronicle *s.a.* 827 (recte 829) in relation to the power held by the West Saxon king, Ecgberht, following his conquest of the kingdom of the Mercians and everything south of the Humber. Ecgberht was said by the chronicler to have been the eighth king who was *brytenwalda* (*bretwalda* uniquely in the A manuscript of the Chronicle), the previous seven being those named by Bede in *HE* II.5. But where Bede had envisaged a wide-ranging kind of power, the chronicler appears to have conceived of an office, or wide rulership. The form *bretwalda* (meaning ruler of Britain, from *bret-* 'Briton' and *-walda* 'ruler' or 'king') is attested only in the A manuscript of the Chronicle and is unlikely to represent the original spelling. Other manuscripts have different forms: *brytenwalda* or *brytenwealda* (BDE), *bretenanwealda* (C). Here *bryten* might be a noun meaning

that, just as one faith and one language *can* unify disparate groups, so, bearing in mind the demonstrable unity provided by the centralising authority of the Church, *could* a single political authority serve as one means of binding otherwise distinct political groups into a common cause: the promotion of the true faith and the making of a people with a single, Christian identity. That such an argument might be translated further in the ninth century by a dynasty which found itself in possession of a power exceeding that of any of its West Saxon predecessors, and that it might (having itself only newly come to power) look to Bede's account for an historical justification or parallel for its own pretensions, seems entirely natural. What Alfred can be seen to have recognised is the potential for his own purpose of the model invented by Pope Gregory and promoted by Bede: one Church, one people and one faith could prefigure a political unity, an ideal which might be made real by a king with sufficient power and ideological energy to promote it.

In making the one nation he created English (and not Saxon) Alfred perpetuated the name for that people coined by Bede. Bede did not invent the term, nor was he unique among Anglo-Saxon writers in using it to define the Germanic people of Britain collectively, but he did use it more consistently than his contemporaries.[66] The author of the Whitby Life of Pope Gregory wrote of the pope's role in ensuring the salvation of the *gens Anglorum* and once made reference to the *sudrangli*, meaning apparently the the people south of the Humber.[67] Boniface's letters frequently alluded to the characteristics of the English race, although he also noted their kinship with the continental Saxons; similarly Bishop Torhthelm of Leicester wrote to Boniface on hearing of the success of his continental Saxon mission, to rejoice at the conversion of *gens nostra*.[68] The anonymous Lindisfarne Life of Cuthbert referred to the bishops of the Saxons, while Stephen, hagiographer of Wilfrid, wrote of both *Angli* and *Saxones*.[69] To outsiders, the Germanic

---

'Britain', but it might alternatively be an adjective *bryten* from the verb *bretoan* 'to break', or 'disperse'; so *brytenwalda* might mean simply 'wide ruler'. See Whitelock in *EHD*, 186 n. 2; Keynes, 'Rædwald the bretwalda', 111.

[66] Wormald, 'Bede, the *Bretwaldas*', 122–3; for a semantic discussion of Bede's use of the word 'Angle' see Wormald, 'The Venerable Bede', 21–3.

[67] Anonymous, *Liber beatae Gregorii papae*, chs. 6, 12, 18, ed. and transl. B. Colgrave, *The Earliest Life of Gregory the Great* (2nd edn, Cambridge, 1985), 82–3, 94–5, 102–3.

[68] Boniface, *Epistola* 46, ed. M. Tangl, *Die Briefe des heiligen Bonifatius und Lullus*, MGH, Epistolae selectae, 1 (Berlin, 1916), p. 74; and compare *Epistolae* 33, 73, 74, 78, ed. Tangl, *Die Briefe*, 57–8, 150–2, 156, 169 and 171. Torhthelm's letter is preserved with Boniface's correspondence: *Epistola* 47, ed. Tangl, *Die Briefe*, 76.

[69] Anon., *Vita S. Cuthberti*, IV.1, ed. and transl. B. Colgrave, *Two Lives of St Cuthbert* (Cambridge, 1940), 110–11. References to the English or *gens Anglorum* are found in *The Life of Bishop Wilfrid by Eddius Stephanus*, chs. 6, 11, 41, ed. B. Colgrave (Cambridge, 1927), pp. 14–15, 22–3, 82–3; to the *Saxones*: chs. 19, 21, pp. 41, 43. Stephen also quoted a letter of Wilfrid's in which he described his country of origin as *Saxonia*: ch. 30, p. 60. A letter

inhabitants of the former Roman Britain did interestingly seem to have a single identity, but it was a Saxon one, they were *Saxones*. The Celtic peoples of Britain consistently called their Germanic neighbours Saxons (a usage which persisted into the modern period).[70] The term Saxon was similarly used by most of the non-insular authors who described affairs in Britain in the fifth and sixth centuries such as the Gallic Chronicler of 452 and Constantius, author of the Life of St Germanus,[71] and this terminology continued to be used in the seventh century.[72]

At variance with all these early external authorities is the sixth-century Byzantine historian Procopius, who in describing the island of *Brittia* spoke of the three populous nations to inhabit the place, each with a king set over it, these nations being the *Brittones* (named from the island), the *Frisiones*, and the *Angiloi* (Αγγιλοι).[73] Procopius's information about Britain was presumably obtained from the group of *Angiloi* whose presence he recorded among a legation sent from the Frankish king to Constantinople *c.* 550, making a claim for Frankish hegemony over the island.[74] One might question how accurately Procopius recorded (and translated) the language used by these foreign enemies, were it not that Pope Gregory adopted the same term, *Anguli*, to described the Germanic inhabitants of Britain. It is not impossible that Gregory's nomenclature was influenced either by Procopius or by

---

of abbot Hwætberht's to Pope Gregory II quoted by Bede in his *Historia abbatum* similarly described England as *Saxonia*: *Historia abbatum*, ch. 19, ed. C. Plummer, *Venerabilis Baedae Opera Historica* (2 vols., Oxford, 1896), I.383, and note II.368. M. Richter, 'Bede's Angli: Angles or English?', *Peritia*, III (1984), 99–114, at 105. In a letter to Pope Zacharias Boniface described himself as born and raised *in transmarina Saxonia*: *Epistola* 50, ed. Tangl, *Die Briefe*, 84.

[70] Richter, 'Bede's *Angli*', 105–7; Wormald, 'Bede, the *bretwaldas*'; 122; L. Colley, *Britons: Forging the Nation 1707–1837* (2nd edn, London, 1994), 13.

[71] Gallic Chronicle of 452, ed. T. Mommsen, *MGH, Auctores Antiquissimi*, IX (Berlin, 1892), 660; Constantius, Life of St Germanus, chs. 17–18, ed. W. Levison, *MGH, SRM*, VII (Hanover, 1919–20), 263, 265.

[72] Wormald, 'Bede, the *Bretwaldas*', 122. Much of this ground was explored by E.A. Freeman, *History of the Norman Conquest* (3rd edn, 2 vols., Oxford, 1877), I.533–48, who argued that the Germanic inhabitants of pre-Conquest England ought to be described as the English, not as the Anglo-Saxons.

[73] Procopius, *History of the Wars*, ed. and transl. H.B. Dewing (5 vols., London, 1914–28), VIII.xx.4–8

[74] Procopius, *Wars*, VIII.xx.8–10. R. Collins ('Theodebert I, "Rex Magnus Francorum"', in *Ideal and Reality*, ed. Wormald, 11–12) ascribed this legation to the time of Theudebert, who died in 548, but Ian Wood (*The Merovingian North Sea*, 12 and 23 n. 77) has argued rather that it should be dated to *c.* 553. For the likelihood that the Franks did have some hegemony over southern England see further I. Wood, 'Frankish Hegemony in England', in *The Age of Sutton Hoo*, ed. M. Carver (Woodbridge, 1992), 235–41, at 235, and I Wood, *The Merovingian North Sea* (Alingsås, 1983), 12–14. Robert Markus has suggested that Pope Gregory's mission to the English might have been conceived on the presumption of continued Frankish domination of southern England as part of a plan for the revitalisation of the Frankish church: 'Gregory the Great's Europe', *TRHS*, 5 ser., XXXI (1981), 21–36, at 26–7.

THE MAKING OF *ANGELCYNN*: ENGLISH IDENTITY 43

the general currency of the term at the Imperial court in Constantinople, where Gregory is known to have been papal apocrisarius *c.* 578–585.

All of Pope Gregory's letters about the mission to Kent referred to the people as the Angles, including those written after he had received some direct information about affairs in Britain and so might have known that this was not the most appropriate term, certainly not for the people whom Æthelberht ruled.[75] The texts associated with Gregory are not, however, consistent in the retention of the third syllable added by Procopius; the brief biography of Gregory in the *Liber pontificalis* referred to the pope's sending of missionaries *ad gentem Angulorum*, but his verse epitaph stated that he had converted the *Anglos* to Christ.[76] The extra syllable makes more plausible the 'not Angles but angels' pun (and in reporting the famous story of the boys in the Roman slave-market the anonymous Whitby hagiographer of Gregory indeed described them as *Anguli* although Bede termed them *Angli* in his own account).[77] In the letter which he wrote in July 598 to Eulogius, bishop of Alexandria, where he described the success of the Augustine's mission, however, Gregory provided an alternative explanation for the name English, referring to the missionaries whom he had sent to the *gens Anglorum in mundo angulo posita*.[78]

Gregory's adoption of the *Angli/Anguli* label, wherever he had obtained it, would have had little influence had it not been taken up by Bede and via his writings gradually acquired a wider currency. A shift is noticeable in the language used by continental writers to describe the Germanic peoples of Britain from the eighth century, perhaps as Bede's Ecclesiastical History began to circulate on the continent through the influence of English missionaries, but there is little consistency of

[75] H. Chadwick, 'Gregory the Great and the Mission to the Anglo-Saxons', *Gregorio Magno e il suo tempo*, Studia Ephemeridis 'Augustinianum' XXXIII (Rome, 1991), 199–212, at 199–200.

[76] *Liber pontificalis*, ed. L. Duchesne (2 vols., Paris 1886–92), I.312: '... misit eos in praedicationem ad gentem Angulorum ut eos conuerteret ad dominum Iesum Christum'. Gregory's epitaph is preserved by Bede, *HE*, II.1, 132, and John the Deacon in his Life of Gregory, IV,68 (*Patrologia Latina*, ed. Migne, LXXV, col 221 C)

[77] *Liber beatae Gregorii papae*, ch. 9, p. 90: 'Cunque responderent, "Anguli dicuntur, illi de quibus sumus," illed dixit, "Angeli Dei".' Compare also ch. 13, p. 94, where the insertion of the additional syllable looks like an error in the transmitted text: 'Thus the name of the Angli, with the addition of the single letter *e* means angels': *ergo nomen Angulorum, si una e littera addetur, angelorum sonat*; had the name originally been given as *Anguli*, the letter *e* would need to be substituted, not added. Bede's account of the same story is found in his *HE*, II.1, 134–5.

[78] *S. Gregorii Magni, Registrum Epistularum*, VIII.29 (ed. D. Norberg, *Corpus Christianorum, series Latina* CXL–CXLA (Turnhout, 1982)), CXLA.551. The same pun is made by Widukind: *Res Gestae Saxonicae*, I.8 (ed. G. Waitz, MGH, Scriptores III (Hanover, 1839), 419–20): 'Et quia illa insula in angulo quodam maris sita est, Anglisaxones usque hodie uocitantur.'

practice, the two names, Saxon and English, being used synonymously.[79] For example Alfred's father Æthelwulf was variously described in the Annals of St-Bertin as king of the English, of the Anglo-Saxons, of the west English as well as king of the West Saxons.[80] The author of the miracles of St Wandrille appears to have viewed Britain as inhabited by only one people (the *gens Anglorum*) although having multiple kings; he reports how at some time between 858 and 866 the *praefectus* of Quentovic, Grippo, was sent by Charles the Bald on a mission *in insula Brittannica ad reges gentis Anglorum*.[81] That there was an association between the Germanic inhabitants of Britain and the continental Saxons was by no means forgotten; Boniface could write to all the *Angli* in the eighth century urging them to pray for the conversion of the Saxons, 'because they are of one blood and one bone with us',[82] and in the tenth century the marriage of Edith, sister of King Æthelstan, to the Saxon king Otto was seen as a reassertion of familial ties between the two peoples, as well as providing the Saxon dynasty with an opportunity to benefit from a more ancient kingship.[83]

It thus appears that before the eighth century the seaborne attackers of Roman Britain and the peoples who settled the south-eastern part of the island in the sub-Roman period were seen generically by outsiders as *Saxones*. Bede also talked of the *aduentus Saxonum*, even though he

---

[79] Richter, 'Bede's *Angli*', 113. See for example *Annales Regni Francorum, s.a.* 786 and 808 (ed. F. Kurze, MGH SRG (Hanover, 1895), at 73 and 127); Einhard, *Vita Karoli Magni*, ch. 25 (ed. G. Waitz, MGH, SRG ius 25 (Hanover, 1911), 30).

[80] Annals of St-Bertin, *s.a.* 839, 855, 856, 858 (ed. Grat *et al.*, 28, 70, 73, 76): *rex Anglorum, rex Anglorum Saxonum, rex occidentalium Anglorum* and *rex occidentalium Saxonum*. The same text, *s.a.* 862 termed Æthelwulf's son, Æthelbald *rex Anglorum*, ed. Grat *et al.* 87. In a ninth-century confraternity book from the northern Italian monastery of Brescia Æthelwulf appears among a list of pilgrims with the appellation *rex Anglorum*, having presumably visited the house during his visit to Rome in 855/6: Brescia, Biblioteca Queriniana, MS G.VI.7, fo. 27v: H. Becher, 'Das königlich Frauenkloster San Salvatore/Santa Giulia in Brescia im Spiegel seiner Memorialüberlieferung', *Frühmittelalterliche Studien*, XVII (1983), 299–392, at 377. I owe this reference to Janet Nelson.

[81] *Ex miraculis S Wandregisili*, ed. O. Hodder-Egger, MGH Scriptores XV (Hanover, 1887), 408–9; quoted by P. Stafford, 'Charles the Bald, Judith and England', in *Charles the Bald: Court and Kingdom*, ed. M. Gibson and J.L. Nelson (2nd edn, Aldershot, 1990), 139–53, at 142.

[82] Boniface, *Epistola* 46, ed. Tangl, *Die Briefe*, 74.

[83] K. Leyser, 'The Ottonians and Wessex', in his *Communications and Power in Medieval Europe: The Carolingian and Ottonian Centuries*, ed. T. Reuter (London, 1994), 73–104, at 74–5. See also E. Van Houts, 'Women and the Writing of History in the Early Middle Ages: The Case of Abbess Matilda of Essen and Aethelweard', *Early Medieval Europe*, I (1992), 53–68, at 57 and 63–4. The so-called *Leges Eadwardi confessoris*, dating from the mid-twelfth century, also preserve a remnant of a sense of common descent and interests between English and Saxons, directing that Saxon visitors should be received as if brothers, for they are born 'from the blood of the *Angli*, that is to say from *Engern*, a place and region in Saxony, and the English from their blood; they are made one people, one kind': ch. 32 C, ed. Liebermann, *Die Gesetze*, I.627–72, at 658; transl. Leyser, 'The Ottonians', 74.

sought to describe the salvation of the *gens Anglorum*. The fact that there was one term in general usage before Bede's time suggests that the Germanic inhabitants of Britain were perceived from the outside as one community with a recognisable identity and distinction from their neighbours. The created notion that this community should be named the *Angli* came gradually to be recognised on the continent from the eighth century, but the consistency of usage found in the earlier period does not persist, except in the Celtic-speaking areas, where the Germanic peoples of Britain remained Saxons.

King Alfred's vision of one people united through a shared history, common faith and opposition to the Danes under a single rulership might have found outward celebration in the ceremonies to mark the general submission of 886, but can scarcely have met without opposition. Those reluctant to accept the concept of the newly created identity or unwilling to accept West Saxon overlordship had, however, few independent means of articulating their alternative perceptions or preferences (or, at least, few are recorded). The Alfredian programme was indeed in part an exercise in controlling knowledge, encompassing as it did 'those books most necessary for all men to know'. Those attracted to Alfred's court were not exclusively English. According to Asser 'foreigners of all races came from places near and far', some in search of money, others looking for a lord of proven ability: 'many Franks, Frisians, Gauls, pagans (*viz* Danes), Welshmen, Irishmen and Bretons subjected themselves willingly to his lordship, nobles and commoners alike'.[84] There were others of 'English' birth who failed to perceive the benefits to be gained from obedience to King Alfred. A charter of Alfred's son, Edward the Elder, dated 901, provides the history of an estate in Wiltshire, recording that it had previously been forfeited by an ealdorman, Wulfhere, 'when he deserted without permission both his lord King Alfred and his country (*patria*) in spite of the oath which he had sworn to the king and all his leading men. Then also, by the judgment of all the councillors of the *Gewisse* and of the Mercians he lost the control and inheritance of his lands.'[85]

Such acquiescence as there was in the unified rule created by Alfred did not extend beyond his death to the automatic acceptance of his heirs. Within Wessex Alfred's son, Edward the Elder, faced a challenge

[84] Asser, Life of Alfred, chs. 101, 76, ed. Stevenson, *Asser*, 87, 60; transl. Keynes and Lapidge, *Alfred the Great*, 107 and 91.
[85] S 362, transl. *EHD*, 100. Discussed together with other instances of disloyalty to Alfred by J.L. Nelson, '"A King Across the Sea": Alfred in Continental Perspective', *TRHS*, 5th series, XXXVI (1986), 45–68, at 53; and by S. Keynes, 'A Tale of Two Kings: Alfred the Great and Æthelred the Unready', *ibid.* 195–217, at 206. For further evidence of reluctance to promote Alfred's plans see Asser, Life of King Alfred, chs. 91 and 106, ed. Stevenson, *Asser*, 77, 93–4; transl. Keynes and Lapidge, *Alfred the Great*, 101, 110.

from his cousin, Æthelwold.[86] The predominantly West Saxon sources imply that the arrangements for the control of the parts of Mercia not under Danish control remained as they were (direct control of the kingdom rested in the hands of Ealdorman Æthelred and his wife Æthelflæd, but under King Edward's overall authority)[87] and Edward continued in his charters to use the royal style his father had adopted: 'king of the Anglo-Saxons'.[88] There is no record in the surviving sources of any objection to these arrangements beyond 903 (although the Mercian Register hints at disquiet when Edward assumed rulership of Mercia on his sister's death in 918),[89] but acceptance of the necessity for Mercian and West Saxon collaboration against a common threat is not sufficient ground for arguing for widespread noble acquiesence in the fusion of the two kingdoms, or the loss of the separate identities of their peoples.

The notion of one English nation continued to have a currency throughout the tenth century and might seem to have had a wider applicability following the unification of England under West Saxon rule first by King Æthelstan and particularly in the time of King Edgar. Ælfric showed signs of national pride in writing c. 1000 that 'the English nation (*angelcynn*) is not deprived of God's saints when in England lie buried such holy people as this sainted king [Edmund], and the blessed Cuthbert and St Æthelthryth in Ely ... There are also many other saints among the English nation (*on angelcynne*).'[90] Did Ælfric attribute

---

[86] The Chronicler reported not only that Essex submitted to Æthelwold, and that he was later joined by the East Anglian Vikings and a Mercian prince, but that Edward had some difficulty in holding his own army together, having to send seven messengers to the men of Kent who persisted in lingering behind against his command: Anglo-Saxon Chronicle 903. Æthelwold's revolt has been discussed by Dumville, *Wessex*, 10.

[87] This has been argued by Simon Keynes on the basis of a group of charters issued in 903 and by references in S 396 (*EHD*, 103) and S 397 issued in 926 to 'the order of King Edward and also of Ealdorman Æthelred along with the other ealdormen and thegns': 'A Charter of Edward the Elder for Islington', *Historical Research*, LXVI (1993), 303–16. In other charters, however, Æthelred and Æthelflæd made grants without reference to Edward: S 221, 224–5; see P. Stafford, *Unification and Conquest: A Political and Social History of England in the Tenth and Eleventh Centuries* (London, 1989), 25–6.

[88] S. Keynes, 'The West Saxon Charters of King Æthelwulf and his Sons', *English Historical Review*, CIX (1994), 1109–49, at 1148–9. The West Saxon chronicle described Æthelred as an ealdorman, but the tenth-century writer of a Latin chronicle based on a lost version of the Anglo-Saxon Chronicle termed him *rex* (*Chronicle of Æthelweard*, ed. A. Campbell (Edinburgh, 1962), 49–50), and Asser described Æthelred's power in terms similar to those he used of the Welsh kings who submitted to Alfred: Asser, Life of Alfred, ch. 80, ed. Stevenson, *Asser*, 66–7; transl. Keynes and Lapidge, *Alfred the Great*, 96. See Stafford, *Unification*, 26.

[89] The Mercian Register for 919 reported that Æthelred's daughter was deprived of all authority in Mercia and taken into Wessex: *Two of the Saxon Chronicles Parallel*, ed. C. Plummer (2 vols., Oxford, 1892–9), I.105; transl. Whitelock, *EHD*, 217.

[90] Ælfric, *Passio Sancti Eadmundi Regis et Martyris*, quoted by C. Fell, 'Saint Æðelþryð: A

to Alfred a responsibility for making this a single people greater than that inherent in his defeat of their enemy, the Danes? [91] He certainly knew of 'the books which King Alfred wisely translated from Latin into English', specifying of these only a *Historia Anglorum*, presumably the translation of Bede's History not now thought to have been translated by Alfred personally.[92] To an outsider in the eleventh century, the English did look to be one people; Cnut wrote to his subjects as 'the whole race of the English' (*totius gentis Anglorum*), and in the preface to the version of his laws which he brought before an assembly at Oxford in 1018, Cnut sought to 'establish peace and friendship between the Danes and the English and put an end to their former strife'.[93] The referent of the term has, however, shifted since Alfred's day. Alfred's English were the Christian people of Kent, Wessex and western Mercia;[94] the English whom Cnut conquered included not only the East Anglians and Northumbrians but men of Danish parentage, born or settled in England. The Normans also saw the people they had conquered as one English *gens*.[95]

Although some continued to perceive the Anglo-Saxon peoples as one nation, and to use the term English to describe them into the eleventh century, this does not demonstrate a linear development of an Alfredian notion of English nationhood through the tenth century, nor the perpetuation of the shared memory that Alfred had sought to cultivate. The potential to unite all the Englishkind under one rule

Historical-Hagiographical Dichotomy Revisited', *Nottingham Medieval Studies*, XXXVII (1994), 18–34, at 18.

[91] *The Old English Version of the Heptateuch: Ælfric's Treatise on the Old and New Testament and his Preface to Genesis*, ed. S.J. Crawford (London, 1922), 416–17; transl. Dumville, *Wessex*, 141: 'In England too kings were often victorious because of God, as we have heard tell—just as King Alfred was, who fought frequently against the Danes until he gained victory and thus protected his people; similarly Æthelstan, who fought against Anlaf and slaughtered his army and put him to flight—and afterwards with his people he [Æthelstan] dwelt in peace.'

[92] Whitelock, 'The Prose of Alfred's Reign', 69.

[93] Cnut's letter to the English of 1027, ed. Liebermann, *Die Gesetze*, I.276–7 at 276, transl. Whitelock, *EHD*, no. 53. I Cnut prologue, ed. Liebermann, *Die Gesetze*, I.278–307 at 278; transl. *EHD*, no. 47.

[94] Interesting in this context is the Chronicle's (alliterative verse) annal for 942, which, describing King Edmund as lord of the English and protector of men, recounts how he 'overran Mercia and thereby redeemed the Danes, previously subjected by force under the Norsemen, for a long time in bonds of captivity to the heathens': ASC 942, ed. Bately, 73; transl. Whitelock, *EHD*, no. 1, 221.

[95] G. Garnett, '"Franci et Angli": The Legal Distinctions between Peoples after the Conquest', *Anglo-Norman Studies*, VIII (1986), 109–37; R.W. Southern, *Medieval Humanism and Other Studies* (Oxford, 1970), 135–8. See also J. Gillingham, 'The Beginnings of English Imperialism', *Journal of Historical Sociology*, V (1992), 393–409. In some senses, however, Northumbria was virtually a separate state *c.* 1100: W.E. Kapelle, *The Norman Conquest of the North: The Region and its Transformation, 1000–1135* (London, 1979), 11–13.

became a reality temporarily only in the reign of King Æthelstan, and permanently only from the time of Edgar. The tenth-century West Saxon kings frequently saw themselves as kings of the English (*rex Anglorum*) but not uniquely or exclusively so; their authority ranged more widely, encompassed peoples of greater ethnic diversity and might extend to governorship of Britain.[96] A grant of King Eadred's of 946 reported that king's consecration to 'sovereignty of the quadripartite rule' on the death of his brother, Edmund, who had 'royally guided the government of kingdoms of the Anglo-Saxons and Northumbrians, of the pagans and the Britons'.[97] It may be that regional separatism was too sensitive an issue to be ignored by southern kings often seen as unwelcome foreigners in Mercia, let alone Northumbria; the problems of imposing unitary rule from the south were considerable, and the loyalty of these regions to Wessex was never certain.[98]

Where there was any notion of the existence of Englishness among the nobility even in Wessex, let alone Mercia or Northumbria, it is likely to have been perceived as only one of a number of possible communities of identity. Those who might at times have defined themselves as English would simultaneously recognise other loyalties: to their king, to their lord, to a village, to a region. Distance from the West Saxon court (or from Canterbury) might alter conceptions of Englishness substantially. Alliance with Scandinavian 'enemies' looked attractive at various times to archbishops of York, and the members of

[96] Numerous tenth-century royal charters style kings as 'king of the English and of the people round about', and the witness lists to these grants reveal the presence at the West Saxon court of Northumbrian and often Welsh princes. For the articulation of imperial pretensions in the charters of Æthelstan and his successors see Dumville, *Wessex*, 149, 153–4, and N. Banton, 'Monastic Reform and the Unification of Tenth-Century England', in *Religion and National Identity*, ed. S. Mews (Oxford, 1982), 71–85, at 72–3 and 80–1.

[97] S 520, transl. *EHD*, no. 105; for discussion of this group of alliterative charters see Whitelock, *EHD*, 372–3. Similarly the early tenth-century coronation *ordo* granted West Saxon kings government of two or three nations: C.E. Hohler, 'Some Service Books of the Later Saxon Church', in *Tenth-Century Studies*, ed. D. Parsons (London and Chichester, 1975), 60–83, at 67–9. For Edgar's imperial coronation at Bath in 973 see Banton, 'Monastic Reform', 82. The pledge made to Edgar at Chester by six British kings in the same year was reported only in the northern recensions of the Chronicle: ASC 973 DE, ed. Plummer, I.119; transl. Whitelock, *EHD*, 228. In the more elaborate account of this ceremony given by John of Worcester, Edgar is reported to have declared afterwards to his nobles 'that each of his successors would be able to boast that he was king of the English, and would enjoy the pomp of such honour with so many kings at his command': *The Chronicle of John of Worcester II: The Annals from 450–1066, s.a. 973*, ed. and transl. R. Darlington *et al.* (Oxford, 1995), 424–5.

[98] D. Whitelock, 'The Dealings of the Kings of England with Northumbria in the Tenth and Eleventh Centuries', in *The Anglo-Saxons*, ed. P. Clemoes (Cambridge, 1959), 70–88; N. Lund, 'King Edgar and the Danelaw', *Mediaeval Scandinavia*, IX (1976), 181–95; Keynes, 'A Tale of Two Kings', 206–8.

the northern Mercian and Northumbrian nobility.[99] Nevertheless, it does appear that one collective identity of Englishness had an enduring currency through the pre-Conquest period, transcending the significant separation brought about by the existence of a multiplicity of different political organisations and ethnic groups among the Anglo-Saxons. Alfred's promotion of the *Angelcynn* as a people with a shared past united under West Saxon rule fostered an awareness that English self-consciousness lay in more than their acknowledgement of a common Christianity centred on Canterbury. Patrick Wormald has already shown how useful the notion of Englishness was to be in the evolution of the early English state; it is worth exploring whether the notion has any potential for the examination of other spheres of pre-Conquest history.[100]

The force of this sense of a common identity is striking, notably its prevalence in sources at least from Bede's time onwards, coupled with the fact that it was clearly recognisable to outsiders. That 'a strong sense of a common unity as a people is not incompatible with a highly particularised local identity' has been demonstrated by the current President of the Society in relation to eleventh- and twelfth-century Wales. Professor Davies has shown that the Welsh defined their common unity in terms of a common descent, the invention of a common mythology to create their identity, a common language and literary tradition, and much that was common in law, together with the coining of names to given themselves a consciously constructed identity as compatriots.[101] This argument—that one can have cultural, legal and linguistic unity without political unity—is equally valid for the pre-Norman English. Alfred's achievement lay in his realisation that by harnessing and focusing these three forms of identity through an appeal to a common memory, and by imposing a cultural hegemony he was able to provide a retrospective and self-consciously historical explanation for the creation of a fourth, national, consciousness. In that sense, while Bede invented the English as a people in the sight of God,[102] they were made one nation by 'Alfred of the English, the greatest treasure-giver of all the kings [Bishop Wulfsige] has ever heard tell of, in recent times, or long ago, or of any earthly king he had previously learned of.'[103]

---

[99] Lund, 'King Edgar', 189–92; W.M. Aird, 'St Cuthbert, The Scots and the Normans', *Anglo-Norman Studies*, XVI (1993), 1–20, especially 3–4 and 6–9.

[100] I hope to pursue this further in a thematic consideration of the history of the English before the Norman Conquest.

[101] R.R. Davies, *Conquest, Coexistence and Change: Wales 1063–1415* (Oxford, 1987), 15–20.

[102] Wormald, 'The Venerable Bede', 24.

[103] Wulfsige, bishop of Sherborne, preface to his translation of Gregory's *Dialogues*; transl. Keynes and Lapidge, *Alfred the Great*, 188.

# ISABEAU OF BAVARIA, QUEEN OF FRANCE (1385–1422): THE CREATION OF AN HISTORICAL VILLAINESS

*The Alexander Prize Essay*

By Rachel Gibbons

READ 28 APRIL 1995

CONSIDERING the high personal profile and influence of Isabeau of Bavaria during her time as queen of France between 1385 and 1422, it is extraordinary that she has not been the subject of more sustained serious academic study in the past, and that so little is known about her. The woman at the centre of such a turbulent period of Anglo-French war and internal conflict is far too often dismissed in the space of a few paragraphs; even then, what is written about her is often one-sided, two-dimensional and, in many cases, plain wrong. The history of Isabeau of Bavaria so far has largely been a fabricated mixture of gossip and propaganda which has been absorbed into historical tradition and repeated so often that, to many, legend has become indistinguishable from fact. For a mere two decades it has been accepted that: 'Isabeau ne mérite point la réputation qui lui fut faite',[1] and it cannot be a coincidence that the few historians who have devoted any time to research on Isabeau all have come to the conclusion that her infamous legacy is not deserved. Yet, the movement for Isabeau of Bavaria's rehabilitation has not been as prominent as it might have been: Vallet de Viriville only wrote a few articles about her, Marcel Thibault never produced the promised second part of his biography and Yann Grandeau sadly died before his research papers could be developed into a complete work. The very first line that Thibault wrote in 1901 makes the claim that: 'L'histoire vraie et complète d'Isabeau de Bavière n'a jamais été ecrite' and, despite recent scholarly work,[2] this still seems to be the case almost a century later.

As even the dates of her birth and death are not universally agreed on, it could be said that not enough is known on any aspect of the life of Isabeau of Bavaria. When her uncle Frederick of Bavaria, fighting with the French in Flanders in September 1383, suggested his niece as

---

[1] Jean Verdon, *Isabeau de Bavière* (Paris, 1981), 252.
[2] Jean Markale, *Isabeau de Bavière* (Paris, 1982), and Verdon, *Isabeau*.

a possible bride for Charles VI, Froissart tells us that he described her as between thirteen and fourteen years old;[3] at the time of her marriage in July 1385, she was not yet sixteen,[4] which leads to the conclusion that she was born in the first few months of 1370, probably in Munich,[5] where she was baptised at the Church of Our Lady with the name of Elisabeth. This was a favourite name of the Bavarian ruling family, for Saint Elisabeth of Hungary had been a distant relative. The sister of the dukes of Bavaria, the duchess of Austria, and Frederick's daughter, the wife of Marco Visconti, had both been christened Elisabeth also, so it seems fair to assume that one of these ladies was godmother to the new baby. Elisabeth/Isabeau was the younger of the two children of Stephen III of Bavaria and Taddea Visconti, another of those marriages between impoverished ancient families and the upwardly-mobile, hugely wealthy dukes of Milan. Matches had already been made between Edward III's son Lionel, duke of Clarence and Violente Visconti; between the duke of Austria's heir Leopold of Hapsburg and Virida, the elder sister of Elisabeth's mother Taddea Visconti; and Jean II of France was prepared to 'sell his own flesh' in the form of his eleven-year-old daughter Isabelle to Gian Galeazzo in return for 600,000 gold florins which helped to pay the ransom he incurred after his capture at Poitiers.[6] The Wittelsbachs of Bavaria had a long illustrious heritage: they were descended from the Merovingians and Charlemagne, and Elisabeth's great-grandfather had been elected Emperor as Ludwig IV in 1314. Consequently, she was not quite the 'nobody' that has been suggested and, even if Froissart's story of Charles V's deathbed wish that his heir marry a German princess is not accepted, it is clear that Charles V himself saw both branches of the Wittelsbach clan as useful potential allies in the continuing war with England. He had betrothed his daughter Marie to William of Bavaria, heir to Hainault and Holland, and his daughter Catherine to Rupert,

---

[3] Jean Froissart, *Chroniques*, ed. S. Luce, G. Raynaud and L. Mirot (13 vols. incomplete, Paris, 1869– ) [hereafter Froissart], xi, 225.

[4] *Istoire et Croniques de Flandres*, in *Collection des Chroniques Belges*, ed. J.M. Kervyn de Lettenhove (5 vols., Brussels, 1880), II, 351.

[5] Isabeau held strong religious beliefs on the cult of the family and always marked significant stages in her life by gifts. If she had been born anywhere else, that town should have figured in the list of bequests in one of her wills. For example, twenty francs were left to the church Our Lady and to the Friars Minor, both in Munich, to perform a requiem mass for her soul in the 1408 version of her will—Bibliothèque Nationale, Paris, fond français 6544 [hereafter BN f.fr.], piece 7.

[6] Lionel and Violente in 1368; Leopold and Virida in 1361; Isabelle and Gian Galeazzo in 1364. And, of course, Valentina, the daughter of Gian Galeazzo Visconti and Isabelle of France, went back to her mother's family, marrying Isabelle's nephew Louis, duke of Orleans.

heir to Rupert of Bavaria, the Elector Palatine, but neither marriage came to fruition.

The marriage of Charles VI to Elisabeth of Bavaria, as told in detail by Froissart, was supported by the duke of Burgundy, and his influence was crucial in the choice of her in preference to a princess from Austria or Lorraine. When her father finally agreed to take the risk of sending her to France, 'on approval' as it were, it was on condition that no one, not even the prospective bride, should know the purpose of the visit. So, under the impression that she was accompanying her uncle Frederick on a pilgrimage to the shrine of Saint Jean the Baptist at Amiens,[7] the fifteen-year-old Elisabeth left Bavaria in the spring of 1385, never to return. She was presented to the eager Charles VI on Friday 14 July, in borrowed French clothes because her own were not considered grand enough, and obviously made a good impression because they were married on Monday 17 July 1385. The new queen's name was replaced by Isabel which she spelt with a 'Y', but historians most commonly call her 'Isabeau', used in reference to her in 1406 by the author of the satirical political poem *La Songe Véritable*. As a number of her ladies-in-waiting also used the name 'Isabeau', as did some in the service of Anne of Brittany, one could suggest perhaps that it was an affectionate pet-name for Isabelle, on the lines of Jehanette, that the family might have used. If this is the case, and a critical poet was calling the queen of France by a nickname, Thibault may well have been correct when he proposed that the use of 'Isabeau' was aimed at being disrespectful. Consequently, it is revealing rather than strange that a number of the queen's 'champions' like Vallet de Viriville and Grandeau choose to go against historical tradition and sometimes call her 'Isabel'. However, this essay will maintain the tradition of designating the queen as 'Isabeau', a name which, despite any unpleasant connotations behind its original use, is at least distinctive.

The marriage of Isabeau of Bavaria to Charles VI and her entry into Paris for her coronation on 23 August 1389 are the most often documented episodes of her life. The births of all her twelve children also appear in the majority of the chronicles and, were it not for the tragedy of her husband's unpredictable fits of madness, she could well have spent the rest of her life in historical anonymity, like the majority of medieval queens. However, possibly because of her prominence, a great deal of her administrative papers and letters have survived, along with chronicle references, to provide some insight into her personality.

---

[7] It was widely believed that the saint's head was enshrined there, although Rome and other shrines also claimed that they possessed the relic. The Bavarians arrival was timed for the annual fête, with public worship centred around the relic. Auguste Vallet de Viriville, *Isabeau de Bavière* (Paris, 1859), 4.

When Charles VI experienced the first attack of what would be a lifelong insanity on 5 August 1392, Isabeau was twenty-two years old and mother to three children, two others having already died in infancy, and must have been as unprepared for ruling responsibility as any other bride from an unimportant ducal house. Yet, on his recovery from this initial bout, Charles ensured that, if he died, as was clearly feared, from this mysterious ailment, Isabeau would have a major role in government as principal guardian of the dauphin, until he reached his majority at thirteen, and as a member of the regency council. However, the struggle for power between the dukes of Burgundy and Orleans, which had escalated from discord into downright aggression by the turn of the century, was the real opening on to the diplomatic stage for Isabeau, in the role of arbiter. Her success in mobilising the other royal dukes with her as negotiators led the king to entrust her with full powers of mediation in March 1402 and, on 1 July, with authority to deal with finance and any other major matters of government business when he was incapable of so doing. These powers were clarified on 26 April 1403, when it was finally recognised that Charles's bouts of insanity occurred too often for an *ad hoc* governmental situation to continue, with whoever the king chose to recognise—in all senses of the word—at the time having full authority by default. Isabeau was acknowledged as the leader of a new regency council, which included all the royal dukes, the Constable, the Chancellor and others of the king's regular councillors, who would rule by majority vote in Charles VI's name until he was sane and could resume power.

The assassination of Louis of Orleans in 1407 began the actual physical conflict of the civil war, and the need of both sides to control the queen and the dauphin in order to be thought of as legitimate rulers led to Isabeau's confused and later criticised factional instability, as she agreed to defensive alliances with whichever magnates seemed the least threatening. When the death of Jean, duke of Touraine, in March 1417 meant that Isabeau's last son Charles became dauphin and, for the first time, the Armagnacs had possession of the heir, as well as control of Paris and the king, Isabeau's position finally was untenable. On the count of Armagnac's orders, she was deprived of her finances, her servants and her liberty, being held in captivity at Tours for six months before being rescued by Burgundy, although it is still debated as to whether this was on her request or his initiative. From now on, there was no real deviation in her actions: maintained, financed and protected by the Burgundians, her name was united with theirs in all government decisions, up to and including the surrender of France to the English that the Treaty of Troyes entailed.

There are many points of contention that surface continually in works on Isabeau of Bavaria, the 'crimes' of which she stands accused in accounts of her life. The major complaint for French writers is her agreement to the Treaty of Troyes and the disinheritance of the dauphin that this led to. Linked to this is the accusation that she was a bad mother. She faces also accusations of adultery, incest, moral corruption, treason, avarice and profligacy, as well as being condemned over her political aspirations and involvements—a heavy catalogue of sins. It is difficult to see how one can start to counter or even discuss these charges in a limited time, but possibly a logical beginning is what initially seems a trivial subject, that of her personal appearance, which is as disputed as any other claims about Isabeau, perhaps because of what May McKisack identified as the 'problem of historical reputation'.[8] Beginning with the many contemporary and historical descriptions of the queen, she was small and brunette, or tall and blonde; she was beautiful and hypnotic, or so obese through dropsy that she was crippled. As far as Isabeau's physiology is concerned, historians seem not to have left the morality theatre: if she is bad, she is ugly; if not so bad, she is allowed to be pretty. Surprisingly, this is not just the case in medieval works, where it could be seen as an acceptable literary device, but also in modern accounts. Conversely, the burden of the researcher is often lessened because it is possible to tell almost immediately what the conclusions of an author are going to be from his description of the queen's appearance. Despite the statement of Villiers de l'Isle-Adam that historians agree on her exceptional beauty,[9] many have chosen to accept the vehement diatribe of the 1406 propaganda pamphlet known as the *Songe Veritable* in which the queen is described as 'envelopée en laide peau'. Through a mistranslation of this as ugly fat,[10] a myth has been developed around her supposed obesity, backed up by fanciful stories about palace doors having to be widened so she could fit through.[11] To take some examples, Lévis-Mirepoix said that she was 'sans réelle beauté',[12] while Margaret Wade Labarge describes Isabeau as 'a gross figure of a women suffering from dropsy',[13] perhaps assuming that the *Songe* gave an accurate picture of her in her thirties. However, those writers who are largely sympathetic to Isabeau tend to believe Froissart's judgment on her as 'moult belle': in 1900, Catherine Bearne claimed her 'extraordinary beauty was the admiration of the

---

[8] May McKisack, 'Edward III and the Historians', *History*, XLV (1960), 1.

[9] P.A.M. Villiers de l'Isle-Adam, *Trois portraits de femmes. Isabeau de Bavière* (Paris, 1929), 59.

[10] As shown in P.S. Lewis, *Later Medieval France. The Polity* (1968), 114.

[11] H. Baudrillart, *Histoire de luxe privé et public* (4 vols., Paris, 1878–80), III, 288–9. He does say that the doors were widened at Vincennes, but only to accommodate the fashionably wide skirts that Isabeau wore.

[12] Le duc de Lévis-Mirepoix, *La France féodale, 987–1515* (Paris, 1975), 193.

[13] Margaret Wade Labarge, *Women in Medieval Life: A Small Sound of the Trumpet* (1986), 69.

court',[14] and Yann Grandeau considers that the adoption by Charles VI in 1394 of a new motto 'J'aime la plus belle' and the wearing of a collar with this device was too public a display to be aimed at anyone other than his queen.[15] However, some of her critics have used Isabeau's reputed beauty as another 'proof' of her evil, such as in the following description by Villiers de l'Isle-Adam: 'Hair red like burning gold, pale with the complexion of a storm, endowed with a languid and fateful beauty, and dangerous charm, Isabeau still did not refuse to use the resources of balms and philtres';[16] that is to say, he accuses her of maintaining her beauty with courtesans' tricks and possibly magic. It is unlikely that Isabeau's real appearance was as dramatic as the above description, but even the critical Burgundian propaganda-allegory *Le Pastorelet* admits that she was pretty, despite being quite short and brunette,[17] which is the image preserved in the few surviving portraits of Isabeau. The earliest work is a sculpture in the Palais de Justice at Poitiers, probably carved in the early 1390s, depicting a young, attractive queen with large, wide-set eyes, an oval face with full, high cheeks, a large expressive mouth and a pointed double-chin that stayed with her throughout her life, if the frontispiece of Christine de Pisan's *Œuvres* is also considered to be accurate.[18] In the illumination, the seated queen is short, pleasant-looking, dark-haired and round-faced; the long nose and double chin imply that, as not unrealistically flattering, this portrait could be as close to life as her tomb at Saint-Denis. This effigy shows a strongly featured elderly woman in a widow's veil which, despite pronounced wrinkles, has many of the facial characteristics of the earlier statue.[19] Despite not apparently conforming to the idealised blonde looks of the period, and perhaps inheriting olive skin from her

---

[14] Catherine Bearne, *Pictures of the Old French Court* (1900), 109.

[15] Yann Grandeau, 'Isabeau de Bavière ou l'amour conjugal', *Actes du 102 Congrès National des Sociétés Savantes Limoges 1977: section de philologie et histoire jusqu'à 1610.*, II: *Etudes sur la sensibilité au Moyen âge* (Paris, 1979) [hereafter Grandeau, 'Amour conjugal'], 139.

[16] Villiers de l'Isle-Adam, *Trois portraits*, 59 (my translation).

[17] *La Pastorelet*, in *Chroniques rélatives à l'histoire de la Belgique sous la domination des ducs de Bourgogne*, ed. J.M. Kervyn. de Lettenhove (3 vols., Brussels, 1873), II, 578.

[18] British Library Harley manuscript 4431.

[19] Carved by Pierre de Thury, this'depicts Isabeau in 1435' according to Sandra Hindman, 'The Iconography of Queen Isabeau de Bavière (1410–1415): An Essay in Method', *Gazette des beaux-arts*, ser. 6, CII (1983), 104. Although Charles VI had been dead since 1422, the joint mausoleum was still not begun before 1432, although part of the royal library in the Louvre had been sold to pay Thury 400 livres of the 1,400 that had been promised to him for the work. Cf. Yann Grandeau, 'La mort et obsèques de Charles VI', *Bulletin philologique et historique du comité des travaux historiques et scientifiques (jusqu'à 1610) du comité des travaux historiques et scientifiques, année 1970* (Paris, 1972), II, 184 [pièce justificative: Bibliothèque Municipale de Rouen, collection Leber 5870, manuscrit Menant]. This being the case, Isabeau's effigy must certainly have been carved very close to her death.

Italian mother which would have been considered plain by some in the north, it should be remembered that Isabeau was thought pretty enough by Charles VI to become queen of France on looks alone: despite not being able to speak a word of French, she impressed the king enough for him to wed her a mere three days after their first meeting, with no contract and no dowry asked for.[20]

A queen's main duties were to secure the succession and support her husband and, unfortunately for Isabeau, this is seen by many commentators as one of her greatest areas of failure. She has been accused of being a poor wife and mother, neglecting her children for a court of libertines, abandoning the care of her mad husband to servants, and indulging in a myriad of adulterous liaisons, including an incestuous relationship with her brother-in-law Louis, duke of Orleans. This is the principal historical image of Isabeau the debauched, uncaring wanton—perhaps because, as is also often the case today, the most accessible weapons for an historian to use against a woman were criticisms of her looks and her sexual conduct, an ugly, adulterous woman who also neglects her children thus being totally beyond redemption. Yet, it is unclear where these accusations originate, and very difficult to state categorically whether there is any truth in them. Opinion on Isabeau's character and conduct tends to take a turn for the worse on all subjects, personal and public, around 1405. This was certainly a significant date for the queen because the death of her friend and mentor Philippe le Hardi in 1404 meant that she no longer had anything to tie her politically to Burgundy, and consequently she had become more dependent on the support of her previous rival, Louis of Orleans.[21] Thibault states that: 'le mort du duc de Bourgogne jeta la Reine dans les bras du duc d'Orléans',[22] but he claims that this was only as a political ally, not a lover. Their governmental activities between 1404 and 1407 were the subject of heavy criticism at the time, so it is tempting to see these two issues as not entirely unconnected. The provision of an official mistress for the king in 1405 is also a significant event in the formation of the myth of Isabeau, as it is used

[20] At least, not in documents that have been found to this date. The monk of Saint-Denis's inaccurate story of the bride being chosen from three portraits even relates that Charles VI found Isabeau's image to be 'très supérieure aux autres en grâce et en beauté'. Religieux de Saint-Denis, *Chronique de Charles VI de 1380 à 1422*, trans. and ed. L. Bellaguet (6 vols., Paris, 1841) [hereafter Religieux], I, 359.

[21] Their previously irreconcilable differences over policy had been greatly alleviated by the death of Gian Galeazzo Visconti (Louis's father-in-law and Isabeau's second cousin) in 1402, who was considered as an enemy by Isabeau because of his usurpation and murder of her grandfather Barnabo Visconti by Gian Galeazzo's father.

[22] Marcel Thibault, *Isabeau de Bavière: la Jeunesse* (Paris, 1903), 426. 'The duke of Burgundy's death threw the queen into the arms of the duke of Orleans.'

as ammunition for charges that she had abandoned her poor insane husband to rule France herself amid a life of decadence.

This essay will now move on to the contemporary allegations that this appalling reputation as a neglectful wife and mother is based on, and examine if is there proof either to Isabeau's culpability or her innocence. To commence with an analysis of Isabeau of Bavaria in her role as a wife and mother, her marriage was begun through attraction to her tall, blonde, handsome husband and continued with what appears to be great affection. As the first New Year's gift that he was able to offer his bride in January 1386, Charles gave Isabeau a palfrey saddle in red velvet and silk, scattered with the intertwined letters K and E, for the Latin names Karolus and Elisabeta, in gilded copper. The next year, he presented her with two gold rings embellished with this 'K/E' device, a symbol that also adorned jewels, tableware, clothing, even the clips of the queen's garters.[23] As far as physically providing for the succession went, it cannot be disputed that Isabeau performed admirably. She spent practically her entire youth in pregnancy, her first seven children arriving between 1386 and 1395 at average intervals of 16.5 months. There is also no reason to believe that she was less of an attentive mother than any other noblewoman of the period. Purchases of clothes, toys and books suitably luxurious as befitting their rank for each of the children are plentiful throughout her accounts; payments to couriers taking letters to them when they were apart from their mother are regular; memorial masses were commissioned for those who did not survive infancy. In June 1399, when plague was approaching Paris, riders of the queen's *écurie* were dispatched around the Île-de-France region to enquire where the royal children might be sent to safety.[24] The children were eventually taken to Vernon, apart from the ninth, the year-old baby Jean from whom the queen did not want to be parted, and it was only at the end of July that she agreed to send him to stay with the king's cousin, Madame Dammartin, near Meulan. These were not the actions of a disinterested mother, and the fact that Isabeau's daughters continued to visit her after they had married and grown up shows that there was some sort of lasting relationship within the family.[25] There is only one contemporary reference that questions whether Isabeau was an attentive parent: the Religieux de Saint-Denis says that in mid-1405 some members of the king's court accused the queen of not seeing to the children's education and, when this reached the king's ears, he questioned the dauphin as to how long it had been

[23] Vallet de Viriville, *Isabeau*, 6.

[24] Archives Nationales, Paris (hereafter AN) KK45, fos. 5 and 9.

[25] As examples, Jeanne, duchess of Brittany stayed with the queen at Melun in January 1415, and Princess Catherine even went to see her mother during her imprisonment at Tours by the Armagnacs in 1417.

since he was embraced by his mother and the child replied 'three months'. The Religieux continues: 'Des personnes qui se trouvaient là m'ont assuré que le roi se montra vivement affecté de tant d'indifférence',[26] but if he had mentioned who these 'people' were, it would be easier to judge the likelihood of the accusation being true. Yet, the charge of negligence has stayed with Isabeau to some extent, with the 'proof' cited in one case as being that only three of her children survived her,[27] clearly an unfair charge for a period when families of each and every class lost offspring to untimely death in infancy, of disease or in childbirth. Isabeau produced twelve children in twenty-one years, seven of them after Charles's first attack of insanity, which was particularly remarkable when it is recalled that one of the most distressing aspects for Isabeau of her husband's seizures was his inability to recognise her, and occasionally his violent reaction to her presence, or even the sight of her coat-of-arms.[28]

As a young woman of twenty-two, previously happy with her marriage, nothing could have adequately prepared Isabeau for the tragedy of 5 August 1392, after which nothing about her life could ever be the same. In the words of Yann Grandeau: 'le prince charmant se muait en bête; c'était l'envers du conte'.[29] One could guess that those close to Charles VI hoped that the bout of madness on the Plain of Mons was an isolated incident and, that when he recovered from it, he was cured. Unfortunately, this was not the case, for the king relapsed into a lengthy bout of insanity in June 1393.[30] It was more from this point rather than the previous year that desperation set in to find a medical solution or divine blessing. Isabeau trusted mainly in God to come to her husband's aid and promised to give the child she was carrying to God if Charles recovered.[31] It was eight months before he was fully well, but the princess Marie who had been born in August did eventually take the veil. Her name was chosen by Isabeau herself in honour of Charles VI's aunt, Marie of Bourbon, who was abbess at the royal nunnery of Poissy, which is where Marie of France spent her life from the age of six. In the winter of 1393, solemn processions were made in Paris on the orders of the queen and the Council;[32]

---

[26] Religieux, III, 291. 'People who were there have assured me the king was greatly affected by such indifference'.

[27] M. Vale, *Charles VII* (1974), 23 n. 4.

[28] Religieux, II, 404, which describes how the king tried to tear down or destroy carvings, windows or other images of the Bavarian arms. Cf. also R.C. Famiglietti, *Royal Intrigue: Crisis at the Court of Charles VI, 1392–1420* (New York, 1986), 15.

[29] Grandeau, 'Amour conjugal', 126. 'Prince Charming turned into the Beast; it was the reverse of the fairy-tale.'

[30] Religieux, II, 87–9.

[31] Ibid., ii, 95.

[32] Ibid., ii, 93.

in January 1396, Isabeau instructed pious processions to be organised throughout France to pray 'pour la bonne santé et prosperité de
mondit seigneur'.[33] Also, perhaps hoping that their innocent voices
would soften the heart of an obviously displeased God, Isabeau sent
her children in 1409 to pray for their father's recovery at Mont-Saint-
Michel,[34] the shrine of the third patron saint of France, after Saint
Denis, the patron of Paris and Saint Rémy, the patron of the Capetian house. Presumably, the naming of the seventh *Enfant de France* as
Michelle in 1395 was also a desperate plea for the intercession of
the king's favourite saint, who had received the credit for his recovery
in 1394.

Yann Grandeau described traditional interpretations of the royal
couple's relationship after the king's insanity as a romanticised diptych:
on one screen, the king, alone, neglected, clothed in rags and half-
starved;[35] on the other, the queen, well-dressed, happy, dancing with
any faceless lover.[36] This is an image that has more than made its
mark, but can only be described as apocryphal, given the queen's
recorded distress at any misfortune befalling her husband. On 29
January 1393, at the wedding feast which became known to history as
the tragic *Bal des Ardents*, the king escaped from serious burns only by
the prompt action of the young duchess of Berry, and the Religieux
tells us that, when she thought the king had died with his friends, the
pregnant queen 'tomba à terre demi-morte de frayeur.[37] Despite her
anguish at his madness, there was very little that Isabeau could do on
a practical basis. A queen of France would not have been expected to
bathe and nurse a lunatic, whether he was her husband or not, and it
is true to say that, if the maddened king wore torn and soiled clothes,
it was because he had torn and soiled them. There are orders from his
household staff for replacements for garments and furniture that he
had ruined, by urinating on them,[38] throwing them on the fire or
breaking them.[39] If he was alone, it was because he had refused the
companionship of his wife. The Religieux of Saint-Denis describes
Charles's rejection of the queen vividly and tragically:

[33] Verdon, *Isabeau*, 74.
[34] AN KK32, fo. 24.
[35] In 1409, a new silver cruet and a silver-plated meat larder were ordered by the king's
kitchen. Purchases such as this would be unnecessary if reality corresponded to myth
and (as in the opera by C. & G. Delavigne [1843]) Charles VI was weeping: 'J'ai faim
... tout le monde m'oublie!' Cf. Charles Barthélemy, *Erreurs et mensonges historiques*, IV: *A
propos de Charles VI et d'Isabeau de Bavière* (Paris, 1876), 215.
[36] Grandeau, 'Amour conjugal', 126.
[37] Religieux, II, 71.
[38] AN KK26, fo. 102 [1398].
[39] BN f.fr. 6745, fos. 16 [1404] and 13.

'Je ne saurais dire combien était profondé la douleur que l'auguste reine Isabelle[40] éprouvait de l'état du roi. Ce qui l'affligeait surtout, c'était de voir que toutes les fois que, fatiguée de pleurer et de gémir, elle l'approchait pour lui prodiguer les marques de son chaste amour, le roi repoussait en disant avec douceur à ses gens: 'Quelle est cette femme dont la vue m'obsède? Sachez si elle a besoin de quelque chose, et délivrez-moi comme vous pourrez de ses persécutions et de ses importunités, afin qu'elle ne s'attache à mes pas.'[41]

This was particularly distressing for Isabeau because the madness was intermittent, attacks succeeding periods of remission. It would possibly have been kinder to her if Charles VI had died in 1392, or remained permanently insane and thus inaccessible to her. However with this impossible situation, when the king recovered his faculties, he retook his place in Council and in the queen's bed,[42] only for insanity to return and him to reject her again. On his doctors' advice, festivities were organised for Charles VI constantly in the 1390s to distract him from the stresses of rule so, to return to that imaginary diptych, if the queen danced then, her partner had the face of the king.

As each year passed and the new century began, the situation grew worse. Charles VI's bouts of insanity were occurring more frequently, with greater intensity, and with shorter periods of remission between them. Isabeau has been accused by a fair number of historians of abandoning her conjugal duties and the care of her husband, moving away to her hôtel Barbette.[43] In fact, from 1398, the time it was given to her, to 1407, she spent a total of only six months there, but it would be unjust to blame her if she did not want to live with a madman. He would not let her see him during his periods of insanity so, short of retreating to the queen's wing of Saint-Pol rather than risk meeting him, there does not seem to have been much that she could do to help in this tragic situation. If Isabeau had seen Charles in one of his more severe bouts, she would probably not have recognised the handsome, chivalrous prince whom she had married. Juvénal des Ursins declared that: 'C'estoit grande pitié de le voir, car son corps estoit tout mangé

[40] The Latin term that the Religieux uses is 'venerabilis regina'.
[41] Religieux, II, 89. 'I would not know how to tell with what profound grief the august queen Isabelle was affected by the king's condition. What distressed her above all was to see how on all the occasions when, fatigued by tears and sobbing, she approached to lavish attention on him, the king repulsed her, whispering to his people: "Who is this woman obstructing my view? Find out what she wants, and stop her from annoying and bothering me, if you can".'
[42] Seven of their twelve children were born after the insanity began in 1392.
[43] For example, Firmin Didot, *Nouvelle biographie universelle* (Paris, 1854), IX, 831.

de poux, et d'ordure'[44] but, unfortunately, the king's sexual appetite was not dulled by his condition. The Religieux de Saint-Denis explains that the fearful situation meant the king could not be allowed to sleep with the queen, so instead the daughter of the *maître des écuries*, Odette de Champdivers, was put forward as his concubine at the end of 1405, with Isabeau's consent. Jean Verdon puts forward this explanation of what might initially seem a strange agreement: 'Quand (the queen) songeait aux maux qui la menaçait, aux violences et aux mauvais traitements déjà supportés par le fait du roi, la pensée qu'entre deux maux il valait meiux choisir le moindre la faisait se résigner à ce sacrifice.'[45] This arrangement might not have meant that the royal marriage was over for good: Monstrelet reports that Isabeau slept with the king on the night of Louis of Orleans's murder, 23 November 1407, when she fled back to Saint-Pol in distress,[46] and Juvénal des Ursins says that the king and queen shared a chamber on 9 March 1408, because she was there when he again succumbed to an attack of insanity.[47] However, even if the peculiarities of Charles's illness meant it was impossible on a practical basis for the king and queen to continue a sexual relationship, or if, understandably enough, Isabeau no longer felt what she had for her husband and largely gave up on the marriage in all but name around 1405, the couple did not stop caring for each other in other ways. Presents were still given to each other, letters were still exchanged, both instituted an obituary mass at Amiens cathedral where they had been married—all of these indicate remnants of affection. Therefore, unless Isabeau really was the amoral whore that some historians believe, it is difficult to ally the above images of her with later rumours that she indulged in an affair with her brother-in-law, who already had Mariette d'Enghien as a mistress and a full relationship with his wife; that she was probably 'the most immoral woman of an immoral age'.[48] It is proving more difficult than one might imagine to find any proof behind the torrid tales of depravity, which leads one to suspect that there may have been a more subtle, political motivation behind the moral condemnation.

During her lifetime, Isabeau was certainly accused of frivolous,

[44] Jean Juvénal des Ursins, *Histoire de Charles VI, roy de France* in *Nouvelle collection de mémoires sur l'histoire de France*, ed. Michaud and Poujoulet (32 vols., Paris, 1836), II [hereafter Juvénal], 438. 'It was pitiful to see him, because his body was consumed totally with lice and filth.'

[45] Verdon, *Isabeau*, 79. 'When she thought of the evils which had threatened her, as well as the violence that she had endured already from the king, it was thought better to choose the lesser of the two evils, so she resigned herself to this sacrifice.'

[46] Enguerrand de Monstrelet, *Chronique, 1400–1444*, ed. Lucien Douet-d'Arcq (6 vols., Paris, 1857–62), I, 161.

[47] Juvénal, 445.

[48] Dinah Lampitt, *The King's Women* (London, 1992), 431.

unseemly behaviour by clerics and chroniclers in her development of outlandish new fashions, and some alleged that members of her court or immediate household behaved scandalously, but there do not appear to be any concrete contemporary charges of this kind levied at Isabeau herself. Modern critics who want to back up their allegations with contemporary evidence often use some phrases from the Religieux of Saint-Denis, but first have to extract them from a piece which does not moralise on any gross moral turpitude, but in fact condemns taxation and purveyance imposed by Isabeau and Orleans during 1405:

> On leur reprochait encore, entre autres actes de tyrannie, d'insulter à la misère publique en faisant grande chère aux dépens d'autrui; ils enlevaient les vivres sans les payer, et quand on en demandait le prix, les pourvoyeurs de la maison royale regardaient cette réclamation comme un crime. Indifférents à la défence du royaume, ils mettaient toute leur vanité dans les richesses, *toute leur jouissance dans les délices du corps*. Enfin ils oubliaient tellement les règles et les devoirs de la royauté, qu'*ils étaient devenus un objet de scandale pour la France* et la fable des nations étrangères.[49]

They 'became an object of scandal' for forgetting the responsibilities of a prince to defend his people from external attack and internal deprivation. Juvénal des Ursins agreed that there was much popular feeling against Isabeau and Orleans during 1405: one could hear them cursed in the streets because they were responsible for implementing this taxation.[50] The Religieux of Saint-Denis expands further on these complaints against war subsidies:

> Les habitants du royaume en rejetaient la faute sur la mauvaise administration de la reine et du duc d'Orléans. On déclamait publiquement dans les villes contre leur insatiable cupidité; on disait que, négligaient la défense du royaume et non contents des exactions ordinaires, ils avaient encore l'année précédente établi un impôt général.[51]

[49] Religieux, III, 267 (my italics). 'They could be reproached also with insulting the people's misery by spending heavily from the payments of others. They took away supplies without paying for them and, when payment was asked of them, the purveyers of the royal household regarded this complaint as a crime. Indifferent to the defence of the kingdom, they (Isabeau and Orleans) put all their vanity in riches, *all their joy in the pleasures of the flesh*. In a word, they so forgot the rules and duties of royalty that *they became an object of scandal for France* and the laughing stock of foreign countries.'

[50] Juvénal, 434.

[51] Religieux, III, 229. 'The people blamed the bad administration of the queen and the duke of Orleans. They were condemned publicly in the towns for their insatiable greed; it was said that, negligent of the kingdom's defence and not content with normal taxation, they had imposed a general levy the previous year.'

The Religieux estimates that this universal taxation would have raised about 800,000 gold *écus*, which they were suspected of keeping for themselves. There is also no reason why the 'pleasures of the flesh' that the Religieux talked about have to be an illicit relationship, for good food, luxurious clothes and lavish lifestyles could also be described in this way. There is clear proof of Isabeau's expensive tastes:[52] for example, she is known to have owned a jewelled headdress encrusted with ninety-three diamonds set amongst sapphires, rubies and pearls, to have got through 68,233 pelts of *vair*, the blue-white squirrel fur, in one twelve-month account,[53] and to have spent 800 *livres parisis* on just two pieces of cloth-of-gold.[54] Condemnation of Isabeau for her extravagance during a period of national crisis and widespread poverty is not a charge that it is possible to defend her against, because it is undoubtedly true. The lavish tastes that she acquired as queen of France were selfish, short-sighted and foolish, but not morally corrupt. After all, one of the most popular queens of England, Philippa of Hainault, was notoriously bad with money but, luckily for her reputation, Edward III was prepared to clear her debts and to supervise her future expenditure. As well as being deprived of her husband's advice, it is possible also that Isabeau's upbringing had not prepared her adequately for the responsibilities that came with great wealth. As was previously mentioned, when Isabeau first came to France in 1385, her aunt the duchess of Holland did not allow her to keep the clothes she arrived in, seeing them as too simple for French tastes, but arranged new ones for her.[55] With the image of what a queen was supposed to be presented so deliberately to a young and presumably impressionable girl, it could be said with some justification that France may well have got the queen she deserved, because France had made her.

The words of Jacques Legrand, the Augustinian friar and preacher, have been used also as proof of the scandalous lifestyle that Isabeau of Bavaria kept. In May 1405, he preached a sermon before the queen, condemning the behaviour and the appearance of those at her court by means of allegorical characters:

> Je voudrais, noble reine, ne rien dire qui ne vous fût agréable, mais votre salut m'est plus cher que vos bonnes grâces: je dirai donc la vérité, quels que doivent être vos sentiments à mon égard. La déesse Vénus règne seule à votre cour; l'ivresse et la débauche lui servent

---

[52] Her *average* argenterie expenses for the five years of 1393–8 were about 9,350 *livres parisis* p.a. For the same time period between 1400 and 1405, the average was about 45,700 *livres parisis*—an average being almost as much as the total for 1393–8.
[53] AN KK42, 10th account (February 1402—January 1403) fo. 61.
[54] AN KK42, fo. 73.
[55] Froissart, XI, 228.

de cortége et font de la nuit le jour au milieu des danses les plus dissolues. Ces maudites et infernales suivantes, qui assiégent sans cesse votre cour, corrompent les mœurs et énervent les cœurs. Elles efféminent les chevaliers et les écuyers et les empêchent de partir pour les expéditions guerrières, en leur faisant craindre d'être défigurés par les blessures . . . Partout, noble reine, on parle de ces désordres et de beaucoup d'autres qui déshonorent votre cour. Si vous ne voulez pas m'en croire, parcourez la ville sous le déguisement d'une pauvre femme, et vous entendrez ce que chacun dit.[56]

Legrand also greatly censured the immorality of the court fashions at the time for which he considered Isabeau to be principally responsible. Eustache Deschamps in his poem *Miroir de mariage* relates how the low-cut gowns worn at court exposed the neck, shoulders, and sometimes even the breasts,[57] so there does seem to be good reason for censure from a monk. However, respectable outrage at the way the court ladies dressed is not an accusation of adultery aimed at Isabeau and, from Legrand's response when condemned by courtiers for saying such things in front of the queen, it is clear that he was not accusing her personally of impropriety, just those around her: 'Je suis bien plus étonné que vous osiez commettre d'aussi méchantes actions et même de pires, que je révélerai à la reine, quand il lui plaira de m'entendre.'[58] If she needed to be told of these offences, Legrand cannot have believed that Isabeau herself was involved. Whether because of outrage equal to that of Legrand, or trying to deflect attention from her own misdeeds as the cynical would say, later that year Isabeau dealt harshly with several members of her household who were tainted with scandal. The dame de Minchière, holder of the queen's seal, was among the attendants dismissed from court, and on 15 August, the vicomtesse de Breteuil and the *écuyer* Robert de Varennes were actually imprisoned.[59]

The chronicler Guillaume Cousinot treated any gossip that was being

---

[56] Religieux, III, 269. 'Noble queen, I would never want to tell you anything disagreeable, but your salvation is dearer to me than your good graces: thus, I will speak the truth, whatever your opinions of me might be. The goddess Venus is the only ruler at your court, Drunkenness and Debauchery serve in her train and turn night into day amidst the most dissolute dances. These confounded, infernal followers, who incessantly besiege your court, corrupt morals and agitate the heart. They make knights and squires effeminate and prevent them from leaving for war by making them scared of being disfigured by injury ... Noble queen, there is talk of these and many other disorders which dishonour your court. If you do not want to believe me, go through town disguised as a poor woman and you will hear what everyone says.'

[57] Eustache Deschamps, *Œuvres complètes*, ed. G Raynaud (Paris, 1894), IX, 49.

[58] Religieux, III, 269–71. 'I am astonished that you dare to commit such wicked deeds, and even worse ones, which I shall tell the queen all about, when it pleases her to listen to me.'

[59] Ibid., III, 331.

peddled around the court and the capital as deliberate slander: he says that, in an attempt to 'mectre les cuers du peuple contre eulx', the duke of Burgundy '... fist semer par cayemans et par tavernes faulses mençonges de la royne et du duc d'Orléans son frère',[60] and it does seem to be the case that, even in 1405, Paris was opposed to the influence of Louis of Orleans and leaning towards its later pronounced Burgundian sympathies. A political pamphlet that surfaced in around 1406, the *Songe Véritable*, strongly criticises the cupidity of Isabeau and the extravagance of her entourage, but does not contain any specific slurs on her private life, even though the harsh language of the allegorical characters shows their distaste at her other actions. Expérience accuses Isabeau of greed and foolish spending, and mentions the discovery made public by the citizens of Metz that she had sent six horses laden with bags of money to Bavaria in 1405.[61] Fortune claims to have endowed the queen with a good reputation, a gift she lost in less than a year, and replies to the pleas of Souffrance:

> Je ly ferai avoir tel honte
> Et tel dommage et telle perte
> Qu'en la fin en sera déserte,[62]

while Raison makes the cruel threat:

> Toy, Royne, dame Ysabeau,
> Envelopée en laide peau
> Se devers moy bientost ne viens
> Je te touldray trestous les tiens
> Et te menray a tel mischief.[63]

Despite the brutality of these words, this poem is in fact a valuable aid in Isabeau's defence against adultery charges, for it attacks the queen venemously but states that her good reputation had previously been intact up to that one year, which must be 1405, and has nothing to say

[60] Guillaume Cousinot, *Geste des Nobles*, in *Chronique de la Pucelle ou Chronique de Cousinot suivie de la Chronique normande de P. Cochon relative au règnes de Charles VI et de Charles VII*, ed. Auguste Vallet de Viriville (1st edn. Paris, 1859; Geneva, 1976), 109.

[61] The Religieux of Saint-Denis recorded public opinion on this issue as fear that she wished to enrich the Germans by impoverishing the French. This money was probably the one-off payment of 57,000 francs that Isabeau gave her brother Louis on 22 July 1405 in return for the revenues of five Bavarian provinces (cf. BN f.fr. 6537, fo. 159), but there were suspicions that this was actually the proceeds of the 1405 tax, being concealed in Bavaria.

[62] *Le Songe Véritable*, ed. H. Moranvillé, *Mémoires de la Société de l'Histoire de Paris*, XVII (1890), 276. 'I will make her feel such shame / and such injury and loss / that in the end she will be desolate.'

[63] Ibid., 296. 'You, queen, Lady Isabeau, / enveloped in ugly skin / if you do not come to me soon / I will take away everything of yours / And lead you into such trouble.'

about a relationship with Orleans. If there had been widespread gossip on such an inflammatory and damaging subject in existence in 1405, it would be highly improbable for this critical author to have no wish to repeat it and to air his own suspicions on the queen's morality.

If the story of Isabeau's reputed adultery did not begin in the chronicles and popular writings of the time, how did the woman whom fifteenth-century writers seem to have admired, whom Chartier described as a 'très-chrétienne' queen[64] and the Religieux de Saint-Denis called 'reginam venerabilem' in 1413,[65] be transformed by the twentieth century into Villiers de l'Isle-Adam's 'la grande gaupe'?[66] The metamorphosis is quite easy for those who think the worst: if one believes that Isabeau was prepared to indulge in a liaison with her husband's own brother, it is not too great a step to imagine her capable of adultery with anyone, for any end. Consequently, if one accepts the conclusion of earlier historians, that she and Louis of Orleans were lovers, one has to be prepared for accusations that there were liaisons with all who supported her, and that she must also have been the mistress of Jean sans Peur, of Jean Villiers de l'Isle-Adam who took Paris in 1418, supposedly because of his infatuation for her,[67] and of Louis de Bosredon, her *grand maître d'hôtel*, whose sudden arrest on 18 April 1417 heralded the queen's captivity in Tours.[68] Rumours about Isabeau and Louis of Orleans seem to have been entirely based on two sources: another famous verse allegory, the *Pastorelet*, and one remark made by Jean Chartier, the royal historiographer, after 1437. The anonymous author of the pastoral poem depicts the rulers of the time as shepherds and shepherdesses with fictitious names, such as Belligère for Isabeau, Tristifer for Orleans and Florentin for Charles VI, but an end glossary is also provided, detailing the real identity of the characters so that there can be no mistake. The *Pastorelet* claims to be a true record of events leading up to the assassination of Jean sans Peur, but its purpose is clearly to glorify the duke of Burgundy. As he confessed to the crime almost immediately, and received a pardon for it, the poem is forced to admit that Burgundy ordered the murder of Louis

[64] Jean Chartier, *Histoire de Charles VII, roi de France*, ed. A. Vallet de Viriville (3 vols., Paris, 1858) [hereafter Chartier], i, 208. Famiglietti assumes that this appellation has the same symbolic significance as the usual description of French kings being 'très-chrétian' (*Royal Intrigue*, 229 n. 35).

[65] Religieux, V, 28. Add to this the fact that a Cabochien spokesman criticised the Dauphin Louis for straying despite the sound moral education given him by his mother, the venerable queen. Ibid., V, 31.

[66] Villiers de l'Isle-Adam, *Trois portraits*, 75.

[67] Ibid., 73.

[68] For accounts on Bosredon's arrest, cf. Cousinot, *Geste des Nobles*, 163–4, and Jean le Fèvre de Saint-Rémy, *Chronique de Jean le Fèvre, seigneur de Saint-Rémy*, ed. F. Morand (2 vols., Paris, 1876–81), I, 292ff.

of Orleans in 1407, but justifies his actions by saying that he was only acting on the king's orders. In the poem, Charles learns of the affair between Louis and Isabeau and swears bloody revenge, at which point Jean sans Peur says that he will take care of it.[69] The adultery is heavily emphasised because it is used in this way to attempt to excuse the murder; obviously Jean's defence in 1407, that Louis was becoming a tyrant in his unchecked political position, was no longer seen as adequate in light of the duke of Burgundy's manipulation of the king's insanity since then.

When Jean Chartier recorded the death and funeral in October 1435 of Isabeau of Bavaria,[70] he laments that the English shortened her life by claiming that her son, the dauphin Charles, was illegitimate. He says that, after learning of this slander, she was so upset that she never felt happiness again.[71] As Chartier calls Charles VII only 'dauphin de Vienne' in this passage, it has been assumed that he is referring to the period before Charles was crowned in 1429, a time that Isabeau spent in English-occupied Paris.[72] This may have been mere anti-English propaganda on Chartier's part, depicting the enemy as low enough to sully the reputation of the 'très-chrétienne' queen,[73] because certainly there is no official English material of this kind. For example, a defence of the legality of the Treaty of Troyes was written in 1435 by Jean de Rinel, secretary to Henry VI, which makes no mention of Charles VII's parentage.[74] If such an allegation had been made at this point, it would certainly have simplified the English position, for the heir to Charles VI's sons under 'Salic law' was Charles, duke of Orleans, in captivity in London for twenty years since the battle of Agincourt in 1415, and hence in no position to defend any claim he might have to the crown. Even the scandal-rich *Chronicle of Tramecourt* written soon after 1420 makes no scurrilous comment about Isabeau, despite record-

[69] 'Léonet' replies to 'Florentin's' outburst with the words: 'Je feray vostre voloir et gaiteray tant que je voia plus à plain les amours en puy ou en plain? *Le Pastorelet*, 636. Cf. Famiglietti, *Royal Intrigue*, 45.
[70] It is possible that he even attended the funeral because he was an officer of the abbey of Saint-Denis in 1435. Cf. C. Samaran, *Chronique latine inédite de Jean Chartier* (Paris, 1928), 9.
[71] Chartier, I, 209–10.
[72] Famiglietti, *Royal Intrigue*, 44.
[73] Chartier, I, 208.
[74] Rinel's defence of the Treaty of Troyes is published in full in *English Medieval Diplomatic Practice*, part 1: *Documents and Interpretation* (1982), II, 648–52. English propaganda posters illustrating the genealogy of Henry VI stressed his *French* ancestry, his blood rights to the crown and his legal rights through the Treaty, as well as discounting Charles VII's claim by stating that he had eliminated himself though his culpability in the murder of Jean sans Peur. Cf. J. W. McKenna, 'Henry VI of England and the Dual Monarchy: Aspects of Royal Political Propaganda, 1422–1432', *Journal of the Warburg and Courtauld Institutes*, XXVIII (1965), 151–3.

ing much of the popular gossip of the time, such as the stories that the dauphins Louis and Jean were murdered, and that Valentine, duchess of Orleans, attempted to kill their older brother Charles with a poisoned apple but that her son ate it instead.[75] The first non-contemporary writer to mention an affair between Isabeau and Orleans seems to have been the Flemish monk Adrian de But, who wrote in the 1480s that he had read a pamphlet about it on a trip to Paris.[76] Soon, the myth had found its way into the writings of more famous authors, such as Brantôme in the sixteenth century; and before long its origins were forgotten and it was, to all intents and purposes, a fact, as much as if it had really happened. The myth of the queen's adultery may also have been promoted to glorify further Joan of Arc, who Jean Verdon describes as being moulded by popular history into Isabeau's 'opposite number': 'La mémoire collective des peuples aime les diptyques bien tranchés: ainsi Isabeau servira de repoussoir à Jeanne; à l'une elle conférara la sainteté, à l'autre des actes démoniaques; la Pucelle dénoue l'ouvrage d'Isabeau la maudite'.[77] Historians have and sometimes still do subscribe to the preposterous and impractical notion of Pierre Cazé that Joan was Isabeau's daughter, the product of an affair with Orleans.[78] The reasoning behind this is unclear, but perhaps it has been felt to be more fitting for someone of Valois blood, however tainted, to redeem France rather than a peasant-girl from Lorraine. This myth persists despite the fact that, if Joan was nineteen as she claimed during her trial in 1431, it would have been a miraculous conception in 1412, considering Louis of Orleans had been dead for five years. However, this fiction does at least give an idea of the effort that has been made to denigrate Isabeau by 'proving' her to be an adulteress once it has been decided already that she is one of history's great villains, and it is clear that irrefutable facts and discrepancies do not prevent this character assassination.

---

[75] Famiglietti, *Royal Intrigue*, 228 n. 31 (chronicle on m/film at Archives départementales du Pas-de-Calais, Arras).

[76] *Chroniques des religieux des Dunes: Jean Brandon, Gilles de Ruyes, Adrien de But*, ed. J.M. Kervyn de Lettenhove (Brussels, 1870), 111. Cf. Famiglietti, *Royal Intrigue*, 229 n. 44.

[77] Verdon, *Isabeau*, 12. 'National consciousness loves clear-cut dichotomies: thus Isabeau serves as a foil to Joan; to one it conferes sanctity, to the other demonic behaviour; the Maid undoes the work of the damned Isabeau.'

[78] Cazé was a sub-prefect in Bergerac who expounded his theory in *The Death of Joan of Arc or the Maid of Orleans* (Libourne, 1805), and *The Truth about Joan of Arc or enlightenment on her origin* (2 vols, 1819). Cf. *Actes du 104e congrès national des sociétés savantes, Orléans 1979: section de philologie et d'histoire médiévale—Jeanne d'Arc, une époque, un rayonnement* (Paris, 1982) for modern comment on Joan as an Orléans bastard. Pierre Marot, 'La genèse d'un roman: Pierre Cazé, l'inventeur de la "bâtardise" de Jeanne d'Arc' refutes the story, while Claude Ribera-Periville, 'Aspects du Mécénat de Lous 1er d'Orléans' actually describes the duke as 'père putatif de Jeanne'.

Despite popular misinformation about its contents, the Treaty of Troyes of 1420 is not a source of evidence for this affair: it contains no mention of the queen's adultery, and does not declare the dauphin, the future Charles VII, to be illegitimate, a bastard of Louis of Orleans or anyone else. The only mention of Dauphin Charles is in one of the very last articles, which states that:

> considerez les orribles et enormes crimes et deliz perpetrez oudit Royaume de france par Charles soy disant daulphin de viennois, Il est accorde que nous ne nostre filz le Roy henry ne aussi nostre treschier filz phelippe duc de Bourgoigne ne traicterons aucunement de paix ou de concorde avecques ledit Charles, ne ferons ou ferons traictier se non du conseil et assentement de tous et chascun de nous trois, et des troiz estas des deux Royaumes.[79]

This description of Charles as the 'soy disant daulphin de viennois' has been taken as a denial of him as the legitimate son of the king, without recognising that it was a common device for insulting one's rivals in legal documentation of the time: for instance, there has never been any suggestion that Charles, duke of Orleans thought Jean sans Peur was illegitimate when he wrote a defiance to the 'soy disant duc de Bourgogne' in 1408.[80] In letters personally issued by Charles VI on 17 January 1420,[81] it was declared that, by breaking the peace with his involvement in the assassination of the duke of Burgundy, his son the dauphin had rendered himself unworthy to succeed to the throne or any other title, so no one was to give him aid, acknowledge his rule or support him. Therefore, the dauphin in fact had been disinherited personally by his father before the Treaty of Troyes was enacted in May: the declarations of the treaty only confirmed his outlaw status, and recognised the conqueror Henry V as heir to the throne of France. This was acknowledged as the situation on both sides of the Channel. In his chronicle, Edward Hall records Henry V acknowledging Charles as 'the kynges sone' but that saying he has been deprived of his dignity as heir because: 'contrary to his promise & against all humaine honestie, (he) was not ashamed to polute & staine him selfe with the bloud and homicide of the valeaunt duke of Burgoyn.'[82] These declarations were

[79] AN X1a 8603, fos. 63–4. 'Considering the horrific and enormous crimes perpetrated in the said kingdom of France by Charles who calls himself dauphin of Vienne, it is agreed that neither we (Charles VI), nor our said son King Henry, nor our very dear son Philip duke of Burgundy shall negotiate any peace or agreement with the said Charles without the advice and consent of all and each of us three, and of the three Estates of our two kingdoms'.

[80] BN f.fr. 3910, no. 82 (reply by Burgundy at no. 83 in similar style, also including the 'soy disant' insult).

[81] *Ordonnances des rois de France de la troisième race* (22 vols., Paris, 1723–1849), XII, 273–7.

[82] Edward Hall, *Chronicle* (1809), 101.

confirmed by the *lit de justice* held jointly by Charles VI and Henry V in Paris on 23 December 1420, at which the *procureur-général* Nicholas Rolin accused the dauphin of complicity in the murder of Jean sans Peur. When the dauphin ignored his summons to appear at the *Parlement de Paris* on 3 January 1421, he was sentenced *in absentia* to disinheritance, in a similar fashion to Edward III of England being 'disinherited' of his Gascon lands in 1337 for harbouring Robert of Artois against the wishes of his liege-lord Philip VI. Thus, the judgment of the treaty was backed up by the French nation as it were, through Parlement and the law.

However, the Treaty certainly did disinherit the dauphin and, because Charles VI was unable to appear on 21 May 1420, Isabeau was his replacement at the ceremony and it is she rather than her husband who has the perpetual responsibility of having sworn away France in the oath to uphold the treaty, and of betraying her son. The murder of Jean sans Peur had irrevocably split the French, and the Burgundians proved by the alliance made between his heir Philip and Henry V on 2 December 1419 that they would rather deal with the English invaders than with the murderous Armagnacs. Yet, despite the humiliations that she had suffered at the hands of the dauphin's supporters during her imprisonment at Tours in 1417, it seems that Isabeau still cultivated some relationship with her son Charles, as indicated by a letter he sent to his mother, dated 21 December 1419: 'Vous plaise savoir que j'ay receu voz lettres et oy la créance qui par vous m'a esté rapportée et ce que vous a pleu moy mander, dont je vous mercye le plus humblement que je puis.'[83] Even at this stage, with all that had happened to separate mother and son, and to set them up as the leaders of opposing political factions, Isabeau had not abandoned Charles and was evidently still working for a reconciliation, despite the Anglo-Burgundian alliance and Philippe le Bon's domination of the king's Council at Troyes. It was not hatred of her son that led Isabeau to conclude the Treaty: it could well have been a sense of self-preservation that some would condemn in a mother, but it must be remembered that Isabeau had other offspring to consider, the duchesses of Burgundy and Brittany, and the princess Catherine, as well as her husband. It is quite possible that she thought that the descendants of their daughter as rulers of France were better than none at all, and one cannot say what further triumphs might have awaited Henry if the Treaty had not been agreed to, as Burgundy was now his ally and the Armagnacs were in continued

[83] E. Depréz, 'Un essai d'union nationale à la veille du traité de Troyes (1419)', *Bibliothèque de l'Ecole des Chartes*, XCIX (1938), 346–7. 'You will be pleased to know that I received your letters and I give credence to what you tell me, and to what you ask of me, for which I thank you as humbly as I can.'

disarray and isolation in the south. Yet, it is still Isabeau—and only Isabeau—who is considered as a traitor, as seen by the sole paragraph that she was felt to merit in a 1990 history of the French monarchy:

> Probablement la plus honnie des reines de France, ce parfait «contre-type» de Blanche de Castille ne mérite guère d'être rehabilitée. Ce ne sont pas tant ses mœurs qui sont à blâmer que son irresponsibilité après la folie d'un mari qu'elle aimait pourtant. Mais sa faute, que l'on retrouvera à un moindre degré chez Marie-Antoinette, fut de ne jamais se sentir française, au point de se tourner vers les Anglais et donc, finalement, contre son propre fils qu'elle n'hésita pas à renier au moment où son aide lui aurait été la plus précieuse.[84]

In *Women in Medieval Life*, Margaret Wade Labarge recognises that it has often been found 'safer and more emotionally satisfying to blame all the trouble on the foreign women rather than take sides among internal factions that often manipulated the queens as their puppets'.[85] However, she herself follows the lead that she condemns by categorising Isabella of France, wife of Edward II, Margaret of Anjou, wife of Henry VI, and Isabeau of Bavaria as 'the most notorious queens of the later Middle Ages'.[86] Margaret of Anjou has been unfortunate in that the image she received in the Yorkist propaganda of the fifteenth-century London chronicles survived through compilation and recompilation to emerge almost intact in the pages of Shakespeare, and from thence to enter the public consciousness. Yet, she and Isabella the 'She-Wolf' of France began to be rehabilitated in the 1980s, as the study of queens came to the fore for the first time and as a re-reading of the sources showed the mythological figures of much historical writing about these women to be at odds with what most of the contemporary material had to say.[87] Isabeau of Bavaria is not so fortunate, in that French history has never been charitable towards its queens: in 1791, Louise K. Robert offered *The Crimes of the Queens of France* to a public ready to

[84]Jean-Philippe Guinle, *Les souverains de la France* (Paris, 1990), 102. 'Probably the most hated queen of France, this perfect "counter-type" to Blanche of Castile does not deserve to be rehabilitated. It is not so much her ways, which are to blame for her irresponsibility after the insanity of a husband whom she still loved. But her fault, found to a lesser degree in Marie-Antoinette, was that she never felt herself to be French, to the point of turning against the English and thus, finally, against her own son whom she did not hesitate to disown at the moment when her help would have been the most precious to him.'
[85]Labarge, *Women in medieval life*, 66.
[86]Ibid.
[87]Cf. Sophie Menache, 'Isabelle of France, Queen of England—A Reconsideration', *Journal of Medieval History*, X:2 (June 1984), 107–24, and Patricia Ann Lee, 'Reflections of Power: Margaret of Anjou and the Dark Side of Queenship', *Renaissance Quarterly*, XXXIX:2 (Summer 1986), 183–217.

believe that queens prior to Marie-Antoinette had exerted a malign foreign influence on the kingdom. Any queen prepared or having to pursue a role apart from her husband or son was portrayed as a perpetrator of heinous crimes against the people of France—if children had fairy tales to acquaint them with wicked queens, the literate public had history books in which the lives of royal women instilled the same lessons'.[88] Isabeau of Bavaria does share some traits with Marie Antoinette: both had Germanic origins, both were condemned as frivolous and extravagant, both sought to forget their royal situation in a pastoral environment.[89] Yet the later tragic queen can be described as just that—tragic: she found her historical champions early in Romantics and royalists, and she tends to be pitied rather than condemned because of the humiliation of her death on the guillotine and her image as a victim. This might well prove to be Isabeau's problem: she is certainly not a saint or a heroine, and her determination to keep her own head above water in the turbulence of her husband's insanity, in a civil war in which her last son ended up on a different side, amid the conquest of France and its surrender to a foreign king, gives her the appearance of anything but a victim. Not fitting conveniently into any characterisation mould, she has tended to be maligned as she cannot easily be praised or pitied. As Grandeau summarised so eloquently: 'Si meurtrie qu'elle fût, elle ne se résigna pas, et peut-être est-ce là tout le secret de sa légende: les historiens virent de l'insouciance dans son refus d'assumer la tragédie.'[90]

[88] Susan Mosher Stuard,'Fashion's Captives: Medieval Women in French Historiography', in *Women in History and Historiography*, ed. Susan Mosher Stuard (Philadelphia, 1987), 65.

[89] Isabeau's farm was called the 'hôtel des Bergeries' and was given to her by Charles VI on 4 March 1398, adjoining her palace at Saint-Ouen. Cf. AN JJ154, fo. 20v°.

[90] Grandeau, 'Amour conjugal', 124. 'If she was bruised, she did not resign herself to it, and perhaps this is the secret to her legend: historians see insolence in her refusal to assume the tragic pose.'

# CHURCH AND CHAPEL IN MEDIEVAL ENGLAND

## By Nicholas Orme

READ 26 MAY 1995 AT THE UNIVERSITY OF BRISTOL

IN Emlyn Williams's play, *The Corn is Green* (1938), an Englishwoman
arriving in Wales is asked an important question: 'Are you Church or
Chapel?'[1] Since the seventeenth century, when non-Anglican places of
worship made their appearance, this question has indeed been important, sometimes momentous. 'Church' has had one kind of resonance
in religion, politics and society; 'chapel' has had another. Even in un-
religious households, people may still opt for 'church' when the bread
is cut (the rounded end) or 'chapel' (the oblong part). The distinction
is far older than the seventeenth century, however, by at least five
hundred years. There were thousands of chapels in medieval England,
besides the parish churches, when religion is often thought of as
uniformly church-based. Although these chapels differed in some ways
from those of Protestant nonconformity, notably in worship, they also
foreshadowed them. Locations, architecture, social support and even
religious diversity are often comparable between the two eras. Arguably,
the creation of chapels by non-Anglicans after the Reformation marked
a return to ancient national habits.[2]

---

[1] *The Corn is Green*, Act 1 Scene 1.

[2] Most writing about medieval chapels has taken the form of individual and county
studies. See, for example, Arthur Hussey, 'Chapels in Kent', *Archaeologia Cantiana*, XXIX
(1911), 217–67; Dorothy M. Owen, 'Medieval Chapels in Lincolnshire', *Lincolnshire History
and Archaeology*, X (1975), 15–22; idem, 'Chapelries and Rural Settlement: An Examination
of Some of the Kesteven Evidence', in *Medieval Settlement: Continuity and Change*, ed. P.H.
Sawyer (1976), 66–71; idem, 'Bedfordshire Chapelries: An Essay in Rural Settlement
History', *Worthington George Smith and Other Studies Presented to Joyce Godber*, Bedfordshire
Historical Record Society, LVII (1978), 9–20; and P.E.H. Hair, 'Chaplains, Chantries
and Chapels of North-West Herefordshire c.1400', *Transactions of the Woolhope Naturalists'
Field Club*, XLV part i (1988), 31–64. Wider studies include Rotha Mary Clay, *The Hermits
and Anchorites of England* (1914), *passim*; A. Hamilton Thompson, *The English Clergy and their
Organization in the Later Middle Ages* (Oxford, 1947), 123–8; C. Kitching, 'Church and
Chapelry in 16th Century England', *Studies in Church History*, XVI (1979), 279–90; Paul
[E.H.] Hair, 'The Chapel in the English Landscape', *The Local Historian*, XXI (1991), 4–
10; *Unity and Variety: A History of the Church in Devon and Cornwall*, ed. Nicholas Orme
(Exeter, 1991), 61–9; and Gervase Rosser, 'Parochial Conformity and Voluntary Religion
in Late-Medieval England', *Transactions of the Royal Historical Society*, 6th series, I (1991),
173–89. The religious and social context is admirably surveyed by Eamon Duffy, *The
Stripping of the Altars* (New Haven and London, 1992).

75

*Origins and the law concerning chapels*

The word 'chapel' is a medieval coinage, derived from the *capella* or 'little cloak' of St Martin which belonged to the Frankish kings.[3] The word was first applied to the church where the cloak was displayed, and then came into general use to describe ecclesiastical buildings smaller than monasteries or parish churches, but with their own identity. A chapel could be part of a larger unit, demarcated by walls or screens like a Lady or chantry chapel. It could also be free-standing and enjoy independent status. Independent chapels in England originated in the Anglo-Saxon period. The wish of Saxon kings to have worship in their houses led to the building of chapels for the purpose, like that in the royal palace at Cheddar (Somerset).[4] When castles appeared at the Conquest, they too included chapels for their lords, castellans and retinues. Bristol, Coventry, Dover, Exeter, Hereford, the Tower of London, Norwich, York and many others had such amenities, sometimes with permanent staffs of clergy.[5] Other early chapels were public places of worship which failed to gain parochial independence from, or lost it to, a neighbouring parish church. St Michael's East Teignmouth (Devon), for example, first recorded in 1044, was subject to its mother church of Dawlish until modern times.[6] Martinstow near Plymouth, on the other hand, described as a church in about 1200, had forfeited its status to Tamerton Foliot by the end of the thirteenth century.[7]

The motives for founding chapels were various. Some were built for personal convenience: private oratories in households, chapels of ease for outlying communities and guild chapels for members of a particular rank, trade or cult. No doubt people's status was often a factor. Having an oratory, with the bishop's permission to hold masses, marked the owner as wealthy and important. Equally, a new town or village gained dignity from possessing a chapel. Some were built as personal acts of devotion. Richard earl of Warwick (d. 1439) was said to have refounded the chapel at Guy's Cliff (Warwick) in the hope of gaining a son, perhaps more truthfully in gratitude for getting one.[8] Tudor tradition

---

[3] *The New Catholic Encyclopaedia* (15 vols., Washington, DC, 1967), sub 'chapel'.

[4] Probably by 930–41 (Philip Rahtz, *The Saxon and Medieval Palaces at Cheddar: Excavations 1960–2*, British Archaeological Reports, British Series, LXV (1979), 203).

[5] *Historic Towns*, ed. Mary D. Lobel (3 vols., 1969–89), *passim*; Norman J.G. Pounds, 'The Chapel in the Castle', *Fortress*, IX (May 1991), 12–20.

[6] P.H. Sawyer, *Anglo-Saxon Charters* (1968), 300, no. 1003.

[7] *Charters of the Redvers Family*, ed. R. Bearman, Devon and Cornwall Record Society, new series, XXXVII (1994), 167–8; *The Registers of Walter Bronescombe and Peter Quivil, Bishops of Exeter*, ed. F.C. Hingeston-Randolph (London and Exeter, 1889), 458.

[8] John Rous, *The Rous Roll* (2nd edn, Gloucester, 1980), section 50, says to gain an heir, but Richard's son Henry was born in 1425 and the licence to endow the chapel is dated 1430 (*Cal. Patent Rolls 1429–36*, 100).

*Plate 1. The Private Chapel: Cotehele House, Cornwall, the late 15th-century chapel built by Sir Piers Edgecombe, rebuilding or replacing a chapel of 1411 (photograph by permission of the National Trust).*

*Plate 2.    The Chapel of Ease: St Michael Porthilly, Cornwall, over two miles distant from its parish church (photograph by permission of the Royal Commission on the Historical Monuments of England: Crown Copyright)*

ascribed the chapel of St Thomas Becket and St George, by the River Tamar below Cotehele House (Cornwall), to Sir Richard Edgecombe's escape from Richard III's men at the spot in 1483.[9] Other chapels were survivals of older larger institutions. St Mary Old Sarum (Wiltshire) stood on the site of the former cathedral of Salisbury, St Mary and St Francis Exeter on that of a Franciscan friary.[10] Redundant priories, hospitals, and parish churches often concluded their lives as chapels before the Reformation, through reluctance to dissolve them altogether.

As Church organisation developed and law was codified, so terminology and laws evolved to define different kinds of ecclesiastical units.[11] The basic element of the Church, ministering to and drawing in all the Christian people of an area, became the parish church (*ecclesia*) representing the universal Church in miniature. A chapel (*capella*) was a part of the parish church, or a separate building subordinate to it, or

[9] Richard Carew, *The Survey of Cornwall* (1602), fo. 114r–v.

[10] *Victoria County History* (hereafter *VCH*) *Wiltshire*, VI, 59; A.G. Little and R.C. Easterling, *The Franciscans and Dominicans of Exeter* (Exeter, 1927), 20.

[11] For the law by the fifteenth century, see William Lyndwood, *Provinciale* (Oxford, 1679), 35, 70, 224, 233, 238, 276.

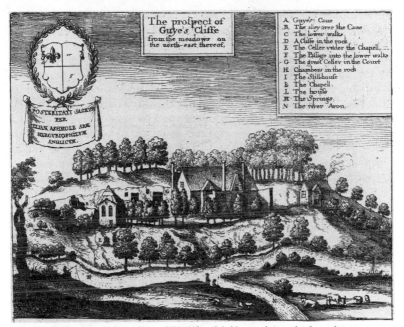

*Plate 3.* *The Cult Chapel: Guy's Cliff, Warwickshire, as it was in the 17th century, showing the chapel and chantry priests' dwelling built by Richard earl of Warwick where the legendary Guy of Warwick was said to have lived as a hermit (William Dugdale, The Antiquities of Warwickshire (1656), p. 194, photograph by permission of the Dean and Chapter of Exeter Cathedral).*

a building in an extra-parochial area.[12] Chapels outside the parochial system were eventually known as 'free chapels'.[13] Every new chapel had to be licensed and dedicated by authority of the diocesan bishop, though the Church complained that secular courts interfered with this system, enabling chapels to establish their independence of parish churches.[14] Episcopal licences allowed the use of chapels for prayer (the divine office) and the mass, but pastoral services (baptisms, marriages, churchings of mothers, funerals and burials) required further permission

[12] On this terminology, see *Dictionary of Medieval Latin from British Sources*, ed. R.E. Latham, fasc. ii (1981), s.v. 'capella'; *The Oxford English Dictionary*, ed. J.A. Simpson & E.S.C. Weiner (2nd edn, 20 vols., Oxford, 1989), s.v. 'chapel'.

[13] *Dictionary of Medieval Latin*, s.v. 'capella (6)'; *Oxford English Dictionary*, s.v. 'chapel 3 (c)'.

[14] *Councils and Synods I: A.D.871–1204*, ed. D. Whitelock, M. Brett and C.N.L. Brooke (2 vols., Oxford, 1981), II, 676, 777; *Councils and Synods II: A.D.1205–1313*, ed. F.M. Powicke and C.R. Chency (2 vols., Oxford, 1964), I, 174, 281, 408–9, 429, 543, 600, 708; II, 766, 1002–6, 1272–3.

because these were rights belonging to parish churches. A third institution was the oratory (*oratorium*), a place for private prayer. Anyone could establish an oratory and such places were not consecrated; they could be used for prayer, but not for masses or other services. However, by the later middle ages, wealthy people could purchase permission from the pope for portable altars and masses to be said even in oratories, blurring the distinction. While the three-fold grade of church, chapel and oratory was legally recognised, it was often modified in practice. Some of the chapels one sees in medieval manor houses were probably oratories in law, though they mimicked the form of public chapels. Equally, a chapel could rival its parish church in size and grandeur, like Holy Trinity Hull or St Bartholomew Orford (Suffolk).

## Numbers of chapels

The topic of chapels is extensive. In principle, it should encompass those in monasteries, cathedrals, parish churches and hospitals, since their architecture, constitution and worship often resembled those of free-standing buildings. However, such chapels are hard to disentangle from the churches around them: both architecturally and in their functions. Our attention will be confined to chapels that stood by themselves—a category which has received less attention from historians. They were a large group; how large is hard to say. Lists have been made in only a few localities, and even detailed local histories often ignore their existence.[15] Such chapels, however, are frequently encountered all over England. Many are found in towns, especially in larger communities. At Hull, which had no church with full parochial status until 1661, all six places of public worship were technically chapels, while Norwich possessed about eight besides the parish churches.[16] At Exeter, six chapels with a semi-public status in and around the city during the thirteenth century grew to about eleven in the early sixteenth.[17] Coventry included about ten throughout the later middle ages, rising to about seventeen if areas further out are included.[18] Bristol, of which the fifteenth-century historian William Worcester has left us a good account, seems to have had about fourteen in the city and its environs.[19] John Stow's sixteenth-century *Survey of London* mentions some twenty-seven in or close to the capital, and there were other

[15] For recent bibliography, see above, n. 2.

[16] *VCH York, East Riding*, I, 76, 287, 294, 297–8, 305; *Historic Towns*, ed. Lobel, vol. II, sub Norwich.

[17] This figure is based on detailed research into local documentary sources.

[18] *VCH Warwick.*, VIII, 321–61.

[19] *Historic Towns*, ed. Lobel, II, 'Bristol'; *Itineraria Symonis Simeonis et Willelmi de Worcestre*, ed. J. Nasmith (Cambridge, 1778), 180, 190–1, 199, 202, 209, 229, 239, 241, 246, 252–3, 270–1.

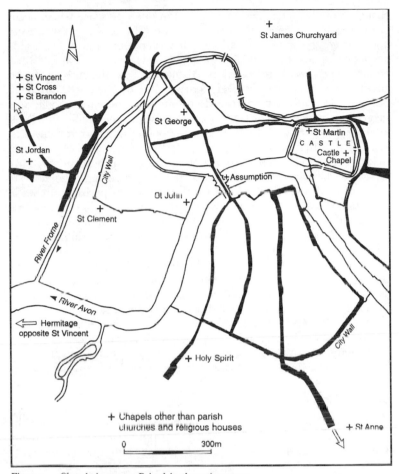

*Figure 1.    Chapels in towns: Bristol in the 15th century.*

suburban chapels within the reach and consciousness of London's citizens.[20] These totals exclude oratories in the houses of the nobility, clergy and merchants, which would increase the urban totals greatly.

Chapels were also widespread in the countryside. Private ones of the nobility and gentry were evidently common to judge from the many casual references to them which occur in romantic literature. The impression is confirmed by the frequent grants of licences for private chapels, portable altars and masses said in one's presence which occur in the registers of popes and bishops. If we were to assume that every noble or gentry family had at least one chapel or oratory, we would need to add five thousand or so in this category nationally.[21] Rural public chapels too were common. A study of Leicestershire has found about 100 of them in just over 200 parishes by the early thirteenth century.[22] In Lincolnshire, records throughout the later middle ages suggest the existence of at least 243, mostly with some public functions, in about 600 parishes.[23] In the highland zone of England, roughly west and north of the line from Exeter to York, parishes were often larger, roads less passable and the proportion of chapels to churches may have increased. Charles Henderson collected documentary references to about twice as many public and private chapels as parish churches in the western half of Cornwall (188 to 95).[24] In Devon, recent research has identified about 1,300 public and private chapels in a county of 409 parishes.[25] Nor are these high figures yet complete, since intimations of other sites exist in archaeological remains and in the names of hamlets, farms or fields like Chapel, Chapel Close and Chapeltown, requiring careful research to verify the evidence. Nevertheless, one conclusion already seems safe. There was a very large body of chapels in medieval England, along with the thousand-odd religious houses and the nine or ten thousand parish churches.[26] Chapels with public roles must have numbered several thousands, and if oratories were added, the total would outstrip any other category of religious buildings. This has important consequences for understanding the role of parish churches.

*Categories of chapels*

Chapels had common characteristics, enabling us to classify them by their locations, their functions and the people associated with them. They were founded by individuals and groups, both greater and lesser

---

[21] N. Denholm-Young, *Collected Papers on Mediaeval Subjects* (Oxford, 1946), 61.

[22] Thompson, *The English Clergy*, 123.

[23] Owen in *Lincolnshire History and Archaeology*, X (1975), 15–22. Other examples include Wootton hundred (Oxfordshire), the area between Oxford and Banbury, with 13 public chapels in 27 parishes by the end of the middle ages, and Kent with at least 140 private and public examples in about 400 parishes (*VCH Oxford*, XI–XII, *passim*; Arthur Hussey, 'Chapels in Kent', *Archaeologia Cantiana*, XXIX (1911), 217–67).

[24] Charles Henderson, 'Ecclesiastical History of the 109 Parishes in Western Cornwall', *Journal of the Royal Institution of Cornwall*, new series, II–III (1953–60), separate pagination. Not all these parishes were independent in the middle ages.

[25] By Mrs Jeanne James, MPhil student, Department of History and Archaeology, University of Exeter.

[26] About 9,500 parishes in 1291 (J.R.H. Moorman, *Church Life in England in the Thirteenth Century* (Cambridge, 1955), 4–5), 8,500 in 1535 (R.N. Swanson, *Church and Society in Late Medieval England* (Oxford, 1989), 4).

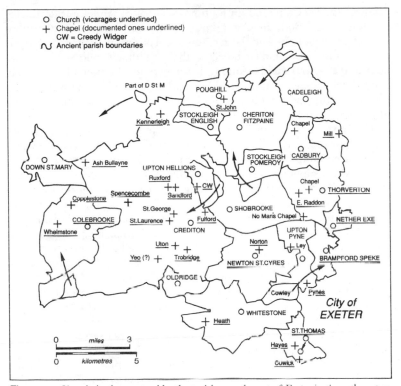

*Figure 2.    Chapels in the countryside: the parishes north west of Exeter in the 15th century.*

in rank. The nobility and gentry set up their own private chapels and
oratories, and were responsible for some of the public ones. Edward
IV built a chapel on the battlefield of Barnet and Richard III, while
duke of Gloucester, on that of Towton.[27] Henry Ley, a gentleman of
Bere Ferrers (Devon), is said to have founded Our Lady of Baselake in
his parish in about 1489, because of a dream he had while campaigning
abroad.[28] Other public chapels originated with clergy. Roger Ive, rector
of Albright Hussey (Shropshire) was the moving spirit in erecting one
on the battlefield of Shrewsbury in 1406, and John Wygwar, chantry

[27] F.C. Cass, 'The Battle of Barnet', *Transactions of the London & Middlesex Arch. Soc.*, VI
(1883), 38; John Leland, *The Itinerary of John Leland in or about the Years 1535–1543*, ed. Lucy
Toulmin Smith (5 vols., 1907–10), I, 43; IV, 77.

[28] Raymond J. Skinner, 'The "Declaration" of Ley: His Pedigree', *Devon & Cornwall
Notes & Queries*, XXXVII (1992), 61.  The source says Spain, but this must be a mistake
for Brittany.

priest of Exeter Cathedral, in founding that of St Anne outside Exeter in about 1417. Both men got help for their enterprises from more important people.[29] The larger town corporations—Bristol, Exeter, London and York—built chapels at their guildhalls, and so did many craft and religious guilds. Among lesser people, the individual (usually a man) who took up the life of a hermit was a characteristic chapel founder: sometimes in a lonely place where he lived, sometimes as part of a bridge that he maintained, or a lighthouse.

The purposes of chapels also differed. The private chapel or oratory catered for the owner's immediate household, while the chapel of ease served a community removed from the parish church. Other chapels tried to draw support as widely as possible. Some of these were attached to public works like bridges, providing a place for travellers to worship and give alms. Some were cult chapels dedicated to the Saviour, Our Lady or other saints, and sought to gather pilgrims as widely as possible. True, in the national league of English shrines, few chapels figured in the premier division which drew crowds from all over the country. In John Heywood's satirical play of the 1530s, *The Four PP*, a professional pilgrim rattles off the names of some thirty places that he has visited: international, national and local.[30] Only two were important chapels, St Anne of Buxton and St Winifred of Holywell (north Wales), both associated with mineral waters. We can add to these St Michael's Mount in Cornwall, which was technically a chapel served by chantry priests after the 1420s and attracted pilgrims from England as well as from Cornwall.[31] Most cult chapels, however, probably drew their supporters chiefly from the neighbourhood. Heywood put two of these into his list—the chapels of Muswell near London and Cattawade on the Essex–Suffolk border—perhaps to give a ludicrous effect by mixing famous and lesser-known places. But small chapel shrines should not be underrated. They appealed to the majority of people who had not time or money to go to Canterbury or Walsingham, and most English pilgrimages were probably short journeys to local sites. The support for small chapels, in aggregate, may have rivalled that of the greatest centres.

Chapels can be further categorised by location. Many occupied picturesque places in the landscape: hills, caves, woods, springs and islands. They represented a wish to Christianise such places, sometimes arising from hermits who sought to live secluded from the world.

---

[29] *VCH Shropshire*, II, 128–31; Nicholas Orme, 'The Medieval Chapels of Heavitree', *Devon Archaeological Society Proceedings*, XLIX (1991), 124.

[30] *The Plays of John Heywood*, ed. Richard Axton and Peter Happé (Cambridge, 1991), 112–13, 248–51.

[31] Nicholas Orme, 'St Michael and his Mount', *Journal of the Royal Institution of Cornwall*, new series, X part i (1986–7), 32–43.

*Plate 4.    Chapels in the Landscape: the rock chapel of St Michael Roche, Cornwall (photograph by permission of the Royal Commission on the Historical Monuments of England: Crown Copyright).*

Hill chapels were frequently dedicated to St Michael, like those on Glastonbury Tor, Brentor (Devon) and the great rock at Roche (Cornwall). There was a notable cave chapel at Knaresborough (Yorkshire), where St Robert, the local hermit, dwelt in the cave named after him until his death in 1218 and was buried in a chapel outside it. A second cave nearby, hewn from the rock and nowadays known as St Robert's Chapel, was originally known as Our Lady of the 'Crag', 'Quarrell' or 'Quarry', and is recorded in 1408.[32] There were chapels in deer parks like Liskeard and Restormel (Cornwall) and forests like Dean and Waltham.[33] Several stood by streams or wells, as at Buxton and Holywell. At Oswestry, the well by St Oswald's chapel was said to have acquired virtue from the saint's arm and formed a local centre of pilgrimage.[34] The well chapel of St Clether (Cornwall) still survives, the

[32] Abbot Cummins, 'Knaresborough Cave-Chapels', *Yorkshire Archaeological Journal,* XXVIII (1926), 80–8.    For other rock and cave chapels, see *Itineraria ... Willelmi de Worcestre,* ed. Nasmith, 180, 184–7, 261, 275; Clay, *Hermits and Anchorites,* 44–5.

[33] Charles Henderson, *The Cornish Church Guide* (Truro, 1925), 125; Clay, *Hermits and Anchorites,* 16–31; *Cal. Patent Rolls 1436–41,* 180; ibid., *1461–7,* 149.

[34] Leland, *Itinerary,* III, 74.

*Plate 5.    The Urban Chapel: the chapel of St William on the bridge of York, demolished 1810 (Francis Grose, The Antiquities of England and Wales, new ed., vol. v (1785), facing p. 171).*

water flowing under the high altar. There were numerous chapels on islands. St Herbert's Island on Derwent Water (Cumberland) took its name from one, and others were scattered all round the coasts of the south-west of England: Brownsea (Dorset), Birr, Drake's and Lundy (Devon), while Cornwall had St Michael off Looe, St Clement off Mousehole and about eight on the Isles of Scilly.

Equally, chapels lay in close proximity to daily life and work. As well as those in dwellings—royal palaces, castles, town halls, manor houses and clergy residences—most public chapels were sited by roads to facilitate access. They stood on the principal bridges of Bristol, Norwich, Reading, Rochester, Wakefield and York. St Thomas Becket's chapel on London Bridge was built midway along the structure in *c.* 1212 and was later enlarged into a polygonal building.[35] Chapels were sometimes placed at river crossings. That of St Tyrioc, whose ruins can still be seen from the Severn Bridges, occupied a rock near the main ferry passage between Bristol and south Wales at Beachley (Gloucestershire), while a chapel of St Margaret lay at the point of passage itself.[36] Further

[35] *Historic Towns*, ed. Lobel, III, 79.
[36] *VCH Gloucester*, X, 75–6.

*Plate 6.  The Churchyard Chapel: 15th-century chapel at Higham Ferrers (Northants.), later used as a school (photograph by permission of the Royal Commission on the Historical Monuments of England: Crown Copyright).*

north, St Leonard at Purton marked a shorter crossing of the river.[37] Most ports acquired chapels, frequently dedicated to St Nicholas the patron saint of sailors, or to the Saviour. St Nicholas chapels stood at the approaches to Ilfracombe, Plymouth and St Ives, and St Saviour chapels at Bridgwater, Exmouth, Padstow and Fowey. At Dover, passengers disembarking from Channel ferries could give thanks at the chapel of Our Lady of Pity on the shore, also known as Our Lady of the Rock; the French ambassador restored it in 1530 after escaping shipwreck.[38] There were chapels in churchyards, close to parish churches but physically detached from them, perhaps because it was simpler and cheaper to build them separately. John Leland, travelling round England in about 1540, noted them at Faringdon (Berkshire), Reculver (Kent) and Sherborne (Dorset), while Weedon (Northamptonshire) had two.[39] A distinct genre of such buildings from the thirteenth century onwards was that of charnel chapels. As graveyards became full, grave digging

[37] *Cal. Patent Rolls 1358–61*, 477.
[38] S.P.H. Statham, *The History of the Castle, Town, and Port of Dover* (1899), 207–8.
[39] Leland, *Itinerary*, I, 10, 125, 295–6; IV, 60.

turned up the bones of previous occupants. These were placed for decency in a charnel house, and several such houses had chapels attached. This was so in the cathedral cemeteries of Exeter, St Paul's, Norwich, Winchester and Worcester, as well as several parish churchyards.[40]

Some chapels recorded events. The murder of St William of Perth near Rochester in 1201 was marked by a chapel, and that of William Lechlade at Exeter Cathedral in 1283 may have been too.[41] By the end of the middle ages, political events were recalled in the same way. In 1399, Henry IV pardoned Matthew Danthorpe, hermit, for building an unlicensed chapel where Henry had landed at Ravenspur on the Humber, and granted him wrecks and foreshore profits to maintain it.[42] There were chapels on battlefields, particularly those of the Wars of the Roses, like Barnet, Shrewsbury and Towton already mentioned. When a battle took place near the existing chapel of Dadlington (Leicestershire), its people decided to exploit what some of them called Dadlington Field. They obtained a royal licence to send out collectors of alms, and circulated printed papers proclaiming the licence and promising indulgences to contributors. The chapel still exists but the name of the battle did not stick; the rest of the world preferred to call it 'Bosworth'.[43]

All chapels supported worship, but not all in the same way. Some, notably chapels of ease, had regular services carried out by a permanent priest provided by the parish rector or paid for by the local inhabitants. In other chapels, worship was less frequent; indeed, it was often restricted so as not to compete with the parish church. At Garrington (Kent), formal services were confined to three days of the week, and at St Bridget Wembworthy (Devon) to the saint's feast once a year.[44] Private chapels were less regulated in this respect, but there too worship were probably often confined to times when the lord or lady was in residence. Pastoral offices—baptisms, weddings, churching of women after childbirth, funerals and burials—were also strictly controlled to preserve the rights of the mother church. Most chapels, however,

[40] Nicholas Orme, 'The Charnel Chapel of Exeter Cathedral', *Medieval Art and Architecture at Exeter Cathedral*, ed. Francis Kelly (British Archaeological Association, 1991), 162–71; Leland, *Itinerary*, I, 270.

[41] Hussey, 'Chapels in Kent', 252; Orme, 'The Charnel Chapel of Exeter Cathedral', 164. At York, the pre-existing chapel on Ouse Bridge accommodated two chaplains after 1268 in expiation for the murder of followers of John Comyn (Angelo Raine, *Medieval York* (1955), 208).

[42] *Cal. Patent Rolls 1399–1401*, 209.

[43] *Letters and Papers, Foreign and Domestic, Henry VIII*, I part i, p. 454; Oxford, Bodleian Library, Arch. A.b.8 (26a-b) (STC 14077c.36).

[44] Hussey, 'Chapels in Kent', 242; *The Register of Edmund Lacy: Registrum Commune*, ed. G.R. Dunstan, Devon & Cornwall Record Soc., new series (5 vols., 1963–72), I, 9.

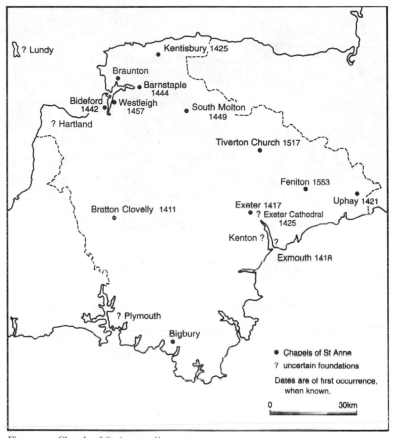

*Figure 3.    Chapels of St Anne in Devon, c. 1400–1550.*

possessed images or relics of their patron saint, and informal devotion
to these may have been the commonest form of worship. Sometimes the saint was Celtic or Saxon, particularly in the west and
north.[45] More frequently, the cult was an international one, the largest
being that of the Virgin Mary. Many of her chapels were centres of
local pilgrimage, particularly Caversham (Oxfordshire), Court-at-Street

[45] In Cornwall, for example, there were chapels of St Anta in Lelant, St Derwa in
Camborne and St Illick in St Endellion (Henderson, *Cornish Church Guide*, 39, 62, 117). A
little-known Saxon saint, Algar, was commemorated in a chapel at Langley near Frome
(Somerset) (W.E. Daniel, 'St. Algar', *Somerset & Dorset Notes & Queries*, IV (1894–5), 119;
E.M. Thompson, 'An Early Somerset Will', ibid., VI (1898–9), 359–60).

*Plate 7.    Cults, Publicity, and Fund Raising: part of a printed indulgence of c. 1510 issued to gather alms for the chapel of St Anne Tottenham (Middx.), showing St Anne, the Virgin, Jesus, and St George, 'Our Lady's knight' (Westminster Abbey, Box 74; photograph by permission of the Dean and Chapter of Westminster Abbey).*

(Kent), Ipswich (Suffolk), Liskeard (Cornwall) and Wakefield (Yorkshire).[46]

Chapels were especially suitable for housing new religious cults, which might encounter resistance or lack of space in parish churches. From about 1350 to 1530, numerous foundations were made in honour of St Saviour, the Holy Spirit, St George, St Roche, St Sythe and, most notably, St Anne whose cult grew popular all over England. Indeed, the latter, which belongs to an age of documentation, offers the best opportunity to study how a medieval saint cult developed in terms of time, space and adherents. In Devon alone, at least a dozen chapels of St Anne were built in the fifteenth and early sixteenth centuries. The earliest known is a private chapel in the rectory of Bratton Clovelly, set up by the rector—an incomer from Winchester

[46] Below, note 94 (Caversham); note 65 (Court-at-Street); *The Complete Works of St. Thomas More*, VI part i, ed. T.M.C. Lawler *et al.* (New Haven and London, 1981), 93–4 (Ipswich); Leland, *Itinerary*, I, 208 (Liskeard); ibid., V, 38 (Wakefield).

diocese—in 1411.[47] The first public one, already mentioned, was built outside Exeter in about 1417.[48] By the end of the middle ages, they had spread from Braunton on the north coast of Devon to Bigbury on the south.[49] The chapel of St Anne two miles east of Bristol and perhaps unusual in its scale is described by William Worcester in about the 1470s. Its building, founded by Lord de la Warr, was nineteen yards long and five wide, supported by nineteen buttresses. Inside, the image of the saint was honoured by thirteen candles and thirty-two silver boats—the latter, worth 20s. each, perhaps for burning incense. The pride of the chapel was two huge 'quadrate' candles, reaching to the vault, one given by local weavers, the other by shoemakers. Each candle cost £5—a good annual wage—and was renewed every year at Whitsuntide.[50]

## The role of chapels

In some respects, chapels fitted into the Church harmoniously alongside religious houses and parish churches. Sometimes they had functions in parish life—particularly in the summer processions popular before the Reformation. During Rogation week, clergy and people walked with crosses, banners and relics from major churches around the neigh-bouring town or countryside, singing litanies and asking God's blessing on the Church and the crops. Chapels might figure in these processions as stations where mass was said, a sermon preached or food eaten before returning. At Long Melford (Suffolk), the furthest point of the parish processions was the chapel of St Anne in Lutons Park.[51] In Cornwall, the parishioners of Crantock, Cubert, Newlyn East and Perranzabuloe met at the chapel of St Nighton near their parish boundaries, placing their relics on four stones and listening to a sermon.[52] All chapel worship was extra to the duty of supporting the parish church, and chapel congregations are sometimes recorded giving such support. At Bodmin (Cornwall), a major rebuilding of the church took place in 1469–72, involving the collection of money from all the parishioners. Some thirty guilds or communities in the town contributed

[47] The Register of Edmund Stafford, ed. F.C. Hingeston-Randolph (London and Exeter, 1886), 35.

[48] Above, note 29

[49] I am grateful to Jeanne James for this list.

[50] Cambridge, Corpus Christi College, MS 210, fo. 107; Itineraria... Willelmi de Worcestre, ed. Nasmith, 190–1. The given height of the candles—80 feet—must be incorrect.

[51] Duffy, The Stripping of the Altars, 137.

[52] Nicholas Roscarrock's Lives of the Saints: Cornwall and Devon, ed. Nicholas Orme, Devon & Cornwall Record Soc., new series, XXXV (1992), 94. Some other boundary chapels may have fulfilled this purpose, e.g. No Man's Chapel in Thorverton (Devon) (SS 913002), equidistant between four parishes.

sums, and several of these were located in the parochial chapels of Bodmin: the Berry, the Bore, St George, St Leonard, St Nicholas and St Thomas in the churchyard.[53]

Equally, there were times when church and chapel fell out. To the church, the chapel was a potential poacher of worshippers and, if it gained rights of sacraments and burials, a subtractor of money as well.[54] To the chapel, the church might seem a distant tyrant, demanding laborious journeys to attend services and exacting additional burdens of maintainance. The litigation of the medieval Church is full of disputes on such matters.[55] Maidenhead (Berkshire) grew up as a village in the thirteenth century on the boundary between the parishes of Bray and Cookham. Between 1263 and 1274, the inhabitants erected a chapel without the permission of either clergyman. The bishop of Salisbury forbade the use of the building, and two of his successors refused to relax the ban. Not until 1324 did the people of Maidenhead succeed in making terms with the two incumbents. What pressures were applied, what favours changed hands, are not known, but an agreement was made to reopen the chapel. Stringent conditions were imposed by the bishop. The people were bound to maintain the fabric of the building and pay the chaplain who served there, yet they had to surrender all the offerings: a third to the vicar of Bray and two-thirds to his colleague at Cookham. Regular worship was allowed, along with the churching of wives, but infants had still to be taken to the mother churches for baptism and the population had to go there too on six major feasts every year. Even the appointment of the chaplain was awarded to the vicar of Cookham, and the appointee had to swear to respect the rights of the parish churches.[56]

Not surprisingly, settlements of this kind did not always satisfy chapel supporters, who sought to escape from their strictness. In King's Lynn (Norfolk), the parish church of St Margaret owned two dependent chapels in the town: St James and St Nicholas. In 1378, St Nicholas got a papal bull granting it powers of baptism, marriage and churching, provided these did not infringe the rights of the parish church. The prior of Lynn, the patron of St Margaret's, summoned a meeting at which the mayor (John Brunham) and seventy-eight burgesses endorsed a letter of protest to the papal court—effectively blocking the bull. In

---

[53] J.J. Wilkinson, 'Receipts and Expenses in the Building of Bodmin Church, A.D. 1469 to 1472', *The Camden Miscellany Vol. VII*, Camden Soc., new series, XIV (1875), 1–41, especially 5–7.

[54] *Councils and Synods II*, ed. Powicke and Cheney, I, 281, 543, 766, 1272–3.

[55] For a good recent case study, see R.N. Swanson, 'Parochialism and Particularism ... Ditchford Frary, Warwickshire', in *Medieval Ecclesiastical Studies in Honour of Dorothy M. Owen*, ed. M.J. Franklin and Christopher Harper-Bill (Woodbridge, 1995), 241–57.

[56] *VCH Berkshire*, II, 30–2; III, 111.

1432, the supporters of St Nicholas, including several merchants, reopened the project. The prior again withstood them and the case went to the bishop of Norwich for arbitration. John Brunham was now dead, but his formidable daughter, Margery Kempe, a leading figure in local religion, was asked to predict the outcome. She prophesied that St Nicholas would not get a baptismal font 'for a bushel of nobles' and prayed God to defend the parish church—successfully, as it turned it. The negotiations broke down and the chapel party lost everything. Margery's autobiography gleefully noted that 'the parish church stood still in her worship and her degree as she had done two hundred year before and more'.[57] Elsewhere, some chapel partisans preferred to ignore the law altogether. At Polruan in the parish of Lanteglos-by-Fowey (Cornwall), three men were accused in 1434 of inciting a chaplain to bless the chapel of St Saviour, which was undedicated. He asked for prayers in the pulpit, distributed holy bread on Sundays and made wills for sick people, in defiance of the mother church.[58] At Templeton (Devon) in 1439, local people egged on by the Knights of St John (the lords of the manor) brought in a friar-bishop to consecrate a chapel and cemetery where baptisms and burials were carried out against the rights of Witheridge church.[59] The bishop intervened on both occasions to defend the churches, as bishops usually did, but the Knights and the people of Templeton won in the end. By the Reformation, the chapel had gained parochial status.[60]

The squabbles between churches and chapels recall those which were to surge up again in England after the Reformation. It is true that worship in pre-Reformation chapels was closer to worship in parish churches than was to be the case after the sixteenth century. The staple diet was similar: masses, the divine office, the veneration of Christ and saint cults. Yet chapel goers might particularise themselves even in these matters. They might revere a different saint, hold masses with different devotions, or meet at different times, from those of the parish church. Moreover, the history of religion shows that forms of services often matter less than those who attend them. Chapels allowed people to worship in groups, rather than as the whole people of God: the aristocracy in their households, the urban elites in their guilds and the cult devotees by their images. Often, such groups chose their own clergyman—a domestic chaplain, guild chaplain, or priest hired for the occasion—rather than the parish rector or vicar. In these respects there were strong resemblances between pre- and post-Reformation chapels.

[57] *The Book of Margery Kempe*, ed. Sanford Brown Meech and Hope Emily Allen, vol. I, Early English Text Soc., ordinary series, CCXII (1940), 58–60, 372–4.
[58] *Reg. Lacy*, ed. Dunstan, I, 285–8.
[59] Ibid., II, 150–1, 153–5, 174–5, 211–21.
[60] *Valor Ecclesiasticus tempore Henrici VIII*, ed. J. Caley (6 vols., 1810–34), II, 333.

Both were voluntary not compulsory institutions; both involved withdrawing from the parish church to worship with like-minded souls under a chosen minister. Chapels in either era might co-exist with the parish church (some Methodists attended church and chapel), or try to be mutually exclusive like those medieval chapels which tried to secede. There were locational similarities. Both kinds of chapels were often sited in peripheral areas: the back streets of towns, suburbs and parish boundaries. People in both eras chose such places to benefit from cheap land, to colonise new territory or to attract adherents from more than one parish. Both medieval and modern chapels were frequently humble buildings, close in form to domestic houses or barns. They even came to share a common name. In the seventeenth and early eighteenth centuries, most dissenters preferred the terms 'meeting' or 'meeting house' for their places of worship. Towards the end of the eighteenth century, however, the Methodists revived the use of the term 'chapel', which gradually spread to most denominations except for the Quakers.[61]

There were even times when medieval chapels, like later ones, became centres of religious enthusiasm. This may have happened more often than the alarm of the Church authorities has recorded. In 1351, Bishop Grandisson of Exeter was disturbed to hear that the canons of Frithelstock Priory (north Devon) had built an unconsecrated chapel in a nearby wood, attracting local pilgrims to an image of Mary. He described the place as a shrine more suitable for 'proud and disobedient Eve or lewd Diana' and ordered the building to be rased to the ground. This was evidently no ordinary cult of the Virgin; there must have been divinations or superstitious ceremonies to prompt the thought of Diana.[62] Different, but also unorthodox, were the activities of the Lollards of Leicester in about 1382. Here, William Smith the literate, vegetarian, teetotal enthusiast and his fellow spirits formed a conventicle in the deserted chapel of St John in Belgrave Gate, outside the walls of the city.[63] They were joined by William Swynderby, the radical local preacher, and started Church reform by burning St Katherine's statue to cook their food.[64] A third famous case of enthusiasm in a chapel is that of Elizabeth Barton, 'the nun of Kent', at Court-at-Street in the parish of Aldington (Kent). The chapel already housed what seems to have been a well-frequented image of Our Lady when, in about 1525, Elizabeth Barton began to experience trances and make prophecies at the house of her nearby employer. After her mentor Edward Bocking,

---

[61] *Oxford English Dictionary*, s.v. 'chapel (4)'.

[62] Nicholas Orme, 'Bishop Grandisson and Popular Religion', *Transactions of the Devonshire Association*, CXXIV (1992), 109–13.

[63] For the location, see *VCH Leicester*, IV, 359.

[64] *Knighton's Chronicle*, ed. G.H. Martin (Oxford, 1995), 296–9.

monk of Canterbury, announced that she would perform a miracle in the chapel, a crowd said to number over 2,000 turned up to see her lie before the Virgin's image for three hours, uttering speeches in metre and rhyme. Although she later moved into a nunnery, Court-at-Street continued to be famous as her chapel; when Leland passed it about a dozen years later, he noted it as the place 'where the nun of Canterbury wrought all her false miracles'.[65]

## Chapels in literature

Another source, romantic literature, helps us to understand the impact made by chapels on people's imaginations. From the late twelfth century, authors of romances viewed chapels as strange places, gateways to the supernatural. Chrétien de Troyes was a pioneer in this respect. The story of his romance *Yvain* (c. 1170s) begins with a magic spring of water next to a 'small but very beautiful chapel'. Whoever takes water from the fountain and spills it on a neighbouring stone arouses an immense and terrible storm, after which he encounters adventures.[66] Similar chapels or chapel-like buildings occur in Chrétien's other works, *Lancelot* and *Perceval*,[67] but it was his successors—the French prose writers of the early thirteenth century—who most developed the chapel as a romantic motif. In the *Prose Lancelot*, which encompasses *Lancelot*, the *Queste del Saint Graal* and the *Mort Artu*, there are several episodes which feature chapels as buildings of mystery and adventure. In one of them, Gawain and Hector see 'an old chapel' while travelling through a 'waste land'. 'The walls were broken and rent, as if they were rotten.' Beside the chapel is a tomb with an inscription, warning them not to enter the nearby cemetery. Through its entrance, thirteen tombs are visible, all burning, with a lance atop each tomb. Gawain attempts to pass the entrance, but the lances rise and drive him back; he tries again, as does Hector, without success. At last they see a message on the door that 'only the son of the dolorous queen can enter this churchyard without shame'. This sets the scene for further happenings.[68]

*Perlesvaus*, alias *The High Book of the Grail*, handles chapels in similar ways. It begins with Guinevere weeping because Arthur has lost the impulse to seek honour; his knights are leaving his court. She urges

[65] *Letters and Papers, Henry VIII*, VI, pp. 418, 624; Leland, *Itinerary*, IV, 66; William Lambarde, *A Perambulation of Kent* (1576), 148–53; *Dictionary of National Biography*, article by Sidney Lee; Alan Neame, *The Holy Maid of Kent* (1971), *passim*.
[66] Chrétien de Troyes, *Yvain*, ed. T.B.W. Reid (Manchester, 1948), lines 380–407.
[67] Chrétien de Troyes, *Lancelot or the Knight of the Cart*, ed. William W. Keller (New York and London, 1984), lines 1829–959; *Le Roman de Perceval ou le Conte du Graal*, ed. William Roach (2nd edn, Geneva, 1959), lines 6340–6518.
[68] *The Vulgate Version of the Arthurian Romances*, ed. H. Oskar Sommer (7 vols., New York, 1969), IV, 339–41.

*Plate 8.    Chapels and Romance: Sir Lionnel du Glac, hermit, and chapel, from a 15th-century Flemish text of the Romance of Perceforest (British Library, MS Royal 19 E III, fo. 133; photograph by permission of the British Library).*

him to go to the chapel of St Augustine in the White Forest, where he may regain the will to do great deeds. The place can be found only by chance. Guinevere warns him that it is dangerous and persuades him (against his will) to take his squire Cahus. However, that night Cahus has a dream in which he goes alone to the chapel, removes a candlestick, and is struck down with a knife by a man on horseback. He wakes to find himself in possession of the candlestick and mortally wounded. Next morning, Arthur goes alone in search of the place. After visiting a second chapel, where he has an adventure, he finds it in the forest. He dismounts and prepares to enter, but is unable to pass the doorway. Watching from outside, he sees the local hermit begin to say mass before the altar. On the hermit's right hand stands a lovely child dressed in an alb with a crown on its head; on the left hand, is a beautiful lady. At the point in the mass when the bread and wine are offered, the lady presents the child to the hermit. The hermit holds the child in his arms, and at the consecration the child turns into a man, crowned with thorns, bleeding from hands, feet and side, before resuming the shape of the child. When the mass is over, woman and child vanish with a great company of the heavenly host. Arthur is now able to enter the chapel. The hermit explains that he was excluded because he was sinful, and warns him to reform his life and his court.[69]

There are about twenty-four episodes concerning chapels in *Perlesvaus*. Sometimes the building is awesome because of its spiritual power: a place to glimpse the real presence of Christ in the eucharist, or Mary's intervention to save the soul of a dying man. Sometimes the chapel is sinister and located in surroundings infested by ghosts or demons. Two of the places mentioned are called the Perilous Chapel and Perilous Cemetery.[70] There were no doubt good reasons why romantic writers chose to use chapels in this way. A monastery could be featured as a place for knights to stay, but monasteries in the real world were comparatively well-regulated bodies. It was less easy for writers and their readers to weave fantasies about them than it was after the Reformation when they had turned into ruins.[71] Parish churches, too, were familiar institutions, hard to exploit romantically. Chapels were better adapted. They could be found in romantic places like rocks and

[69] *Le Haut Livre du Graal Perlesvaus*, ed. W.A. Nitze and T.A. Jenkins (2 vols., Chicago, 1932–7), I, 26–38; *The High Book of the Grail*, trans. Nigel Bryant (Cambridge, 1978), 21–7. Further material on chapels will be found in *The Continuations of the Old French Perceval of Chretien de Troyes*, ed. William Roach, 4 vols. (Philadelphia, 1949–71).
[70] *Perlesvaus*, ed. Nitze and Jenkins, I, 220–1, 340–3; *The High Book of the Grail*, trans. Bryant, 143, 220. The perilous cemetery is discussed in *Perlesvaus*, ed. Nitze and Jenkins, II, 308–9.
[71] A change of direction seen, for example, in Shakespeare, Sonnet 73, line 4; Donne, Satyres, 2, line 60; Webster, *The Duchess of Malfi*, Act 5, Scene 3, lines 1–9.

forests. They tended to lack permanent clergy and were more likely to be staffed, if at all, by hermits, who were more fantastic figures. Some chapels were deserted and tumbledown, increasing their forlorn and disquieting character.[72] One, St John the Evangelist at Beausale near Warwick was nicknamed 'Cuckoo church'; another, on the border of Thorverton parish (Devon), came to be known as 'No Man's Chapel'.[73] Seizing on such examples, 'Gothic' writers—as early as the thirteenth century—depicted chapels in the manner of Gothic revival.

The treatment of chapels by the French writers duly spread to England where their romances were read, translated and imitated. Malory's fifteenth-century Arthurian cycle includes twenty-two episodes featuring chapels, most of them taken from the *Prose Lancelot*.[74] Here again, some of the buildings are ancient and decrepit, like that upon a mountain where Lancelot 'found a chapel passing old, and found therein nobody, for all was desolate'.[75] The late fourteenth-century romance, *Sir Gawain and the Green Knight*, is another story about chapels; indeed, *Sir Gawain and the Knight of the Green Chapel* would be a more accurate title. In this realistic poem, chapels are part of the indoor furnishings of great houses. Arthur's court at Camelot has its chapel and chaplains, and so does the castle of Hautdesert where Gawain spends Christmas. The latter contains a chancel where the lord and his guest sit during worship, with a separate closet for the lady and her maidens. These civilised indoor chapels are balanced by the mysterious chapel which gives the Green Knight his name, 'the knight of the green chapel men know me many', and whither Gawain (like Arthur) must make his way.[76] There were several White Chapels in England[77] and a Black Chapel in the Arthurian cycle,[78] but when Gawain finds the green one it is not a man-made building. Instead, it is a mound with holes in it, 'nobut an old cave or the crevice of a crag'. Perhaps this

---

[72] Thus in 1301, the chapel of Rawridge (Devon) was ruinous (*The Register of Walter de Stapeldon, Bishop of Exeter*, ed. F.C. Hingeston-Randolph (London and Exeter, 1892), 397); in 1470–7 Abbot Wisbech of Crowland restored the chapel of Peakirk (Northamptonshire) 'which had lain level with the ground' (*The Crowland Chronicle Continuations: 1459–1486*, ed. N.Pronay and J. Cox (1986), 140–1).

[73] J.E.B. Gover, A. Mawer and F.M. Stenton, *The Place-Names of Warwickshire*, English Place-Name Society, XIII (1936), 262; *The Victoria History of the County of Warwick*, ed. L.F. Salzman, vol. III (1945), 119–20; Exeter, Devon Record Office, Glebe Terriers, 51, Brampford Speke.

[74] *The Works of Sir Thomas Malory*, ed. Eugène Vinaver and P.J.C. Field (3rd edn, 3 vols., Oxford, 1990); *A Concordance to the Works of Sir Thomas Malory*, ed. Tomomi Kato (Tokyo, 1974), s.v. 'chapel' etc.

[75] Malory, *Works*, ed. Vinaver, II, 887; cf. II, 893–4.

[76] *Sir Gawain and the Green Knight*, ed. J.R.R. Tolkien, E.V. Gordon and N. Davis (2nd edn, Oxford, 1967), lines 451, 454.

[77] Near London, in Haltwhistle (Northumberland), and in Witheridge (Devon).

[78] Below, note 82.

heightens the tension, allowing Gawain to imagine it as a place where
the devil might say his mattins at midnight.[79] Perhaps, too, it accords
with a poem which (despite its romantic plot) prefers realistic settings
to fantastic ones, whether indoors in castles or outside in the wild.[80]

*Chapels in folklore*

Romantic perceptions of chapels are also apparent in folklore. Sometimes literature caused people to identify romantic places with real ones
in the way that popular culture likes to do. This was especially true of
Arthurian legend. During the fourteenth century, the monk John of
Glastonbury inserted into his chronicle an episode about King Arthur
and his squire copied from that of *Perlesvaus*, implying it to be historical.
He changed the setting to Avalon and located the chapel at the
hermitage of St Mary Magdalene at Beckery near Glastonbury.[81] John
Harding, a fifteenth-century writer, made a similar conjecture that the
Black Chapel in the *Mort Artu*, where Arthur went after his final battle
and lay buried, was the Lady Chapel of Glastonbury Abbey.[82] Malory
claimed that the chapel in Dover Castle was the burial place of Sir
Gawain. 'And there yet all men may see the skull of him, and the same
wound is seen that Sir Lancelot gave in battle.'[83] Another story which
inspired chapel folklore was that of Guy of Warwick, a romantic hero
first written about in the mid-thirteenth century.[84] Guy was not an
historical figure and his romance portrays him implausibly as a crusader
in the reign of King Athelstan. After an heroic career, he returns to
Warwick in disguise and lives, unknown to his wife, at Gybbecliff, a
real hermitage not far from the town. He dies there in an odour of
sanctity, and his body is taken to Lorraine by his friend Terri de
Guarmeise, who buries it in an abbey.[85] The story became accepted as
a fact. Thomas Beauchamp, earl of Warwick (d. 1401) is said to have

---

[79] *Sir Gawain and the Green Knight*, lines 2180–96.

[80] A further unique depiction of a chapel occurs in the fifteenth-century carol 'Mery
hyt ys in May mornyng', with the thrice repeated line 'And by a chapel as I came' (*The
Early English Carols*, ed. Richard Leighton Green (2nd edn, Oxford, 1977), 197, 428). The
singer tells how, as he passed a chapel, he saw Jesus going to mass there with his disciples:
a portrayal of a chapel as a gateway between earth and heaven like that of Arthur's
vision of Jesus in the mass.

[81] *The Chronicle of Glastonbury Abbey*, ed. J.P. Carley (2nd edn, Woodbridge, 1985), 76–9;
J. Armitage Robinson, *Two Glastonbury Legends* (Cambridge, 1926), 20–3; discussed in
*Perlesvaus*, ed. Nitze and Jenkins, II, 105–20.

[82] *The Chronicle of John Hardyng*, ed. Henry Ellis (1812), 147.

[83] Malory, *Works*, ed. Vinaver and Field, III, 1232; cf. I, p. cxliv.

[84] M. Dominica Legge, *Anglo-Norman Literature and its Background* (Oxford, 1963), 162–71.

[85] *Gui de Warewic*, ed. Alfred Ewert (2 vols., Paris, 1933), II, lines 11375–632; *The Romance
of Guy of Warwick*, ed. J. Zupitza, Early English Text Soc., extra series, XXV-VI (1875–
6), lines 10475–8; ibid., XLII, XLIX, LIX (1883–91), 610–27.

renamed Gybbecliff 'Guycliff' and to have rebuilt the hermitage there. His son Earl Richard (d. 1439), the master of the young Henry VI, added a chantry of two priests and a house for them to live in. Richard made the place part spa, part theme park, building wells enclosed with stone, a pavilion to shelter visitors from the rain and an image of Guy 'great like a giant'. According to the antiquary John Rous (d. 1492), who was one of the chantry priests, pilgrims came to the place to be healed and often experienced miraculous cures.[86]

Nor were these the only chapels to acquire romantic associations. When John Leland visited Gainsborough (Lincolnshire), he was told of a chapel said to have many Danes buried there,[87] and at Richmond (Yorkshire) he saw one 'with strange figures in the walls of it. The people there dream that it was once a temple of idols.'[88] At Maidenhead, really Maidenhythe or 'landing place', he learnt that the name was derived from the head of one of St Ursula's 11,000 virgins, 'to the which offering there was made in a chapel'.[89] St Michael's Mount was another chapel site encrusted with legends. According to William Worcester who went there in 1478, the archangel personally manifested himself at the Mount, which was previously called 'le Horerok in the Wodd', i.e. the grey or white rock in the wood. Nothing less woodlike than the Mount can be imagined today, but Worcester goes on to say that the place was originally clad in dense forest. It lay six miles from the sea and 'there were both woods and meadows and ploughlands between the said Mount and the Scilly Islands'.[90] Seventy years later, Leland observed 'near the low water mark' on the shore by the Mount, 'roots of trees in diverse places'.[91] The roots, which still exist, are in fact the remains of a petrified forest.

## The reformation of chapels

Chapels were so intimately connected with late medieval religion that they were bound to be affected by the Reformation, which attacked that religion in so many respects. The first assaults they received came from Henry VIII's Injunctions of 1536 which discouraged devotion to images, and those of 1538 which ordered the removal of images attracting pilgrimages or offerings.[92] This struck at the many chapels which housed such things. By the late summer of 1538, royal agents

---

[86] *The Rous Roll*, sections 22, 32–3, 48, 50, 57; Leland, *Itinerary*, II, 45.

[87] Leland, *Itinerary*, I, 33

[88] Ibid., 79.

[89] Ibid., V, 232.

[90] William Worcester, *Itineraries*, ed. John H. Harvey (Oxford, 1969), 38–9, 98–103.

[91] Leland, *Itinerary*, I, 320.

[92] *Visitation Articles and Injunctions of the Period of the Reformation*, ed. W.H. Frere and W. McC. Kennedy, Alcuin Club Collections, XIV-XVI (3 vols., 1910), II, 5–6, 38.

were taking action against cult chapels. In August, Sir William Bassett reported to Thomas Cromwell that he had destroyed the shrine of St Anne of Buxton. He took away the image, the wax offerings, crutches, shirts and sheets offered by those healed, and locked up the baths and wells.[93] Next month, John London suppressed the cult of Our Lady of Caversham (Oxfordshire), 'whereunto was great pilgrimage'. He removed the silver-plated image, the coats, cap and hair it had worn, the lights, shrouds, crutches, wax images and 'many pretty relics' including the daggers said to have killed St Edmund and Henry VI.[94] John Leland, who toured England during the following years, observed the results of the Injunctions in several places. Although many chapels still existed, those with pilgrimage cults had lost them and some buildings had already been closed or turned to other uses. Pilgrimages had ceased at St Anne Bristol, St Helen Isles of Scilly, Our Lady in the Park at Liskeard, Our Lady of Grace at Hamble (Hampshire), and St Oswald's chapel at Oswestry. At Sherborne, St Thomas Becket's chapel 'standeth but uncelebrated', the same saint's chapel at Barnstaple was 'prophaned', so was the chapel near Portsmouth harbour, while St Mary Shrewsbury was 'now pulled down'.[95] The Henrician Reformation, by its attack on chapels, dealt one of its greatest blows at traditional religion.

Further measures against them followed in the reign of Edward VI. The Chantry Act of 1548 abolished the chantry priests who had ministered in some chapels (actually, in but a small proportion), and did away with the religious guilds which had more widely maintained lights and images.[96] Only in a few chapels of ease were arrangements made for chantry priests to continue as curates. The Book of Common Prayer of 1549 replaced the Latin mass by a new English communion service and prohibited communion from being celebrated in chapels 'except there be some to communicate with the priest'—thus ruling out private masses.[97] Neither these statutes nor others of the period concerned themselves with chapels directly in a major way, but the tide of the English Reformation turned against them as certainly as it was silent. Negatively, Reformers could not but dislike the cults which so many chapels had promoted. Positively, they wished the people of God to meet together for worship in parish churches, not apart in private coteries. Robbed of reasons to continue, and probably sometimes actively reprobated, large numbers of chapels—especially cult chapels—were closed and even dismantled. At St Paul's London, the charnel

[93] *Letters and Papers, Henry VIII*, XIII part ii, 95.
[94] Ibid., 143, 147.
[95] Leland, *Itinerary*, I, 196, 154, 169, 190, 200, 200, 282, III, 74; V, 111.
[96] *The Statutes of the Realm* (10 vols., Record Commission, 1810–24), IV part i, 24–33.
[97] *The English Rite*, ed. F.E. Brightman (2nd edn, 2 vols., 1921), II, 714.

chapel was demolished in 1548, the chapel in the Pardon Churchyard in 1549 and the charnel chapel at Exeter in about the same period.[98]

In the short term, the Reformers had some successes; in the long term they were less effective. There were too many chapels. The private gentry ones could not be touched as a group; they often stayed intact, and some of them formed a basis, after 1559, for establishing Catholic nonconformity. Even public chapels frequently survived in recognisable shapes: disused, converted to barns or cottages, but remembered for what they had been. An enquiry into ninety-two Devon parishes in about 1755 revealed 115 chapels still extant as buildings or thought to have once existed.[99] The attempt to confine all public worship to parish churches, while meeting with much success, progressively encountered more resistance and collapsed in the later seventeenth century. By 1689, large numbers of the laity had reacted against religious uniformity and gained toleration for separate worship. A new proliferation of chapels ensued. The history of all this appears to teach us that chapels spring from deep human yearnings. People yearn for variety, both in devotion and in companionship. In seeking such variety, those who lived in the middle ages have more in common with people today than either share with the leaders of the Reformation.

[98] *Chronicle of the Grey Friars of London*, ed. J.G. Nichols, Camden Soc., old series, LIII (1852), 57–8; Orme, 'The Charnel Chapel', 169.

[99] Oxford, Bodleian Library, MS Top. Devon b. 1–2, a survey carried out by Jeremiah Milles, precentor of Exeter Cathedral.

# 'AN AIRIER ARISTOCRACY': THE SAINTS AT WAR

*The Prothero Lecture*

## By Christopher Holdsworth

READ 28 JUNE 1995

The Latins are much like Arabs, as we say at Radcliffe;
decay of infeud scattered the Scottish clans,
but ours is an airier aristocracy:...[1]

I want to plunge into my subject by adopting that practice well known
to our medieval predecessors, namely to use an *exemplum*, because at
once it transports us into the heart of the problem to be addressed.
The event is recounted by Orderic Vitalis in Book Six of his *Ecclesiastical
History*, and describes the practice of a Norman priest called Gerold
who served in the household of the great earl of Chester Hugh of
Avranches (1071–1101). Gerold was, apparently, a devoted priest who
regularly said the offices for the day and offered Mass, but beyond this
he wanted the men of the earl's household to live a better life. That
desire he discharged by telling them about how some of their forebears
had lived:

> To great lords, simple knights, and noble boys alike he gave salutary
> counsel and he made a great collection of tales of the combats of
> holy knights, drawn from the Old Testament and more recent records
> of Christian achievements, for them to imitate. He told them vivid
> stories of the conflicts of Demetrius and George, of Theodore and
> Sebastian, of the Theban Legion and Maurice its leader, and of
> Eustace, supreme commander of the army and his companions, who
> won the crown of martyrdom in heaven. He also told them of the
> holy champion, William, who after long service in war renounced
> the world and fought gloriously for the Lord under the monastic
> rule. And many profited from his exhortations, for he brought them
> from the wide ocean of the world to the safe haven of life under the
> Rule.[2]

[1] Robert Lowell, *Notebooks* (1970), 111. I must here acknowledge the many helpful points
made in the discussion which followed the reading of this paper, some of which have
been adopted in this printed version. In the following notes when citing Latin sources I
have usually cited an English translation in brackets.

[2] *The Ecclesiastical History of Orderic Vitalis*, VI.2, ed. Marjorie Chibnall ( 6 vols., Oxford,
1969–80) [hereafter Orderic, HE], III, 216–17.

Here we catch a glimpse of one of the ways in which stories about soldier saints were passed on from one generation to the next, and Orderic's sequel tells how five men were sufficiently impressed to leave the world and become monks at his own house.³ Their presence at Saint-Évroul, indeed, provides some assurance for us of the truth of the story, for we may reasonably believe that Orderic would not have invented something which some of his fellows could have denied. The story also opens up a much wider theme, namely the part played in early medieval warfare by holy men and women who together make up what, following Robert Lowell, I have called 'an airier aristocracy'. Perhaps such a warrior theme may be peculiarly apposite in a year when the ending of the Second World War has been recalled, or indeed in a month in which an American airman having been shot down in Serbian controlled Bosnia, when rescued from his precarious position, burst out with thanks not only to his rescuers but to the Almighty. Certainly, the terrain for exploration is vast, and in one paper I can do no more than indicate some of its most important landmarks.

The first area to view lies around those heroes whose names Orderic gave us. Who were they, how did Gerold know about them, and why did he chose stories about those particular holy men? They fall into two very unequal and distinct groups: the first consisting of six martyrs of the early church, and the other of one man who died during the reign of the emperor Charlemagne. Let us turn to the larger, and more complex, group first.

Most of them, that is to say, Demetrius, George, Theodore, Sebastian and Maurice, probably met violent deaths during the last period of fierce persecution of the Christian community, during the reign of Diocletian.⁴ Eustace, on the other hand, may be little more than a romantic myth. That formidable scholar Delehaye minced no words on the matter: 'what strikes one when reading his Passion, is the impossibility of discovering in it the least trace of contact with reality'.⁵ But since now our concern is not primarily with that reality but rather with the use to which stories, however mythical, were put, we need not linger over Eustace's solidity. He, like his five associates, was known to Orderic's world as someone who had met his death because he had refused to sacrifice to the Roman gods. Eustace and the others, with one curious exception, also shared another characteristic; they had been soldiers. The odd man out is George, the best known to a modern audience for whom he is inextricably linked both with soldiering, and,

³ *Ibid.*, VI.4 (III, 227).
⁴ I follow here David Hugh Farmer, *The Oxford Dictionary of Saints* (Oxford, 1978), and *Bibliotheca Sanctorum* (12 vols., plus indices, Rome, 1961–70).
⁵ H. Delehaye, 'La légende de S. Eustache', in *Mélanges d'hagiographie grecque et latine* (Studia hagiographica, XLII, Brussels, 1966), 217.

of course, with the hunting of a dragon. But he lacked these attributes in the story circulating in Oderic's time.[6] There he was a layman suffering martyrdom because he, like the other soldiers, had refused to make proper acknowledgment of the gods.[7] Now to our second question: how could Gerold have known about these Christian heroes?

The probable answer is that he knew about them from his daily experience of the liturgy, that regular worship of the church, which, Orderic emphasised, Gerold punctiliously attended. We can distinguish at least two aspects of the liturgy which would have made their names, and to a lesser extent their lives, familiar to him. In the first place, the litanies used during the mass referred to nearly all of the earlier group.[8] The one possible exception is Demetrius. Michael Lapidge's recent edition of Anglo-Saxon Litanies,—we have, alas, no equivalent for the Anglo-Norman period—shows that he occurs in only one set of nearly fifty litanies, in the so-called *Portiforium* of St Wulfstan probably produced in Worcester in the second half of the eleventh century. The comparative numbers of occurrences for the others in ascending order are Theodore 6, Eustace 15, Sebastian 23, Maurice 25 and George 26. It is, therefore, highly likely that Gerold would have repeated their names among the martyrs whose prayers he sought every day.

The other kind of liturgical experience occurred once a year on the feast day of each saint. Nineteen calendars produced in England before 1100 included all the military martyrs, with the single exception of Demetrius, while less abundant evidence from missals and prayer books dating between the late ninth and later eleventh centuries suggests that the same five men were remembered with special prayers at the mass on their high and holy days.[9] These feasts were indeed marked with

---

[6] Alison Goddard Elliott, *Roads to Paradise: Reading the Lives of the Early Saints* ( Hanover and London, 1987) [hereafter Elliott, *Roads*], 157 n. 115; Veronica Ortenberg, *The English Church and the Continent in the Tenth and Eleventh Centuries* (Oxford, 1992) [hereafter Ortenberg, *English Church*], 211, refers to three tympana in England showing the fight with the dragon, citing Charles E. Keyser, *A List of Norman Tympana and Lintels* (1927). It is likely all postdate 1120; cf. George Zarnecki, *Later English Romanesque Sculpture* (1953), 12,13,14,36,55. There is need for further discussion of early images of George in England and Normandy.

[7] See the discussion of Aelfric below at n. 12.

[8] *Anglo-Saxon Litanies of the Saints*, ed. Michael Lapidge, *Henry Bradshaw Society* [hereafter *HBS*], CVI (1991), *passim* for the rest of this paragraph.

[9] *English Kalendars before A.D. 1100*, ed. Francis Wormald, *HBS*, LXXII (1934, repr. 1988), *passim*. One may note also that Demetrius has a different day in each case: 19 Sept. (West Country, late XIc), 8 October (Worcester, later XIc, a XIIc addition), 10 November (Glastonbury, *c.* 970); below I refer to saints by initials only: *The Durham Collectar*, ed. Alicia Corrêa, *HBS*, CVII (1992), 174(S), 176(G), 196(T); *The Missal of the New Minster, Winchester*, ed. D.H. Turner, *HBS*, XCIII (1962), 62(S), 87(G), 166(M), 179(E), 180(T), includes the Durham collects, adding others with Epistles and Gospels (these are not given for E and T); *The Winchcombe Sacramentary*, ed. Anselme Davril, *HBS*, CIX (1995),

some solemnity, though the prayers say not a word of their military activity. That kind of information was, however, available in martyrologies and legendaries, which, one must suppose, were read either in church, or in refectory, on the appropriate days. Martyrologies, indeed, make it very likely that the quartet George, Maurice, Sebastian and Theodore were commemorated in England from the seventh century onwards with the reintroduction of Christianity. All their names occur in the fifth-century Martyrology wrongly attributed to Jerome and widely known in the western church, whilst Bede in his Martyrology provided short accounts of each individual's passion.[10] Eustace and Demetrius were unknown to pseudo-Jerome and Bede, as well as to the anonymous compiler of the vernacular Old English Legendary, written in the late ninth century, but he did know about Sebastian, George and Maurice.[11] Aelfric, on the other hand, composing his Catholic Homilies about a century later, was well aware of Eustace's fabulous adventures.[12] This suggests that he entered into English liturgical consciousness during the tenth century. Demetrius, on the other hand, with his single calendar entry and lack of special prayers, may well be the one early martyr in Gerold's group whose cult had scarcely taken off anywhere in England before the end of the eleventh century.

This somewhat protracted consideration needs making because it has sometimes been suggested that all the military saints owe their popularity in Europe to the First Crusade when they made miraculous appearances, in the Holy Land, encouraging the pilgrim soldiers.[13] The

143(S), 154–5(G), 189–90(M), 199(T), has the same prayers as New Minster; *The Leofric Missal*, ed. F.E.Warren (Oxford, 1883), 140 (G), 161 (M), 166 (T); *The Portiforium of Saint Wulfstan*, ed. Anselm Hughes, HBS, LXXXIX and XC (1958–60), 118 (S), 122 (G), 144(M), 148( E and T), has one collect for each like those at New Minster, but adds two more for E which are distinctive. I have not consulted Benedictionals.

[10]Michael Lapidge, 'The Saintly Life in Anglo-Saxon England', in *The Cambridge Companion to Old English Literature*, ed. Malcolm Godden and Michael Lapidge (Cambridge, 1991), 250–2. *Martyrologium Hieronimi* in *Acta Sanctorum, Nov. II, i*, 11(S), 46(G), 124(M), 141(T); Bede, *Martyrology*, Migne, *Patrologia Latina*, 94, cols. 816–17 (S), 886–7 (G), 1050–1 (M), 1009–10 (T). I have not been able to use *Edition pratique des martryloges de Bède, de l'Anonyme lyonnais et Florus*, ed. J. Dubois and G. Renaud (Paris, 1976).

[11]*Das altenglische Martyrologium*, ed. Günter Kotzor, *Bayerische Akademie der Wissenschaften*, Phil.-Hist. Klasse, Neue Folge, LXXXVIII/1–2, (Munich, 1981), 21(S), 58–62 (G), 214–15 (M). Kotzor shows that two of his five manuscripts were written between c.1050 and c.1200: 75*, 56*.

[12]On Aelfric as hagiographer see Lapidge (as n. 10 above), 256–8. *Aelfric's Lives of Saints: Being a Set of Sermons on Saints' Days*, ed. Walter W. Skeat, Early English Texts Society, Orig. Ser. LXXVI, LXXXII, XCIV, CXIV (2 vols. in 4 pts, 1881–1900; repr. in 2 vols., Oxford, 1966), I, 117–47 (S), 316–19 (G), II, 159–69 (M), 191–219 (E).

[13]Carl Erdmann, *The Origin of the Idea of Crusade*, transl. Marshall W. Baldwin and Walter Goffart (Princeton, N.J., 1977) [hereafter Erdmann, *Origin*], 275–7, where Erdmann's cautious words, first published in 1935, are modified by Baldwin's notes. Maurice Keen, *Chivalry* (New Haven and London, 1984), 47, follows Erdmann without modification.

evidence just surveyed suggests that this can not be the case: the quartet seem well and truly at home long before then, and even Eustace to be settling down.

But litanies and calendars also make it clear that Gerold must have been making a conscious selection because other soldier martyrs were invoked, their feast days celebrated. One may mention the forty soldiers martyred in Cappadocia, or the Maccabees, whose stories were told by Aelfric.[14] What, we should ask, may have influenced Gerold's selection? Here there can be no certainty, but one may suggest that another liturgy, of a more secular kind, played its role, namely that of the *Laudes* sung before a ruler. By the eleventh century it is clear that in Normandy praises sung periodically at great ceremonial courts included appeals to George, Sebastian and Maurice.[15] Theodore, one may note, did not feature there, although he is found in Franco-Roman *Laudes* from the early ninth century where he occurs in the exclamation 'Exaudi Christe exercitui Romanorum et Francorum vita et Victoria. Sancte Teodore tu illos adiuva.'[16] Demetrius and Eustace, on the other hand, do not occur in such texts.

Here, it must be emphasised, England and Normandy were in no sense the only places in western Europe where these early martyrs were celebrated. Maurice, for instance, supposedly killed with his companions near Agaune in Gaul, had a basilica built in his honour soon after, which gave its name to Saint Maurice in the Valais, and by the mid-sixth century his cult had spread to the Loire.[17]

But is there, one must now ask, a plausible reason why these early martyr soldiers appealed to 'popular' enthusiasm both in England and

Ortenberg, *English Church*, 69–70 (G), 180(M), 210 11 (E), is much more nuanced, but does not mention D or E. Franco Cardini, *Alle radice della cavalleria medievale* (Florence, 1981) [hereafter Cardini, *Cavalleria*], 227–41, a broad-ranging discussion to which Richard Barber kindly directed me.

[14] Lapidge, *Anglo-Saxon Litanies*, and Wormald, *Kalendars*, *passim*: Aelfric, *Lives*, I.241ff, II. 87ff.

[15] Ernst H. Kantorowicz, *Laudes Regiae: A Study in Liturgical Acclamations and Mediaeval Ruler Worship* (Berkeley and Los Angeles, 1958), 167.

[16] Ibid., 105: 'Grant O Christ to the army of the Romans and Franks life and victory. Saint Theodore help them.' Cf. Michael McCormick, 'The Liturgy of War in the Early Middle Ages: Crisis, Liturgies, and the Carolingian Monarchy', *Viator*, XV (1984), 1–23, espec. 17.

[17] Ian Wood, *The Merovingian Kingdoms 450–751* (1994), 183. M. Wallace-Hadrill, *The Frankish Church* (Oxford, 1983), 78, the oldest surviving MS of a saint's life is for Maurice. Gregory of Tours, *Decem Libri Historiarum* [hereafter *HF*], X.31 (trans. Lewis Thorpe, *Gregory of Tours. The History of the Franks* (Harmondsworth, 1974), 601–2), for his discovery of Maurice's relics in St Martin's church and transfer of them to the cathedral. For later embroderies on these events see Sharon Farmer, *Communities of Saint Martin. Legend and Ritual in Medieval Tours* (Ithaca and London, 1991) [hereafter Farmer, *Communities*], 54–5, 232–5, 287.

in mainland Europe throughout the central middle ages ? Perhaps two rather different attractions may have been at work; they provided Christian Europe with ancient prototypes for the soldiering profession, and, secondly, these models may have been the more acceptable in that most of them were not associated by birth with any one of the successor kingdoms of the west. According to their legends all, save Sebastian, were in a sense incomers from the eastern mediterranean and so they could be adopted by a world which was absorbing far more numerous settlers from the Germanic world. There is in this second aspect a parallel to the way that 'new' cults spread in the pre-Christian empire, an indication of a set of similarities which we shall notice elsewhere.[18] Beyond this one may suggest that the very ways in which they experienced death, and were, of course, believed to have overcome it, were specially apposite for soldiers.[19]

Sebastian and George were pierced by arrows and swords, both types of weapons met with in battle, whilst George also experienced being heated up, a suffering shared by soldiers when hot liquids were decanted on them from above.[20] Eustace suffered death by fire in a brazen ox in which he was roasted with his friends, after he, rather like Shaw's Androcles, had outfaced a lion.[21] Their bodies, incidentally, emerged unmarked by fire, 'whiter than snow' as Aelfric puts it.[22] Maurice and his companions faced their persecutors having thrown away their swords; they could serve, therefore, as models for soldiers who could easily face being forcibly disarmed themselves. So, although the passions of these early martyrs had little to say directly about conduct in ordinary battles, they might yet speak about the way death lurking on every battlefield could be overcome.

William of Gellone, on the other hand, differed from them in this respect, as in so many others. He died in his bed, but he had been a valiant soldier, although this was a career of which he ultimately tired. When Orderic wrote in the early 1130s his cult had not spread into England, and, indeed, there is no evidence that it ever received formal recognition here.[23] Two questions pose themselves: how had Gerold come to know about him, and why was he, perhaps, a saint who failed to take off as widely as the early military martyrs? Orderic himself

[18] Robin Lane-Fox, *Pagans and Christians* (Harmondsworth, 1986) [hereafter Lane-Fox, *Pagans*], 82.

[19] Aelfric provides an accessible source for the legends, see n. 12 above.

[20] Philippe Contamine, *War in the Middle Ages*, trans. Michael Jones (Oxford, 1984) [hereafter Contamine, *War*], 297, for S as patron saint of archers.

[21] Elliott, *Roads*, 144–67, brings together much evidence about early saints, especially martyrs, and animals.

[22] *Lives of Saints*, II, 219.

[23] Orderic, *HE*, III, xiv (for date), 218–27 (Orderic's summary of the *Vita*).

confessed that it had been hard to find genuine information about William until a monk from Winchester had passed through Saint-Évroul carrying with him a Life.[24] This he copied down in abbreviated form into his *History*. It was, in fact, hot from the press since it had only been written within the previous decade, but Gerold, of course, living in the earl's household late in the eleventh century, cannot have read it. He could, on the other hand, have picked up a sketch of William's life from the much older Life of Benedict of Aniane, and it is possible that already what Orderic dismissed as *vulgo cantilena*, which we might translate as a popsong about William, was going the rounds in the mouths of jongleurs.[25] Yet, as I have already remarked, William seems not to have taken root in England, although vernacular poems and stories circulated widely.[26] The only explanation I can offer for his failure to enter into the liturgical life of the Anglo-Norman world is that by the time his long *Vita* was available, soldier saints were two a penny.

From Gerold and his heroes let us now move back to a second area, to the time when the early soldier saints lived. Was there then any perception that the combination soldier and Christian was unusual?

The evidence for there being Christians within the Roman army exists from around a hundred years before Gerold's heroes lived, namely from the late second century onwards.[27] We do not know whether they had been converted in the army, or before they joined it, but one must assume that they had had to make some compromises over taking part in pagan ceremonies which were part and parcel of army life. Whether they were conscious of having to compromise over whether killing other people was compatible with being a Christian is also unclear.

The complex question of what the early church thought about this issue could well occupy a separate paper; here I must be brief.[28] Most scholars, I think, would argue that whereas some Christians in the period before the conversion of Constantine took a line which one can broadly call pacifist, others did not. As we shall see in a moment, the fact that after the emperor's conversion most Christians ceased to be pacifists suggests that even before that this was becoming the pre-

[24] Ibid., 218–19; *English Benedictine Kalendars after A.D. 1100*, ed. Francis Wormald, HBS., LXXVII, LXXXI (1939, 1946), have no entries for William.

[25] Orderic, *HE*, III, 218: 'Vulgo canitur a ioculatoribus de illo cantilena....'

[26] For the vernacular texts see R.R. Bezzola, *Les origines et la formation de la littérature courtoise en occident* (5 vols., Paris, 1958–60), II.494 n.1.

[27] Lane-Fox, *Pagans*, 304, 319, 553, but 588 under Constantine 'the random sample of the soldiery remained overwhelmingly pagan'.

[28] Louis J. Smith, *The Early Fathers on War and Military Service* (Wilmington, Delaware, 1983) [hereafter Swift, *Early Fathers*], is a useful guide. I am grateful to Ian Markham for having drawn my attention to it.

dominant position. But, on the other hand, the existence for many centuries of texts which imposed penances on soldiers killing in a public war suggests that the conviction about its incorrectness survived. How seriously it was regarded may be indicated by the fact that early medieval penitentials prescribe the same penance for killing in battle as for masturbation, namely forty days.[29] There is, one need scarcely add, something of a gap here between medieval and modern perceptions.

The church from an early date seems to have been clear that it was wrong for priests to join the army, a prohibition extended to monks by the Council of Chalcedon in 451.[30] These survived to pass into the body of canon law. Here it looks as though the church adopted a stance which had its parallel in the pagan world where priests were exempt from conscription into the army.[31] Perhaps it may be correct to suggest that the growth of a more relaxed view about Christians serving in the army (of which the emergence of cults of warrior martyrs was a part), just as Christianity was becoming a really significant force in the Graeco-Roman world, may have helped the church make a crucial transition. As it became first an allowed, and then the official, religion of the empire it had to meet many new demands. It is striking that when Constantine campaigned against the Persians in the mid-330s he took bishops with him and had priests serving the army, the first time that military chaplains are mentioned in western history, as Lane-Fox remarked.[32] It is relevant to observe too that just as the church shifted its stance on soldiering, it was softening the very harsh discipline it used to employ on adulterers. Both sets of sinners now could be relatively easily reconciled with the Christian community.[33]

Such things create the impression that the transition on war occurred

---

[29] *Medieval Handbooks of Penance*, trans. John T. McNeill and Helena M. Gamer (Records of Western Civilisation Series, New York, orig. edn, 1938; repr. 1990), Pentitential of Archbishop Theodore, cap.IV,6 (187): I,9 (185), whereas a priest only has three weeks' fast, VIII,4 (191). Other texts (225, 317) also have the forty-day penance. Cf. A.J. Frantzen, *The Literature of Penance in Anglo-Saxon England* (New Brunswick, N.J., 1983), 76, 111–12. There is no mention of killing in battle in the Irish texts, which are severe on killing in general: *The Irish Penitentials*, ed. Ludwig Bieler, *Scriptores Latini Hiberniae*, V (Dublin 1975). Later there are signs of a more severe view: Contamine, *War*, 268, his last example follows the battle of Hastings.
[30] Swift, *Early Fathers*, 157; Contamine, *War*, 269; F. Prinz, 'King, Clergy and War at the Time of the Carolingians', in *Saints, Scholars and Heroes. Studies in Honour of C.W. Jones*, ed. M.H. King and W.M. Stevens (Collegeville, 1978), 302–3; Timothy E. Powell, 'The "Three Orders" of Society in Anglo-Saxon England', *Anglo-Saxon England*, XXIII (1994), 103–32, espec. 124–5 on Prinz.
[31] Swift, *Early Fathers*, 55, citing Origen, *Contra Celsum*, 8.73, though this relates to wartime.
[32] Lane-Fox, *Pagans*, 16–17.
[33] Swift, *Early Fathers*, 92f, noting how soldiers who had killed were allowed back into

without much internal struggle. The same message comes across in the historical works of Eusebius of Caesarea, an outstanding feature of the landscape to which we now turn.

At first sight his history has little relevant to our theme: there are, for example, no saints leading men into battle (which we shall find later), but there are other things which are very significant. In the first place Eusebius says a good deal about martyrs, and he talks about them with a special military language, even though most of them were not soldiers in the strict sense. A group of Gallic martyrs, for example, 'charged into the fight' when they withstood 'abuse and punishment', whilst their deaths are hailed as 'the greatest war they fought'.[34] Elsewhere a martyr in Alexandria 'fights like a hero in the great war for the Faith', or martyrs are likened to an army with Jesus as their commander.[35] It is not, of course, difficult to trace such language back to the Bible, especially to the epistles of Paul, and also to many historical passages in the Old Testament. Joshua, for example, had a vision of a man standing against him (the language here is reminiscent of that used by Greeks and Latins for the appearances of gods to men), holding a drawn sword in his right hand, who in answer to a question reveals himself as 'Commander- in -chief of the army of the Lord', whom Joshua at once worships (Jos. 5, 13–15).[36] Eusebius cites this passage twice at least.[37] Such passages had created for him and the early church as a whole a view that humankind was involved in a cosmic battle between the divine forces of good and the demonic powers; military metaphors inevitably sprang readily to their minds.

It is not surprising to find, therefore, that for Eusebius the battle is exemplified by the life of his hero, the emperor Constantine. He triumphs at the Milvian Bridge because he has God's help which he had prayed for beforehand.[38] Similarly when Licinius is his ally, he defeats Maximin because God has given him victory, but when Licinius turns against Constantine and his son, whose allies are God and Jesus, he is easily defeated.[39] The language of two later works, the *Encomium* addressed to Constantine and the *Life* about him, is stronger; for example, Constantine's triumphs occur because he is 'armed with the

the church after three years and then shorter periods. Lane-Fox, *Pagans*, 556–60, 597, 666, shows a less rigorist view on sin emerging in the third century, and becoming predominant after Constantine's conversion.

[34] Eusebius, *The History of the Church* [hereafter Eusebius, *History*], 5.1, 5.2 (trans. G.A. Williamson, rev. edn, Andrew Louth (Harmondsworth, 1989), 139, 149).

[35] Eusebius, *History*, 6.40, and 10.4 ( 212, 310–11).

[36] Cf. E.R. Dodds, *The Greeks and the Irrational* (Berkeley and Los Angeles,1951), 105–6.

[37] Eusebius, *History*, 1.2, 10.4 (6, 309).

[38] Ibid., 9.9 (293).

[39] Ibid., 9.10, 10.9 ( 297, 332).

standards given him by the Saviour', which enable him to subdue in
battle and chasten 'the visible enemies of truth'.[40]

So through Eusebius we can see that with the arrival of a Christian
emperor—we must sidestep here over a tricky piece of ground—the
powers of this world have become hard to separate from the powers of
God. Indeed, Eusebius was completely certain that the higher power
had given Constantine a very strong lift upwards.

Eusebius records, too, without any adverse comment, the existence
of Christians serving in the army: in Alexandria, in Palestinian Caesarea,
in the army under Licinius, and much earlier, under the emperor
Marcus Aurelius facing the Germans.[41] This last episode where Christian
soldiers prove their worth as rainmakers, and so save the army from
dying of thirst, created later the legend of the thundering legion, a
precedent for the Theban Legion of which Maurice was a member.
What strikes one in all this is how normal the presence of Christian
soldiers within the army appears in Eusebius. Sometimes they have
difficulties—the last great persecution begins, according to him, with
them—but he betrays almost no sense that there might be any con-
tradiction between their faith and their profession.[42] The only possible
exception occurs in his story of the Christian Marinus serving in the
army in Palestine.[43] About to be promoted an officer he is denounced
by a rival as a Christian who does not sacrifice to the emperors. The
judge after questioning him about his beliefs gives him three hours to
think the matter over, during which the local bishop takes him into a
church and makes him choose between the Bible placed on the altar
and the sword which hangs from his side. Marinus chooses the Bible,
returns to the judge, reaffirms his Christian beliefs and suffers instant
execution. What Eusebius does not say, however, is that Marinus was
executed because he would not kill: everything hinges on his unwillingness to sacrifice. Indeed, even a cursory reading of Eusebius betrays
the fact that many Christians had adjusted to taking part in warfare
long before any co-religionist had provided a theoretical justification
for this shift. It was Ambrose who first provided this in his *De Officiis
Ministrorum* and to do this he turned back to Cicero, not to the Bible,
to help him define the circumstances in which a war could be just. The
much better-known words of Augustine on war dominated later medieval thinking, but it was the bishop of Milan who has left us with the
first recorded Christian prayer for victory which still may shock when
first encountered: 'Turn, O Lord, and raise the standards of your faith.

[40] Swift, *Early Fathers*, 85 (citing *Encomium*, 2.3); other extracts, 84–7.
[41] Eusebius, *History*, 6.42, 7.15, 5.5 ( 213, 232, 151).
[42] Ibid., 8.1 (257).
[43] Ibid., 7.15 (232–3).

No military eagles, nor flight of birds here lead the army but your name Lord Jesus and your worship.'[44]

From the world of Eusebius to the world of the historians of the Germanic settlements is in some areas a large step, but as far as the saints at war are concerned it seems to be a fairly small one, though the variety of their ways in warfare has diversified. It is worth pausing with Jordanes, Gregory of Tours, Adomnan, Bede and Paul the Deacon. Adomnan, whilst not strictly a historian of the settlements, is included as a near contemporary of Bede and one who offers a valuable insight from the Scotto-Irish world. Although Jordanes wrote in the mid-fifth century and Paul about two hundred and fifty years later, all these authors, with one exception, have remarkably similar views about saints and war. The odd man out is Jordanes whose history of the Goths is full of wars, which he attributed to the devotion of the human race for its kings, ' for it is at the mad impulse of one mind (that) a slaughter of nations takes place...', [45] yet saintly intervention occurs not at all. Perhaps the explanation for this gap is that at the time he wrote people in Italy had not been forced back on heavenly defenders as later generations were forced to do.

All of them, even Jordanes, believed that what happened in this world reflected the will of God, perhaps especially what happened in battle, one of the most hazardous experiences in any period. Jordanes attributed the defeat of the emperor Valens at the battle of Adrianople to God, who was displeased that when the emperor had allowed the Goths to become Christian, they had adopted the Arian heresy.[46] Many events for Gregory reflected either divine favour, or disfavour: for example, God makes Clovis's enemies submit, and God causes the walls of Angoulême to collapse.[47] But on at least one occasion he attributes something to both divine response to prayer and to human skill: ' No one has any doubt that the army of the Huns was really routed by the prayers of the Bishop about whom I have told you; but it was the patrician Aetius, with the help of Thorismund, who gained the victory and destroyed the enemy.' [48] His 'no one has any doubt'

---

[44] *De Fide*, II.xvi.141–2, a prayer for Gratian fighting the Goths, cited by J.E. Cross, 'The Ethic of War in Old English', in *England before the Conquest. Studies in Primary Sources Presented to Dorothy Whitelock*, ed. Peter Clemoes and Kathleen Hughes (Cambridge, 1971), 269–82, at 270, a fine, wide-ranging article.

[45] *Jordanes: The Gothic History*, cap. XXXVI (trans. Charles C. Mierow, Cambridge and New York, 1915; repr. 1966, 105).

[46] Ibid., XXVI (90). One may note that Gregory, *HF*, I.41 (92) attributed Valens's defeat and death to his earlier having forced monks to do military service, something later forbidden by the church: see n. 30 above.

[47] *HF*, II.40, II.37 (156, 154), and many others. Cf. Walter Goffart, *The Narrators of Barbarian History* (Princeton, 1988) [hereafter Goffart, *Narrators*], 151, God's vengeance is 'nothing less than God's own feud in support of his servants'.

[48] *HF*, II.7 (118).

alerts us to the fact that almost certainly many *had* doubted the power of prayer. Bede demonstrates the general belief too: for example, the coming of the Saxons to Britain was 'ordained by the will of God so that evil should fall on those miscreants', the British.[49] On the other hand those very Britons prospered for a time under Ambrosius Aurelianus 'with God's help'.[50] But many events lack such comments: why was this ? Perhaps the fundamental conviction was so widely accepted it only needed stressing in exceptional circumstances, at an event which could not be otherwise accounted for. But what about saintly intervention in war?

Here we find that the holy men appear but not regularly or consistently. Their power, *virtus* is the word Gregory likes, is demonstrated 'unexpectedly, one might say irrationally', as Walter Goffart puts it in his tour-de-force, *The Narrators of Barbarian History.*[51] But if we ask which saints are now involved they are not the soldier martyrs of the earlier period, but rather people much closer to the age of the writers. This is something to which I shall return. Let us now examine some examples of these moments of power when the saints (I quote here Goffart again) 'multiply, almost as nerve ends, God's capacity to be a living presence among men'.[52] Their transmission of power may be observed in three circumstances.

The first occurred when the saint offered advice to a warrior king, rather in the way that oracles and individuals thought to be inspired had advised pagan rulers.[53] So, the emperor Constans, according to Paul the Deacon, consults a solitary holy man only to receive the disturbing news that he will not succeed in conquering the Lombards in Italy because the Lombard queen had built a basilica in honour of St John who has successfully interceded for her people with God.[54] Ecgfrith of Northumbria is advised by another saint with a solitary bent, Cuthbert, not to attack the Picts, but goes ahead, is ambushed and killed. For Bede the explanation is that the preceding year Ecgfrith had sent troops to Ireland, a people who had done him no harm, and who in their distress had cursed him.[55] Near to Ireland and well to the

[49] *Bede's Ecclesiastical History of the English People* [hereafter Bede, *HE*], I.14, ed. Bertram Colgrave and R.A.B. Mynors (Oxford, 1969), 48–9. Bede's anti-British bias has often been noticed, most recently Clare Stancliffe, 'Oswald, "Most Holy and Most Victorious King of the Northumbrians"', in *Oswald Northumbrian King to European Saint,* ed. Claire Stancliffe and Eric Cambridge (Stamford, 1995), 37, 76.
[50] Bede, *HE*, I.16 (54–5).
[51] *Narrators*, 142.
[52] Ibid., 151.
[53] Lane-Fox, *Pagans*, 229.
[54] *Historia Langobardorum*, V.6, ed. L. Bethmann and G. Waitz, *Monumenta Germaniae Historica, Scriptores rerum Langobardorum* (Hanover, 1878), 146–7.
[55] *HE*, IV.xxvi (426–9). This reads like a reflection of Augustine's attack on aggressive war.

north-west of Northumbria, in Iona, Columba, a saint from over the
sea, prophesies that another ruler will have a victory but that it will be
'an unhappy one'. By this he means that there will be heavy casualties,
and when the news comes back to Iona they hear that no less than
three hundred and three men had been killed.[56] One could cite other
examples. Nearly all show the living saint in gloomy, warning mood:
there will be victory only if the ruler refrains from doing something on
which he has set his heart.[57] Was this, I wonder, a reflection of
the current in earlier Christian thinking which held that war was
fundamentally not a good thing?

The same question is raised in a less acute form by some of the
evidence about the second arena where the saint showed his paces,
when praying about war. Most of these events take place, one should
realise, against a background in which the church, from at least the
fifth or sixth century, had built prayers for victory into its liturgy.[58]
Again, one may note, there are parallells in the pre-Christian empire,
as well as in the Old Testament.[59] Adomnan, for instance, records
baldly that some kings were defeated and others were victorious
according to Columba's prayers, but how he chose whom to favour
Adomnan does not tell us.[60] Gregory, on the other hand, seems to have
had no doubt that prayer offered by King Sigismund at the tomb of
the Theban legion at Agaune saved him from death when he was
defeated by Chlodomer.[61] These saints come across as powerful people,
indeed so powerful that their energy could be dangerous for those who
lost their patronage. Another writer of this era, Eddius Stephanus,
comments that when King Ecgfrith was on good terms with bishop
Wilfrid all went well with him, including the gaining of glorious
victories, but that when he and the king fell out, royal triumphs, like
other good things, came to an end.[62] Praying in battle for a ruler
proved spectacularly dangerous for the British monks who gathered

[56] Adomnan, *Life of Columba*, I.18 ( *Adomnán of Iona Life of St Columba*, trans. Richard
Sharpe (Harmondsworth, 1995), 119).

[57] E.g, Gregory, *HF*, III.6, IV.51 (166–7, 247–8)

[58] Michael McCormick, 'The Liturgy of War in the Early Middle Ages: Crisis, Liturgies,
and the Carolingian Monarchy', *Viator*, XV (1984), 1–23, at 18; Cardini, *Cavalleria*, 222–
6. One may note that Origen, often considered a pacifist, thought that if the Romans
put their mind to praying to God they could conquer more enemies than Moses had:
his pacifism did not exclude getting God to do the dirty work; Lane-Fox, *Pagans*, 626.

[59] E.g. I Sam vii. 6–11, Jonah iii.1f; Lane-Fox, *Pagans and Christians*, 120, for relics and
statues in battle.

[60] *Life of Columba*, I.i (110).

[61] Gregory of Tours, *Gloria Martyrum* [hereafter *GM*], c.74 (*Gregory of Tours, Glory of the
Martyrs*, trans. Raymond Van Dam (Liverpool, 1988), 96–7).

[62] *The Life of Bishop Wilfrid by Eddius Stephanus*, cap. XIX, ed. and trans. Bertram
Colgrave (Cambridge, 1927), 41–3.

behind the lines at Chester to invoke divine support for their ruler for they were slaughtered by Aethelfrith of Northumbria who recognised the threat which they presented.[63] Gregory's pages contain many mentions of the power of prayer in battle, or seige. Saragossa, for example, survives an attack from the Franks because it was defended by prayers offered to St Vincent, whose tunic was also within the city.[64] One of his most interesting stories concerns the seige at Bazas by the Huns.[65] Within the city the bishop, whom Gregory considered to be a saint, leads his people in saying prayers and singing psalms. The beseigers at night see people dressed in white carrying lit candles going round the town, but when Ganseric the Huns' king asks some locals what is going on, they have no idea; they had seen nothing untoward. The same thing happens another night when the Huns see a ball of fire coming down on the city: the inhabitants see nothing. This induces Ganseric to say 'If they do not know about these things, it is obvious that their God is helping them', and having said this he retreats and gives up the seige. On the other hand, praying was not always efficacious. Gregory wrote of one man that he was killed even though he had prayed to St Martin, explaining that he had never prayed with a contrite heart.[66] This was surely an irrefutable explanation, for who could judge the real state of another's heart?

Other stories about the efficacy of prayer reveal what Gregory and some of his contemporaries thought happened to their prayers when they reached the saints in heaven. Aetius's wife travelled to Rome to pray for the safety of her husband. One night a drunk got locked into St Peter's church and overheard two men talking, one of whom declared that he had lost patience with the woman's tearful requests that her husband should come home safe from Gaul. However, he went on, 'God in his wisdom has decreed otherwise, but nevertheless I have obtained this immense concession that Aetius should not be killed.'[67] God's will was, so to say, believed to be mutable if one appealed to him through the right go-betweens. That those holy intercessors had their hierarchy in heaven, just as earthly lords had here below, emerges from a story about Metz. Someone there had a vision of St Stephen arguing with Peter and Paul that his oratory there should not be destroyed by the Huns, a boon he asked so that he should be shown

---

[63] Bede, *HE*, II.2 ( 140–3). Bede here was in a difficulty since the Britons were Christians, but got round that by linking their fate with Augustine's prophecy that because they had refused to work with him they would die.

[64] *HF,* III.29 (186–7).

[65] *GM*, c.12 (32–4).

[66] *HF,* VII.29 (411).

[67] Ibid., II.7 (117).

to have 'some influence with the Lord'.[68] Here one can surely discern how the visionary experience helped to explain the curious fact that only this one oratory, out of many, survived the fire. It is not surprising either that heaven was pictured in similar terms to an earthly ruler's court with its mass of plaintiffs and its smaller group of people with the ruler's ear, jostling to establish which of them carried most clout. Another image of the heavenly court springs from Gregory's pages, for he writes of his favourite saints dancing in heaven.[69] One can not help wondering to which measure they tripped. Perhaps it was some version of the Willibrord Hoppe, that dance which still lumbers down the streets of Echternach on the saint's feastday, and in which at least one distinguished Fellow has taken part. Venantius Fortunatus, on the other hand, seems in his *Life of Martin* to have visualised the celestial inhabitants in different guise: 'less as a court than as a great army of legions, squadrons and cohorts, gloriously equipped and commanded by Christ, its king,' as Wallace-Hadrill memorably put it.[70]

More rarely the sources disclose to us appearances of saints in battle, our third and last circumstance where the heavenly ones worked. They did not, as far as I can see, in this period appear in armour like some of the soldier saints of the Byzantine world from the tenth century, but, nonetheless, they were recognised.[71] The earliest western appearance seems that of Paulinus at Nola when it was attacked by barbarians, which Augustine reported.[72] Much later, Oswald, for example, has a vision of Columba just before his battle with Cadwallon, urging him 'Be strong and act manfully....'[73] Here the saint himself is supposed to have told Oswald who he was, though we may suppose that a fifteen-year exile among the Picts and Irish must have familiarised him with descriptions of the saint. But it was otherwise, according to Paul the Deacon, for the Lombard duke Ariulf who only realised that St Sevianus had protected him in battle when afterwards he saw his likeness in the church dedicated to him in Spoleto.[74] Occasionally we read of relics of saints being carried into battle, something whose equivalent, the use of statues, is found in the pagan world too, but these, like prayer, did not

[68] Ibid., II.5 (115–16).

[69] Gregory of Tours, *Liber de passione et virtutibus sancti Iuliani martyris*, 50 ( trans. Raymond Van Dam, *Saints and their Miracles in Late Antique Gaul* (Princeton 1993) [hereafter Van Dam, *Saints*], 194).

[70] M. Wallace-Hadrill, *The Frankish Church* (Oxford, 1983), 87.

[71] Michael McCormick, *Eternal Victory. Triumphal Rulership in Late Antiquity, Byzantium and the Early Medieval West* (Cambridge and Paris, 1986), 170–1, appearances of George and Theodore in the tenth century.

[72] *De cura pro mortuis gerenda*, XVI (19), cited Erdmann, *Origin*, 7 n. 9. Augustine was certain about his informants: 'non incertis rumoribus, sed testibus certis'.

[73] *Life of Columba*, I.11 (110–11).

[74] *Hist. Lang.*, 121–2.

always 'work'.[75] Gundovald having heard of a Byzantine ruler who took the thumb of saint Sergius into battle, decided to get a piece of a finger for himself. His wish proved hard to effect for under repeated blows the relic splintered, and bits, as Gregory puts it, 'dropped out of sight in different directions.' Such primitive surgery clearly displeased Sergius since Gundovald was killed soon after in a particularly violent manner.[76]

Saints, dead or alive, needed careful handling, and one cannot help recalling Gerald of Wales's observation about Irish saints of which Robert Bartlett has recently reminded us. Where there were no castles, he said, you needed 'particularly active[,] vindictive and protective saints'.[77] Here we should remind ourselves that war was but one end of a spectrum of aspects of life in which the power of the holy man could be demonstrated. This occurred most frequently in the conquest of illness: every saint—is there an exception ?—was believed to have healed, if not in their lifetime, then afterwards. Many of them also freed prisoners, and many defended possessions which had been given to them while they lived, or to the churches where they were believed to be present even after death. Both liturgical objects, and lands with the people and their animals who lived on them could profit from such heavenly defenders who worked in ways like those they used in war. What is striking, however, is that among those historians whom we are considering, only Gregory provides examples of this kind of intervention. I cannot resist sharing one extreme case which involved the assailant on the saint's property in an enforced and fatal athleticism. A soldier tried to reach with his lance the gold dove hanging above the tomb of St Denis in Paris. As he climbed up on to the tomb his legs slipped, splaying out on either side of the tomb, crushing his testicles. Then, somehow or other, the saint ensured that as he fell further the point of his lance entered his side and killed him.[78] Was this kind of saintly protection story missing from Bede and Paul because English and Italian kingdoms were better governed than Frankish Gaul, or was something else involved ? The former seems unlikely, so the explanation may lie in the different ways in which authors looked at their worlds.[79]

[75] Farmer, *Communities*, 30, for *cappa* of Martin; Lane-Fox, *Pagans*, 121, the pagans in Rome trying in 394 to protect the city with images of Zeus and his golden thunderbolts known because Augustine mocked at it in the City of God: 133–4, other examples of statues placed to defend territory, in the last case the Christian emperor, Theodosius II, ordered their removal. When this was done three tribes invaded 'one for each statue'.

[76] *HF*, VII.31, VII.38 (413–14, 423).

[77] *The Making of Europe. Conquest, Colonization and Cultural Change 950–1350* (Harmondsworth, 1993), 79.

[78] *GM*, c. 71 (94–5); other examples *GM*, c. 60,65, 78( 84–5, 89–90, 101f). *HF* has many more.

[79] Cf. Wallace-Hadrill's suggestion, *Frankish Church*, 399, that Bede could have painted English history as dark as Gregory did that of Francia, if he had wished to.

On the other hand *some* aspects of saintly intervention differ because of different social structures. Gaul, and to a much lesser extent, Italy, have stories about the defence of towns: England lacks any in this early period.

So far I have not adduced any examples of peace being brought about through saintly intervention even though Jesus blessed the peacemakers, not those who made war. I only know of one example from the settlement historians I have just been discussing, and I suspect that that is not untypical of other sources.[80] Later, in the tenth and eleventh centuries, saints did play a large part in the Peace of God movement. Then huge gatherings of relics were orchestrated to induce fractious nobles to keep the peace, but that is another theme I have not time to follow now.[81] What, however, I must say here is that holy women are, in rather more cases than men, recorded as peacemakers. Radegund, notably, wrote letters to kings urging them to make peace rather than war.[82] What success she had we do not know. But she and other female holy ones, were generally described in the same militaristic language as men, although they almost never involved themselves with war.[83] Genovefa of Paris, who organised what a recent scholar has called a 'prayer marathon' to save Paris from the Huns, is a notable exception.[84]

These historians of the settlement period have concerned us so long because they set the stage for the way that saints were supposed to intervene for the rest of the middle ages and well beyond. The main parameters within which holy people were believed to work did not change out of recognition. These underlying continuities in the place of the saints in warfare and disorder may say something about the influence of works of history as well as the stability of society. After all Bede, Paul the Deacon and Gregory survive in large numbers of manuscripts, testifying to their being read all over Europe, and being recopied over many centuries.[85] One may, however, briefly observe

---

[80] Gregory, *HF*, IV.49 (246).

[81] Cf. *The Peace of God, Social Violence and Religious Response in France around the Year 1000*, ed. Thomas Head and Richard Landes (Ithaca and London, 1992).

[82] *The Life of Radegund by Baudonivia*, 10 (*Sainted Women of the Dark Ages*, ed. and trans. Jo Ann McNamara, John E. Halborg with E. Gordon Whatley (Durham N.C., and London, 1992) [hereafter *Sainted Women*], 93, cf. 9, female peacemakers could also be powerful friends and dangerous enemies); Van Dam, *Saints*, 34, on Radegund and peace.

[83] *Sainted Women*, 12–14, and 162 (Jonas of Bobbio on Burgundofara [603–45] in his *Vita S. Columbani*, II.11), 229 (anon., *Vita Sanctae Gertrudis* [628–58], miracle 2). Both of these are late seventh-century texts.

[84] *The Life of Genovefa, a Virgin of Paris in Gaul*, 10–11 (*Sainted Women*, 23–4, and 4, for the comment)

[85] Bernard Guenée, *Histoire et Culture historique dans l'Occident médiéval* (Paris, 1980), 250, for Bede and Gregory. For Paul see Goffart, *Narrators*, 329.

that during the second invasion period the 'territorialise ion' of the saints went much further, to include the development in the late tenth and eleventh centuries of ways to stir up a sluggish sain to act on behalf of his earthly followers. This subject has recently been fascinatingly discussed by Lester Little in a book with the pithy title *Benedictine Maledictions*.[86] It is interesting that the earliest references to such practices among Christians, in which a saint's relics were literally grounded, and a liturgical strike proclaimed, go back to Gregory's time.[87] Then when some fields belonging to St Andrew's church at Agde had been taken by the count, the local bishop piled briars on top of Andrew's tomb, blocked the entrance to the church in a similar way, and threatened the saint with a blackout around his tomb, and a musical silence until he ensured that the stolen estate was restored.

So, by the time Gerold told his stories of ancient heroes, and of one much nearer to his day, the idea that a holy person could intervene in war, either during their lifetime or afterwards, was very much part of the contemporary thought-world. All sorts of saints, even someone who refused to fight for the emperor once he had become a Christian, like Martin, developed warlike capacities, sometimes long after they were dead.[88] So Cuthbert, who emerges from the early lives as a peaceful person, became the protector of the folk living in the north-east, able to strike the Conqueror with an unseasonable heat so that he had to retreat from Durham.[89] Durham, we may remind ourselves, was still in a disputed border between different kingdoms in the eleventh century, just as Tours had been in Gregory's time, and it was too an area, like Ireland, with few castles.[90] The saints were badly needed there.

[86] *Benedictine Maledictions. Liturgical Cursing in Romanesque France* (Ithaca and London, 1993).

[87] *GM*, c. 78 (101). Little does not mention this but refers, 84, to another case involving the tomb of St Mitrias; Gregory, *Gloria Confessorum*, c. 70 (*Gregory of Tours. Glory of the Confessors*, trans R. Van Dam (Liverpool, 1988), 73–4). For a pagan equivalent in which a statue of Ares, the war god, was chained to protect a town against local bandits see Lane-Fox, *Pagans*, 133–4.

[88] Cardini, *Cavalleria*, 149, suggesting the change had occurred by 459, little more than sixty years after his death (397). Cf. Farmer, *Communities*, 24–6.

[89] David Rollason, *Saints and Relics in Anglo-Saxon England* ( Oxford, 1989), 93, draws attention to a miracle in the Anonymous Life occurring while Cuthbert was 'in camp with the army, in the face of the enemy' suggesting that before his conversion he was a typical noble. For the posthumous saint defending his people see W. Aird, 'St Cuthbert, the Scots and the Normans', in *Anglo-Norman Studies*, XVI (1994), 1–20, at 17.

[90] Bartlett, *Making of Europe*, 79, citing Aelred of Rievaulx's statement that when the Scots invaded *c.* 1079 the English had 'no fortification to flee to'. In contrast Benedicta Ward, *Miracles and the Medieval Mind* (1982), 97, suggests that the dead Becket was not needed to defend Christ Church's estates because other means were available to the monks.

Looking back across the whole terrain which has been surveyed it becomes clearer just why the saints became so involved with warfare.[91] They were needed from the fifth century onwards in societies which usually lacked rulers strong enough either to keep the peace within their realms, or to defend them from outside attack. In such an unstable situation the great shrines which had grown around the tombs of holy men and women, with their conspicuous wealth and great estates, were peculiarly vulnerable. Their guardians, lacking sufficient earthly defenders, turned to their heavenly patrons, and then, when it seemed that their prayers had been answered, made what they could of those interventions in verbal propaganda, of which we hear an echo in chronicles and miracle stories. Some saints by the late eleventh century, like Maurice in the Empire, had been adopted by a ruling house so that they became quasi-national patron saints, but nowhere in Europe was there a place far from a wonderworker who might, perhaps only occasionally, come to the defence of his people, of his special community.[92] Sometimes, as at Martin's Tours, Julian's Brioude or Cuthbert's Durham, there seemed to be a kind of *cordon sanitaire* around the shrine to be penetrated at one's peril.[93] Part of its danger arose from the utter undependability of the saints' intervention: their capriciousness increased the terror with which they were invested, just as was the case with earthly lords.

But until Gerold's time none of the early military saints, with the one exception of Maurice, had put down such deep roots into patches of western European soil. None of them was the most important saint for any great land-owning church until after Orderic was writing, and so had not become the inescapable defender of any particular part of the world like Martin or Denis, Cuthbert, Patrick or Swithun. The chaplain Gerold knew tales of the early military saints but probably most of them were old stories from distant places. Any modern miracles

[91] There is much else which could have been mentioned: e.g. the inscription of Christian talismans on armour, rituals to bless armour and those who wielded it.
[92] For Maurice see Ortenberg, *English Church*, 46–9: Henry Mayr-Harting, 'The church of Magdeburg: Its Trade and its Town in the Tenth and Early Eleventh Centuries', in *Church and City 1000–1500. Essays in Honour of Christopher Brooke*, ed. David Abulafia, Michael Franklin and Miri Rubin (Cambridge, 1992), 129–34. For national patron saints see *Saints and their Cults. Studies in Religious Sociology, Folklore and History*, ed. Stephen Wilson (Cambridge, 1983), espec. Gabrielle M. Spiegel, 'The Cult of St Denis and Capetian Kingship', 141–68.
[93] Tours: Gregory *HF*, II.37 (151–2); Brioude: Gregory, *Vita Juliani*, 13 (171–2); Durham: see Aird 'St Cuthbert', n. 89 above. For similar sacred precincts in early Irish ecclesiastical legislation and later Welsh Lives: Kathleen Hughes, *Early Christian Ireland: Introduction to the Sources* (1972), 80–2; Wendy Davies, 'Property Rights and Property Claims in Welsh "Vitae" of the Eleventh Century', in *Hagiographie, Cultures et Sociétés IVe-XIIe siècles* (*Etudes Augustiniennes* (Paris, 1981)), 515–33. I am indebted to Dr Julia Crick and Professor Davies for drawing these to my attention.

about the earlier military saints which he might have known would almost certainly have come to him from returning Crusaders, for in the east, as we have seen, they had been active in battle for a very long time.[94] He chose, one may suggest, to speak of those saints, rather than of awkward local, 'territorialised' holy men, to his knightly audience because they had actually lived and died as soldiers, rather than as bishops, monks or even kings. And although the less venerable saints of the settlement period, and indeed their later successors, continued to watch over their lands for many centuries, in some sense a more surprising future lay with the oldest group of military martyrs.[95] As Orderic wrote they were coming into renewed significance as military men across Europe came to share a common outlook with common ideals. Behind that change was the coming into being from the mid-eleventh century onwards of a more stable political situation across the region, allowing knights to find models in the lives of professionals in a distant imperial age. For many earlier centuries their deaths for the faith had been had recalled in the ceremonies of the church, but now they could ride out again as models for living and fighting.

[94] See n. 71 above.
[95] One may refer to the emergence of military fraternities dedicated to George, or of Sebastian as patron of archers, for example.

# WILLIAM COBBETT: PATRIOT OR BRITON?

## By John Stevenson

READ 20 OCTOBER 1995 AT THE UNIVERSITY OF EDINBURGH

COBBETT remains best known to historians and to a wider audience as one of the two or three major figures in the popular radicalism of the early nineteenth century: one of the leading actors in the agitations which eventually led to the Great Reform Act of 1832 and a persistent tribune of the people at a time of profound economic and social change. Fundamental to his influence and reputation was his career as a popular journalist, in his own time regarded as a phenomenon and capable of almost single-handedly turning the labouring poor from machine-breaking and insurrection into more peaceful and productive paths. Famously, Cobbett was envisaged in Bamford's *Passages in the Life of a Radical* as the instrument whereby the disturbances of the post-war years were channelled into parliamentary reform. Opening his account of 1816 with a great litany of riot, insurrection and distress, Bamford noted that it was also in 1816 that Cobbett wrote his *Address to the Journeymen and Labourers*, published in November 1816 as the sole contents of the first cheap edition of the *Register*, priced at twopence. Cobbett's linking of 'our present miseries' to the need for parliamentary reform had an immense circulation, reaching an estimated 200,000 within two months. Its effects were no less dramatic according to Bamford:

> ... the writings of William Cobbett suddenly became of great authority; they were read on nearly every cottage hearth in the manufacturing districts of 'South Lancashire, in those of Leicester, Derby and Nottingham; also in many of the Scottish manufacturing towns. Their influence was speedily visible; he directed his readers to the true cause of their sufferings—misgovernment; and to its proper corrective—parliamentary reform. Riots soon became scarce, and from that time they have never obtained their ancient vogue with the labourers of this country."[1]

In spite of a degree of *post hoc* reasoning, Cobbett's influence and reputation was to remain singular. Whatever else, he must be regarded as one of the most successful and prolific writers in early nineteenth-century England. For over thirty years he produced his *Political Register*,

[1] S. Bamford, *Passages in the Life of a Radical* (Fitzroy edn, Dublin, 1967), 13.

week in week out, whether in prison, in exile or at home. It has been estimated that during his long journalistic and literary career he published between ten and twenty million words, contributing several thousand each week to the *Register* as well as producing a stream of pamphlets, essays and books on a very wide range of topics. An advertisement for his works near the end of his life, in 1831, itemises fifteen titles in print under four sub-heads: first, books for teaching languages, including Cobbett's English and French Grammars; second, books on 'Domestic Management and Duties', such as Cobbett's *Cottage Economy* and *Advice to Young Men*; third, books on 'Rural Affairs', which included *Cobbett's English Gardener* and *Cobbett's Woodlands*; and, lastly, his works on the 'Management of National Affairs', *Paper Against Gold*, the *Rural Rides* and the *Poor Man's Friend*.[2] Even this fairly formidable list of works in print excluded a mass of earlier projects, set down or sold to others to meet debts and obligations, including Cobbett's *Parliamentary Register*, now known as *Hansard*, and his separate *Parliamentary History*. It excluded the voluminous writings of his first incarnation as Peter Porcupine in the United States in the 1790s and the work Cobbett himself regarded as his most successful publication after *Rural Rides*, his *History of the Protestant Reformation in England and Ireland*, first published in letter form in 1824–7. Undoubtedly vastly popular in its day, Cobbett claimed that *only* sales of the Bible outstripped those of his *History of the Protestant Reformation*. Although we may see Cobbett being tempted to hyperbole, his most diligent biographer, the late George Spater, puts the sales figures for this work within two years of publication at 700,000 copies. It is hardly surprising, therefore, that in Robert Altick's list of nineteenth-century 'best-sellers', Cobbett appears no less than five times.[3]

Moreover, besides his astonishingly wide and successful printed output, Cobbett maintained a voluminous correspondence with members of his family, his various literary co-adjutors, and with political allies, friends and acquaintances on both sides of the Atlantic and further afield. Only a fraction of Cobbett's correspondence has been published, yet much of it has the spontaneity, directness, verve and, it must be said, occasional brutality of his printed work. Recently I have been working through an uncatalogued folio of Cobbett's letters written while he was in Newgate Prison in 1810 and listed as 'missing' by George Spater in his biography. They represent a fascinating and

[2] Endpiece to *Cobbett's Two-Penny Trash or Politics for the Poor* (London, 1831), 262–3.

[3] For a recent review of Cobbett's literary output, see L. Nattrass, *William Cobbett: The Politics of Style* (Cambridge, 1995), 1–5; G. Spater, *William Cobbett: The Poor Man's Friend* (2 vols., Cambridge, 1982), II, 443–5; R. Altick, *The English Common Reader* (London 1957), Appendix B. The last reference I owe to F.G.A.M. Aarts, 'William Cobbett: Radical, Reactionary and Poor Man's Grammarian', *Neophilolopus*, LXX (1986), 606.

entirely characteristic cross-section of Cobbett's concerns—many of them intensely practical, concerning such matters as the settling of his troublesome financial affairs in the wake of his fine and imprisonment, the management in his absence of the affairs of his farm and property, including detailed instructions to his young son, William, about managing the farm, the obtaining of a steward, the regulation of his labourers and setting their tasks, the organisation of relays of the Cobbett household to come and live with him in Newgate to assist him in his literary work, as well as correspondence with his brother-in-law in Spain to obtain some Merino sheep.[4] Cobbett's letters, scattered across more than a score of libraries and depositories in both England and the United States, as well as even further afield, offer to add yet more hundreds of thousands of words to the Cobbett canon.

But to his contemporaries, however, and perhaps even now, Cobbett was seen above all as the greatest and potentially most effective political journalist of his day. Indeed, as Bamford suggested, Cobbett's most influential period came after the long wars with Revolutionary France when in 1816 and 1817 his cheap version of the *Political Register* was achieving a circulation of between 40,000 and 70,000 copies a week. At this time it was alleged that Cobbett was read by everyone, from government ministers to handloom weavers. Hazlitt was to sum up his influence most pithily when he called Cobbett a virtual 'Fourth Estate' in the politics of the country.[5] Leigh Hunt eulogised Cobbett's virtual invention of the popular press:

> The invention of printing itself scarcely did more for the diffusion of knowledge and the enlightening of the mind than has been effected by the Cheap Press of this Country. Thanks to Cobbett! The commencement of his twopenny register was an era in the annals of knowledge and politics which deserves eternal commemoration.[6]

Cobbett was thus portrayed as one of the great engines of improvement, a diffuser of useful knowledge, and a genuine friend to the poor by advising them to seek their remedies through education, the acquisition of political rights and the pursuit of reform. Put simply, Cobbett's message in the post-war years was to try to persuade the poor and distressed that it was through parliamentary reform that they could better their lot, that the real cause of their sufferings was corruption of government and elections, that their poverty and hardships stemmed

[4] Nuffield College Library, Cole Collection, Cobbatt Papers, Vol. XXIX, Letters 1806–12.

[5] W. Hazlitt, 'Character of Cobbett', in *The Complete Works of William Hazlitt*, ed. P.P. Howe (21 vols., London, 1931), VIII, 50.

[6] Leigh Hunt, *White Hat*, 13 Nov. 1819, quoted in W.H. Wickwar, *The Struggle for the Freedom of the Press, 1819–1832* (London, 1928), 52–3; cited by Nattrass, *William Cobbett*, 5.

from waste and misgovernment, amplified by Pitt's funding of the Napoleonic Wars. Throughout his political career he was to cling to what might be called the 'Country' platform, that the country required reform, not revolution, expressed in his remark:

> I know of no enemy to reform and of the happiness of the country, so great as that man who would persuade you that we possess *nothing good* and that all must be torn to pieces ... We want great alteration, modification to suit the times and circumstances; but the great principles ought to be, and must be, the same, or else confusion will follow.[7]

Cobbett's other great influence has been upon the historiography of the industrial revolution and as a commentator upon the changes being wrought in the pivotal years through which he lived, almost from the accession of George III to the accession of Queen Victoria, the classic period of the first industrial revolution as described by the Hammonds, Ashton and Cole. It was G.D.H. Cole who referred to Cobbett as the spokesman of the first generation of industrial workers 'torn from the land and flung into the factory'.[8] Right up to our own day, Cobbett's most famous work, his *Rural Rides*, has been seen as one of the classic contributions to the debate on the transformation of Britain from a rural, agricultural society to an urban and industrial one. If a single sentiment can be said to animate it, it is that the social conditions he saw about him in the rural counties in the 1820s represented a disastrous deterioration from those he had known in his youth. Cobbett's lament about a lost Golden Age for the labourers and yeomen of rural England provided one side of that powerful stream of criticism of the process of urbanisation and industrialisation of which the other lay in the exposure of conditions in the new environment through the 'condition of England' novels and the Parliamentary Blue Books.[9] Cobbett provided the sense of a lost rural idyll, an ideal of harmony and prosperity, already being undermined in the era after the Napoleonic Wars by a new world of commerce and social antagonism. This view has tended to shift appreciation of Cobbett towards the debate about the nature and consequences of the industrial and agricultural revolutions—a proponent of 'the world we have lost' and the celebration of a land lost and scarred, blighted forever by the rise of commerce and industry. Hence Cobbett figures prominently in the so-called 'Wiener thesis', British culture's apparent resistance to and devaluing of entrepren-

---

[7] *Political Register*, 11 Feb. 1816.
[8] G.D.H. Cole, *The Life of William Cobbett* (3rd edn, London, 1947), 11.
[9] See J. Stevenson, 'Social Aspects of the Industrial Revolution', in P. O'Brien and R. Quinault (eds.), *The Industrial Revolution and British Society* (Cambridge, 1993), 229–32, 249–51.

eurship and enterprise, and even attracted attention as a forerunner of ethical socialism.[10]

But Cobbett's intellectual pedigree did not lie in the world of Peel and Cobden, rather it belonged to the great maelstrom of events which burst over the Atlantic world from the 1770s. One of Cobbett's earliest memories was of attending the great hop-fair at Weyhill in the autumn of 1776 when news of the British capture of Long Island, carried by an Extraordinary *Gazette*, burst upon the assembled company, provoking lengthy and acrimonious debate. Cobbett and his father were among that part of the company which retired to an apartment where 'Washington's health, and success to the Americans, were repeatedly toasted'.[11] Cobbett joined the army after the loss of America; his formative years were spent as a soldier on Britain's imperial frontier in Canada; and received his discharge and returned to England two years after the fall of the Bastille. As with so many others of his generation his 'mental furniture' was to be dominated by the turbulent intellectual climate of the French Revolution, the event that produced such a prodigious diaspora of mind and feeling. This was the generation for whom Hazlitt attempted to provide an epitaph:

> Kind feelings and generous actions there always have been, and there always will be, while the intercourse of mankind shall endure: but the hope, that such feelings and such actions might become universal, rose and set with the French revolution. That light seems to have been extinguished for ever in this respect. The French revolution was the only match that ever took place between philosophy and experience: and waking from the trance of theory to the sense of reality, we hear the words, *truth, reason, virtue, liberty*, with the same indifference or contempt, that the cynic who has married a jilt or a termagant, listens to the rhapsodies of lovers.[12]

Cobbett can be seen as a late entrant to this debate and one whose apparently maverick and multifarious concerns create problems as to where he should be placed. As Ian Dyck has reminded us, Cobbett has had a diverse range of admirers and commentators, a notable company which includes Karl Marx, Matthew Arnold, G.D.H. Cole, G.K. Chesterton, A.J.P. Taylor, Raymond Williams, Michael Foot, Asa Briggs, Edward Thompson, the former editor of *Private Eye*, Richard Ingrams and the late Lord Grimond. Although the majority of these figures belong to left of centre, it is apparent that Cobbett cannot be

[10] See M.J. Wiener, *English Culture and the Decline of the Industrial Spirit, 1850–1980* (Cambridge, 1981).
[11] Cole, *Cobbett*, 19.
[12] *The Collected Works of William Hazlitt*, ed. A.R. Waller and A. Glover (12 vols., London, 1902), II, 156.

claimed exclusively by either the Left or the Right. Cobbett's distinguished career as an advocate of parliamentary reform and a champion of the common people had been preceded in the 1790s by a decade of vehement pro-government propaganda as Peter Porcupine, when Cobbett had defended Pitt and the British Constitution, denounced Paine, Priestley and the radicals, and fiercely upheld the necessity of war with France. Moreover, Cobbett's liberal credentials have always had to contend with his fierce prejudices. His railings against a range of minorities, including Quakers, Methodists, Jews, Scots and intellectuals in general have raised difficulties for his biographers and commentators. Cobbett, hailed by A.H. Halsey as an 'ethical socialist', has also been seen by W.D. Rubinstein as an exponent of the 'dark side of populism'.[13] As the latter has pointed out, it is not difficult to find examples throughout Cobbett's writings of condemnation of any of those whom he saw as parasites upon the 'real' England, often lumped together in a veritable bestiary of *bêtes noires*. Thus Cobbett on the growth of middlemen in the food trade—the Quakers: 'There was that numerous sect, the Quakers, engendered by the Jewish system of usury. Till excises and loan mongering began, these vermin were never heard of in England. They seemed to have been hatched by that fraudulent system, as maggots are bred by putrid meat.'[14] On the Jews, in 1826, well into Cobbett's career as a champion of popular radicalism:

> The debt, gentlemen, amounts to eight hundred millions of money ... Let me remark that this debt, this horrible and incredible parcel of money has been lent us; the fundholder, the money-broker, the stock-jobber, and Jews and all the vermin of this description who prey upon the vitals of the people, tell us they lent us this money; lent us what?
>
> Is it possible! What! the Jews to lend *us* ten times as much money as ever was in this world! Where did they get it?[15]

The Scots too were the butt of his wrath expressed as both a general and a particular prejudice. Eighteen months before his tour of Scotland in 1832 he was writing

> Base and degraded indeed are we if we suffer in silence those beggarly burgoo-eaters to swagger over us, while they are sucking our blood ... These vagabonds have contributed largely towards the ruin of England: they have been sucking its blood ever since James

[13] W.D. Rubinstein, 'British Radicalism and the "Dark Side" of Populism', in *Elites and the Wealthy in Modern British Society* (Bighton, 1987), 339–73; see also K.W. Schweizer and J.W. Osborne, *Cobbett in his Times* (Leicester, 1990), 70–7.
[14] W. Reitzel (ed.), *The Autobiography of William Cobbett* (London, 1957), 193.
[15] Ibid., 190.

I ... but ever since George III mounted the throne, they have been eating up our very flesh ... They will *not work*; they depend on the taxes in all countries whether they go....[16]

To the Scots as universal scroungers Cobbett added his venom against the Scottish intellectuals, dredging the sump of his venom he referred to the 'Scotch Jews', or more simply 'Scotch feelosophers':

The truth was, that these men were mere writers: they were writers by trade: they understood that trade pretty well: but they knew nothing of the real situation of this or any other country. Such men knew a great deal about words, but, what the devil could they know of men and things; they were extremely enlightened; but they had no knowledge. Hence all this stupid stuff in praise of manufacturing establishments: hence all their exaltations at the prosperity of Manchester and Paisley, hence all their everlasting clamour in praise of paper money.[17]

Space prevents pursuing further the full range of the objects of Cobbett's vigorous range of prejudices, many of them, I am sure, already familiar: London, tea-drinking, tithes, birth control, paper money. What, if anything, informed this apparent rag-bag of prejudices? Some lines are clear enough, Cobbett's contempt for the corrupt money-men whom he saw as the authors of the nation's ills. Jews, Quakers and Scots were on the receiving end of Cobbett's vulgar attack because they were the financial exploiters of the country through the funding system and paper money. These views are startling to those who would wish to see the radical tradition as tolerant, rational and progressive. But it was now many years ago that Geoffrey Best urged us to recognise the 'flag-waving, foreigner-hating' side of popular politics.[18] It has led some to see in Cobbett's adoption of racial abuse and stereotyping, in his agrarianism, in his populism, in his anti-intellectualism and his 'Little Englandism', something of the prototype for an authentic English 'populism' that might in another age have verged upon the kind of blood and soil fascism found in the twentieth century.[19] But models for Cobbett's views lie much nearer to hand in his own period. One of the most fertile explanatory tools for the discussion of eighteenth-century politics is what is variously described as the 'Country', 'Patriot' or Country-Tory platform. As Professor Speck has demonstrated in his volume on Society and Literature in the

---

[16] See D. Green (ed.), *Cobbett's Tour in Scotland by William Cobbett* (Aberdeen, 1957), 193.

[17] Reitzel, *Autobiography*, 194–5.

[18] G. Best, 'The Making of the English Working Class', *Historical Journal*, VIII (1965), 278.

[19] See Rubinstein, 'Dark Side', *passim*.

early eighteenth century, Addison's character, Mr Foxhunter, introduced in the *Freeholder* in March 1716 already articulated a set of attitudes which find direct responses in Cobbett. These formed the prototype of the Tory Squires caricatured by Macaulay in his famous Third Chapter. According to Macaulay:

> His opinions respecting religion, government, foreign countries and former times ... were the opinions of a child ... His animosities were numerous, and bitter. He hated Frenchmen and Italians, Scotchmen and Irishmen, Papists and Presbyterians, Independents and Baptists, Quakers and Jews. Towards London and Londoners he felt an aversion which more than once produced important political effects.

Macaulay's Country Squire was based on his reading of the literature of the late seventeenth and early eighteenth centuries. Mr Foxhunter holds just these opinions, so with some important modifications does Swift, Cobbett's acknowledged mentor.[20] Thus when we hear Cobbett's condemnation of London, as the great 'Wen', literally a giant cyst, drawing to itself the goodness of the body—the Body Politic—we are on the familiar ground of Country Party ideology. Cobbett's denunciation of 'The Thing'—the web of capital, speculation and finance which so much offended him as the source of high taxation and therefore poverty, echoes Mr Foxhunter in 1716:

> He expatiated on the inconvenience of Trade, that carried from us the Commodities of our Country, and made a Parcel of Upstarts as rich as Men of the most ancient Families in England ... He would undertake to prove, Trade would be the Ruine of the English Nation ... to which he added two or three curses upon the London Merchants, not forgetting the Directors of the Bank.[21]

It is clear from this why Cobbett might be ascribed the title of a 'one-man Country Party', applying to the conditions of the late eighteenth and early nineteenth centuries the strictures of a Swift. As Professor Dickinson has reminded us, the primary concern of the Country Party interest was the fear that the Court had acquired the means of corrupting the constitution.[22] For Cobbett, those visible signs became evident during the 1800s after his return from America. Cobbett opposed the Peace of Amiens because he felt it allowed France to enjoy

[20] W.A. Speck, *Society and Literature in England, 1700–60* (Dublin, 1983), 1–13. For the fullest exposition of 'Country Ideology' see H.T. Dickinson, *Liberty and Property: Political Ideology in Eighteenth-Century Britain* (London, 1977), 153–92.
[21] Speck, *Society and Literature*, 6–7.
[22] Dickinson, *Liberty and Property*, 169–70.

too many of her gains and displayed a supine weakness on the part of the Government.[23] Shocked, too, by what he perceived as the falling off of the living standards of the labourer, Cobbett became a parliamentary reformer when he considered standing at the Honiton Election of 1806. Cobbett's prescription then for remedying of the abuses of the County was simple—the ending of the corruption of elections. According to Cobbett, the abandonment of treating, bribery and the trade in seats would *in itself* be a cure-all for the ills of the nation. Cobbett opined:

> But, Gentlemen, as it is my firm determination never to receive a farthing of the public money, so it is my determination equally firm, never, in any way whatever, to give one farthing of my own money to any man, in order to induce him to vote, or to cause others to vote, for me; and, being convinced, that it is this practice of giving, or promising to give, money, or money's worth, at elections, being convinced, that it is this disgraceful, this unlawful, this profligate, this impious practice, to which are to be ascribed all our calamities and all the dangers that now stare us in the face, I cannot refrain from exhorting you to be against all attempts at such practices, constantly and watchfully upon your guard.[24]

Cobbett retained this Country Party faith in the possibility of purifying the constitution. Towards the end of his life, when his faculties were still in full working order, he declared famously that 'I wanted to see no innovation in England. All I wished and all I strove for, was the Constitution of England, undefiled by corruption.'[25] Although Cobbett was eventually pushed along the road to a more extensive view of parliamentary reform, he always approached it from the view of one who saw the task as the restoration of something lost—a return to things as they were in the 'golden age' of his youth.

The other vital theme Cobbett inherited from the eighteenth century, and which is crucial to an understanding of his writings, is that of the 'Patriot', understood both as a genuine love of country and as an oppositionist stance. Cobbett's early career as a soldier left him with an innate sense of the place of England in the world. It is important to remember that Cobbett was an expatriate in North America on three separate occasions, as well as spending time in France. Cobbett's stance as a pro-Government journalist based in America during the 1790s was steadfastly bellicose. Not only did he oppose peace with France but he prepared anti-invasion tracts and co-operated with Windham in advocating a well-trained volunteer force to resist a French

---

[23] Reitzel, *Autobiography*, 89.
[24] *Political Register*, 7 June 1806.
[25] Reitzel, *Autobiography*, 214.

invasion. Nor was this only a feature of his earlier life, writing to an American friend in 1832, he made a wholly characteristic observation:

> You will see, that we are going to have the *Reform* that I used to talk so much about. Those terrestrial devils, Castlereagh, Liverpool and Canning, are all gone to their father below. We shall have as cheap a government as yours and (which I tell you as a secret), we shall not let the 'American Navy' swagger about the world as it does now; and mind I tell you so. I like your country very well; but the world was not made for any navy but that of England to swagger in.[26]

But to assert Cobbett's patriotic credentials takes us to the heart of the complexities of ideological definitions in the Revolutionary era: a world in which the terms 'patriot', 'conservative', 'loyalist' and 'Briton' jostle in a confusing kaleidoscope. Arguably, one of the most important features of Britain after 1789 is the way in which the forces of patriotism were marshalled in defence of the existing order. The established order, it has been argued, was especially successful in appropriating the language and symbols of patriotism during the war years. Conservatives having embraced patriotism during the fervent years of the French Wars, were not inclined to allow their opponents to repossess the language of patriotism in peace-time.[27] Linda Colley has entertained the powerful argument that in Britain, in contrast to the other opponents of Revolutionary and Napoleonic France, the language of patriotism was decoupled from its anti-establishment and potentially radical inheritance. Radicals vacated the realm of conventional xenophobic patriotism and left it to the élite to exploit for defensive purposes.[28] Patriotism in Britain, unlike for the supporters of the Spanish Constitution of 1812 or the War of German Liberation, became, it is argued, conservative property. We would have to say that whatever general truth this may hold, it does not hold for Cobbett. Cobbett was one of those, Leigh Hunt was another, who sought to justify redress for the ills of the country in the language of the 'true Patriot'. Cobbett may have been the kind of Patriot who *in extremis* might have cut off the head of his king to save his country, but we would be mistaking our man if we failed to recognise that he retained an attachment to the land and people of England, to its army and navy, to its monarchy and to its traditional social order. He was persistent in his defence of the landed interest: he complained that the 'Ancient nobility and gentry of the kingdom' had been thrust out of public employment and that 'a

[26] Huntingdon Library, letter to Mr. John Tredwell, 28 March 1832.
[27] See D. Eastwood, 'Patriotism and the English State in the 1790s', in *The French Revolution and British Popular Politics*, ed. M. Philip (Cambridge, 1991), 146–68.
[28] L. Colley, 'Whose Nation? Class and National Consciousness in Britain, 1750–1830', *Past and Present*, CXIII (1986), 97–117.

race of merchants and manufacturers and bankers and loan jobbers and contractors' have usurped their place. Cobbett wanted to see the nobility and gentry restored to their rightful dominance and the return of 'those assemblages and sports, in which the nobleman mixed with his peasants, which made the poor man proud of his inferiority and created in his breast a personal affection for his lord'. He found repugnant all signs of foreign 'effeminacy' of habits and manners in which capacious hold-all was stored items as varied as Italian opera and tea-drinking.[29] He gloried in what he saw as 'English' manners and habits, such as rural sports. Nor were these idle words, spending a considerable amount of time resurrecting the dying martial game of single-stick fighting at Botley where 30 guineas was awarded as the first prize. Thousands of spectators travelled from all over southern England to witness a post-harvest spectacle of two combatants at a time, each with one arm tied behind his back and equipped in the other with a stout stick, attempting to 'break' the head, as it was put, of his opponent by drawing one inch of blood from his skull.[30]

Cobbett nearly always referred affectionately to the army and the navy and retained a strong allegiance to an ideal monarchy. Nor was this abandoned when Cobbett adopted a more openly anti-governmental stance from the post-war years. In the autumn of 1820, only months after returning from forced exile in the United States, to escape what he was convinced was the threat of prosecution, he was quite literally playing the courtier to Queen Caroline, the estranged wife of George IV, freshly returned to London to claim her rights to the throne. Cobbett's daughter Anne described how he had dressed himself in a black satin suit and played 'Blind Man's Bluff'. If there is something faintly ludicrous about the Botley tribune turned courtier, there is no doubting his genuine grief at her death in 1821.[31] A champion of the common people, Cobbett found little difficulty in maintaining his patriotic stance. He did, however, distinguish between patriotism and loyalism, identifying the former with a pure love of one's country and the desire to see all the people prosperous and happy, the latter, the perquisite of those having some measure of privilege in society, who supported their government only in order retain their privileges.

But was Cobbett, in the terms we have learned from Professor Colley, a Briton? Colley has argued powerfully the case for the creation of a British identity very largely in the years spanned by Cobbett's lifetime. That identity we have been urged was forged primarily of two elements,

[29] Nattrass, *William Cobbett*, 21–2.

[30] See I. Dyck, *William Cobbett and Rural Popular Culture* (Cambridge, 1992), 21.

[31] See J. Stevenson, 'The Queen Caroline Affair', in *London in the Age of Reform*, ed. J. Stevenson (Oxford, 1977), 123, 134; also Nuffield College, Cole Collection, vol. XXX, William Cobbett to Samuel Clarke, 17 Aug. 1821.

anti-Catholicism and the long succession of wars—the second Hundred Years War—against France. 'Protestant warfare' helped larger and larger numbers of the inhabitants of the United Kingdom to think of themselves as British. Now Cobbett offers a useful test case for her thesis and perhaps one to give pause for thought. An often bellicose patriot as we have seen, certainly, but one who stands right at the intersection of so many of the crucial issues raised by Colley's *Britons*.[32] Cobbett used the words English and British often indiscriminately, and tended when speaking of the British to subsume all the constituent parts as honorary English, unless being singled out for condemnation. What was most striking, given his many prejudices, was Cobbett's inclusion of the Irish as fellow countrymen. Thus he wrote:

> I have never been able, for one single moment, to look upon Ireland or Scotland, other than as parts of my native country. I have never been able, for one single moment, to view an Irishman as other than as my own countryman. Therefore I have always considered the wrongs done to Ireland (and they are beyond all number and beyond all magnitude); I have always considered these wrongs as participated in by myself.[33]

But what is most striking and contradictory is Cobbett's attitude to Catholicism. His *History of the Protestant Reformation* was an astonishing publishing success. In it, Cobbett argued that the Protestant Reformation had been a disaster for both England and Ireland. Convinced by reading the Catholic historian John Lingard's *History of England*, first appearing in 1819, Cobbett eulogised the communal functions of the medieval church and the monasteries in particular.[34] He ripped into Henry VIII and Elizabeth as despoilers of the people's inheritance with a gusto and venom which makes the *Protestant Reformation* still a brilliant, if absurdly one-sided, polemic. Cobbett's outrage at the destruction of ancient tombs and memorials almost outdoes Burke in his regard for the relics of the past. What Cobbett asserted was a kind of 'Tudor Yoke' where the lands and wealth taken from the monasteries had been appropriated by the monarchy for their own purposes, squandered on favourites and made the foundation of the fortunes of many of the great houses now foremost in resisting reform and in extracting pensions and sinecures. Here was the origin of 'The Thing'— here lay the beginnings of the ruin of the common people. Cobbett's eulogy of medieval Catholicism and of its harmonious social order

[32] L. Colley, *Britons: Forging the Nation, 1707–1837* (New Haven and London, 1992), esp. 1–9.
[33] *Political Register*, 11 March 1834.
[34] For Cobbett's use of Lingard, see Nattrass, *William Cobbett*, 157–82, esp. 172 ff.

suggests a somewhat more complex relationship between a 'British' identity and anti-Catholicism. It places Cobbett in the romantic context of Pugin's *Contrasts* and 'Young England'. Nor is this absurd, for his work is permeated with the individualism of the Romantic movement, its love of landscape, its self-conscious sense of the past, extravagance of prose and expression of natural feeling. In this context, Cobbett bears comparison with writers such as Scott and Chateaubriand.[35]

Cobbett can also be seen articulating sentiments which would become more familiar later in the nineteenth century. Amongst his best sellers referred to earlier were his Advice books and Grammars, which herald many of what might later be called 'Victorian values' of hard work, sober habits and a happy domestic life. There are many elements in Cobbett the self-made man which parallel his near contemporary Francis Place and, later, the work of Samuel Smiles. Cobbett left little excuse for the idle and the self-indulgent:

> I learned grammar when I was a private soldier on the pay of sixpence a day. The edge of my berth, or that of the guard-bed, was my seat to study in; my knapsack was my bookcase; a bit of board lying on my lap was my writing table; and the task did not demand anything like a year of my life. I had no money to purchase candle or oil; in winter time it was rarely that I could get any evening-light but that of *the fire*, and only my *turn* even of that. And if I, under such circumstances, and without parent or friend to advise or encourage me, accomplished this undertaking, what excuse can there be for *any youth*, however poor, however pressed with business, or however circumstanced as to room or other conveniences?[36]

But most unlikely of all, and hard as it can be to believe with some of Cobbett's most aggressive, abusive and bullying rhetoric ringing in our ears, is the Cobbett who carried forward from the eighteenth century the language of sensibility and feeling. Amongst his conduct books is his *Advice to a Lover* in which, characteristically, he called upon his own experience when courting a girl in Canada while a young soldier:

> ... my affection for her was very great: I spent no really pleasant hours but with her; I was uneasy if she showed the slightest regard for any other young man; I was unhappy if the smallest matter affected her health or spirits: I quitted her in dejection, and returned to her with eager delight: many a time when I could get leave but for a day, I paddled in a canoe two whole succeeding nights, in

[35] See W. Stafford, *Socialism, Radicalism, and Nostalgia: Social Criticism in Britain, 1775–1830* (Cambridge, 1987), p. 264.
[36] W. Cobbett, *Advice to Young Men* (1829), para. 44.

order to pass that day with her. If this was not love, it was first cousin to it; for as to any criminal intention, I no more thought of it, in her case, than if she had been my sister. Many times I put myself the question 'What am I at? Is not this wrong? Why do I go?' But still I went.[37]

We might say that with Cobbett the Country Party met with the Man of Feeling and produced Self-Help. He belongs to no one age nor does he fit easily into any simple transition from 'Patriot' to 'Briton'. Cobbett's identity and self-image were composed of overlapping ideas and sentiments drawn from the late eighteenth century but often more internally consistent than his apparently maverick prejudices would appear to allow.

[37] W. Cobbett, *Advice to a Lover* (London, 1937), 60–1.

# 'TO PLUCK BRIGHT HONOUR FROM THE PALE-FACED MOON'[1]: GENDER AND HONOUR IN THE CASTLEHAVEN STORY

## By Cynthia Herrup

READ 24 MARCH 1995 AT THE UNIVERSITY OF CAMBRIDGE

FOR Hotspur, honour was a thing self-evident—easy to recognise and to defend. As his name suggests, the younger Percy equated honour with battle, with the supposed clarities of spilt blood and martial conquest. We can all agree, I think, that honour was a touchstone for both the fictional and the authentic Percies, as well as for most other early modern people. However, from the distance of three centuries (as well, of course, as from the perspective of other characters in *Henry IV*) the concept seems considerably more complicated than Hotspur's claims imply.

More than fifteen years ago, Mervyn James, in a still invaluable essay on the subject, argued that early modern England experienced a transition between two distinct aristocratic views of honour—a traditional version defined by lineage, competitiveness and a propensity for violence (that is, a view very much like Hotspur's) and a second strain more meritocratic, moralistic and pacific than the first. The older view, James argued, valued autonomy and style over outcome; the newer notion replaced independence with obedience and fortuna with Christian providence.[2] But James's article, useful as it is, has begun to show its age. Its focus is too aristocratic, too male and too prescriptive.

---

[1] *Henry IV, Part 1*, I.iii. This paper relies on ongoing research into the trial of the 2nd earl of Castlehaven. It has benefited from the research assistance of Scott Lucas and Philippe Rosenberg as well as from the critical comments of Susan Amussen, Judith Bennett, Barbara Donagan, Barbara J. Harris, Kristen Neuschel, Linda Levy Peck and William Reddy. I also appreciate the comments received when I presented an earlier version of this essay at Vanderbilt University in November 1994. I would like to thank Lady Braye for permission to cite the Braye manuscripts on deposit in the Leicestershire Record Office, the Lamport Hall Trust for permission to cite the Isham Lamport manuscripts on deposit in the Northamptonshire Record Office, and Barbara Harris, Caroline Hibbard and Linda Pollock for allowing me to cite their unpublished work. This essay is dedicated to the memory of Sir Geoffrey Elton.

[2] Mervyn James, 'English Politics and the Concept of Honour 1485–1642' first published as *Past and Present*, supplement no. 3 (1978) and reprinted in *Society, Politics and Culture: Studies in Early Modern England* (Cambridge, 1986), 308–415.

137

It masks the fact that whatever the male elite may have believed, defining honour was neither their prerogative nor their monopoly. It tells us much about what a powerful group wanted honour to be, but not enough about how it was. And its chronology is too simple, making survivals from an older ethic anomalies rather than continuing competitors for authority. As careful as James was, his analysis deflects attention from some of the most important and most impenetrable qualities of early modern honour—its ubiquity, its tenacity and its complexity. Since 1978, the work of many people has shown us how much there is to be gained from broadening our perspective outward from the study of male aristocratic ideals of honour, from adopting a dialogic rather than a 'trickle-down' approach to the social mapping of the subject, from studying the influence of honour in the street, the tavern and the kitchen as well as the battlefield, the tilt yard and the library. And how much is to be gained as well by taking honour off its pedestal, by looking less at ideals of honour and more at how those ideals were breached and sustained through particular interactions and institutional forms.[3]

Reading early modern authors on the subject of honour, what comes through most strongly is not transition, but multi-vocality, even self-contradiction.[4] Tracing the workings of honour in particular circumstances, what seems most striking is not transparency, but plasticity. The essence of honour, we are told, was virtue, without which it was worthless, false coin, nothing 'but as a stape [stamp] set upon base bullion', yet virtue was almost as much of a jumble as was honour.[5] As

---

[3] See particularly Richard Cust, 'Honour and Politics in Early Stuart England: The Case of Beaumont v. Hastings', *Past and Present*, no. 149 (November 1995), 57–94; Laura Gowing, 'Gender and the Language of Insult in Early Modern London', *History Workshop Journal*, 35 (Spring 1993), 1–21; Laura Gowing, *Domestic Dangers: Women, Words and Sex in Early Modern London* (Oxford, 1996); Anthony Fletcher, 'Honour, Reputation & Local Officeholding in Elizabethan and Stuart England', in *Order and Disorder in Early Modern England*, ed. A. Fletcher and John Stevenson (Cambridge, 1985), 92–115; Anthony Fletcher, *Gender, Sex and Subordination in England 1500–1800* (1995), esp. ch. 7; Caroline Hibbard, 'The Theatre of Dynasty', in *The Stuart Court and Europe*, ed. Malcolm Smuts (Cambridge, forthcoming); Lyndal Roper, *Oedipus & the Devil: Witchcraft, Sexuality and Religion in Early Modern Europe* (1994), esp. chs. 3, 5; and the essays in this volume.

[4] Some of the discussions I have found most useful include John Norden, *The Mirror of Honour* (1587); Robert Ashley, *Of Honour* (c. 1596), ed. Virgil B. Heltzel (San Marino, 1947); William Segar, *Honour Military and Civil* (1602); John Cleland, *Institution of a Young Noble Man* (1607; facsimile repr. New York, 1948); Thomas Milles, *The Catalogue of Honour* (1610); Gervase Markham, *Honour in his Perfection* (1624); Francis Markham, *The Book of Honour* (1625); Richard Brathwaite, *The English Gentleman* (1630); Richard Brathwaite, *The English Gentlewoman* (1631); Fulke Greville, 'An Inquisition upon Fame and Honour', and 'A Letter to an Honourable Lady', both in *Certain Learned and Elegant Works of the Right Honourable Fulke Greville, Lord Brooke* (1633).

[5] Cleland, *Institution*, 10.

it appears in early modern discussions of it, honour was less a single value than a selection from a medley of values. It was both quality and commodity, inborn and achieved, self-generated and bestowed, activist and stoical. Honourable men could be quick to action or disinterested, quick to prayer or self-reliant, quick to success or unambitious, martial or peaceable, learned or plain, independent or obedient. Honour was both inherited and earned, aristocratic and meritocratic, dependent upon royal favour and upon community approval. Honour was its own reward, yet truest when publicly acknowledged, yet diminished by any concern for that acknowledgment. Honour, Francis Markham wrote in 1625, was 'the greatest gift belonging to this life', but also, it seems, one of the most slippery.[6] In part this was a response to changing circumstance, to a world where wealth and lineage seemed ever less invariably twinned, where appearances seemed ever more important and more deceptive. But to some extent, circumstances are always changing, and at a deeper level, the comprehensiveness of definition reflects honour's inherent sociability. Prescriptive writers attempted to stabilise the ideal by taking an ecumenical approach to its definition; comprehensiveness allowed honour to mean different things in different situations and allowed different people to mobilise different aspects of the concept's rhetorical power. Honour was desirable, valuable and never secure. And its reliance on public recognition, however narrowly defined, made its possession permanently impermanent.[7]

And, this, I think, helps to explain the growing concern in the sixteenth and early seventeenth centuries with honour as reputation. Reputation was the interpretive transaction through which discrete incidents became or did not become imbued with honour. Reputation was the gauge of one's public compatibility. Reputation translated acts into words. It was based not on character, but on presentation; it was not only of the moment, but also transcendent; it was not about what you did, but about what people thought about you did. Honour and reputation were symbiotic, but not identical. The potential disjuncture between them was a site of considerable anxiety,

[6] Markham, *Book of Honour* 25.

[7] England was not an honour/shame society in the classic sense, but the insecurity of honour is one way that early modern England does fit the Mediterranean model made famous in *Honour and Shame: Values of a Mediterranean Society*, ed. J. G. Peristiany (1965). This remains the classic anthropological discussion of honour, but for challenges to its wider applicability, see *Honour and Shame and the Unity of the Mediterranean*, ed. David Gilmore (special publication of the American Anthropological Association no. 22, 1987); Frank Henderson Stewart, *Honour* (Chicago, 1994). Scott Lucas suggested to me that in a society such as early modern England, it might also have been dangerous for writers to deny the validity of any particular claim to honour.

one that encompassed disquiet about the relationship of both behaviour to belief and individual to social group. In a society where direct action in defence of honour was increasingly discouraged, words and with them, reputation, took on ever greater import. This, despite the recognition that words were even less controllable than were actions.[8]

I want to use this paper to look at the workings of both honour and reputation in the trial for felony of Mervin Touchet, Baron Audley, known more commonly by his Irish title, the 2nd earl of Castlehaven. Castlehaven was tried and convicted in April, 1631, by a specially convened Court of the Lord High Steward on charges of rape and sodomy.[9] His reported victims were his second wife, Anne (he had allegedly assisted her servant in raping her, but since the law of rape recognised no accessories, he appeared as a principal), and his footman. His initial accuser was his son and heir, James. The earl was beheaded about three weeks after his conviction, having not only contested the charges, but also maintained his innocence at trial and on the scaffold. He claimed to be the victim of a conspiracy organised by his son and his wife, the one eager for his inheritance, the other for a younger sexual partner. Castlehaven's trial is *sui generis*—the number of peers tried for felony is tiny, the number executed is even smaller, and no other noble died solely for crimes that were quite so personal and quite so scandalous.[10] But for our purposes, this case has several distinct advantages. It was exceptionally elaborate.[11] It focused on both male

[8] Kristen Neuschel, *Word of Honour: Interpreting Noble Culture in Sixteenth-Century France* (Ithaca, 1989); Ann Rosalind Jones, 'Nets and Bridles: Early Modern Conduct Books and Sixteenth-Century Women's Lyrics', in *The Ideology of Conduct: Essays in the Literature and History of Sexuality*, ed. Nancy Armstrong and Leonard Tennenhouse (1987), 39–72; J.A. Sharpe, *Defamation and Sexual Slander in Early Modern England: the Church Courts at York*, Borthwick Papers 58 (York, 1980); Gowing, 'Language of Insult'; Laura Gowing, 'Women, Status and the Popular Culture of Dishonour', in this volume.

[9] When Parliament was not in session, peers were tried for felony or treason in a court presided over by a Lord High Steward (who was specially appointed for the occasion) sitting with a number of peers as jurors and the judges of the common law as advisers. See Luke Owen Pike, *A Constitutional History of the House of Lords* (1894), ch. XI.

[10] Most serious charges against peers involved treason and/or murder. The most notorious English counterparts to Castlehaven in this period were the earl and countess of Somerset (condemned for murder, but later pardoned); Charles, Lord Stourton and Thomas, Lord Dacre of the South, (each executed for murder);and Walter, Lord Hungerford (executed for treason and sodomy).

[11] Among aristocratic trials in this period, only the trial of the earls of Essex and Southampton in 1601 (*The Complete Collection of State Trials*, ed. Thomas Howell (1809–26) [hereafter *ST*], I, cols. 1333–69) brought more witnesses into court; only the defensive claims of the duke of Norfolk in 1571 (*ST*, I, cols. 957–1050) and the duke of Somerset in 1550 and 1551 (*ST*, I, cols. 510–28) were equally sophisticated.

and female aristocrats.[12] And it was a cause célèbre.[13]

However comprehensive a concept honour may have been in early modern England, it clearly was not broad enough to accommodate a man convicted of rape and sodomy or a woman who traded sex for murder. But stories of honour traduced can be every bit as revealing as stories of honour realised. If in this story, we ask how each of the principals reacted to their humiliation, we learn new things not only about the narrative, but also about the contingency of honour.

The Castlehaven story is an apt illustration of the value of studying honour through particular case studies. Because it concerns an aristocrat tried before aristocrats, this case reveals both the privileges of honour accorded a peer at law and the demands that honour placed upon peers trying one of their own in public. It shows the importance of institutional circumstance in the expression of honour, and the critical role of class in that expression. We have taken peers to be the 'honour community' *par excellence*, but the publicness of a legal setting demanded that peers display their honour before others as well as before their aristocratic brethren. Peers showed their virtue by being willing, on the one hand, to apply (at least occasionally) a moral code that proclaimed their ordinariness, while insisting, on the other hand, that they would only enforce that code through procedures that accentuated aristocratic particularities.[14] Castlehaven's peers condemned him, but to do so effectively, they had to respect the forms of legal and aristocratic custom. To do otherwise would delegitimate their actions.[15] The trial

---

[12] The other incidents involving both male and female peers were the trials of the earl and countess of Somerset (*ST*, II, cols. 951–1022), of Queen Anne Boleyn (*ST*, I, cols. 410–34) and of Queen Catherine Howard (*ST*, I, cols. 445–52). However, in the first instance, the pair were not at odds with one another, and in the trials of the two queens, where the king was the accuser, there were denials, but no countercharges.

[13] Manuscript versions of the trial began to circulate even before the earl was executed, and the first in a series of pamphlets on the case appeared in 1633. A large number of contemporary diaries and letters include comments upon the trial and/or execution. For details, see my work in progress, *Sex, Law and Patriarchy: The Trials of the 2nd earl of Castlehaven*.

[14] On English peers and the legal autonomy, see Public Record Office State Papers Domestic [hereafter PRO SP] 12/112/51 summarised in Penry Williams, *The Council in the Marches of Wales under Elizabeth I* (Cardiff, 1955), 61; C. Barber, *The Theme of Honour's Tongue: A Study of Social Attitudes in the English Drama from Shakespeare to Dryden* (Gothenburg Studies in English, 1985), 42–3; Lawrence Stone, *The Crisis of the Aristocracy 1558–1641* (Oxford, 1965), 235–9, 249ff; Hibbard, 'Theatre of Dynasty'; V.G. Kiernan, *The Duel in European History: Honour and the Reign of Aristocracy* (Oxford, 1986), especially c. 9. See also Ellery Schalk, 'Under the Law or Laws unto Themselves: Noble Attitudes and Absolutism in Sixteenth and Seventeenth Century France', *Historical Review/Revue Historique*, XV, 1 (1988), 279–92; Jay Smith, 'Our Sovereign's Gaze: Kings, Nobles and State Formation in Seventeenth-Century France', *French Historical Studies*, XVIII, 2 (1993), 396–415. More work needs to be done on the relationship of elites in England to the law.

[15] The Crown's convenient reinterpretation of the law regarding sodomy did, in fact,

shamed the earl not only by its accusations of criminal behaviour, but also by the spectacle of his public admission of both his and his son's cuckoldry, yet it also offered him the opportunity to explain his predicament and to try to save his reputation. He could be condemned unbelieved, but not unheard. And the language of aristocratic male honour was varied enough to offer the earl a dialect through which to claim first innocence and then redemption. He did not need to argue that he was honourable as his prosecutors had explained honour; honour was comprehensive enough that Castlehaven could claim that he had followed other, equally legitimate, aspects of it, aspects that he could reasonably expect his fellow peers to understand. His response suggests that class and circumstance determined the shaping of honour in ways more complicated than a simple status model can allow.

The gap between the options honour made available to the earl and to the countess, moreover, reveals how honour worked to reinforce established hierarchies of gender within as well as between classes. It is no revelation to say that the limits of proper behaviour in early modern English life were stricter for women than they were for men, although they were neither so continually strict nor simple as we once believed.[16] But only if we move beyond prescription to see how the limits that were there divided the experiences of women and men can we glimpse the ways that gender really functioned in this society. Castlehaven could hope to regain his reputation through his public presence; the countess's best hope to regain hers was through the words of others in her absence. The conventions of modesty demanded that her defence be by proxy; without further risk to their honour, aristocratic women could neither fight duels nor make their own cases in or beyond the courtroom.[17] Castlehaven could use his status to negotiate his standing; in this instance, convention denied his wife that same agility. What distinguished the men of the elite in early modern England was not that they had a monopoly on honour, but that they had extraordinary access to its public display. Other folks had honour too, but only males of a certain status, it seems, could pluck that value back when it threatened to escape them.

---

come close to endangering the verdict this way. See Herrup, *Law, Sex and Patriarchy.*

[16] Felicity Heal, 'Reputation and Honour in Court and Country: Lady Elizabeth Russell and Sir Thomas Hoby'; Faramerz Dabhoiwala, 'The Construction of Honour, Reputation and Status in Late Seventeenth- and Early Eighteenth-Century England'; Garthine Walker, 'Expanding the Boundaries of Female Honour in Early Modern England', all in this volume.

[17] On the 'problem' of women in court, see John Hawarde, *Les reportes del cases in Camera Stellata 1593–1609*, ed. W.P. Baildon (1894), 39,161; W. R. Prest, 'Law and Women's Rights in Early Modern England', *The Seventeenth Century*, VI (1991), 182–3; David Lindley, *The Trials of Francis Howard: Fact and Fiction in the Court of King James* (1993), ch. 3, 185–6; cf. Heal, 'Reputation and Honour'; Gowing, 'Language of Insult'.

The trial of an earl for felony, much less felonies as salacious as these were, was a major public event. And it was an event adorned from its outset by the perquisites justified by aristocratic claims to honour. Noblemen and noblewomen were tried in special tribunals with particularly elaborate ceremonial. Their juries were drawn from their status group rather than from their neighbours, were chosen deliberately rather than randomly, were of various sizes rather than the standard dozen. The peers acting as jurors wore their hats within the court; they took no oaths and could not be challenged. They decided cases by a majority of at least twelve votes rather than by unanimity.[18] And even the executions of peers were exceptional. Tradition spared peers, as it did certain other groups in early modern society, from the ignominy of a common felon's death. Condemned peers routinely received time for repentance (and to negotiate a pardon), met their ends on Tower Hill rather than at Tyburn and died on the block rather than on a gibbet. These prerogatives, it is important to emphasise, were not badges of immunity. A peer was less likely than anyone else to find himself a defendant, but indicted of felony, the aristocrat probably had less chance of acquittal. More ordinary defendants could challenge the qualifications of the jurors, and they could be saved from condemnation by a single stubborn voice. The anomalies between peers and others reflected the distinctive position of peers before the law in England, but unlike their other privileges, these spoke to ideological position, not to juridical result.[19] Peers on trial for felony had little chance of acquittal, but the way that they were tried reminded observers that although they were ultimately subjects, even when felons, peers were not like other subjects.[20]

In addition to the legal distinctions, visual markers of honour also set the stage for the trial of a peer. In Castlehaven's case, the physical layout of the court, with a raised gallery for participants and specially constructed scaffolds for observers, acknowledged the publicness of the event and exploited it. The opening ceremonies, magnificent and formulaic, proclaimed the esteem and the unity of the court. The organisation of the participants was itself a sort of map of honour. In

---

[18] Pike, *Constitutional History*; Colin Rhys Lovell, 'The Trial of Peers in Great Britain', *American Historical Review*, LV (1949), 69–81.

[19] The prerogatives of English peers were particularly focused on their status before the law. English peers could not be arrested except on allegations of felony, treason or breach of the peace, could not be imprisoned for debt, could not be subjected to torture, could not be outlawed or compelled to testify under oath. They were immune from the power of most forms of summons and could be tried only by other peers, even in civil actions. Michael Bush, *Noble Privilege* (New York, 1983), 66–9.

[20] Acquittal was so unlikely that Francis Hargrave, one of the early editors of *ST*, justified the inclusion of the case against William, Lord Dacre, despite its 'triviality', specifically on that score; *ST*, I, col. 407.

the centre of the gallery, the adjudicating peers (including almost every current member of the Privy Council) sat in order of their precedence at a long low table.[21] At their head, beneath a canopy of state, sat the king's representative, the Lord High Steward (in this instance, Thomas Coventry, the Lord Keeper). At his entry, the Lord High Steward saluted the assembled peers; they returned the salute. When the earl of Castlehaven was brought before them, he, too, saluted and was saluted by the adjudicating peers. During the earl's arraignment, all of the noblemen, judges and privy councillors in the court sat with their heads covered; by the Lord High Steward's order, anyone else doing so might be imprisoned. After the earl entered his plea and requested trial 'by god and my peers', the peers took off their hats, and the trial itself officially began.[22] The spatial arrangements of the court and the symbolics of the arraignment emphasised the discreteness of the peerage, their power and their cooperation with the king. The peers and the Lord High Steward, rather than the judges or lawyers or even the defendant, were the visual focus of the courtroom. They alone greeted one another and the defendant. They alone began the trial (by their uncovering). They alone judged the case. As the Lord High Steward explained to Castlehaven, seeing that 'in the opinion of the world you have generally lost your reputation' this was the only forum before which he might reestablish himself, 'so by the verdict of these your noble judges you may publicly be acquitted of the scandals, and again restored (if you be innocent) to your lost good name...'.[23]

In fact, even before the opening of the trial, honour had been the earl's companion. While the Privy Council investigated the charges made against him (from December 1630 until late the following April) Castlehaven was kept close prisoner in the Tower of London, but the Council ensured that even there, he could live in a manner appropriate to his dignity. Between December and April, the Council allowed the

[21] The only privy councillors among the English peers not on the jury were the earl of Bridgewater (Castlehaven's brother-in-law), the earl of Exeter and the earl of Lyndsey.
[22] Folger Library MS [hereafter Folger MS] V.b.328/2–6v; Northamptonshire Record Office Isham (Lamport) [hereafter NRO IL] MS 3339, 2–5. Throughout this paper, where ever possible I have cited from NRO IL MS 3339, which I believe to be the earliest of the more than forty different extant versions of the trial. However, because the language of the fullest text (Folger MS V.b.328) is clearer, I have sometimes quoted from that, slightly later, version and then cited the comparable earlier passage. Folger MS V.b.328 is more fully discussed below, see below, pp. 155–56. The best-known printed text of the trial (ST, III, cols. 401–18), a collation of three still later accounts, is neither as complete nor as accurate as the earlier versions. The history and uses of these texts will be discussed more fully in my book. The assistance of Scott Lucas on the genealogy of these manuscripts has been invaluable. Similar preparations accompanied the trials of other peers; cf. ST, I, cols. 296, 957, 1249, 1334–6.
[23] Folger MS V.b.328/5; NRO IL MS 3339, 2–3.

earl to spend £600 of his own money on his accommodation.[24] His inventory in the Tower included four beds and their equipment (one of crimson taffeta, presumably for himself), chairs, stools, tapestries, three Turkish table coverings, two dozen plates, two silver flagons, various pots, basins, dishes and other serving things plus a silver voider knife with a chamber pot. As was typical in the case of privileged prisoners, the items came from the earl's residences in Wiltshire and London at his own expense, but were arranged for and carried by men employed by the Privy Council.[25] The earl conducted estate business from the Tower, and his longtime steward continued to manage the family's properties. In the Tower, and later on Tower Hill, the earl was attended by his personal servants.[26] Magnificence was critical to a noble, critical because it set him apart from the people, and, critical because, as Kristen Neuschel has pointed out in her study of early modern France, it suggested that he could create abundance both for himself and for others.[27] 'Without means', Henry, 5th earl of Huntingdon, advised his son, 'thy honour will look as naked as trees that are cropped.'[28] To project a sense of control over one's environment even when that environment was a prison suggested the triumph of one's lineage over even the most demeaning circumstances, and, by implication, the triumph of one's self over false accusation. For someone such as Castlehaven, whose position in the peerage, both financially and hierarchically, was relatively modest, these sorts of aggressive displays would have been especially important.[29]

Castlehaven was indicted on three charges of felony—one count of rape and two counts of sodomy. The case for the king was put by the Attorney-General (Sir Robert Heath), the Solicitor-General (Sir Richard Shelton) and Sir Thomas Crew, king's sergeant. Eight of the twelve judges of the common law, including all three chief justices, acted as legal advisers. As in any trial, the prosecutors here wanted to condemn the defendant and he, in turn, wanted to escape that condemnation. Since honour in early modern England was a language with several dialects even within the confines of the aristocracy, and since honour conditioned the form as well as the substance of the trial of a peer, the

---

[24] *Acts of the Privy Council* [hereafter *APC*] entries for 29 Dec. 1630; 23 Feb. 1630/1; 20 April 1631.

[25] *APC*, 20 Dec. 1630; 7 Jan. 1630/1; 10 Jan. 1630/1.

[26] PRO SP 16/189/56.

[27] Neuschel, *Word of Honour*, 169–70; see also Felicity Heal, *Hospitality in Early Modern England* (Oxford, 1990), 24–5.

[28] Historical Manuscripts Collections [hereafter HMC] *Report on the Manuscripts of the Late Reginald Rawdon Hastings* (1928–47), 'Directions of Henry, 5th earl of Huntingdon for the guidance of his Son Ferdinando', IV, 332.

[29] On the family's finances, Stone, *Crisis*, appendices viii-ix; on precedence: G. Squibb, *Precedence in England and Wales* (Oxford, 1981), 32n, appendix 2.

language of honour was a logical grounding for each side's rhetoric. The prosecution equated the honour of the peerage with practised virtue and providential Protestantism. Using that measure rather than ancient lineage, they declared the earl no longer worthy of nobility. Castlehaven, in turn, tried to convince the peers to acquit him *because* he was one of them; a man honoured by his birth whatever his misfortunes. The jurors heard not only two versions of what happened, but also explanations rooted in two different dialects of honour.

The Lord High Steward and the Attorney-General began the trial with speeches defining the peers as men of honour. The peers acting in the trial, Coventry explained, were men 'whose hearts are as full of integrity, justice and truth, as their veins [are full] of noble blood'.[30] These were men whose probity the law so trusted that they would 'do that for justice, which others do for oaths'.[31] They would not be deceived. The Attorney-General declared the jurors to be 'honourable peers, such as of whose wisdom and sincerity there can be no questions, but to have an honourable hearing'.[32] Extravagant flattery was in the Crown's interest, to be sure, but the acclaim here was quite specific. Peers might be peers by blood, but what ennobled them, the language suggests, were learned attributes not inborn ones. These were men of integrity, of wisdom, of responsibility, men of Mervyn James's more pacific sort of honour (or so Heath claimed). They were men who would be directed by reason and by God, exactly the two forces to which, the prosecution was about to argue, Castlehaven was immune. It was not, of course, a crime to be ignoble, but if Castlehaven lacked the benign virtues of other peers, claims of his degeneracy became not only more credible, but also more serious. His sins, the prosecution implied, betrayed rank as well as nature. His expulsion from the community of peers would uphold the integrity of their claims to honour. Having defined the peerage as a community of honour based on virtue, the prosecutors worked now to separate the defendant from that community.[33] The earl, the prosecution argued, was not an errant brother—he was a foreign being, transformed by his behaviour into something wholly other. Heath likened him to the pagan emperors, adding that 'never poet invented nor historiographer [ever writ] of any [crimes] so foul'; each of the prosecutors stressed not only the rarity of the alleged crimes, but also their fundamental unEnglishness. Castlehaven was allied with a catalogue of legendarily destructive political, moral and financial forces—the pagan emperors of Rome, the Biblical

[30] NRO IL MS 3339,2–3.
[31] NRO IL MS 3339,5.
[32] NRO IL MS 3339,6.
[33] For similar tactics, see the trials of the earl of Arundel (*ST*, I, cols. 1252–3) and of the earl of Somerset (*ST*, II, col. 970).

debauchees of Sodom and the Lombard bankers of medieval England.[34] The accident of noble birth, Crew and Heath explained, gave one opportunities for honour, but the earl's actions deprived him of the thing itself. 'The prisoner is honourable, the crimes dishonourable', Heath began his speech. The earl's position gave him greater than normal obligations, not greater than normal latitude. 'As he is great in his birth so should he have been good in his example', Heath concluded.[35]

And in this context, unEnglish and unaristocratic also meant un-Christian, or at the very least, unProtestant. The Attorney-General called Castlehaven a Catholic sympathiser and an atheist, explaining his demise as a logical result of religious inconstancy—the earl's exploration of religion led him to irreligion, and from there, Heath argued, any sin was realisable. He concluded that he had 'never observed to be such a concurrence and confluence of vices in the person of any one man'.[36] And because this man was a peer, that confluence defiled not only Castlehaven, but also his household, the peerage and the nation. Heath's argument endorsed the commonplace expressed by Robert Ashley decades earlier, '... by honour are cities kept, families preserved, the society of men quietly and peaceably continued, the commonwealth defended ... without honour no one thing can be well administered or worthily effected'.[37] Beyond his specific crimes, it was alleged, the earl's behaviour taught profligacy to his son, promiscuity to his wife and daughter, and self-importance to his servants.[38] His disorder was a hazard in itself and in its example. His position made him willingly or not a pedagogue. The crown case could almost have been summarised by the moralist Owen Feltham, who in 1628 had declared that 'Earth hath not any thing more glorious than ancient nobility, when 'tis found with vertue, ... [but] a debauched son of a noble family, is one of the intolerable burdens of the earth, and as hateful a thing as hell.'[39]

---

[34] NRO IL MS 3339, 5; Henry E. Huntington Library Ellesmere [hereafter HEH EL] MS 7976/12. The importance of Englishness appears as well in the trials of the duke of Norfolk (*ST*, I, col. 969) and of the earl of Somerset (*ST*, II, cols. 970–1).

[35] NRO IL MS 3339.5. The relation between birth and merit as grounds for honour was one of the subject's most heated areas of early modern discussion.

[36] HEH EL MS 7976/11.

[37] Ashley, *Of Honour*, 30.

[38] In addition to felony, Castlehaven was accused of diverting his son's inheritance and encouraging the adultery of his daughter-in-law; NRO IL MS 3339, 7–8,12; BL Hargrave MS 226/311v, 312–12v. On the particular horror of such accusations, see Barber, *Honour's Tongue*, 36–7; Greville, 'Letter to an Honourable Lady', 290.

[39] Owen Feltham, *Resolves: A Duple Century One New an Other of Second Edition* (1628), 86. Feltham's work was originally published in 1620. The 1628 edition was dedicated to Thomas, Lord Coventry, the man later to preside over Castlehaven's trial. On loss of honour as a slippery slope to anarchy, see Gervase Markham, *Honour in his Perfection*, 4; Herrup, *Law, Sex and Patriarchy*.

The earl's response to the charges against him was to deny them all and he continued to do so to his death. Like other peers before him, Castlehaven attacked the technical deficiencies of the case against him—the credibility of the witnesses, the definition of the crimes, the absence of the accusers from the courtroom.[40] But since his alleged victims were neither dead nor royal, the earl also countered with an explanation for his plight that portrayed him as a man victimised by his sense of honour. He used the courtroom and later the scaffold as a platform to explain the honour in his actions, and why he believed that he ought to regain his reputation. His appeal spoke directly to the prosecution's attempt to isolate him. And regardless of its persuasiveness, his desire to vindicate himself showed that he still valued honour, and that he recognised his peers to be its arbiter.[41] The very fact of his defence belied the prosecution's picture of him as an outsider.

Throughout his life, the 2nd earl of Castlehaven had shown a considerable concern for ancestry and its privileges, an irony for a man who would die accused by members of his family for crimes committed against them. In 1611, the earl, then only the eldest son of an English baron, caused an uproar in Dublin when he publicly refused to cede precedence to members of the Irish Privy Council. 'It was much noted, and somewhat reprised at, insomuch as some of the Barons' eldest sons then in this town spake of it, as if they intended to do likewise', the Lord Deputy reported when he referred the case to London.[42] The next year, inspired by 'some doubts lately moved in that behalf, concerning himself and his younger brothers and sisters', Sir Mervin submitted a list of broader questions concerning precedence to the commissioners for the Earl Marshal.[43] In 1614, as a knight of the shire for Dorset, Sir Mervin's only recorded remarks in Commons addressed the declining condition of the ancient peerage.[44] And in a letter to his brother the day before his trial, the earl spoke of his son not as having

---

[40] See the trials of the duke of Somerset (ST, I, col. 520), the duke of Norfolk (ST, I, cols. 965–7, 985, 992, 1001–2) and the earl of Arundel (ST, I, cols. 1253–64). Sir Nicholas Throckmorton, accused of treason in connection with the Wyatt Rebellion in 1554, mounted the most elaborate and most successful defence of the day; see ST, I, cols. 869–902, and Annabel Patterson, *Reading Holinshed's Chronicles* (Chicago, 1994), c. 8.

[41] On how shame could offer an opportunity to display one's sense of honour, see William Ian Miller, *Humiliation and Other Essays on Honour, Social Discomfort and Violence* (Ithaca, 1993), 117–24.

[42] British Library [hereafter BL] Cotton MS Titus B, X/210. Linda Levy Peck first suggested that I look through these papers.

[43] PRO SP 14/71/39, 40.

[44] He preferred a bill against high legal fees and moved to broaden restrictions on luxurious apparel; *Proceedings of the Parliament 1614* ed. Maija Jansson (Philadelphia, 1988), 75.

harmed him, but as having 'undone his house'.[45] Castlehaven was not very prominent locally or nationally, but what we know of his public personality suggests a man quite familiar with a traditional understanding of aristocratic honour, one rooted more in lineage and protocol than in service or in piety.

The same concern with the public respect accorded to the peerage underlay the earl's explanations of his behaviour in 1631. The core of his defence was an identification with his jurors; he argued that his dilemma was situational not personal. He denied the charges against him and went on to argue that he was a casualty of his position, a victim of a conspiracy organised by a son impatient for his inheritance and a wife insatiable with sexual desire. Castlehaven insisted that he was not 'the most wicked of men' as Heath had made him seem, but 'the most unfortunate of the living'.[46] He told the court that he had been betrayed by his subordinates, undone by the malice of those whom he commanded. What had happened to him, he said, could well happen to them. 'It is not, my Lords, my sins that make me this day a spectacle to the world ...' he concluded. 'it is the ingratitude of a son and the wickedness of a wife. I am so conscious of mine own innocencie', he said, 'that I make no question, but God Almighty (the just revenger of all injuries), will, in his own time, bring their malice to light.'[47] Moreover, Castlehaven's difficulties, he insisted, were not random afflictions; his tribulations, he claimed, were the direct consequence of his own position and integrity.

By integrity, he meant not only noble lineage, but also his concern for public respectability. His wife, he told the peers, was so licentious that she had born a bastard; he had concealed the fact 'for her honour ... twas my ill fortune to wear the hornes, though I put them in my pocket'. His thanks was that she now falsely charged him with abetting rape. Her accusation freed him from his reticence; 'she cries whore first', he argued.[48] He claimed to have been equally tender of the reputations of his son and daughter-in-law. According to evidence deposed, but not repeated in court, the earl charged that their marriage

[45] PRO SP 16/189/25.

[46] Folger MS V.h.328/20v; NRO IL MS 3339, 11–12.

[47] Ibid. The tensions inherent in a family structure so tied to the dissemination of property have been much studied; for important recent assessments, see Linda Pollock, 'Domestic Dissidence: Women Versus Women and Women Versus Men in the Early Modern Elite Home', unpublished paper presented to the North American Conference of British Studies; Barbara J. Harris, *Of Noble and Gentle Birth: English Aristocratic Women 1450–1550*, to be published by Oxford University Press; Heal, 'Reputation and Honour'.

[48] NRO IL MS 3339, 12; Folger MS V.b.328/21. On the added dishonour of making private business public, see Linda Pollock, 'Living on the Stage of the World: Concepts of Privacy among the Elite in Early Modern England', in *Rethinking English Social History*, ed. Adrian Wilson (1993), 88–9; Fletcher, *Gender*, 144–5.

was a shambles. He claimed that his daughter-in-law had told him that her husband was impotent (or at least unresponsive to her), and that she wanted a divorce. Again, Castlehaven explained that he had chosen decorum over dishonour. He said that he had begged his daughter-in-law 'not [to] make herself and her husband an open shame and scandal to the world', and later, that he had turned a blind eye to her promiscuity, since complaining of it 'was to no purpose'. His son's public treachery, he said, made a sham of such discretion.[49] And as for the servants who testified against the earl, 'impostors falsely seduced to take away a guiltless life' as he called them, their motives were revenge, not justice. They had fled the strictness of his discipline, and now, coaxed by his son, they saw an opportunity to destroy him. The details of this story, Castlehaven argued, were particular, but the dangers it revealed were not.[50] Peers deserved protection from inferiors who would use the law against them; wives should not be allowed to testify against their husbands nor servants against their masters nor inferiors against barons.[51] In Castlehaven's view, his loyalty to the claims of lineage, public decorum and hierarchy had endangered him, and the court's unwillingness to support him in these principles would endanger the security of every peer.

If honour in seventeenth-century England was still as it may once have been primarily a quality realised only in public, one assessed by how a person adapted to the exigencies of fate, then perhaps an earl insulted by his family in private or one who insulted his family in private could be honourable. But even were that so, the breach of familial confidence in the complaint by Castlehaven's son destroyed the conditions upon which such a claim could have been grounded. That the son, James, could do this with so little harm to his own reputation says something about how the predominant terms of honour had shifted by 1631; the priorities implicit in his act—loyalty to a national rather than a natal family, to an indirect rather than a direct forum for vengeance, to virtue over lineage—contrasted sharply with his father's.[52] By 1631, to many peers, Castlehaven's honour was like a dialect from a different region—familiar, comprehensible, but received as if through the static of another grammar. We cannot directly know

[49] Leicestershire Record Office DE 3128/184.
[50] Folger MS V.b.328/24; NRO IL MS 3339,12; BL Hargrave MS 226/312v-13.
[51] NRO IL MS 3339, 11.
[52] James, 'Concept of Honour', 339–40. One of the striking aspects of the Castlehaven case is that the son's honour, despite making accusations that impugned his intimates, and declared his own cuckoldry, seems not to have been permanently damaged. He regained his English title and most of his father's property. His younger siblings married well. I have found no libels at his expense and the gossip surrounding the case generally ignores him. For his later history, colourful in its own right, see Herrup, *Law, Sex and Patriarchy*.

how the earl's presentation of his plight struck his jurors, but we do know that they deliberated an exceptionally long time before returning with their verdicts, and that the verdicts they returned were exceptionally divided.[53] Their reluctance may have signalled doubt about the earl's guilt, or merely sympathy with some of his complaints about the case.[54] But Castlehaven's defence both helped and hurt him. In alleging that his wife and daughter were promiscuous, his servants disobedient and his son rebellious, the earl was admitting to his own inadequacies as a ruler. The publicly acknowledged disorder of the Castlehaven household was *prima facie* evidence of his dishonour.[55] His attempt to shift the blame to others was, from this perspective, nonsensical, even shameful. Castlehaven hoped to restore his reputation by claiming innocence, but he undermined that assertion by confessing to a failure of control. And his defiance disrupted the peace as much as did his guilt or innocence; it guaranteed not only his dishonour, but also the defaming of all those associated with him.[56] The earl's story was made up of remnants from a familiar, if old fashioned, code. There was never much chance that the jurors would acquit him; but through his marshalling of a plausible vocabulary of honour, Castlehaven seems to have been able to give at least some of his listeners some hesitation about his fate.

The conventions that provided the earl with a construct, however askew, upon which to build an explanation of his behaviour, served in a different way to frame the conduct of the countess. Castlehaven's peers were (indirectly) hers as well. The Touchets were an older noble family than her family, the Stanleys, but in terms of influence, the Stanleys were far more powerful. Anne Stanley Brydges Touchet was the eldest daughter and co-heir of the 5th earl of Derby. Through her

[53] Having debated for more than two hours, the jurors convicted the earl on the count of rape by twenty-six votes to one and on the counts of sodomy by fifteen votes to twelve. PRO Baga de Secretis KB 8/63m10; HEH Hastings Manuscripts Legal Papers Box 5(2) #2.

[54] On the merits of those complaints, see Herrup, *Law, Sex and Patriarchy*. Anxiety about exposure from wives and from servants certainly had some resonance. On wives, see Fletcher, *Gender*, c. 1; Elizabeth Foyster, 'A Laughing Matter? Marital Discord and Gender Control in Seventeenth-Century England', *Rural History*, IV, 1 (1993), 5–21; Elizabeth Foyster, 'Male Honour, Social Control and Wife Beating in Late Stuart England', in this volume; Gowing, 'Women'; on servants, HMC Hastings, IV, 333; on the view from service, Katharine Hodgkin, 'Thomas Whythorne and the Problems of Mastery', *History Workshop Journal*, XXIX (1990), 20–41, and more generally, Cust, 'Honour and Politics', 81–3.

[55] Roper, *Oedipus*, 61; Bertram Wyatt-Brown, *Southern Honour: Ethics and Behaviour in the Old South* (New York, 1982), 303–4, for similar results in different settings.

[56] This possibility was first suggested to me by my colleague, Kristen Neuschel. The sense of the earl's disruptiveness may have been heightened further by the dissension his case caused among his jurors; see above n. 53.

paternal grandmother, Margaret Clifford, she had a substantial claim to the throne. Her mother, the redoubtable Alice Spencer Stanley Egerton, was a patron of Spenser and later of Milton. Her brothers-in-law were the earls of Huntingdon and of Bridgewater. She could count both relatives and close allies of her family among the jurors—but that did not, of course, give her a place among the brethren of the peerage. At no point was the countess allowed either the grandness or the freedom of her husband. She accepted the grudging hospitality of the bishop of Winchester from the time of her husband's accusation until after his death, and made do with a single trunk with 'some necessary provisions' brought from Salisbury.[57] The Council allowed her and her guardians £130 for expenses (i.e. about one quarter what the earl spent), even though, according to her mother, the countess was 'destitute'.[58] There is no mention at any time of the countess being attended by her servants. And the conventions of honour dictated that she had literally no presence in the courtroom. 'For modesty's sake', the Chief Justice affirmed her examination privately, in a small chamber nearby in the Court of Wards. Having been spared the ordeal of facing her husband, the countess lost any opportunity to respond to his counter charges against her character. The belief that verbal women were probably unchaste and that women willing to talk publicly about sex were almost certainly so complicated her position further—had she wanted to defend herself, it is hard to imagine how she could have done so without undermining her virtue by the fact of her presentation. The earl had a chance to save his own reputation, but the conventions of honour forced the countess to entrust hers to the defence of others.[59]

As with the earl, two very different representations of the countess appear in the trial, but, in contrast to Castlehaven, these descriptions are like a single vernacular uncorrupted by regional dialects, mirror images constructed of the same materials. The precepts for aristocratic women as revealed here contain neither the tensions nor the variety of male honour. The stories, pro and con, turn on the adherence of the countess to an accepted standard; the standard itself goes unquestioned. And the axis of the standard, it will surprise no one to hear, was chastity. We have been too quick to conflate female honour with sexual purity; ongoing research is revealing the varied canvas of social possibilities through which women might display honour.[60] But in this

---

[57] *APC*, 14 Dec. 1630; 31 Dec. 1630.

[58] *APC*, 23 Dec. 1630; 23 Feb. 1630/1; 25 Feb 1630/1; PRO SP16/198/18.

[59] HEH EL MS 7976/9v; Gowing, 'Women', and the sources cited above, n. 17.

[60] See, for example, Dabhoiwala, 'The Construction of Honour', and Walker, 'Expanding the Boundaries of Female Honour', in this volume. The circumstances of this case would have made untenable two of the alternative possibilities for claims to honour suggested by Walker, good housewifery and good mothering. Additional alternative

case, perhaps because it was so public, perhaps because it took place in a forum where men controlled the discussion, perhaps because the crimes themselves were sexual, perhaps because it involved a wife accused rather than supported by her husband, chastity was the essence of the discussion. When, as in this instance, a woman's closest male relatives were also her accusers, and no other male acted specifically to protect her, the broader possibilities for honour collapsed.[61]

The countess, Heath declared, was 'high by birth, noble by her first marriage, great in fortune, but most unfortunate by her last...'. And from the beginning of their marriage, the prosecution alleged, the earl of Castlehaven had attacked his own wife's virtue, inclining 'to have his wife naught, which the wickedest man that ever I heard of before would have virtuous and good'. He had forced her to witness servants exposing themselves. He had urged her to accept various servants as sexual partners. He had deprived her of an allowance in order to force her to sleep with his favourite. And when she responded with patience and resistance, he had helped her own page to rape her. As the earl would claim about his humiliation, the prosecution contended that the countess's humiliation resulted, too, from integrity rather than from flaw. She had merely obeyed her husband, they maintained, but unlike him, she could not control her fate. Through his commands, the prosecutors conceded 'she must make a shipwreck of her honour...'.[62] The earl's depiction of his wife, not surprisingly, was very different from the prosecution's, yet he, too, worked from an ideal of female honour based on purity and submission. In his telling, the countess was sexually voracious; she chose several lovers from among the servants, and even bore a child by one of them. She rejected the earl, she disobeyed him, and now she was seeking to dishonour and to disable him.

Since the countess never spoke at the trial, we have only glimpses of her own views about the foundations of her honour. What we can infer is conventional, if perhaps disingenuously literal. That after her first husband (Grey Brydges, 5th Baron Chandos) died, the countess asked

measures of female honour might include the defence of property, the honourableness of one's children (especially sons) or the redeeming of one's spouse or child by pardon or petition. It is worth noting the greater emphasis on familial achievement than in comparable male options, although Scott Lucas has pointed out to me that literary patronage provided at least one non-familial arena for the indirect attainment of honour by a woman.

[61] Barber, *Honour's Tongue*, 36, 47; Lindley, *Trials*; Keith Thomas, 'The Double Standard', *Journal of the History of Ideas*, XX (1959), 195–216; Harris, *Of Noble and Gentle Birth*. See also Wyatt-Brown, *Southern Honour*; Robert Nye, *Masculinity and Male Codes of Honour in Modern France* (New York, 1993).

[62] Folger MS V.b.328/11 for the first and last quotes; NRO IL MS 3339, 7 for the second.

the Privy Council to restore her to the position befitting the daughter of an earl reveals her concern for precedence. That once remarried, she never invoked her father's higher status, suggests her respect for the prerogatives of marriage.[63] Her narrative of her behaviour while married to the earl, relayed in her deposition, affirms her belief in patriarchy, hierarchy, obedience and chastity. According to her examination, Castlehaven told his wife that sins committed at his urging would fall upon his head, that 'if she lay with any man with his consent, it was not her fault, but his'.[64] When the rape compromised her decency, she said, she would have killed herself immediately had her attacker not prevented it.

The conflict as revealed to the peers by the countess and the prosecutors was not between older and newer forms of honour, but between the dictates of obedience and chastity. However narrow the possibility that the earl might escape reproach, his chance was a broad avenue compared to what faced the countess. I can think of no other case that stretched the bonds of obedience as far as this one did, and the starkness of a distressed wife's options as presented here is considerably overdrawn. Women, and certainly elite women, were not and were not expected to be mindlessly obedient. Even the strictest precepts of obedience excluded acts against the laws of God, for example.[65] But the routine analogising of household and state, wife and subject, made the public exculpation of any act of resistance highly problematical. As Fulke Greville counselled another unhappy noble woman, '[Nature] ... gave honour more wings than one to the end, those which cannot have it in commanding might have it in obeying ... I cannot advise you either to complain or to mutiny against the stronger ... pay your tribute, do your homage, and make your reward to be the secret peace of well doing....'[66]

Yet even passivity could not redeem the countess; the earl's insistence

[63] Squibb, *Precedence*, 62–6; appendix 1. Nor did she petition for a return to her original status after her second husband's death.

[64] NRO IL MS 3339,8. Folger MS V.b.328/16v adds her claim that the earl told her that if 'it were his will to have it so, she must obey, and do it'; HEH EL MS 7976/10 has the countess adding that although she deferred to her husband's wishes, 'she never consented in her heart'.

[65] Harris, *Of Noble and Gentle Birth*; Linda Pollock, 'Teache her to Live under Obedience: The Making of Women in the Upper Ranks in Early Modern England', *Continuity & Change*, IV (1989), 231–58; Alison Wall, 'Elizabethan Precepts and Feminine Practice: The Thynne family of Longleat', *History*, LXXV (1990), 23–38. Barbara Donagan reminded me of the particular exemption for acts against divine law. That claim never surfaced in contemporary comment about the case.

[66] Greville, 'Letter to an Honourable Lady', 277, 278, 279; Thomas, 'Double Standard', 196, 214, citing the marquis of Halifax and Juan Luis Vives offering similar advice; Richard Snawsell, *A Looking Glass for Married Folks* ... (1610; repr. 1631), n.p.; Roper, *Oedipus*, 109–10.

upon his innocence had guaranteed her dishonour. If the jurors believed the earl, then she was a whore; if they believed the countess, then she was obedient, but still to be shamed for her adultery; if they disbelieved both parties, then both would be dishonoured. An aristocratic wife's dignity was linked inextricably to her husband's, but her reputation, once tarnished, was not as easily redeemed. 'Ages and sexes have their distinct laws', Greville wrote, 'Our reputations not easily shaken, and many ways repaired; theirs [women's], like glass, by and by broken and impossible to be healed.'[67]

Given that the earl died a felon and that the countess survived unchallenged by the law, it is a delicate task to argue that he had the kinder fate. But in terms of honour, the idea is not entirely ridiculous. In the weeks before his death, Castlehaven drew yet another nugget from the treasury of possibilities for honourable behaviour. Refusing to become, as was expected, the apologetic postulant, he became the Christian stoic, still defiant, but piously preoccupied. He refused to request a pardon or even the respite of hanging routinely granted to a nobleman, claiming that he was 'no more ashamed of hanging in a rope, then Christ was for his sins upon the cross'.[68] He had his coffin built and brought to his chambers to help him to contemplate his death. He regularly saw spiritual advisers, took communion and declared a renewed devotion to his faith in the Church of England. He never admitted the justice of his conviction and used the scaffold as a platform from which again to affirm his innocence. The future earl of Clarendon (who had been unmoved by the defendant's reasoning at the trial) visited the prisoner the night before his death and reported that Castlehaven was 'as full of piety as ever any martyr was, and as void of passion ... none, but an innocent man could have put on that confidence'.[69]

And before the year had ended, a lengthy disquisition framing the

[67] Greville, 'Letter to an Honourable Lady', 066; Hawarde, Reportes, 341; cf Harris, Of Noble and Gentle Birth.

[68] HMC, The Manuscripts of his Grace the Duke of Portland (1891–1931), II, 122. A few texts suggest that he did ask for pardon or exile; see HEH EL MS 7976/14, 15 as an example. The king did respite the form of execution, but it is unclear at whose request, PRO E371/818m7–8.

[69] BL Additional MS. 17, 017/1–2; On the importance attached to style in death in early modern England, see Beach Langston, 'Essex and the Art of Dying', Huntington Library Quarterly, II (1950), 109–29; W.L. Ustick, 'Changing Ideals of Aristocratic Character and Conduct in Seventeenth-Century England', Modern Philology, XXX (1932–3), 149–50. For a provocative discussion of the possibilities of such a moment, see Carlin Barton, 'Savage Miracles: The Redemption of Lost Honour in Roman Society & the Sacrament of the Gladiator and the Martyr', Representations, XLV (Winter 1994), 41–71.

trial with a discussion of the earl's character was circulating throughout the country. This text, which survives in multiple versions, recast the story of the earl as one of honour undone and redone.[70] The view of honour proposed here was emphatically not the earl's. While the earl had admitted no stain upon his honour, the author of this text rooted honour in values similar to those of the prosecution. Admitting Castlehaven's guilt, he or she nonetheless made the earl into a figure of sympathy and even dignity by redesigning the story as one about redemption rather than degeneracy.

> The late earl [the text proclaimed] was extracted from the loins of noble progenitors, so well qualified with gifts of nature, that he gave no small hopes of augmenting that original honour by his personal actions... A great part of his life he spent honourably and religiously, till at the last he made shipwreck of both... If the prison had not filed away all the rust of corruption, sure in the furnace of his trial, he was refined, and after the sentence of death was passed upon him, seemed then most worthy to live....

Castlehaven's life, the anonymous author concluded, seemed 'a real comment of the apostle's speech, where sin abounded there grace did much more'.[71]

There was no similar rehabilitation of the countess; instead she faced continued humiliation and questions about her chastity. In a dynamic still all too familiar, the fact of a sexual accusation, regardless of its outcome, compromised her. If admitting to the disorder in his household shamed the earl, the public discussion of her chastity shamed the countess, particularly when the truth remained contested. She could second Stephan Guazzo's dictum written fifty years before,

> Where the honour by this fault (unchastity) doth, according to the opinion of men, but a little blemish his honour, the woman altogether looseth her good name, and remaineth spotted with such infamy

---

[70] Lindley, *Trials*, 182ff, on such publications as mechanisms to restore reputation. Though never published, the Castlehaven text has narrative qualities that suggest it was compiled for publication. In addition to the trial, the fullest and most common versions recount the earl's execution, the trial and execution of his co-defendants, the earl's confession of faith, his last letters to his son and to his sisters, the petition to King Charles from Castlehaven's sisters for his pardon and 'a compendious description of Mervin, late earl of Castlehaven, wherein the true picture of his mind and affections towards the latter end of his time is faithfully represented'. Folger MS V.b.328 seems to be the earliest version of this text, but there are many variants, all undated. See Herrup, *Law, Sex and Patriarchy* for a fuller discussion.
[71] Folger MS V.b.328/37, 37v, 38v, 39v.

that she can never recover her honour again, neither by any repentance, nor by amendments of her life.[72]

The earl's scaffold speech carried accusations of the countess's perfidy to a new audience, and every report of his defiance included his allegation of her treachery. She had to appear publicly at the trial of the servant who allegedly had raped her.[73] And at his execution, that servant again proclaimed his innocence, and particularly forgave the countess 'and all the world, who have wronged me'.[74]

Nor initially was there much private succour. Her mother at first refused even to see her until she had been pardoned. In a letter written a week after the earl's execution, the dowager countess of Derby told Secretary of State Dorchester that she was

> much perplexed and afflicted with grief for my daughter Castlehaven and grandchild Audley in that they have so infinitely offended God & the king, by their wicked crimes ... And that my daughter and she may be so happy to receive their pardon from the king and till such time I shall never willingly yield to see either of them.[75]

She did eventually receive the now dowager countess of Castlehaven, while continuing to press the king to grant her a full pardon. The absolution came in November, 1631, for crimes of 'adultery, fornication and incontinency'.[76] The countess never remarried, seems to have had little to do with either her children or stepchildren and maintained virtually no public presence. She seems to have lived with her mother at Harefield in Middlesex until the latter's death in 1637, and then, helped by a maternal bequest of some jewelry, a fitted coach-and-two, six milk cows and a 'competent' number of swine and poultry, she moved to Heydons, a mansion originally intended for her younger son.[77]

---

[72] *The Civil Conversation* (1581), 90–1, cited in Lindley, *Trials*, 171; Greville, 'Letter to an Honourable Lady', chs. 2, 4; cf. Harris, *Of Noble and Gentle Birth*.

[73] At the earl's trial, there were two potential witnesses in the charge of rape: the countess and Giles Broadway, the servant actually accused of the act. After the earl's execution, however, the countess was the only witness, and so her presence, particularly when Broadway requested it, was critical to the case. She came to court, confirmed and clarified her earlier examination, affirmed her shame, her lack of malice and her respect for God, and then left 'with as much privacy as might be into her coach'. *ST*, III, col. 419.

[74] Folger MS V.b.328/34–v; cf. *ST*, III, col. 424, where she has become 'the wickedest woman in the world', someone 'wholly delighting in lust'.

[75] PRO SP16/192/11.

[76] PRO C66/2578m6.

[77] PRO Prob 11/174 (70 Goare). Her income from her jointure lands was something less than £1,000 per year, a modest, but not impossible income for the wife and daughter of peers; cf. Stone, *Crisis*, appendices XXXI and XXXII; Amy L. Erickson 'Common Law Versus Common Practice: The Use of Marriage Settlements in Early Modern

The dowager countess survived until 1647, but reminders of the trial and her role in it punctuated her remaining years. Castlehaven's sister, Lady Eleanor Douglas, denounced her as a Jezebel, first in a private petition to the king and then in two published pamphlets.[78] The texts that bestowed Castlehaven with new integrity gave no quarter to the countess. They not only repeated all of the earl's and his servant's denigrations, but alleged that in contrast to her husband, the countess remained unrepentant.[79] The most popular libel circulating after the trial seems to have accepted at least some part of the earl's version of the story, portraying Castlehaven not as a sodomite nor as a rapist, but as a cuckold.[80] And in 1640, in a fruitless quest to regain Fonthill Gifford, the 3rd earl (the dowager countess's stepson and son-in-law and the earl's original accuser) again brought the discussion of her chastity to a public forum. In a petition to the House of Lords, he rehearsed the history of the trial, alleging among other things, that the inability of his father directly to confront the countess invalidated his condemnation.[81] However, there was at least one reminder for the countess of her life before the aspersions on her honour, a negation, if not a refutation, of her dishonour. In the upper chancel of the parish church of St Mary's, Harefield, stands an enormous hearse monument to Alice, dowager countess of Derby, built before her death, allegedly by Maximilian Colt. Representations of Alice's three daughters kneel in niches carved into the west wall of the tomb, accompanying coats of arms and the words in the inscription identifying them for eternity. The earl of Castlehaven and the dishonour of that association is completely absent. Anne Stanley Brydges Touchet is here reclaimed as Anne Stanley Brydges, daughter of the earl of Derby, wife of Grey, Baron Chandos, and no other. Ironically, today this is the most public and the most permanent of the remains associated with the trial.[82]

---

England', *Economic History Review*, 2nd series, XLIII, 1 (1990), 30. My colleague Bill Reddy pointed out to me how difficult it is to distinguish what in Lady Castlehaven's later actions results from shame and what from an honourable withdrawal from society.

[78] BL Additional MS 69, 919; *Woe to the House* (1633), *The Word of God to the Citie of London, from the Lady Eleanor: Of the earl of Castlehaven* ... (1644/5).

[79] Folger MS V.b.328/38v–9.

[80] 'I need no trophies to adorn my hearse / My wife exalts my hornes in every verse / And placeth them so full upon my tombe. / That for my arms there is no vacant room. / Who will take such a countess to his bed / That first gives hornes, & then cuts off the head' BL Harleian MS 738/328 among many other places. On the libels surrounding the trial, see Herrup, *Law, Sex and Patriarchy*.

[81] House of Lords Record Office Parchment 179/21; Main Papers Parchments/60.

[82] PRO Prob 11/174 (70 Goare); Katherine A. Esdaile, *English Church Monuments 1510–1840* (1946); N. Pevsner, *Middlesex. Buildings of England*, III (Harmondsworth, 1951). Nigel Llewellyn's presentation at the conference for which this paper was originally written inspired me to consider further the meaning of the Derby monument.

We return, then, to where we started, to the importance of circumstance in the articulation of honour, to the fact that this was a conversation of the courtroom rather than of the battlefield, and a conversation between men and women and among peers. This trial and its aftermath are vivid illustrations of the ways that the codes of honour reinforced the social hierarchies of early modern England, most particularly the hierarchies of gender. A man defamed acted 'naturally' to defend his honour. Whether credibly or not, he could try to assert himself back to a good reputation. A woman shamed had fewer options. But aristocratic women are not all women. The status of the principals is crucial to understanding both the scandal and the mystery of this trial—although it was the 'all in the family' nature of the accusations that may have determined the outcome of the case, it was the rank of the participants that made its prosecution critical. Had the countess not been a Stanley, her charges might have seemed less credible; had Touchet not been an earl, his might have seemed less dangerous. Translated outside of the aristocratic vernacular, the dynamics of honour and reputation themselves would have been transformed.[83]

We need, then, a sensitivity to gender and to class that can complement the receptiveness to change over time so well developed by scholars such as Mervyn James. But we also need to revise James's chronology with one that recognises both the importance and the incompleteness of the transition that he charted. The law said that the countess of Castlehaven was a victim; honour left her reputation irredeemably tarnished. The law said that the 2nd earl of Castlehaven was a felon; honour offered him some space and language with which to try to defend and reclaim his reputation. One might conclude that this was mere opportunism, but it was much more than that. Richard Cust, Caroline Hibbard and Felicity Heal have provided examples of multi-vocality used by the elite to claim honour in much less dramatic instances, and here we add a case from the heart of what has conventionally been called the 'honour community', and from a moment quite literally of life and death.[84] Looking at when and where people invoked honour, at how different fora shaped the opportunities and rhetorics credibly available to them will allow us to understand honour's continuing appeal as well as its continuing elusiveness. Considering action as the equal of prescription shows how easily and apparently sincerely people adapted honour to suit their needs, how even among aristocrats in seventeenth-century England, the path from 'old' to 'new' was not a path at all, but instead a motley pattern.

[83] Dabhoiwala, 'The Construction of Honour', and Walker, 'Expanding the Boundaries of Female Honour', in this volume; Gowing 'Language of Insult.'

[84] Cust, 'Politics and Honour'; Hibbard, 'Theatre of Dynasty'; Heal, 'Reputation and Honour'.

# REPUTATION AND HONOUR IN COURT AND COUNTRY: LADY ELIZABETH RUSSELL AND SIR THOMAS HOBY

## By Felicity Heal

READ 24 MARCH 1995 AT THE UNIVERSITY OF CAMBRIDGE

*I*

IN 1576 William Cecil, Lord Burghley, was engaged in one of the most
painful disputes of his distinguished career: a bitter conflict with the
earl of Oxford who had married, and then repudiated, his beloved
daughter Anne. Cecil's distress erupted in a series of memoranda
enumerating the injuries inflicted by the earl. At the end of the most
comprehensive of these documents he briefly resumed his other role,
as mentor and Polonius to the young de Vere. Remember, he begged
him, who he was and what the world expected of him: above all
remember that 'the gretest possession that any man can have is honor,
good name, good will of many and of the best sort'. This appeal to
honour as good reputation among the wisest and best was unlikely to
move his renegade son-in-law, whose understanding of the honour
code, if we may judge by his actions, is that it provided justification for
the wilful individualism of the nobleman. But Cecil's choice of language
has resonance in the broader context of thinking about reputation in
the late sixteenth century. It eschews excessive personal pride in favour
of a balanced appeal to the judgment of one's peers, yet it is scarcely
an elevated perception of virtuous Protestant honour of the kind
associated with another of Cecil's protégés, Philip Sidney. Here, as
elsewhere, Burghley's instincts are pragmatic and conservative: a good
name is an essential prerequisite for proper action within the world of
Elizabethan politics. In his famous *Precepts* to his son the point is made
even more clearly. The essence of intelligent social accommodation, he
argues, is a careful calculus about appropriate outcomes: 'Be not
scurrilous in conversation' because 'it pulleth quarrels on your head';
undertake few suits against anyone, and then only when right is on
your side, but 'spare neither cost nor paines to accomplish' suits
successfully to deter other litigants. It was essential to act prudently

161

and to have this wisdom acknowledged in the theatre of the world: this was the essence of honour.[1]

At the end of the sixteenth century the political consequences of the nobleman's honour code were revealed alarmingly in the Essex rebellion. The earl identified himself to the end as the natural leader of the community of honour and the embodiment at court of the 'way of arms'. His Cecilian opponents were despised as men of the robe: lawyers always prone to the dishonour involved in the petty calculus of interests, and in the manipulation of the 'rigour and quirks' of the legal system for their own benefit. Burghley's prudential maxims, carefully balancing the good opinion of the world against the vigorous pursuit at law of political and individual goals, were always potentially at odds with Essex's views. So also was his belief that personal honour had to yield to public necessity. But it was the Cecilian vision that triumphed in 1601. Honour in the public sphere must now be pursued in ways that modulated the arrogance of individual ambition; that above all accommodated honour to the legitimate interests of crown and state. Men in the Jacobean court, said John Holles, sought 'to walk by the true rule of the Kings honor and thir owne', or at least they were obliged to express their belief in this identity. Though such sentiments were not new they assumed particular significance during the difficult years of transition from Tudor to Stuart rule. Patronage and law provided the mechanisms through which honour as public reputation could be expressed and the interests of individual and crown could be adjusted.[2]

Within the extended family of the Cecils these years produced two famous legal disputes which raised, in microcosm, problems of honour as acute as those found in the Essex revolt. The cases involved a mother and son: the mother Lady Elizabeth Russell, born a Cooke, sister-in-law to Cecil and first married to Sir Thomas Hoby; the son Sir Thomas Hoby the younger, always known as Posthumous from the circumstances of his birth. Through their Cecil kin, and through Lady Russell's second marriage to John, Lord Russell, the two were closely linked to many of the Elizabethan political establishment. It was unlikely that their major quarrels would pass through the courts without some invocation of these patronage networks. It might also be expected that when the

[1] *Historical Manuscripts Commission: Salisbury MSS* [hereafter *HMC Salisbury*], II, 145. William Cecil, *Certain Precepts* (1618), 13–15. On Sidney and honour see M. James, *Culture, Society and Politics in Early Modern England* (Cambridge, 1986) [hereafter James, *Culture*], 387–91.
[2] Essex, for example, accused Francis Bacon of failure to act nobly, despite the latter's initial support for him; on this and the Essex revolt see James, *Culture*, 416–65. *The Letters of John Holles, 1587–1637*, ed. P. Seddon (3 vols., Thoroton Record Society, 31, 35, 36, 1975–86), II, 175.

cases raised issues of honour and reputation the protagonists would refer themselves to the values espoused by their kin in the service nobility. In practice some of the ambiguities of the honour code are revealed by these cases as varying cultural norms were invoked by Lady Russell and her son.[3]

The two pursued their cases through the Star Chamber, the most effective way of engaging the Privy Council in the resolution of their legal grievances. Lady Russell's dispute essentially concerned property: her claims and rights in the castle, park and manor of Donnington in Berkshire. The principal defendant was Charles Howard, earl of Nottingham and Lord Admiral. Howard was constable of Windsor Castle, and keeper of the forest of Windsor, which had Donnington within its boundaries. In 1600 he had been given Donnington Castle by Elizabeth I in outright gift as a reward for his naval services. Lady Russell, who had previously held the keepership of Donnington from the early years of her second widowhood, had little intention of yielding to Howard. Her grievance was finally brought into court in 1606 because the castle had been repossessed by the earl's servants, who were then charged with riot and affray for denying entry to the lady. Material issues were in dispute, but, as we shall see, it was the wound to her honour that Lady Russell chose to place at the heart of her complaint.

Four years earlier the Council in Star Chamber had heard a very different form of complaint of riot from Sir Thomas Posthumous Hoby. He and his wife, the former Margaret Dakins, lived on her inherited manor of Hackness in the North Riding of Yorkshire. They were zealous Protestants in a country still predominantly Catholic, and they made no secret of their alienation from the values of local society. Conflicts with some of the leading families in the region culminated in 1600 in an unusual charivari, or ritual humiliation. A number of youthful gentlemen sought hospitality from the Hobys, supposedly after a hunting trip, and proceeded to mock their godly behaviour in their own home. There was sufficient disturbance for Sir Thomas to appeal first to the Council of the North and then, when satisfaction was denied him, to London and the Privy Council. Here, even more explicitly than in Lady Russell's case, issues of honour, familial loyalty and the different

---

[3] The best evaluation of the two individuals, together with much relevant material on their disputes, is in the introduction to *The Diary of Lady Margaret Hoby*, ed. D.M. Meads (1930) [hereafter *Hoby*], 13–22, 40–3. See also H.M. Gladstone, 'Building an Identity: Two Noblewomen in England, 1566–1666' (Ph.D. thesis, Open University, 1989) [hereafter Gladstone, 'Building an Identity']. I am grateful to Dr. Nigel Llewelwyn for drawing my attention to this dissertation. A.L.Rowse, 'Bisham and the Hobys' in his *Times, Persons, Places: Essays in Literature* (1965), 188–218.

values of different sections of the landed elite were aired at length in the proceedings of Star Chamber.[4]

## II

Lady Elizabeth Russell was a woman with unusual educational skills: like her blue-stocking Cooke sisters she was an able Latinist, who late in life published her girlhood translation of Martin Bucer's *A Way of Reconciliation in the Sacrament.* She employed her sharp mind in her legal disputes, though she never made any explicit claim to distinction as a consequence of knowledge. Her gender was inevitably far more important than her learning when she faced the public world. A woman's honour, as contemporaries endlessly reiterated, lay in chastity and in guarding her private virtue for the collective benefit of her family. A widow might experience some easing of the constraints of marriage, and indeed might be expected to engage in some public defence of familial honour at law. She could not readily transcend the categories of female modesty and assert a view of reputation similar to that of her male peers. Like many of her sex, Elizabeth often found it expedient to emphasise the vulnerability of the woman in order to protect her interests. In 1597, towards the end of a conflict with Windsor tradesmen about debt, she wrote to her nephew Robert Cecil thanking him 'with all my heart for defending my poor part in honour'. Another letter in the same series asserts that she would not have been insulted by mere tradesmen demanding payment had she possessed a 'husband honourable'. In the Star Chamber case she made much of the refusal of Nottingham's men to allow her to take her coach up to the castle, and of the subsequent incident in which she sat up all night outside the castle lodge. These and other Lady Russell statements migrate between the purely manipulative—the use of her position as a means of attracting male sympathy—and vigorous resentment at her inability to use female honour as a means of empowerment.[5]

It is unlikely that appeals to feminine vulnerability would in themselves have served Elizabeth Russell well in the competitive world of the court. Of much greater effect was her claim to high status, based upon her second marriage. Noblewomen, she never tired of repeating, partook of the standing of their spouses living or dead. Imperiousness

---

[4] On Hoby see F. Heal and C. Holmes, *The Gentry in England and Wales: 1500–1700* (1994), 1–5. The Russell case is Public Record Office [hereafter PRO], STAC8/245/7, with preliminary disputes at PRO STAC5/R15/31 and R36/31; the Hoby case is PRO STAC5/H16/2, H22/21, H42/12 and H50/4.

[5] On female honour see R. Brathwait, *The English Gentlewoman* (1631). Good examples of the manipulation of the ideal are in A. Wall, 'Elizabethan Precept and Feminine Practice', *History*, LXXV (1990), 23–38. *HMC Salisbury*, VII, 296–7.

of language, however, barely concealed the uncertainties of her true position. Lord Russell had never inherited the title of the earldom of Bedford to which he was heir, and he had only held the barony as a courtesy title before predeceasing his father. Lady Russell and her daughters, Anne and Elizabeth, therefore had to claim their rights against those of the new earl and his family. At some point after Elizabeth and Anne became maids of honour to the Queen in the 1590s, their mother addressed a passionate complaint to her brother-in-law, Lord Burghley. She argued that her daughters were humiliated by being given places of precedence below that of the wife of Sir William Russell, and that the 3rd earl of Bedford should show his arms differenced to demonstrate his true standing as a younger son. If none of this could be changed by Cecil's influence 'they [Elizabeth and Anne] shall lyve elsewhere rather than in Courte, to the disgrace of my dead hosband. . .'. Long before she raised these problems in a court of law, Lady Russell sought for her family the full panoply of individual noble status; seeking honour through old systems in order to secure their position in a newer environment.[6]

With her inferiors Lady Russell was more confident than she could be in the face of the earl of Bedford. Her extended conflict with one of the Berkshire JPs, Robert Lovelace, raised the question of honour in her own lands. 'Shall a lady of my place', she wrote to Robert Cecil, 'be touched so deeply in honour by a riot in her own liberty, where no sheriff has to do; and in her own manor and parish where she dwells: and have no recompense to his shame and her relief?' Another letter complains of the humiliation she had suffered in a connected dispute with Lovelace's daughter, who had previously been in her service. 'Thus in mine own manor to be cozened for my kindness', she lamented, 'I think too great a dishonour and disgrace.' When she went to law others were prepared to acknowledge some of her claims to rank and her assertion of the significance of reputation in the face of 'base churls' and 'mere servants'.[7]

Her problem was that these claims were not modulated to take account of the realities of political power so well understood by her Cecil kin. She was as likely to attack a nobleman or a royal justice as a minor JP. 'Good Mr. Secretary', she wrote to Robert Cecil about one of the justices of Common Pleas, 'let him know his duty since he knoweth not honesty nor justice . . . my place had deserved more regard of justice . .'. In defending her treasured reputation Lady Russell often

[6] Gladstone, 'Building an Identity', 194. G.E. Cockayne, *Complete Peerage*: Bedford. Russell was summoned to the 1580 Parliament and sat regularly as a baron thereafter. Bodleian Library Rawlinson MS B.146, fo. 87v.
[7] *HMC Salisbury*, XIV, 192; XI, 563.

appears as the epitome of Bourdieu's image that rank and status require you to 'become what you are'. A subjective imperative drove her onwards, and that imperative had its objective correlative in the demands she made upon others to affirm her position. Little space was left for the processes of social and political accommodation that marked Cecilian attitudes to honour. The law-reporter Hawarde noted as the essence of the Donnington dispute a remark of Elizabeth's that would not have disgraced the earl of Essex. She told the JP Thomas Dolman that she would not accept Nottingham's attempts at compromise because 'she scorned to be a keeper to anye subiecte'.[8]

There was, of course, a more practical and material basis to Lady Russell's disputes than her language might suggest. She was a widow without a particularly large estate, and her ambitions, especially for her daughters, demanded great revenues. She therefore valued the keeperships of Donnington, and was for a long period a suitor to the queen to have the manor in lease. Not only, she wrote to Robert Cecil in 1600, had his father promised her the lease, but she had expended large sums in gifts to the queen to gain it. With her usual dis-ingenuousness she listed the items offered as *douceurs*, including a gown and petticoat 'of such tissue that it could have been the Queen of Scots wedding dress'. The outright grant of the property to the Lord Admiral was therefore a sharp rebuff, felt in both purse and person. Even Lady Russell recognised that it was necessary not to blame the monarch, who was always the embodiment of honourable behaviour, so at the 1606 trial the queen was represented as horrified by the loss of Donnington: ' "God's deathe! my Castle of Dunnington! I think he will have my Crowne and all".' A mere widow, however vocal and well connected, could scarcely compete with this ambition, and in practice Lady Russell seems to have settled at first for access to the castle and park, and the ability to profit from her keepership in the years when she was making a grand alliance for her younger daughter with the son of the earl of Worcester.[9]

Early in James I's reign this uneasy settlement broke down when Nottingham sought possession of the castle in order to entertain the king and queen on their journey to the west. Then Lady Russell chose to see her honour as more wounded than her financial prospects. The

[8] *Calendar of State Papers Domestic* [hereafter *CSPD*] *1591–94*, 379. *HMC Salisbury*, XVII, 436–7; XIV, 192; XI, 423–4. P. Bourdieu, 'Rites as Acts of Justification', in *Honour and Grace in Anthropology*, ed. J.G.Peristiany and J.Pitt-Rivers, (Cambridge, 1992), 84–5. J. Hawarde, *Les Reportes del Cases in Camera Stellata*, ed. W.P. Baildon (1894) [hereafter Hawarde, *Les Reportes*], 273.

[9] *HMC Salisbury*, X, 51–2. *CSPD 1595–7*, 147–8. Hawarde, *Les Reportes*, 276. There is a good account of the marriage of Anne to the son of the earl of Worcester in R. Strong, *The Cult of Elizabeth* (1977), 23–30.

threat 'to make a Star Chamber matter of it', uttered to Nottingham's servants before many witnesses, was apparently born of a furious desire to revenge herself on the earl. She petitioned the king at Newbury for his aid: his response was to urge her to seek arbitration, that honourable route for mollifying aristocratic egos. But Elizabeth repeatedly called for 'law and justice', and in the end had little option but to bring the matter before the Council. In Star Chamber even her own lawyers found it profoundly unconvincing that they were prosecuting a senior peer for trespass and riot on his own property. Faced in court with the likelihood of failure Lady Russell took the even more remarkable route of speaking herself as prosecutor and lecturing the Privy Council on the justice of her cause. She embarked upon what Hawarde aptly calls 'a large discourse', which no man in the court had the wit or capacity to halt. The immediacy of her complaint coruscates through the measured prose of the reporters. Hawarde noted that 'revenge by her tounge semed to be the summe of her desyre'. The burden of her speech was of honour and dishonour. The court, she claimed, was abused for allowing the earl to answer not upon his oath, but upon his honour—the nearest that she could perhaps come to a direct charge of lying. She was even more bitter about Nottingham's denial that she was dowager to Lord Russell and began to argue for her status, only to be interrupted by the earl of Northampton who told her that indeed there could be no dowager beneath the status of earl. 'Upon that shee plucked him by the cloake and tolde him the lawe was otherwyse before he was borne'. What finally compelled the councillors to stop her in mid-flow, however, was her claim that the queen had taken £1,500 from her for Donnington, and that she had seen no return. In her anger Lady Russell had finally forgotten the conventions of political discourse. She was silenced, and judgment was later given against her.[10]

How should we locate Lady Russell's story in the shifting concepts of honour discussed at the beginning of this paper? In many ways she depended on very traditional assertions of a noble honour code, using Star Chamber as an environment in which to articulate beliefs which she had no power to enforce in reality. She also exploited her family connections in ways that were essentially traditional. Burghley, who often had little time for his sister-in-law's strident tone and aggressive management of her family, nevertheless took her part against Lovelace, lecturing him for ingratitude to Elizabeth and her son who were 'the chief founders of him and his ancestors'. Robert Cecil, who was more

[10] Moore (K.B.) 786–7, in *The English Reports* (178 vols., 1900–30), LXXII, 906. Hawarde, *Les Reportes*, 271–8. The Star Chamber threat, taken from *Merry Wives of Windsor*, act 1 sc. I, has been linked with Lady Russell's Windsor disputes. The play is usually dated to 1597 or 1600 so any connection, if it does exist, must be with the Lovelace disputes.

patient, was the recipient of endless requests to support the honour of the Russells. At the same time Elizabeth used the mechanisms of new centralist political authority: appeal to the support and patronage of the monarch and the public pursuit of her objectives through the courts. At least one lawyer and politician reminded her that she could not have it both ways. Sir Edward Coke, consulted about the Lovelace case, made the appropriate noises about honour, but stressed that if Lady Russell took the issue to court and was proved to have broken the law her status would not save her. It was wisest, he suggested, to settle out of court 'seeing there is so great inequality of persons, I would not have them suffer equal punishment'. An endeavour to affirm old views of honour by new means was always likely to encounter conflict of this order.[11]

Coke's advice suggests that he, like others, saw Lady Russell's problem as a misunderstanding of the exigencies of politics and law. Hawarde describes how the councillors were scandalised in 1606 by her outburst in court: they 'severallye...much distasted theise fonde speeches...all condemninge greatelye the pryde and wyllfullnes of the plaintiff'. Some of this failure was explained for contemporaries by her gender: when judgment was passed against her Northampton (still no doubt resentful that his sleeve had been plucked) delivered himself of the dark comment that 'by the Civill lawe the wyves are favoured in Cases of treason, *propter imbecillitatem sexus*'. Hawarde noted that Lady Russell spoke 'in a verye boulde and stoute manner, without any shewe of any dis-temparature...but shewinge a very greate spirite and undaunted Courage, or rather will, more then womanlike...'. Thus he raises, but also partially dismisses, the issue of gender. The passions employed were feminine: they were employed in ways that set Elizabeth apart from her sex. More important was his subsequent comment that what would have been called malice in an ordinary person, 'in her, beinge honorable, learned and indued with many excellente guyftes, we grace it with "a greate spirite", which I feare the worlde conceavethe to be more then blemyshed, if not utterlye extinguyshed, with extreame pryde'. Nottingham, on the other hand, possessed a properly controlled understanding of honour, in which the pride of a noble meshed with the prudence of a high officer of state. Chief Baron Fleming singled him out as having ' "done honorablye and discreatelye" ', and Ellesmere praised him as being ' "honorable, and [of] great temper and good respectes" '.[12]

Lady Russell is therefore condemned in part for the same defects of

[11] British Library Lansdowne MS [hereafter BL Lans.] 10/38; 33/85. *CSPD 1595–7*, 148. *HMC Salisbury*, V, 7; XIV, 192.
[12] Hawarde, *Les Reportes*, 275–7, 309–12.

pride and misjudgment that had marred the career of the earl of Essex. Often thwarted in her attempts to use the patronage system and the proximity to the throne that service under Elizabeth gave her family, she resorted to the narrower standards of aristocratic honour. But as a woman the only effective defences of her honour were her family or the law courts. Neither could fully serve her purposes, especially when her opponent stood high in royal favour and her own legal claims were shaky. So her behaviour was labelled as deviant, 'self-willed' as Nottingham argued, and she existed in an uneasy limbo excluded from full acknowledgment by the honour community.

## III

Sir Thomas Posthumous Hoby's route into the Star Chamber can be described rather more briefly. He had married Margaret Dakins in 1596 and immediately begun the process of defining a position for himself in Yorkshire politics. In 1597 he was junior partner to Sir John Stanhope at the famous disputed county election when Stanhope was defeated by Sir William Savile. His sustained efforts at influence-seeking were, however, focused upon the North Riding, where he quickly became a JP, and was frequently used in other commissions, especially against recusancy. His known zeal for godly Protestantism, and his court connections, marked him out as an appropriate agent of central government. In the course of establishing himself in the locality he displayed a political sensitivity that must surely betray his mother's early influence. He came into conflict with several of the leading gentry families of the region, especially the Cholmleys, who dominated Whitby. Henry Cholmley was charged with recusancy, and a group of his dependants were presented by Hoby to the recusancy commission. He also attempted to carve a separate manorial liberty out of the Cholmleys's Liberty of Whitby Sands. Aggressive Protestantism also alienated Hoby from the leading magnate of the area, Ralph, 3rd Lord Eure, who presided over a clan that ranged in religious sentiment from occasional conformists to outright recusants. In August 1600, after three years of this intrusion, the local families took their revenge.[13]

Ritual humiliation by charivari was a common form of popular justice, but not a method usually employed within the 'honour community' among men of substance and status. In the detailed depositions and arguments that were generated by Sir Thomas's Star Chamber

[13] *Hoby*, 8–12, 27–32; *The Fortescue Papers*, ed. S.R. Gardiner (Camden Soc., n.s., 1, 1871), vi–xxii. H. Aveling, *The Catholic Recusants of the North Riding of Yorkshire 1585–1790* (1966), 118–20. G.C.F. Forster, 'North Riding Justices and their Sessions, 1603–25' *Northern History*, X (1975), 108–11. T.H. Brooke, 'The Memoirs of Sir Hugh Cholmley' (B.Litt Oxford University, 1937) [hereafter Brooke, 'Cholmley'], 43–6.

suit against his revelling guests we therefore have a very unusual insight
into different understandings of reputation. The three predominant
elements in Hoby's complaints were that the defendants intended a
public shaming in order to inhibit him in the performance of his
magisterial duty; that they also assailed his private identity as a patriarch
within his household; and that they challenged his religious beliefs,
which were those of all true subjects.[14]

The public consequences of the humiliation were emphasised in
Hoby's bill of complaint and in the depositions of some of his servants
precisely because they were likely to secure governmental sympathy
and provide added force to the legal action. The morning of the visit
by the riotous youths was one on which Hoby had to preside at a
subsidy commission. Robert Nettleton, one of the servants, deposed
that countrymen arriving for the commission were thought by Sir
William Eure to be 'the country roused'. His nephew William Eure
'said he cared not for the Commission, he wolld teare it'. Another
servant, John Walsh, deposed that the uproar had delayed the collection
of the subsidy. These particular points became illustrative of the more
general intention of opposing Hoby as a magistrate. In these 'frozen
parts', he claimed, it was a matter of honour to be backward in
promoting the crown's interests. At the very least, partiality in the
execution of policy was expected: but now the Eure clan, claimed Hoby
'could not attayne at his handes such favors exemptions and discharges
as in regard of the countenance and protection of the said Lord Eure
they had bynne formerly accustomed unto'.[15]

There are no clear counterclaims from the Eures on these matters, but
it can be presumed that one objective of the charivari was to subvert
Hoby's position and neutralise his advantage of access to central patronage networks. The charivari depended on so dishonouring the man in the
face of local society that he would be forced to retreat from the public
stage. This was done most effectively not by aiming directly at the JP and
cousin of Robert Cecil, but at his personal honour and his authority over
his household and tenantry. A hostile witness claimed that well before the
incident Sir Christopher Hillyard was saying that 'there was a sorte of
younge fellowes in Yorkshire wolled plaie him [Hoby] a tricke ere it were
longe and when it were done he shoud not mende himselfe'.[16]

There was also a parochial dimension to the humiliation of the
Hobys. Both husband and wife were deeply invested in their roles as
lord and lady of the manor of Hackness, which was coterminous with

[14] On the nature and significance of charivari in England see M. Ingram, 'Ridings,
Rough Music and "the Reform of Popular Culture" in Early Modern England', *Past and
Present* CV (1984), 79–113.
[15] PRO, STAC5/H16/2. *HMC Salisbury*, X, 303. PRO, STAC5/H22/21.
[16] PRO, STAC5/H22/21, testimony of Michael Wharton.

the village. They provided extensive physical and spiritual care for the community, following the Calvinist precepts on the construction of a godly commonwealth. But, as so often, this vigorous care produced opponents. At least one of the visitors of 1600 was a local man, George Smyth, who used the sanction of his betters as a way of assailing his landlord. It was Smyth who caused much of the damage by galloping around a newly made driveway, and one of the servants claimed that he had previously broken the village stocks 'because the plaintiff did use to punish poore folkes in them'. It was also alleged that in his cups he had proposed to pull down the local church 'becawse the Lord of the Mannor was tyed to buyld yt agayne'. A reformation of manners constructed out of puritan godliness was clearly not to the liking of some of Hackness's traditionalists.[17]

The most visible aspect of the young gentlemen's behaviour, however, was their challenge to Sir Thomas's authority within his household. Their visit probed the limits of his commitment to an honourable ideal of hospitality. They came at evening unannounced and in considerable numbers: they played cards and drank healths, both actions known to be deeply offensive to their host. They interrupted the saying of houschold prayers with noises that were variously described as 'very lowde straunge and wylde', 'a catch or a song of prynce Arthurs' or a deliberately structured 'black sanctus'. Next morning they were drunk, riotous in the courtyard and probably careless enough to have broken a few windowpanes. Robert Nettleton summed up the reaction of the houschold most fully: since all men knew of Hoby's austere views

> and that yt would greve the plaintiff very much to have the lawes of hospitalitye by them so greatly vyolated as they woold be yf the sayde defendants whoe came unsent for and under pretence of kindnes shoold not content themselves with sich thynges and lawfull enterteyne as the plaintiff doth usually geve to all such as does vysyte him.... [18]

It would have been surprising if rioters so bent on revenge had not extended their insults into the arena of personal and sexual defamation. This was, after all, a charivari, and as such was popularly focused on an assault on improper sexual relationships. Hoby's situation and person provided easy opportunity for such taunts. He and his wife were childless after four years of marriage; he had married an heiress and

---

[17] PRO, STAC5/H50/4, testimony of John Reynes. Lady Margaret's diary is rich in references to care for the community, and it is known from other sources that the Hobys repaired their parish church and that Sir Thomas later built a separate upland chapel dedicated to St Margaret: *Victoria County History: Yorkshire: North Riding*, II, 531.

[18] PRO, STAC5/H50/4, testimony of Robert Nettleton; H50/4, testimony of William Jordan and Peter Campelman.

come north with no fortune of his own to assert authority over her; and he had a puny physique. The last we know not just from the comments of his enemies, but from his delightful mother, who in a letter to Lord Burghley remarked 'what his owne infirmitiyes and insufficiency by want of stature, learning and otherwise be I know'. It seems that sexual innuendoes were part of the rioters' language: several witnesses, for example, deposed that young William Eure denounced Sir Thomas, calling him a 'spyndle shanked ape'. But Hoby chose to dwell on the threat of action implicit in such defamatory words. Nettleton deposed that George Smyth looked at stags' horns on the hall wall and wished that they 'were as hard nailed or as hard fastened upon Sir Thomas his heade', and that Eure had threatened to 'sett upp hornes at his gate and be gone'. Sir Thomas himself complained that Eure in his drunken frenzy claimed that he would 'play young Devereux', a reference to Lady Margaret's first husband. Finally Eure was reported to have said that had Mr Rhodes, the chaplain and intimate of Lady Margaret, been present 'he woold have gelded him'.[19]

Richard Rhodes emerges from the case and from the evidence of Lady Hoby's diary as a key actor in the affairs of Hackness. Apparently a Cambridge graduate, he was already at Hackness when the diary begins in 1598, and seems to have been a far more important influence on Margaret's religious life than her husband. Sexual innuendo about their relationship would not have been surprising: even the modern editor of the diary speculates on affection between the two. The importance of Rhodes in the Hackness household gave the rioters an ideal opportunity to conflate sexual suggestion and anti-Protestant sentiment: one of the servants testified that it was generally believed in the community that the intention was to humiliate either Hoby or his chaplain. There seems to have been an earlier complaint to the Privy Council by Hoby about the insulting behaviour of William Eure. The latter claimed that he had resolved the matter partly by showing the Council 'such gestures as [the] preacher did use in his evening exercises, and that your Honour [Robert Cecil] did laugh very heartily at it'. Now Eure had a more direct opportunity for revenge: and Lady Margaret's waiting woman suggests that he was deliberately hunting for the chaplain when he invaded her mistress's chamber on the morning of the visit.[20]

When William Eure challenged Hoby's patriarchal authority directly

---

[19] PRO STAC5/H22/21. BL Lans. 10/38. Another insult was that he 'useth to draw up his Breeches with a shooing-horn', PRO STAC5/H50/4.

[20] Venn identifies a Richard Roodes who matriculated as a sizar at St John's in 1591, was an MA in 1598 and had been ordained in 1597. Rhodes was at Hackness in 1598, evidently at an early stage of his career: J. and J.A. Venn, *Alumni Cantabrigiensis to 1751*, III, 447. *Hoby*, 267, and *passim* for the presence of Rhodes in the household. *HMC Salisbury*, X, 325. PRO STAC5/H50/4.

and forced his way into Lady Margaret's presence, his host no longer felt bound by the laws of hospitality and threw his guests out unceremoniously. It is very difficult to judge how far the revellers intended this provocation. The formal depositions of the Eures and their adherents are at pains to stress that no insult was intended to Lady Margaret, indeed some comments suggest that she was respected by her neighbours. Yet these assurances do not fully conceal the point that a challenge to Sir Thomas's patriarchal authority and his Protestant values was also an attack on his wife. It was necessary to demonstrate that the ordered, sober, hierarchical household of the Hobys was in fact the inversion of all true order. And it was Protestant zeal, the rioters were determined to show, that was the inception and locus of this world-turned-upside-down.

Lady Margaret's diary indicates that her husband reacted almost immediately to the humiliating visit. Less than a week later he was in York, lodging a complaint of breach of the peace before the Council of the North; then early in October he and his wife were en route to London to present a complaint directly to the Council. Hoby receded his London visit by writing to Robert Cecil on 5 September, giving his version of the crisis, and arguing that he could expect no redress locally since Lord Eure was vice-president of the Council of the North. His period in London was spent initiating his Star Chamber suit, but there were powerful pressures from the Eures, and from other members of the Council of the North to follow 'the custom of the country' and put the issue to arbitration. In 1601, with Hoby's cousin, the 2nd Lord Burghley now active as president of the Council of the North, the couple were again persuaded to visit York, where Margaret gives a vivid account of the persuasions used to encourage them to 'take up our sute with the lord Eure'. 'But', she continues, 'perceavinge our selves to be wrongd, in regard that an end was sought which would have tended much to our discredets, and that the truth of our Iniuries Could not be considered, we Came away Abruptly.' Their case was heard in Star Chamber in February 1602: judgment was given for the Hobys and fines imposed on the defendants. It was with unconcealed satisfaction that Margaret recorded in May 1602 that Lord Eure's men had come to Hackness to pay £100 in recompense for the damage done:

> and so it fell out that, as it was done in the sight of our tenenates, so many of the tenants were bye when the mony was brought: which I note, as seeinge the Istuice and mercie of god to his servants in manifestinge to the world, who litle regardes them, that he will bringe downe their enemies unto them.[21]

[21] Hoby, 142–3. HMC Salisbury, X, 302, 325; XI, 11–12, 456, 546; XII, 22. PRO STAC5/H22/21. Hoby, 185, 189, 197–8.

It is difficult to know what expectations the Eures and Cholmleys had of Hoby's response when they embarked on their visit. They probably did not expect him to conform to norms of the community of honour by offering any direct challenge to his adversaries. When the case first came to York Lord Eure's response combined a contempt for Hoby's complaints with a prudential suppression of the commission binding over the rioters to keep the peace. According to Hoby 'the said lord Eure then and there [did] use a long discourse unto the plaintiff of the manier of dewelles and noble combates...saying...that he the said plaintiff must know that men hadd not swordes onelie to weare but sometimes to drawe them to defende theire reputacions'. To Sir Thomas this was yet another indication of the culture of violence and of political disorder that dominated northern society: to Eure an assertion of proper gentlemanly behaviour in a dispute focused above all on honour. Lord Eure, it must be stressed, was no mindless northern thug, nor exclusively a man of the sword. He was employed by the government not only in the northern marches, but later as lord president of the Council of Wales and as an ambassador to Denmark. He was well educated, having attended both Cambridge and the Inns of Court, and been on a European tour where he acquired his linguistic skills. However, his humanist abilities were combined with a general sympathy for the old faith, and an acceptance of the violent elements of the honour code. In 1598, for example, Chamberlain reported to Carleton that Lord Eure and his brother had been set upon in London by members of the Witherington clan, with whom they had 'a country quarrell'. Hoby's use of the courts, and of central government influence, to defend his honour, must merely have affirmed his baseness in the eyes of such a family.[22]

Yet Eure must always have expected that Sir Thomas would appeal to the Council and to his cousin as a ways of salving his wounded pride. He may have hoped that the affair would be regarded as insignificant, to be dismissed as an earlier conflict had been dismissed by young William Eure's playacting. He had not allowed for that strong sense of dishonour experienced by the Hobys and well expressed in the quotation from Margaret's diary given earlier. They believed that they had a strong case at law: they also calculated that this time Robert Cecil would lend them the necessary support. This did indeed happen, and so it is necessary to ask why Robert Cecil should on this occasion

[22] PRO STAC5/H22/21, from the series of interrogatories designed by Hoby to be administered to Henry Cholmley. Venn, *Alumni Cantabrigiensis*, II, 111 . Two of Ralph's younger brothers attended Cambridge and a William Eure, who may well be the brother in the 1600 story, was at Queen's, Oxford: J. Foster, *Alumni Oxoniensis 1500–1714*, II, 468. *CSPD Add. 1580–1625*, 53, 85, 98. *Letters of John Chamberlain*, ed. N.E. McClure (2 vols., American Philosophical Society, Philadelphia, 1939), I, 36–7.

have taken his cousin's posturing seriously? Was Cecil in any way identified with the perception of honour adumbrated by Hoby?

Sir Thomas was of utility to the Privy Council in the North Riding, especially in the work of monitoring the arrival of Catholic priests on the coasts. In 1599 Sir John Ferne of the Council of the North had observed, 'I do not knowe of any [other] faithfull assistance in the cuntry.' Hoby's quarrels and self-importance were no doubt an irritant, but Cecil could scarcely undermine so useful a figure in this dark corner of the land. If this consideration was always relevant, the timing of the Star Chamber case was fortunate for both Sir William Eure and Richard Cholmley were caught in the fringes of the Essex rebellion. Eure was imprisoned for questionable conversations with James VI, probably on Essex's behalf; Cholmley, who was in London at the time of the rising because of the Hoby dispute, took some minor part for the earl. Cholmley was eventually released with a £200 fine, although Hoby typically tried to prove that he had the 'hollow hearts' of his country behind him. Support for his kinsman in his dispute was therefore a signal to Lord Eure and his adherents to avoid any involvement in dubious politics by their younger and wilder spirits. It may also be that appeals to familial honour were particularly telling for Cecil at a time when Essex had held him up to contempt. His father had, after all, advised in his '*Precepts*' that kin should always be welcome at a gentleman's table, since they provided so many voices to speak for him.[23]

It is not necessary in these explanations to foreground any specific concern for honour on the part of Cecil or the Council in London. The Eures' shaming ritual offended only in so far as it represented disorder, and a threat to royal authority in an insecure part of the realm. The humiliation of his allies and servants at the hands of Star Chamber did nothing to arrest the progress of Lord Eure's career: within a year of the decree he had been approached to serve on the embassy to Denmark. Nor did Robert Cecil apparently feel the need to follow Sir Thomas's victory by offering any great marks of favour to him: in 1604 he became *custos rotulorum* of the North Riding bench, and eventually he became a member of the Council of the North, but higher office eluded him. It was in a local context that Hoby's victory meant more, since it demonstrated that he could not be displaced by regional means of revenge. There were local losers as well, most notably the Cholmleys who were locked in a vendetta with Hoby for much of the early Stuart period. A generation later Sir Hugh Cholmley reported

[23] PRO, SP12/270/99. *HMC Salisbury*, XI, 14–15, 39–40, 198. *Letters of Chamberlain*, I, 113. Cecil, *Certain Precepts*, 13.

*Bisham tomb of Lady Elizabeth Russell.*

Hoby's comment of him: 'his grandfather once crossed me thus on the bench, but I made him repent it, and so will I this man'.[24]

Where in these stories should we therefore situate honour? It seems that the Eure charivari depended for its impact on an acceptance that honour and shame were major values, able to change the position a gentleman possessed in his local community. Its perpetrators were not wholly wrong, for Sir Thomas Hoby remained ever afterwards the 'spindle shanked' knight, a butt of jests even among those who were not natural allies of the Eures. The memory of the events of 1600 may even have circumscribed his later career. In his turn Hoby could argue that the true honour of an office-holder under the crown had been vindicated in that most public of forums, the Council sitting as a law court. Here the Hoby case mirrors that of Lady Russell very closely, though in the latter instance it was Lady Elizabeth who was condemned for her challenge to order. Finally we might note that it was important to Sir Thomas that his honour should be vindicated, but that his Protestant ideology would probably have offered an alternative form of solace if the support of his cousin and the Council had been denied. The very formulation of Margaret's response to the payment of the fines indicates this: victory was a 'special providence' for the saints, but the reverse outcome would presumably have indicated their necessary suffering in the face of a despiteful world. Here the idea of honour could be wholly internalised, owing nothing either to the affirmation of the local community or to the support of the crown.

'Honour', says Julian Pitt-Rivers, looking at the subject with the eye of a modern anthropologist, 'is too intimate a sentiment to submit to final definition: it must be felt. . . .' There seems no doubt that both Lady Russell and Sir Thomas Hoby felt the blows to their pride displayed in the actions of the earl of Nottingham and the Eure clan. Both used the mechanisms of law to bring their grievances into the public forum. This was partly because as a woman and a physically weak man traditional forms of violent redress were not open to them, but more significantly because they perceived the political and ideological advantages of linking their particular complaints to the vision of honour espoused by their family of service nobility. This proved reasonably effective as a technique for assuaging Sir Thomas's sense of injury. But the law and the patronage system that sustained her son failed Lady Russell when she pitted her honour in a weak cause against that of the Lord Admiral. Her response to this defeat is interesting: not for her, despite her firm Protestantism, only the suffering of the saints in a hostile world. Her life-size portrait done at about the time of the case has an inscription from the Psalms, 'cast thy burden

[24] PRO STAC8/12/11. Brooke, 'Cholmley', 249.

upon the Lord', and verse which continues 'he shall never suffer the righteous to be moved'. But confidence in the Lord was more than matched by the braving display of family pride on her magnificent Bisham tomb, erected towards the end of her life (see Plate 1). There she adopts the viscountess's coronet to bolster her claims as a dowager, and expresses confidence both in the continuity of her lineage and her own high standing. Honour here is a quality that has to be displayed so that it may be reclaimed: reclaimed from any taint of the manipulation of the law, or of failures in using the patronage system, reclaimed even from the indifference or hostility of the crown. Honour can here be left to the judgment of her posterity and of history.[25]

[25] Peristiany and Pitt-Rivers, *Honour and Grace in Anthropology*, 4. There are two good descriptions of the Russell tomb: P. Begent, *The Heraldry of the Hoby Memorials in the Parish Church of All Saints, Bisham, in the Royal County of Berkshire* (Maidenhead, 1979), and Gladstone, 'Building an Identity', 301–12. Gladstone suggests that the portrait, which still hangs at Bisham, was done in preparation for work on the tomb. It does not include a coronet, though in other respects the clothing worn by Lady Russell is the same in both cases.

# HONOUR IN LIFE, DEATH AND IN THE MEMORY: FUNERAL MONUMENTS IN EARLY MODERN ENGLAND

By Nigel Llewellyn

READ 24 MARCH 1995 AT THE UNIVERSITY OF CAMBRIDGE

## *Introduction*

IN the parish churches and cathedrals of England and Wales stand many thousands of early modern funeral monuments. Typically, these are elaborate structures of carved stone, often painted and decorated in bright colours and trimmed with gilding. Their complex programmes of inscribed text, allegorical figures, heraldic emblazons and sculpted effigies are set within architectural frameworks. With a few exceptions, such as the famous memorials to Queen Elizabeth, William Shakespeare or John Donne, these monuments are relatively little studied and little known. However, they were extremely costly to their patrons and prominently displayed in churches in purpose-built family chapels or against the wall of the sanctuary. Contemporary comment reveals that they were accorded high status by both specialist commentators, such as antiquaries and heralds, and by the patrons who invested in them so heavily. All-in-all, they represent what was the most important kind of church art made in the post-Reformation England, a period when there was a great deal of general uncertainty about the status of visual experience and particular worries about the legitimacy of religious imagery.[1]

The high cost of early modern funeral monuments and the care evidently taken by patrons and tomb-makers over their appearance suggests that weighty responsibilities were expected of them. Indeed, they were intended to establish in the collective memory and set for ever the honourable reputation of the subjects they commemorated. The monuments performed this function by acting in various and precise ways as indices of the social status of the deceased. Such precision was consequent on two factors: first, their specificity to certain individuals and families by virtue of their use of systems of signs such

---

[1] Much of the material presented in this paper may be found in a more fully developed form in two books: Nigel Llewellyn, *Signs of Life: Funeral Monuments in the Visual Culture of Post-Reformation England* (Cambridge, in press), and Nigel Llewellyn, *The Art of Death: The Visual Culture of the English Death Ritual, c.1500—c.1800* (1991).

as heraldry and verbal text and second by their siting, materials and design.

This distinctive role must be set in the context of the elaborate rituals of death which were accepted practice amongst the ranks of honour in post-Reformation England. In their form and function the monuments registered the central importance in the ritual of continuity, that is, of the need to find ways to counter the potential damage to the social or communal fabric caused by the demise of a particular individual. For the monument was intended to replace that individual and by means of its siting and its design, to suggest the continuity of the memory and of the subject's lineage. As time passed, the natural body of the individual, that is, the biological reality of the decomposing corpse, might of necessity sink into corruption and decay, yet imagery and representation could sustain the memory and the reputation of the social body. In this property, funeral monuments were joined by portraits of various kinds and by verbal texts, memoirs and the like. In this sense, the functions of funeral monuments were not unique to church art; for they were, in addition, extremely active in the secular sphere.

One of the ways that the reputations of the honoured could be sustained by means of funeral monuments was through a process that Protestant theologians called *memoria*, or exemplification. This principle required the monument to function as a moral example to the ranks of the living, to set them on the path of righteousness and to remind them of the worthiness of the deceased.[2] These are the kinds of arguments that we find in the official or semi-official written defences made against iconoclastic assaults on monuments, that they deserved to be left alone as an example to the people.[3] Of course, late medieval monuments had often spoken to the living, warning them of the need to look to the future of their souls and beware of the potential pain of immortality rather than to set excessive store by the actual pleasures of the mundane world. Funeral monuments had a place in the vital world of the *memento mori*, a world of popular representation that also embraced prints, wall paintings, verses, homilies and other cultural manifestations. However, the Reformist statutes of the 1550s and 1560s had set fault lines in some of the patterns of belief upon which the traditional iconography of funeral monuments had been established, for example, the customary saying of masses for the souls of the dead imagined as residing in purgatory. In rejecting purgatory in favour of the ideology

[2] For *memoria* see *Death in the Middle Ages*, ed. H. Braet and W. Verbecke (Louvain, 1983).

[3] On iconoclasm see Margaret Aston, *England's Iconoclasts: Laws against Images* (Oxford, 1988), and Nigel Llewellyn, 'Cromwell and the Tombs: Historiography and Style in Post-Reformation English Funeral Monuments', in *L'Art et les Revolutions*, IV, ed. A. Chatelet (Strasburg, 1992), 193–204.

of *memoria*, Protestantism emphasised the need to supply models for the living from amongst the reputations of the dead. In early modern England, it was the ranks of honour, above all other, that supplied such reputations.

## The economy of monuments

Before returning to a more detailed examination of the ways that were open to tomb-makers and patrons to create monuments that effectively set the memory of their subjects for ever in the ranks of honour, we need to understand the economic and design history of early modern funeral monuments and acquire a more vivid sense of their place in the wider visual culture of death.

Although elaborate carved stone funeral monuments were highly successful at establishing and sustaining the reputations of the higher social orders, they were but one kind of memorial art. There were other more modest kinds of commemorative object such as the carved stone tablet, the engraved brass and the painted wooden panel, specimens of all of which have survived from this period (though not in such great numbers as versions in stone). There is, as yet, no comprehensive survey of England's monuments; however, field work and case studies reveal that they were spread (and have survived) right across the country and through time in ways suggestive both of their role as indices of local wealth and prosperity and of their vulnerability to religious controversy and shifts in taste. In the sixteenth and seventeenth centuries, there was a steady rise in the numbers of monuments being erected. However, during the uncertain years around 1550 (and again in the 1640s and 1650s), monuments came to be regarded with suspicion from certain quarters; some even thought them dangerous and took to damaging them. Neither of these conditions encouraged lively rates of production; even so, the picture across the realm changes according to local circumstances.

Insufficient details are known to set out with any real certainty the full production history of early modern monuments although it is clear that the choice and potential of the materials used and questions about transportation were important. A figure such as Sir Edward Denny, on the fringes of the court, had a monument costing £100 erected to his memory in 1600–1 at Waltham Holy Cross, Essex (Plate 1).[4] Within a few years people such as the Denny family were spending hugely larger sums on monuments. The Denny tomb was erected at Waltham Abbey and was delivered at no extra cost having been made at the London

[4] R. C. Fowler, 'The Denny Monument at Waltham Abbey', *Transactions of the Essex Archaeological Society*, new series XVI (1923), 57–9, which includes a transcription of the contractual document.

**Plate 1**   The monument to Sir Edward Denny (died 1600) and his wife
Margaret, made in 1600–1 by Bartholomew Atye and Isaac James, Waltham
Abbey, Waltham Holy Cross, Essex.

workshop of Bartholomew Atye and Isaac James, the latter, as were so many tomb-makers *c.* 1600, an immigrant from the Low Countries. Their chosen material for carving the 'two lieng pictures' (that is, the two recumbent effigies) and some of the rest of the fabric was a kind of roughish limestone which was relatively soft to the point where it did not allow for any very complex undercutting or hard polishing. Effectively, that stone itself disallowed any very fine detail and the tomb-makers relied instead on creating somewhat generalised sculpted impressions finished off by detailed paint work.

All across the country we find local variations of this creative theme; comparatively poor materials constraining the hands of the carvers but offering a reasonable deal to the patrons who otherwise were obliged to involve themselves in the costly transportation of higher quality materials, for example, imports from the continent. For most of the 1500s, as had been the case for several generations, the Midlands alabaster pits had supplied statuary stones of this grade and the Midlands alabasterers had worked them. However, in the high Elizabethan period we find that it is the London workshops which increasingly secure a larger and larger share of the market. The London tomb-makers continued to use Midlands alabaster but gradually this native material was supplanted by more costly foreign imports offering a wider range of visual possibilities as well as a more responsive statuary medium. Purer white marbles from southern Europe, black stones from the north-west of the continent and rance, a kind of mottled red dolomite limestone, were amongst the most used of this crop of alternatives.

The real alternatives to carved and decorated stone were few and little used. There are some effigies carved from oak and there are others cast from the symbolically potent metal alloy gilded bronze but what is much more important is the question of location, that is, the choice of site for the erection of a monument or set of monuments. The question of location perhaps reveals more than all others the acute sensitivities that characterised the complete processes of monumental patronage and the complexity of that process. For location was imposed on patrons. It was rarely a matter of an open choice for there were, invariably, powerful political forces at work to maintain the structures against which location was understood. In establishing an appropriate place for a monument, as in so many aspects of the commemorative pattern, ritualised processes played a leading role. By convention, the bodies of the dead were reincorporated amongst those of their ancestors and monuments were frequently set up in the family chapel or in the church adjacent to the family estate. In the post-Reformation period, the high incidence of changing land ownership created many new ancestral burial sites. Even when death had occurred away from home, perhaps at court in London or abroad on an embassy, the deceased was often carried back to lie for ever with his or her ancestors. So it was that monuments were erected in precisely those ecclesiastical sites where the deceased or the bereaved family had the necessary influence or even ownership to ensure that an appropriate commemorative place could be marked out and filled. Even before a monument was put up, ecclesiastical law required that the patrons obtain a faculty, a legal instrument that needed the agreement of the patron of the church.[5]

There are some important exceptions to this convention of local reincorporation and these exceptional sites signal the emergence of an increasingly open and apparently commercial market especially in one or two markedly prestigious buildings such as cathedrals—where bishops were usually buried—and venues in London such as [Old] St Paul's Cathedral and Westminster Abbey. The Abbey, as a royal peculiar and associated with an increasingly centralised government focused on the court, became the most prestigious site for the commemoration of courtiers during the second half of the 1500s and thereafter. Once the Tudor dynasty had made a serious, royal recommitment to the Abbey and once the early Stuarts had reconfirmed its status as the premier national mausoleum, there was no holding the honoured ranks of courtiers and other worthies in their jostling to secure a commemorative place in the chapels radiating from the eastern ambulatory.[6] However, permission to erect a monument had to be obtained from the monarch and under Elizabeth it seems clear that it was felt especially appropriate for noble women to be commemorated there. In general, funeral monuments supported the principle that an honourable reputation was legitimately an ambition for noble women, as it was incontestably in the domain of noble men. However, the tombs in Westminster re-emphasise for us this point with dramatic clarity.[7] Examples of monuments erected here to the memory of women include those to the daughters of kings and nobles such as James I's young children, the princesses Sophia and Mary, commemorated by the royal tomb-maker Maximilian Colt in a kind of crèche at the extreme west end of Henry VII's Chapel, and Elizabeth Russell (died July 1600) the daughter of the earl of Bedford.[8] In addition, the sacred spaces of the Abbey were

[5] There is no complete account of faculties in relation to monuments, however, see Brian Burch, 'Faculty Records and Church Monuments', *Bulletin of the International Society for the Study of Church Monuments*, VI (1982), 97–114.

[6] For the Tudor and Stuart commemorative investment in the Abbey see Nigel Llewellyn, 'The Royal Body: Monuments to the Dead, for the Living', in *Renaissance Bodies. The Human Figure in English Culture c.1540–1660*, ed. L. Gent and N Llewellyn (London, 1990), 218–40.

[7] For an account of stylistic development in monuments in the Abbey see Adam White, 'Westminster Abbey in the Early Seventeenth Century: A Powerhouse of Ideas', *Church Monuments*, VII (1989), 16–53.

[8] For monuments to children see Jean Wilson, 'Seated Children on Seventeenth-

used to commemorate women indisputably of noble status but for whom commemoration in other locations might have proved inconvenient, indecorous or even an embarrassment to their relicts. For example, Lady Margaret Douglas (1515–78), countess of Lennox, mother of Lord Darnley, daughter of Margaret Tudor and granddaughter of Henry VII (so at one point in the sixteenth century amongst the highest ranking women in the two kingdoms), lies near to Mary, Queen of Scots, then newly restored in reputation by means of a monument to her memory erected by her son James on his accession (Plate 2). Margaret Douglas was commemorated by means of a free-standing tomb-chest which she herself had put up before her death in 1578.[9] In the St Nicholas Chapel, there is a monument to Mildred, second wife of William Cecil, Lord Burghley (1520–98) and mother to the earls of Salisbury and Exeter. Mildred Cecil (died 4 April 1589) is accompanied on a lofty and elaborate monument by the recumbent effigy of her daughter Anne (died June 1588), countess of Oxford. But other male Cecils are commemorated near to their country estates. Mildred's husband William Cecil, Lord Burghley, the great patriarch and founder had himself commemorated at Stamford alongside another monument he had had erected to the memory of his parents, as part of a comprehensive commemorative programme almost certainly triggered by the death of his mother in 1587. This date coincided with the completion of Burghley House, an event which perhaps allowed for the release of some additional funds. Mildred's son Robert, earl of Salisbury (?1563–1612 ) is at Hatfield on the northern fringes of the metropolis and Thomas (1542–1623), the eldest son, has his own monument at Westminster designed to accommodate both himself and his two wives, although the second of these was, in fact, buried at Winchester leaving an empty berth in the St John Baptist Chapel. Elizabeth Manners (died 1591) the young wife of William Cecil, later (from 1623) second earl of Exeter, has her own fragmentary monument in another Westminster chapel, that dedicated to St Nicholas. We find this pattern repeated amongst other noble families: the countess of Sussex lies alongside Mildred Cecil at Westminster and her husband is commemorated with his male ancestors at Boreham, Essex.[10] Never-

---

Century Tombs', *Church Monuments Society Newsletter*, VIII (ii) (1993), 47–9, and for the Russell tomb see H. C. Gladstone, *Building an Identity: two noblewomen in England 1566– 1666* (D. Phil. thesis, Open University, 1989).

[9] The *DNB* is wrong to claim that the monument to Lady Lennox was erected by James I after his accession, her will (Public Record Office MS PROB 11/60 fo. 93 recto), dated 26 February 1577 (that is, 1578) states 'And my bodie to be buried in the greate churche of Westminster in the monument, Sepulture or Tombe, alreadie bargayned for, and appointed to me made and sett uppe in the saide churche ....'

[10] Henry Holland, *Heruulogia Anglica hoc est clarissimorum et doctossimorum* ... (1620), 113.

**Plate 2**   The monument to Margaret Douglas, countess of Lennox (1515–78), made in London *c.* 1579, artists unknown, south aisle of Henry VII's Chapel, Westminster Abbey, London.

theless, there were tensions in this ritual of courtly reincorporation and sometimes the commemorative process was required to be effective in more than one site. The antiquarian observer Holland noted that the body of the first Lord Burghley lay in state in the Abbey for six days prior to its long journey up the Great North Road and obsequies were performed for the dead statesman at both Stamford and Westminster on the same day.[11]

Elsewhere across the country, bishops lie in their cathedrals, dons in their college chapels, the very location of these monuments testimony to their role in setting and maintaining continuities in the face of Death's chaos.

## Visual qualities

With a clearer sense of the role of monuments in establishing a reputation of honour on an individual or family and with some sense of the economies and hierarchies that determined their cost, manufacture and the choices of materials and locations, we need to engage with their visual qualities, the qualities that allowed the monuments adequately to represent their subjects.

There are two important observations which have to prefix any discussion of the visual character of early modern English funeral monuments; first, that monuments were built in a range of forms, a range which accommodated new types and possibilities as well as allowing for the continuation of certain traditional poses and shapes. Second, that a single formal analysis does not do justice to complex images as monuments communicating as they do through interlocking sets of signals, by deploying architectural shapes, verbal and heraldic signs as well as the figurative forms of effigial and allegorical sculpture.

The range of forms embraced two basic types. The first of these was the monument set on the floor with effigies lying on a tomb-chest according to a long-standing tradition. The second saw the monument moved from the floor up the wall and this type usually depicted the subject apparently alive but half-length. This type was a new development which paralleled the very substantial increase in the numbers of monuments being produced from the final years of the 1500s into the early seventeenth century. What is more, the growth of popularity of this second, so-called epitaph type, matched as it was by a general increase in the numbers of monuments, can be shown to have made a particular impact on patrons in the social ranks then seeking access to the community of honour; the professional classes of lawyers, scholars and clerics.

[11] John Weever, *Ancient Funerall Monuments* (1631), 634.

Around the central core of the tomb-chest and its recumbent effigies—even today the most evocative of all monumental types and that most readily associated with an ancient lineage—the patrons and tomb-makers developed a wide range of variants. The chest might be set up with one, two or even three full-sized effigies on its top in open floor space. It might be attached by an end or along its side to a wall and several variations of cover or superstructure might be set up over it. Free-standing forms of such covers might be carried on four, six or eight columns and comprise complex architectural canopies displaying allegorical sculpture or heraldry. Wall tombs used similar patterns often based on the triumphal arch motif and so linking splendid architecture with a reference to the Christian belief in the resurrection as a triumph over death and to the social realities of the survival of the lineage beyond the demise of an individual's natural body.

Despite their smaller scale, the wall-mounted epitaph presented a kind of miniature version of the complex of imagery that was so characteristic of the larger kinds of monuments. Such complexity is epitomised in an enormous monument such as the Earl of Hertford's in Salisbury Cathedral (?1539–1621) where we find the elements of text, column, pattern and figure carving also encountered in more modest epitaphs such as Bodley's tomb at Merton College, Oxford.[12] The Hertford monument (Plate 3), probably erected c. 1625 by William, second duke of Somerset, grand-son of the subject, is intended to establish in perpetuity the honour and reputation of a nobleman who was himself amongst the most prolific of early modern tomb-patrons.

In Westminster Abbey alone Edward Seymour built tombs to his mother (died 1587, in the chapel of St Nicholas), to his sister (died 1560, in the chapel of St John the Baptist) as well as to his second wife (died 1598, in the chapel of St Benedict). At Salisbury, all the available devices are deployed to achieve the desired effect, that of lofty magnificence, an assured and respected dynasty and an honourable reputation sustained in perpetuity. The monument is set in the Retrochoir of the Cathedral where it benefits from the generous dimensions of its architectural setting which affords ample viewing space. Such facilities were not always available and many such tall monuments remain hard to see. Edward Seymour was the son of the Protector to another Edward, Henry VIII's only surviving son, Edward VI. What is more, Seymour's first wife had been Catherine, sister to Lady Jane Grey and Catherine's royal blood explains the precedence given her in the monumental

---

[12] For the Hertford monument see Thomas Fuller, *The History of the Worthies of England* (1662), part vi, 144, and Richard Symonds, 'The Diary of the Marches Kept by the Royal Army ...', ed. C. E. Long, *Camden Society*, LXXIV (1854), 134; for the Bodley monument see most recently Jean Wilson, 'The Memorial by Nicholas Stone to Sir Thomas Bodley', *Church Monuments*, VIII (1993), 57–62.

**Plate 3** The monument to Edward Seymour, earl of Hertford (?1539—1621) and members of his family, made in London in the mid-1620s, artists unknown, Retrochoir of Salisbury Cathedral, Wiltshire.

composition which has her effigy set higher than that of her husband. Hertford's close association with the crown was the key component in the design of the Salisbury monument, just as it was central to Seymour's status and his self-image. The middle vertical core of the monument carries the main epigraphic texts, unabashedly élitist in their deployment of the Latin language and esoteric abbreviations and heraldry. Around the lower panel of inscription, which sets out Seymour's blood lineage and progeny, we find a decorative bordering of shields-of-arms and topping off the central composition is an achievement-of-arms on a prodigious scale. Sculpted representations of Seymour and his family are set at the foot of the monument and so available for close inspection by the viewer. To the left and right, kneeling upright and armoured within columned niches, are the effigies of his two sons, their presence signalling the essential continuity of the lineage, a theme picked up symbolically by the obelisks above. In the centre, lie Seymour and his first wife, their horizontal pose and clasped hands showing them in their devotions and awaiting the resurrection of the righteous. The blood line is carried from the eldest progeny by the first marriage; such issues as these show the basic elements of the code of honour set in stone by funeral monuments.

### The chosen subjects

These combinations of forms were chosen by patrons and tomb-makers because they were regarded as suitable to a commemorative process that was in itself representative of the security and good order of the state. One of the standard topics in contemporary comment about funeral monuments was that they had to be protected from anarchic assault because they epitomised the ideological backbone that the community of honour set into the bodily fabric of the nation's commonwealth. The heralds complained about faulty commemorative coats-of-arms on the grounds that such errors undermined the very precedence upon which good order was established; the antiquaries complained when for reasons of fashion, new forms and iconographies started to appear and Elizabeth I herself complained by means of a decree promulgated early in her reign when schismatics and bigots started to run amok and damage the fabric of some monuments.[13]

Clearly, work as serious as the design and manufacture of funeral monuments could not be left to the mere mechanicals who made up the ranks of the tomb-makers. Indeed, it is evident from the various surviving manuscript sources relating to the patronage process that the patrons themselves reserved rights over the significant, sign-bearing

---

[13] The decree reprinted by Weever, *Ancient Funeral Monuments*, 52–4.

aspects of monuments, without, of course, unduly concerning themselves with technical matters. Substantial monuments were completed in accordance with the terms of formal contracts which set out size, cost, rate of payment, types of materials and the time to be allowed for the completion of the work. But in such texts little was said about the kinds of formal questions which would have demanded a complex aesthetic vocabulary still to be developed in early modern England.[14] A few contract drawings survive for large and expensive monuments and these must have been needed to support the kinds of verbal description set out in the contract itself. The patrons were responsible for supplying the text of the inscriptions and the details of the heraldry which the tomb-makers—illegally for the most part—would then set on the monument.

Some of these decisions were taken about monuments erected to honour the living as well as the dead, for it is one of the most fascinating—if to the modern eye somewhat puzzling—aspects of the study of early modern England that so many tombs were put up to the memory of subjects in their own lifetimes. Until a full survey of the material has been undertaken it will not be possible to be anything other than vague about the numbers of monuments erected in the lifetimes of their subjects; however, the incidence is certainly 30 per cent and probably higher. In church after church across the early modern realm and on countless occasions through this period, members of the local gentry and their spouses must have knelt down in prayer alongside their own effigies. Often it was the death of a spouse, perhaps that of a young wife in childbirth, that suggested that a monument was needed. Nothing concentrates the mind on one's own mortality better than the death of a loved one. Just as the image of the deceased would set in stone for perpetuity a social image to counter the decaying natural body hidden in the grave, so would the patron's own statue set himself or herself for ever in the very midst of life. For this reason we must always treat the effigial sculpture of this period as an idealised form, not as a minute replication of the natural body of the deceased but rather as fictions in stone packed round with other potent forms of signification to establish a collective image of the ranks of honour set in time for ever.

[14] Important work on this subject has been undertaken by Lucy Gent in her *Picture and Poetry, 1560—1620* ... (Leamington Spa, 1981), and ' "The Rash Gaze": Economies of Vision in Britain, 1550—1660', in *Albion's Classicism: The Visual Arts in Britain, 1550—1650*, ed. Lucy Gent (New Haven and London, 1995), 377–93.

*Verbal texts*

How did the many constituent elements in tomb design combine to establish the honourable reputation of the subject in life, death and in the memory? Verbal signs, socially distinctive as well as precise and authoritative, played an important role and these fell into several different categories. Some inscribed texts were overtly biographical and registered the family history and lineage of the deceased together with an exposition of their individual merits and virtues. Such texts often paid lip service to the heavily gendered expectations of the two sexes in the community of honour. In the terms of Mervyn James's analysis, aristocratic men would be commemorated in monuments bearing inscriptions attesting to qualities such as their strength of lineage, their competitiveness (perhaps on behalf of their prince) and to the potential violence of their lives as soldiers.[15] Towards the end of the sixteenth century we find a continuing shift towards a stress on merit, a new emphasis on morals and on the pacific. Both these kinds of male honour—the aristocratic and the developing meritocratic—were paralleled by female equivalents; for example, a woman's social status confirmed through marriage to establish a framework for the subsequent fulfilling of the expected categories of female exemplification, to bear and bring up children, to undertake charitable works, to be obedient, devout and chaste.

Other shorter inscriptions—essentially captions allowing the onlooker to identify sculpted effigies—remind us of the importance for the lineage of precision in commemoration. On a monument erected after his wife's death in 1625 at Much Dewchurch, Herefordshire, the Jacobean courtier and lawyer, Walter Pye (1571–1636) had listed the names of his sons and daughters beneath the row of kneeling figures (with the sons to the superior heraldic dexter side): 'Johannis, Robertus, Jacobus, Johannis, Wilimus, Walterus, Rogerus; Margaret, Bridget, Joyce, Anna, Alicia, Maria, Francisia, Eliz.' (Plate 4).[16] The essential function of a memorial, to replace the individual in order to repair the damage to the social fabric caused by the loss of the deceased, required just such precise identification. To support the system of precedence and hierarchy upon which the codes of honour relied, it was essential to know absolutely whom was related to whom, precisely which wives had carried which children, and how the association of honour was

---

[15] This is a general reference to the ideas pursued by James in several publications, typically in *Family, Lineage and Civil Society. A Study of Society, Politics and Mentality in the Durham Region, 1500–1640* (Oxford, 1974).

[16] This monument is fully catalogued in volume 2 of my unpublished Ph.D. thesis, 'John Weever and English Funeral Monuments of the Sixteenth and Seventeenth Centuries' (Warburg Institute, University of London, 1983).

**Plate 4** The monument to Sir Walter Pye (1571–1636) and his wife Agnes (died 1625), made in London, probably in the later 1620s, artists unknown, nave of St David's church, Much Dewchurch, Herefordshire.

spread through the community and through the clan.[17] It cannot be over-emphasised the extent to which heraldry acted in the same way, as a means precisely of identifying the individual within the ranks of honour.

A final type of verbal text was the scriptural quotation which gave additional emphasis to the monument as an exemplar of moral virtue.

The complex programme of inscription and portrait carving on the Watton monument at Addington, Kent, illustrates how verbal texts can continue to revive the fortunes of a monument through successive generations of use and addition. Within the pediment at the top, in inverse location to the viewer's probable expectations of a family tree, is a panel commemorating the patriarchal figure of Edward Watton who died in 1527. Beneath him to the left and right are further inscriptions to two generations of Thomas Watton, died 1580 and 1622 respectively. Still further down and terminating the central panel are portrait busts of William Watton, died 1651, and his wife Elizabeth Simmons. In the predella at the very bottom and flanking a panel of inscription to William, are described his progeny, in particular his children in low relief, kneeling and two more panels of text about another William (died in 1703).

An alternative and less familiar juxtaposition of text and image is offered by the celebrated Fettiplace monuments at Swinbrook, Oxfordshire, where the effigies of the armoured ancestors appear in a series of shelf-like places each with its own explanatory label. Sir Edmund (died 1613) lies at the top of the set with his ancestors supporting him.

*Heraldic signs*

Heraldry was the esoteric language of the ever-expanding ranks of the armigerous who used it to set themselves apart from the lower orders and to differentiate themselves one from the other according to the ranks of degree. Early modern monuments abound in heraldry and as a consequence are strongly redolent of honour. Indeed, some monuments place such stress on heraldry that they appear to be primarily vehicles for its complex signs rather than for text or sculpture.

Armigerous status was in itself not only a sign of honour but as often as not a reward for honour. The use of armour to signal knightly status and a supposed readiness to fight for one's prince often sat alongside other monumental displays that attest to virtue and humility. Each knight had an heraldic supporter, a beast or other motif, set at the foot

---

[17] See Nigel Llewellyn, 'Claims to Status through Visual Codes: Heraldry on Post-Reformation English Funeral Monuments', in *Chivalry in the Renaissance*, ed. S. Anglo (Woodbridge, 1990), 145–60.

of the effigy as a perpetual reminder of status and such heraldic devices cut across the ranks of early English tomb patrons in disregard for other allegiances such as religious belief. The Mildmay monument in St Bartholomew's the Great, in the City of London, records the Protestant piety of the founder of Emmanuel College, Cambridge, in the form of a simple but dignified architectural panel surrounding a passage of inscription, heavily decorated by an impressive array of eight heraldic shields (Plate 5). Sir Walter Mildmay (?1520–89) had a spectacular political career and despite, or perhaps because of, his Puritan sympathies he retained an active interest in cultural matters. It is interesting, given his knowledge of and contact with Nicholas Hilliard, the miniaturist, that his monument rejects figure sculpture in favour of text and shield-of-arms. Of course, figure sculpture was expensive and in Mildmay's will there is no reference to a preferred burial site and it is a document which gives voice to a familiar Puritan wish to avoid vain funeral pomp.[18] Rather, monies are left for The Word to be preached in church. His Latin inscription epitomises the constituent elements of the code of honour: 'Here lies Walter Mildmay, Knight and Mary his wife; he died on the last day of May 1589, she on 16 March 1576. They left two sons and three daughters; he founded Emmanuel College, Cambridge, and served the Queen as chancellor, deputy treasurer of the exchequer and as counsellor' (my translation). Mildmay's will describes him as of Apelthorpe and given the advice he offered to his son, there is an irony in his being commemorated not in the heart of the Northamptonshire countryside but in the heart of the ancient City: 'Know the Court but spend not they life there, for Court is a very chargeable place. I would rather wish thee to spend the greatest part of they life in the country than to live in this glittering misery.'[19]

Elsewhere and indeed across the country Mildmay's doctrinal enemies, the adherents to the old, Roman faith, were equally enamoured of such monumental heraldic displays.

## Figurative imagery

Honour could be displayed through figure sculpture and in subtle ways each of the several different kinds of effigy encouraged the setting and sustaining of an individual's reputation. Carved figures on early modern monuments fall into three categories: representations of the subject of the monument, that is, effigies of those commemorated; representations

---

[18] The will can be found in PCC 51 Leicester, that is, Public Record Office MS PROB 11/74 fo.1 recto.

[19] Conveniently available in *Elizabethan People. State and Society*, ed. Joel Hurstfield and Alan G. R. Smith (1972).

**Plate 5**    The monument to Sir Walter Mildmay (?1520—1589) and his wife Mary, made in London, probably *c.* 1590, artists unknown, south aisle of the church St Bartholomew the Great, City of London.

of the subject's family and third, other representations, usually allegorical personifications but sometimes decorative figures of relatively free signification.

For many generations before the Reformation, the recumbent effigy had been popular and its antiquity clearly carried immense prestige well into the sixteenth century and beyond. Of all sculpted forms, the recumbent effigy had the most powerful associations with the community of honour and there are many cases where it is clear that patrons have carefully selected the form to create an impression that would have been beyond mere verbal biography. All across England, ambitious new men lay commemorated amongst fictitious ancestors emblazoned with coats-of-arms of recent purchase in direct emulation of the kind of timeless authority sought and found in the recumbent images of medieval knights and princes. Sir John Kyrle, Bart., took over an old chapel at Much Marcle, Herefordshire, in 1628 on the death of his wife Sybil and had them both set recumbent on a tomb-chest in its very centre. Kyrle himself was not to die until 1650.

Of all the many variants of the recumbent pose, perhaps the most redolent of longevity and an honoured line was that of the armoured male, cross-legged. The pages of the heraldic and antiquarian literature were packed with discussion about the meaning of this pose. In *The True Use of Armorie*, William Wyrley argued that the pose signalled not a pre-Conquest date, for it had come into use after the Palestine war; however, there was general agreement that it was a most effective signifier of venerability.[20] Of the Temple Church, the geographer John Norden noted, 'many very auncient monuments of famous men, shaped in Marble armed, their legges crosse, whose names are not to be gathered'[21] A few years later, Frederic Gerschow, writing the diary of the London visit of Philip Julius, duke of Stettin Pomerania, thought that these crossed Templar's legs meant that the subject had been slain in battle, other poses signifying other deaths.[22] Others confirmed what has become virtually an urban myth reconfirmed over and over again in countless church guides, that crusader knights were shown with their legs crossed. In the mid-seventeenth century, Thomas Dingley identified and illustrated just such an anonymous effigy in Bristol Cathedral as of a member of the Berkeley family who had been in Palestine.[23]

Clearly the connotations between a medieval heritage and a cross-legged knightly pose were extremely powerful. There is some evidence that the origins of the pose lie with reclining figures of the patriarch

[20] (1592), 26.

[21] *Speculum Britanniae The first parte. A ... discription of Middlesex* (1593) 33.

[22] See G. von Bülow's edition of the diary in *Transactions of the Royal Historical Society*, new series VI (1892), 9.

[23] *History from Marble*, ed. J. G. Nichols (1867), I, lxiii.

Jesse; at the foot of an ancestral tree there were many precedents for this composition both actual, fictive and recorded. Dingley drew a medieval figure which bore a marked similarity to the much disputed figure of Sir John de Hauteville at Chew Magna in Somerset and to the kings on the west facade at Exeter Cathedral. These two sources, the local Devonian reference and that to the tree of Jesse, perhaps account for the use of the pose inside the Cathedral on the monument (probably dated 1589) to Sir (?) Gawen Carew (died 1583 and son of Richard Carew 1464–1513) in the north-east chapel (Plate 6). The monument, which is heavily restored, shows a fully armoured figure representing Sir Gawen above his relation Sir Peter Carew (1514–75), a soldier and a hero who died in Ireland and is shown lying with legs crossed. An inscription on Sir Peter's own monument, in the south transept, notes that he was buried at Waterford, so the cross-legged pose at Exeter is, in fact, displayed on a cenotaph. The natural body is missing, a suitable omission in a monument intended to commemorate a soldier, dead and buried in a foreign country.

As kneeling effigies slowly became more acceptable to the honoured classes they too showed the trappings of knightly valour as ways of registering the code of honour. The correlation between armour, effigies and honour was such that the antiquarian Richard Symonds (1617–92?) felt obliged to note and even illustrate in a drawing an early effigy without armour: 'This is observable, for never afore have I scene a thing of that age (unless a churchman) without armour.'[24]

But the male virtues of valour were not the only kinds of honour and reputation celebrated by early modern funeral monuments. As we have already noted, there was towards the close of the sixteenth century a marked expansion in the ranks and numbers of people accorded monuments and those new subjects had other kinds of reputation to sustain. Such a breadth of possibilities was there that many monuments displayed a quite bewildering array of subsidiary allegorical figures referring to the widest possible range of virtues. The sets of cardinal virtues and the Pauline triad of Faith, Hope and Charity can be found on endless numbers of monuments, all attesting to the good qualities of the individual in life. Often such figures were joined by other standard references to the endless struggles with Death and Time.

*Connotations and conclusions*

In conclusion, it is clear that there was a leading role to be played by early modern funeral monuments in establishing reputation and ensuring the recognition of honourable status. Just as the contemporary

---

[24] *Diary*, ed. C. E. Long (for the Camden Society), LXXIV (1859), 202–3.

**Plate 6** The monument to Sir (?) Gawen Carew (died 1583) and members of his family, erected (?) in 1589, artists unknown, chapel of St John the Evangelist, Exeter Cathedral, Devon.

discourse on monuments, their legitimacy, their style, their location and their history, was coincidental with so much of the discourse of honour, much of the imagery on monuments has to be interpreted in the context of debates about honour. Inscriptions attest to the strength of the line, heraldry attests to the purity of blood and marriage, costume attests to status and rank, pose attests to piety and chivalry attests to character. Monuments existed to preserve continuities between the present, the future and the past. They sought to act as didactic images, as exhortations to the living to follow the model set by the deceased. Their emphasis was firmly on the establishment of reputation and on the eradication of any lingering stain of dishonour. Monuments only tell such full and persuasive stories with the help of historical research, they are fictions and testaments.

# THE CONSTRUCTION OF HONOUR, REPUTATION AND STATUS IN LATE SEVENTEENTH- AND EARLY EIGHTEENTH-CENTURY ENGLAND

## By Faramerz Dabhoiwala

READ 25 MARCH 1995 AT THE UNIVERSITY OF CAMBRIDGE

NOTIONS of honour and reputation were ubiquitous and important in early modern England for a variety of reasons. They were part and parcel of how individuals in this society conceived of the relationship between the personal and the public, and between the projection and the perception of one's character. More particularly, they lay at the heart of two crucial issues: how people thought about social status, and about the differences between men and women.

It is now generally appreciated that the language and concepts of reputation were important throughout society, but that they also differed significantly according to rank and context.[1] Terms such as 'quality', 'honour', 'credit', 'name', 'fame', 'carriage', 'conversation' and 'condition' were all part of a broad value system; but each described social or moral status in a subtly different way. On the other hand, it has also been demonstrated that honour and reputation were highly gendered

---

[1] See e.g. Mervyn James, *English Politics and the Concept of Honour 1485–1642*, Past and Present Supplements, III (1978); J. A. Sharpe, *Defamation and Sexual Slander in Early Modern England: The Church Courts at York*, Borthwick Papers, LVIII (York, [1980]); Donna Andrew, 'The Code of Honour and its Critics: The Opposition to Duelling in England 1700–1850', *Social History*, V (1980), 409–34; Jonathan Powis, *Aristocracy* (Oxford, 1984), ch. 1; Anna Clare Bryson, 'Concepts of Civility in England, c. 1560–1685' (D.Phil. thesis, University of Oxford, 1984); Fenela Ann Childs, 'Prescriptions for Manners in English Courtesy Literature, 1690–1760, and their Social Implications' (D.Phil. thesis, University of Oxford, 1984); A. J. Fletcher, 'Honour, Reputation and Local Officeholding in Elizabethan and Stuart England', in *Order and Disorder in Early Modern England*, ed. Anthony Fletcher and John Stevenson (Cambridge, 1985), 92–115; Martin Ingram, *Church Courts, Sex and Marriage in England, 1570–1640* (Cambridge, 1987), esp. ch. 10; V. G. Kiernan, *The Duel in European History: Honour and the Reign of Aristocracy* (Oxford, 1988), esp. chs. 4–10. A useful bibliography of relevant literature in European languages is Annemieke Keunen, 'Bibliografie "Eer en belediging"', *Volkskundig Bulletin*, XVIII (1992), 432–40.

concepts, different for men and for women.[2] Yet thus far the inter-action between these two fundamentally different ways of construing reputation has been comparatively neglected. In particular, historians of seventeenth- and eighteenth-century women have explored the ideology of honour mainly from a gendered perspective, concentrating on its apparent obsession with female sexual conduct, and stressing the extent to which this differentiated the way that male and female reputation were perceived.

This is a serious over-simplification, in part derived from sources—conduct books, legal suits for defamation and libel, even funerary monuments—that were necessarily concerned to prescribe or project an unambiguous, coherent ideal. Yet in truth, as in the case of other powerful early modern ideologies—the rule of law, notions of social order and hierarchy, or Christian doctrine—much of the potency of ideas about reputation derived from the fact that they pretended to universal standards, but could potentially be manipulated in rather more subjective fashion. In addition, they were not static but subject to considerable fluctuation over time. And finally, as any survey of more banal and more varied evidence will show, ideas about honour and reputation themselves overlapped with and were contradicted by other patterns of thought (religious standards, notions of social order, and the like): so that in everyday practice their expression was often mixed up with elements from a much wider conceptual vocabulary.[3]

The aim of this essay is to provide a truer picture of how notions of honour and reputation fitted into the mental world of men and women in the later seventeenth and early eighteenth centuries, especially in London and with particular attention to two points. One is the general

[2] In addition to the works of Sharpe, Bryson, Childs and Ingram cited in the previous footnote, see e.g. Susan Dwyer Amussen, *An Ordered Society: Gender and Class in Early Modern England* (Oxford, 1988), ch. 4; Anna Clark, 'Whores and Gossips: Sexual Reputation in London 1770–1825', in *Current Issues in Women's History*, ed. Arina Angerman *et al.* (1989), 231–48; Laura Gowing, 'Women, Sex and Honour: The London Church Courts, 1572–1640' (Ph.D. thesis, University of London, 1993); *idem*, 'Gender and the Language of Insult in Early Modern London', *History Workshop Journal*, no. 35 (1993), 1–21; *idem*, 'Language, Power and the Law: Women's Slander Litigation in Early Modern London', in *Women, Crime and the Courts in Early Modern England*, ed. Jenny Kermode and Garthine Walker (1994), 26–47; Tim Meldrum, 'A Women's Court in London: Defamation at the Bishop of London's Consistory Court, 1700–1745', *London Journal*, XIX (1994), 1–20. Amongst the growing body of 'historicist' work on the literature of the seventeenth and eighteenth centuries that also addresses this issue, see notably Michael McKeon, *The Origins of the English Novel 1600–1740* (Baltimore, 1987), esp. 150–9, 255–65, 364–400; Clare Brant, 'Speaking of Women: Scandal and the Law in the Mid-Eighteenth Century', in *Women, Texts and Histories 1575–1760*, ed. Clare Brant and Diane Purkiss (1992), 242–70.

[3] For other patterns of thought that impinged upon notions of sexual honour, see Faramerz Dabhoiwala, 'Prostitution and Police in London, *c.* 1660—*c.* 1760' (D.Phil. thesis, University of Oxford, 1995), ch. 2.

relationship between male and female reputation; the other the question of change over time. It will argue first that both male and female reputation should be understood as a compound of moral and social factors; indeed, that the importance of the latter was so great that in both sexes the ideology of honour had the potential to subvert orthodox sexual norms. Secondly, and of necessity more briefly, it will suggest that the relationship between sexual conduct, gender and reputation changed significantly over the course of the seventeenth and eighteenth centuries.

*I*

Although reputation was important to all men, its attributes varied according to rank and position. For those who regarded themselves as men 'of honour' or 'of quality', adherence to a specific code of honour set them apart from their inferiors; and across the social spectrum, men in different ranks and circumstances attached greater or lesser importance to lineage, wealth, occupation and conduct as measures of reputation. On the other hand, honour, reputation or credit in its totality was also measurable according to a crude unitary standard: it could increase or decrease, and men could be ranked accordingly. Both these aspects of male reputation are exemplified by Samuel Pepys: as he rose through society his overall 'honour', 'reputation', 'credit' and 'condition' were increased, and as this happened their component parts (that is, the attributes of status) changed as well. The most obvious of these attributes was dress;[4] but equally important were things like whom one associated with;[5] what work one did and how one carried it out;[6] even how one travelled. By 1667, Pepys felt himself 'a little dishonoured' and 'almost ashamed to be seen in a hackney', and decided 'in respect to honour', 'condition' and 'degree' to keep his own coach and horses.[7]

Apart from such socio-economic factors, male reputation was also affected by moral conduct. These two indices of male reputation could

[4] *The Diary of Samuel Pepys*, ed. Robert Latham and William Matthews (11 vols., 1970–83) [hereafter Pepys, *Diary*], IV. 343, 357; V. 65, 269; VII. 329; VIII. 115; cf *Boswell's London Journal 1762–1763*, ed. Frederick A. Pottle (New York, 1950), 59–60; Bryson, 'Concepts of Civility', 364–5; Jeremy Boulton, *Neighbourhood and Society: A London Suburb in the Seventeenth Century* (Cambridge, 1987), 148–9; Robert B. Shoemaker, *Prosecution and Punishment: Petty Crime and the Law in London and Rural Middlesex, c. 1660–1725* (Cambridge, 1991), 101.

[5] See e.g. Pepys, *Diary*, II. 119; V. 30, 41, 263, 330; VII. 53, 173–4; VIII. 124, 307, 442.

[6] See e.g. *ibid.*, I. 252; III. 171, 210; IV. 166, 231, 289, 347; V. 83, 312, 313; VIII. 73, 527; IX. 60, 66, 104. More generally, Pepys felt his own honour and credit to be bound up with that of the Navy Office as a whole, and similarly conflated the reputations of other men with those of their office. This important, corporate understanding of reputation deserves further attention.

[7] *Ibid.*, VIII. 174, 205, 209, 246; cf. *ibid.*, V. 126; IX. 383, 545, also 551.

overlap (for example, if one were 'dishonest' in business);[8] or they could be considered separately. And this contingency was reflected in the language of reputation. Within the wider discourse, certain concepts were relatively exclusive: 'virtue', 'honesty' and 'character',[9] for example, usually referred to moral standing, whilst 'rank' or 'quality' generally applied only to worldly position. But several central terms conflated social and moral assessments: 'honour', 'reputation' and 'credit', for example, could refer to either or to the compound of both.[10]

Sexual conduct was a natural part of the moral index; yet because male reputation as a whole was so multifaceted, it was normally only of subsidiary importance.[11] Even the imputation of cuckoldry—normally the most serious slur on a man's sexual worth—could be flattened by the weight of one's social reputation: when in 1667 the duke of Richmond married Frances Stuart, widely reputed to have been the king's mistress, Pepys observed that 'it is pretty to consider how his *quality* will allay people's talk, whereas had a meaner person married her, he would for certain have been reckoned a cuckold at first dash'.[12] In addition, male sexual norms were acknowledged to be highly subjective and far from unitary. Clearly, there existed not one universal standard of male sexual conduct, with varying degrees of adherence to it, but several different and conflicting codes.

At one extreme of this spectrum lay Christian principles of reputation, according to which unchastity was not merely sinful but dishonourable in both sexes and amongst all ranks: thus whoremongers could only 'pretend to be men of Honour', because inevitably their practices led to 'the ruine of [their] Health, Estates and Reputations'.[13] Yet such a

[8] *Ibid.*, VIII. 100, 155; Ingram, *Church Courts*, 297–8, 302–3; Amussen, *Ordered Society*, 102, 104; Craig Muldrew, 'Interpreting the Market: The Ethics of Credit and Community Relations in Early Modern England', *Social History*, XVIII (1993), 163–83, here esp. 179–81.

[9] This specific usage of the last term (as in men, women or people 'of character', or 'of *some* character') appears to have been an eighteenth-century evolution: see e.g. *Oxford English Dictionary*, ed. J. A. Simpson and E. S. C. Weiner (2nd edn, Oxford, 1989) [hereafter *OED²*], *s.v.* 'character', ¶13; Corporation of London Record Office, GJR/M1, 1 June, 3 June (1752); GJR/M2, 16 Oct., 3 May, 6 May (1761); GJR/M3, 10 May, 11 May (1762).

[10] For typically subtle and illuminating juggling of these concepts, from one particularly influential perspective, see *The Tatler*, ed. Donald F. Bond (3 vols., Oxford, 1987), e.g. I. 342–7 (no. 48, 30 July 1709), 531 (no. 78, 8 Oct. 1709); II. 73–7 (no. 92, 10 Nov. 1709), 140–4 (no. 105, 10 Dec. 1709); *The Spectator*, ed. Donald F. Bond (5 vols., Oxford, 1965), III. 463–6 (no. 390, 28 May 1712).

[11] Cf. *Spectator*, I. 416–19 (no. 99, 23 June 1711).

[12] Pepys, *Diary*, VIII. 120 (my emphasis); cf. *ibid.*, VIII. 132.

[13] [John Dunton], *The Night-Walker: Or, Evening Rambles in Search after Lewd Women, with the Conferences Held with them, &c. To be Publish'd Monthly, 'till a Discovery be Made of all the Chief Prostitutes in England, from the Pensionary Miss, down to the Common Strumpet*, 2 vols. of 4 issues each (1696–7) [hereafter *Night-Walker*, vol./issue], vol. I, issue 1, sig. [A4r] (the

negation of sex and rank was never more than an ideal to be worked towards; and in the meantime, proponents of Christian standards decried the actual state of affairs. 'Where the Crime is the same, why should the Disgrace [to the man be] less'? lamented Jeremy Collier. Why is 'a Lewd Person ... not as infamous as a Thief'?; why 'is wealth a Privilege for Lewdness?'.[14]

There was nothing new about the belief of religious moralists like Collier that their age was a particularly vicious and debauched one: such sentiments had buttressed recurrent calls for moral reform throughout the later sixteenth and early seventeenth centuries.[15] But their concerns over the encroachment of rival norms of sexual behaviour—rather than insufficient adherence to Christian ones—were more topical and pertinent. For regardless of any decline in the strength of religious standards, the development during their lifetime of libertinism as an influential and coherent code of conduct created a powerful polar opposite to the Christian ideal: one in which sexual debauchery was held actually to enhance male reputation.

The emergence after 1660 of this new, '"unofficial" norm ... not just a loose failure to live up to official norms', as a specific response to the unique social pressures and competitiveness of later seventeenth-century London, has been skilfully expounded by Anna Bryson. A number of themes in her account are particularly pertinent here. One is the centrality of sexual rapacity to this code; another, its development as part of a social context in which the inherent tensions between the assertion and perception of status and reputation were greatly heigh-

nature of this source is elucidated in Dabhoiwala, 'Prostitution and Police', appendix B). Cf. *The Life and Errors of John Dunton Late Citizen of London; Written by Himself in Solitude* (1705), 371, 393, 398; and for the notion that the unchastity of a man was as John Milton put it—'much more deflowering and dishonourable' than that of a woman, see Edward Le Comte, *Milton and Sex* (New York, 1978), 18.

[14] Jeremy Collier, 'Of Whoredom', in *idem, Essays upon Several Moral Subjects* (3 parts, 1705), III. 113–55, quotations from III. 121, 123, 134. Cf. [Richard Allestree], *The Whole Duty of Man, Laid Down in a Plain and Familiar Way for the Use of All, but especially the Meanest Reader* (1658), in [*idem*], *The Works of the Learned and Pious Author of the Whole Duty of Man* (2 vols., Oxford, 1684), I. 121; *Tatler*, I. 400–3 (no. 58, 23 Aug. 1709), Keith Thomas, 'The Double Standard', *Journal of the History of Ideas*, XX (1959), 195–216, here 203–5; Andrew, 'Code of Honour and its Critics', 416–17.

[15] Joan Kent, 'Attitudes of Members of the House of Commons to the Regulation of "Personal Conduct" in Late Elizabethan and Early Stuart England', *Bulletin of the Institute of Historical Research*, XLVI (1973), 41–71; Keith Edwin Wrightson, 'The Puritan Reformation of Manners, with Special Reference to the Counties of Lancashire and Essex, 1640–1660' (Ph.D. thesis, University of Cambridge, 1974); Keith Thomas, 'The Puritans and Adultery: The Act of 1650 Reconsidered', in *Puritans and Revolutionaries: Essays in Seventeenth-Century History Presented to Christopher Hill*, ed. Donald Pennington and Keith Thomas (Oxford, 1978), 257–82; Martin Ingram, 'Reformation of Manners in Early Modern England', in *The Experience of Authority in Early Modern England*, ed. Paul Griffiths, Adam Fox and Steven Hindle (forthcoming, 1996).

tened; and a third, related to this, its function as a means of social differentiation, provoked by the cultural imitation of gentry and aristocratic manners in general, yet inevitably sparking similar emulation of its own norms.[16]

As Bryson stresses, the importance of libertinism lay as much in the power of its stereotype as in the actual behaviour or the numbers of those who adhered to its code; and this continued to be true after 1685, the terminal date of her study. But equally its tenets did gradually spread well beyond a narrow circle, even into the clergy. Aboard ship in mid-Atlantic around the turn of the century, for instance, the Reverend Thomas Bray found himself cooped up with a fellow minister, a man qualified to be a professor of Greek and Hebrew, yet one whose morals might have derived straight from the Restoration court—'who tended to Libertinism, and to defend Debauchery', 'to say, that he would prove it to be true in Reason, and Religion both, ... to F--k', and who 'asserted, that when one comes to 17, a man must either have a whore, or commit Buggery'.[17] Unquestionably the perceived prominence of such principled defences of lust had important consequences for assumptions about male immorality in general. For almost three decades, sexual rapacity was held by many in the most influential circles of metropolitan society to be an essential characteristic of any man of fashion and thus a pre-eminent means of social differentiation. In consequence, it was not easy to separate the two issues after the demise of the Restoration court, especially as libertine behaviour itself was less overt but hardly less prevalent in polite circles.[18] That the

[16] Bryson, 'Concepts of Civility', ch. 7; for these particular themes see esp. 344–7, 370–1; 361–3, 367, 369–71; 347–50, 352–3, 362 9.

[17] Thomas Bray to James Blair, 3 Apr. 1700, University of Maryland Archives, Thomas Bray Collection, Case 10, fos. 220r-2r. For further illustration of how libertine and 'reasoned' assumptions about sexual conduct infiltrated clerical circles towards the end of the seventeenth and over the first half of the eighteenth centuries, cf. 'A Young Clergyman' [i.e. Daniel Maclauchlan], *An Essay upon Improving and Adding to the Strength of Great-Britain and Ireland, by Fornication; Justifying the Same from Scripture and Reason* (1735), whose authorship and context is elucidated by Norah Smith, 'Sexual Mores and Attitudes in Enlightenment Scotland', in *Sexuality in Eighteenth-Century Britain*, ed. Paul-Gabriel Boucé (Manchester, 1982), 47–73, here 61, 71–2 n. 68.

[18] See e.g. *Journaal van Constantijn Huygens, den zoon, van 21 October 1688 tot 2 Sept. 1696*, Werken van het Historisch Genootschap, new ser., XXIII and XXV (Utrecht, 1876–7), supplemented by F. Boersma, 'Het ongelukkige lot van een dagboekschrijver: Herwaardering voor Constantijn Huygens jr., secretaris van Willem III', *Groniek*, no. 101 (1988), 29–53. A telling illustration is the behaviour of Sir Charles Sedley, libertine par excellence. On the surface, he renounced debauchery in the 1690s, supported the 1699 Immorality Bill, and passed down into history as the archetypal 'reformed rake': see Bryson, 'Concepts of Civility', 354, and references given there; David Hayton, 'Moral Reform and Country Politics in the Late Seventeenth-Century House of Commons', *Past and Present*, no. 128 (1990), 48–91, here 63, 90. In fact, as Lawrence Stone has uncovered,

aristocracy and gentry ought to revert to Christian standards was a recurrent theme of the 1690s; but it was all too soon transmuted into the simple assumption that many men of quality were inherently and irredeemably rapacious, and that women were constantly under threat of libertine seduction.[19]

On the face of it, norms of female reputation were more uniform and accorded much more closely with religious standards of sexual conduct. The rhetoric of reputation paralleled that of sin, for example, in the notion that a single act of unchastity would lead inevitably to others, and into a downward spiral of general moral depravity; and in the related assumption that unchastity always betrayed itself in every aspect of a woman's behaviour. Indeed, if anything reputation was supposed to be more absolute in its characteristics than spiritual character. As the author of the authoritative *Whole Duty of Man* put it, the act of whoredom had several distinct consequences for a woman. It was in the first place a sin, a grave 'injustice to her soul'; but all sins could be redeemed. Secondly—and less easy to rectify—it set her both spiritually and socially 'in a course of the horridst wickedness ... from which it is probable she may never return'. But finally and irredeemably, 'in respect of this world', it constituted the loss 'of her credit, making her abhorred and despised, and her very name a reproach among all men': for in theory a woman's 'credit' or 'reputation' was identical with her chastity, and once lost was irrecoverable.[20] In other words, repentance and reformation were possible in the eyes of God, but they could not redeem a lost reputation.

In this orthodox understanding of female reputation, there was a clear and absolute distinction between honest women and whores: the one was the defining antithesis of the other. A second central assumption, informed by biblical archetypes, was that all whores were immediately recognisable through their conduct and appearance—as well as a prime cause of female whoredom, improper 'luxury in diet and apparel' was therefore the unmistakable mark of an unchaste woman.[21] Throughout

he continued to engage in sexual intrigue: *Uncertain Unions: Marriage in England 1660–1753* (Oxford, 1992), 57–8, 64–5.

[19] Cf., e.g., *Night-Walker*, I/1, sigs A2r-Br, and *An Account of the Societies for Reformation of Manners in London and Westminster, and other Parts of the Kingdom* (1699), 93–7, with *Spectator*, II. 216–19 (no. 182, 28 Sept. 1711); IV. 370–71 (no. 525, 1 Nov. 1712), 382–4 (no. 528, 5 Nov. 1712). For the continued association between sexual debauchery and male 'honour' at the middle of the eighteenth century, see e.g. Denison Cumberland, *A Sermon Preached before ... the Magdalen-House Charity, on Thursday the 5th of April, 1764* (1764), 15.

[20] [Allestree], *Whole Duty*, I. 87; cf. *ibid.*, I. 121.

[21] See e.g. [Richard Allestree], *The Ladies Calling* (1673), in [*idem*], *Works*, II. 10; Richard Baxter, *A Christian Directory: Or, a Summ of Practical Theologie, and Cases of Conscience* (2 parts, 1673), I. 402–3; *Night-Walker*, I/1, pp. 13, 16; I/2, pp. 1, 10–13, 25–6; I/4, pp. 3, 12, 23; II/2, sig. [A4v]; 'Andrew Moreton' [i.e. Daniel Defoe], *Every-Body's Business, is No-Body's*

the seventeenth and eighteenth centuries, as has been explored in some detail by historians and literary critics, this normative ideal of female reputation, equating it essentially with chastity, was commonplace and extremely powerful.[22]

Yet like the ideology of social order, that of reputation combined notions of gender with ideas about distinctions of rank and status. And even when, as in the case of female sexual conduct, it pretended to absolute judgments of morality, subjective social considerations often impinged. In practice, female sexual dishonour was thus a Damoclean sword, not a patriarchal ton of bricks.

For a start, in normal circumstances and for the vast majority of women, chastity was essentially a prerequisite, rather than a measure of reputation. As long as her sexual 'honesty' was not called into question, a woman's overall 'honour', 'reputation', 'credit' or 'condition', like that of a man, was linked to her social and economic position. Hierarchies of status amongst 'honest' women depended upon similar worldly factors—lineage, wealth, probity in business—and not upon degrees of chasteness. So, too, a woman's honour, credit or reputation could increase or decrease through matters that had nothing to do with sexual continence. For example, women in lawsuits could be accounted of greater or lesser 'credit and estimation' mainly on the grounds of their social and economic standing;[23] and (as is clear from the records of secular courts) women, like men, were frequently slandered as thieves and cheats.[24] At the other end of the social scale, women were equally

---

*Business; or Private Abuses, Publick Grievances: Exemplified in the Pride, Insolence, and Exorbitant Wages of our Women-Servants, Footmen, &c.* (1725), 17–18; Saunders Welch, *A Proposal to Render Effectual a Plan to Remove the Nuisance of Common Prostitutes from the Streets of this Metropolis* (1758), 4–5.

[22] See above, n. 2.

[23] For a typical example of the complex of social, economic and moral factors that could be adduced at law in estimation of a woman's 'credit', see Public Record Office, London, KB 9/919, certiorari 5 (Trinity 1671), which encapsulates proceedings in both ecclesiastical and secular courts. Parallel findings emerge from research by Dinah Winch into slander litigation in later seventeenth-century Sussex and Cheshire; I am most grateful to her for allowing me to read some of her work in progress.

[24] The centrality of sexual conduct to acceptable female behaviour was a commonplace of defamation cases brought by women at the church courts; but to a large degree this was simply because most other types of slander were actionable only in secular courts, notably at Quarter Sessions. Although the nature of sessions records makes it very difficult to recover the wording or even to quantify the incidence of non-sexual slanders, about 7 per cent of all recognisances returned to Quarter Sessions in Middlesex and Westminster between 1660 and 1725 were issued explicitly for defamation—a total of well over a hundred cases a year, many more than were brought before the equivalent ecclesiastical court. In addition, the sessions dealt with a huge number of cases of assault involving women, many of which undoubtedly involved verbal abuse. Unfortunately, however, recognisances seldom record the precise form of words in either type of case. For figures, see Shoemaker, *Prosecution and Punishment*, 50 (Table 3.3), 316 n. 16; Meldrum,

deemed 'of Honour', 'of Quality', or to have 'qualities of honour' on the grounds of rank, not of sexual conduct.[25] In short, for most women 'reputation' was derived from social and economic status.

Moreover, even if a woman's sexual probity was in some way doubtful, the rhetorical vulnerability of her reputation was counterbalanced by the continued importance of social factors. Much of the power of sexual defamation, for example, derived precisely from its conflation of moral with *social* judgments. Because all whores were supposed to be automatically recognisable through their appearance and conduct, the rhetoric of chastity—calling a woman a 'whore'—could be used simply to express disapproval of a woman's conduct or appearance. This is clear from the background to countless suits for defamation; but even more strikingly from the common, casual use of the insult. Samuel Pepys was not the only husband to call his wife a 'whore' simply in argument 'about her ribbands being ill mached and of two Colours'.[26]

Of course there remained a substantial difference—not least at law—between such individual opinions and the 'public' or 'common' fame and repute of a woman's moral and social standing that carried much greater weight, and that was supposed to be a more considered aggregate of received neighbourly views. Yet often, especially in a metropolis the size of London, one had no prior knowledge of a woman's character. Reputation in such circumstances was thus once again assessed in terms that inevitably conflated moral and social judgments—that is to say on the basis of a woman's 'civility', her 'air' or her 'carriage'; or, above all, of the way that she dressed. At a time when gentility—and gradations of rank in general—were increasingly defined through cultural attributes, and the emulation of new fashions was an important part of social competition, clothing was the preeminent way of establishing the social position of unknown men and women;[27] yet plainly it could be a highly problematic index. Particularly confusing was the fact that whores might consciously affect fashionable dress. For example, Restoration gentlewomen often wore vizards in public to conceal their identity, but before very long the adoption of

---

'A Woman's Court in London'. For examples, see Greater London Record Office, WJ/SR/1602, recognisance 85 (Oct. 1681); WJ/SR/2632, recognisance 189 (Apr. 1735); MJ/SR/2016, recognisances 105, 109 (Sept. 1703); and MJ/SR/2409, recognisance 251 (Aug. 1723), whose slander combined sexual and non-sexual slurs: '"bitch, whore, common whore, cheating all people in ye weight of her butter", with other vile and opprobrious language'—how typical this was is now impossible to ascertain.

[25] See e.g. Pepys, *Diary*, I. 48; II. 179; III. 32; IV. 341; VIII. 71, 212. Cf. *ibid.*, II. 210–11; IV. 114; V. 30, 250; VI. 90; VII. 299, 314; [Allestree], *Ladies Calling*, II. 1.

[26] Pepys, *Diary*, II. 235; cf. *ibid.*, VII. 120, 238. For a very different situation, when the word was made to carry tremendous weight between them, see *ibid.*, IX. 369–71.

[27] Peter Borsay, *The English Urban Renaissance: Culture and Society in the Provincial Town, 1660–1760* (Oxford, 1989), 226–7, 237–41; and above, n. 4.

this fashion by prostitutes had rendered ambiguous the moral status of any woman walking the streets in a mask; and similar appropriations occurred throughout this period.[28] Naturally such blurring of sartorial codes was a matter of degree: and just as many prostitutes were obviously and self-consciously visible, the dress of other women proclaimed them to be patently respectable. Yet in between these two poles there was always, both in reality and in terms of subjective perception, at least some room for debate. When Daniel Defoe lamented in 1726 that it was possible to mistake strumpets in taverns for honest, reputable 'Women of Condition', he therefore epitomised a central paradox in the construction of female reputation: in theory one could tell a whore by her appearance and behaviour; but in practice unchastity was *not* always visibly manifested—indeed, it was often disguised rather than revealed by dress and other social attributes.[29]

Tension between social and moral status was most explicit, however, in women who were openly unchaste. Clearly, according to the rhetoric of chastity, no such woman had any honour or reputation at all; and evidently this was an interpretation that was widely accepted. Yet it remained possible even in the case of such openly immoral women to conceive of female 'honour' and 'reputation' in very different terms—terms which continued to acknowledge the overriding importance of social factors. The countess of Castlemaine, Charles II's long-standing mistress, was called a whore in public, in private, by her own relatives, by the king himself;[30] yet none of these judgments detracted from the reality of her social position, or from the fact that to many, the latter was part and parcel of her overall 'honour' and 'reputation'. In the words of one admiring obituary:

Whatever *Character* has been given to this Lady, rais'd to those *Dignities* she enjoyed, by satisfying the Pleasures of a Prince, which *condition* is always attended with much Envy, we cannot but take notice, that her Birth and *Quality*, was otherwise very Noble. ... [She

[28] See e.g. Pepys, *Diary*, IV. 181 and n. 3; VIII. 423; IX. 220; Lodewijk van der Saan, 'Verscheyde Concepten en Invallen, Aengaende mijne Verbeeteringe te Soecken', Universiteitsbibliotheek Leiden, MS BPL 1325, fo. 42v (*c.* 1696).

[29] [Daniel Defoe], *Some Considerations upon Street-Walkers. With a Proposal for Lessening the Present Number of them* [1726], 4. By mid-century, it had become something of a moralist commonplace that honest women aped the fashions of prostitutes: see e.g. Henry Fielding, *The Covent-Garden Journal and A Plan of the Universal Register-Office*, ed. Bertrand A. Goldgar (Oxford, 1988), 312; *Reflections Arising from the Immorality of the Present Age: In which some Self-Evident Facts are Pointed at, which Seem to Call for a more Immediate Redress, than any other Article in our Policy* (1756), 52–8; John Conder, *A Sermon Preached before the Society for the Reformation of Manners* (1763), 27.

[30] For the last two incidents, see Pepys, *Diary*, III. 68; VIII. 331.

was courted by the king] till by the alluring bait of *Honour* and Preferment he won her to his Embraces.[31]

In other words, Lady Castlemaine's moral status, her 'character', may have been in question; but her social standing, her 'condition' and 'quality', were very great, and 'honour' was something she *gained* rather than lost through her unchastity.

Such understandings of female 'honour' and 'reputation' were not confined to the Restoration, or solely to the highest ranks of society. They were part and parcel of how men and women thought about sexual behaviour throughout the later seventeenth and early eighteenth centuries; and they can be inferred from equivalent forms of 'concubinage' amongst all classes of metropolitan society.[32] When the successful author and publisher John Dunton addressed the young women of London in the 1690s, he too noted that 'temptations of honour' often led women to *commit* unchastity, because so many people thought an association with a man of quality brought 'preferment' rather than shame.[33] A generation later, the *Tatler* regarded the matter as a commonplace: 'Conscience, Honour and Credit', it observed, should ideally be the same thing; but in reality the 'Force' of 'Honour' all too often led to unchastity. Any courtesan could tell you that 'if Conscience had as strong a Force upon the Mind, as Honour, the first Step to her unhappy Condition had never been made'.[34] In short, it was widely acknowledged that, whether as 'bait', 'temptation' or 'force', such relative, social understandings of 'honour' might act as an important inducement *to* sexual immorality.

Over time, as notions of personal privacy increasingly transmuted the nature of social relations, and both male and female reputation became more explicitly secularised, this potential tension between absolute standards of morality and relative norms of reputation was recognised with diminishing alarm and increasing frankness. By the 1740s, the term 'demi-rep' had come into use, a linguistic acknowledgment that even a woman of suspect chastity could retain at least 'half' her reputation on social grounds.[35] 'She who is not known to be' a prostitute, declared the founders of the Magdalen House unequivocally

---

[31] *Memoirs of the Life of Barbara, Dutchess of Cleveland, Divorc'd Wife of Handsome Fielding* (1709), 2 (my emphasis).

[32] See Dabhoiwala, 'Prostitution and Police', 55–9; and cf., for later decades, Clark, 'Whores and Gossips'.

[33] *Night-Walker*, II/4, sig. [A4r]; cf. *ibid.*, I/4, p. 23; II/3, p. 23; II/4, pp. 17–18.

[34] *Tatler*, I. 346–7 (no. 48, 30 July 1709). Cf. *A Congratulatory Epistle from a Reformed Rake, to John F------g, Esq; upon the New Scheme of Reclaiming Prostitutes* [1758], 11–12.

[35] *OED*: first recorded usage 1749. Derivations such as 'demi-reputable', 'demi-reputation', 'demi-monde' and the like are all nineteenth-century coinages. Cf. also Fielding, *Covent-Garden Journal*, 312.

by the later 1750s, 'is supposed to have a *character*': the eyes of men were not the eyes of God.[36]

The preceding pages have argued three things about reputation: most obviously, that its rhetoric and concepts were highly flexible; secondly, that both male and female reputation should be understood as a compound of social and moral status; and finally, that this is true even of the most gendered aspect of reputation, namely that relating to sexual behaviour. In broad terms, this model of male and female reputation appears to be valid not just for the later seventeenth and early eighteenth centuries, but for early modern England more generally. On the other hand, there were clearly important changes over the course of the seventeenth and eighteenth centuries in the relationship *between* male and female reputation. As this development has thus far received little attention, it might be useful to end by highlighting very schematically how it was shaped by the broader social and intellectual shifts of the period.

## II

The first gradual change was in assumptions about the social consequences of immorality. Well into the later seventeenth century it remained a commonplace that all immoral, disreputable conduct was inherently harmful to the community (at every level—household, neighbourhood, parish, town, and the nation as a whole), and was therefore a matter of public concern. Towards the beginning of the eighteenth century, however, this organic, holistic view was gradually stretched into one that distinguished much more clearly between personal or 'private' behaviour on the one hand, and 'public' matters on the other.[37] One aspect of this conceptual and practical shift was the declining political importance of sexual immorality; another, the gradual decriminalisation of adultery and fornication. But above all, it led to a marked decline in the importance of sexual conduct to male reputation. Early in the seventeenth century, the reputation of men had clearly still been quite sensitive to sexual aspersions.[38] By the middle of the eighteenth

[36] [Jonas Hanway], *A Plan for Establishing a Charity-House, or Charity-Houses, for the Reception of Repenting Prostitutes. To be Called the Magdalen Charity* (1758), 16 (italics in original).

[37] With specific regard to sexual immorality, see Dabhoiwala, 'Prostitution and Police', chs. 2–6; for an introduction to the more general historiography of this topic see e.g. John Brewer, 'This, That and the Other: Public, Social and Private in the Seventeenth and Eighteenth Centuries', in *Shifting the Boundaries: Transformation of the Languages of Public and Private in the Eighteenth Century*, ed. Dario Castiglione and Lesley Sharpe (Exeter, 1995), 1–21.

[38] See e.g. Martin Ingram, 'Ridings, Rough Music and the "Reform of Popular Culture" in Early Modern England', *Past and Present*, no. 105 (1984), 79–113; Adam Fox, 'Ballads, Libels and Popular Ridicule in Jacobean England', *Past and Present*, no. 145 (1994), 47–83; Richard Cust, 'Honour and Officeholding in Early Stuart England: The

century this was much less apparent, as is epitomised not least by the growing acceptance (whether in affirmation or condemnation) of libertine assumptions about male sexual conduct. As a consequence, even if understandings of female reputation also acknowledged with growing explicitness the importance of social, rather than moral differentiation, the gap between the sexes in this respect had widened significantly.

This development was compounded by a swing in assumptions about the relative lustfulness and rapacity of the sexes. Until the end of the seventeenth century, it was commonly assumed that women were at least as libidinous as men. By the middle of the eighteenth century, however, the balance had shifted considerably, towards the notion that men were the more libidinous sex, the more dangerous seducers; and that women needed to be constantly on their guard against such rapacity. This was a highly complex transformation: one that drew upon well-established notions of gender, and one that was bound up with a sharpening of assumptions about the differentiation of moral standards according to rank. But again, in broad terms one of its effects was clearly to validate the sexual immorality of men (especially socially exalted men) as 'natural' or 'uncontrollable', whilst simultaneously increasing the social pressures on women to guard their chastity.

All in all, these gradual changes over time appear to have had two effects. First, as we have seen, they made increasingly explicit the possible contradictions between the social and the moral aspects of reputation, especially in the case of women. But secondly, they re-shaped and increased the separation between male and female reputation as a whole. By the latter half of the eighteenth century the two were much further apart than they had been at the start of the seventeenth.

In sum, this essay has suggested two main ways of broadening and deepening our understanding of early modern ideas about honour and reputation. The first is by paying closer attention to the interaction between norms of reputation based on social status and those derived from ideas about personal conduct. The second is by examining how ideas about honour and reputation mutated over time, and how such changes were related to wider social and ideological developments. This survey has done no more than scratch the surface; but plainly these are useful places to dig if we want to find out more about how and why ideas about reputation differed by sex, by social status and over time.

---

Case of Beaumont *v.* Hastings', *Past and Present*, no. 149 (1995), 57–94; Felicity Heal, 'Reputation and Honour in Court and Country: Lady Elizabeth Russell and Sir Thomas Hoby', in this volume.

# MALE HONOUR, SOCIAL CONTROL AND WIFE BEATING IN LATE STUART ENGLAND[1]

## By Elizabeth Foyster

READ 25 MARCH 1995 AT THE UNIVERSITY OF CAMBRIDGE

IN seventeenth-century England honour was a concept which had meaning for men in the private or domestic spheres as well as in the public spheres of their lives. Indeed, failure to prove an honourable man at home could exclude men from entering any honour community outside it. Above all else, men from whatever social status were only held worthy of honour if they could demonstrate control over their wives, children and servants. Hence honour was a concept which was vital to the upholding of male power. To achieve that power or control men were encouraged to adopt behaviour which laid emphasis on two key gender characteristics which were thought to distinguish them from women: physical strength and reason. As Sir Thomas Smith explained in 1583, God had intended to give the male 'great wit, bigger strength, and more courage to compel the woman to obey by reason or force'.[2] Men used their claim to reason to legitimise their authority over women; the first Marquis of Halifax explained to his daughter in a letter of 1688:

> That there is Inequality in the Sexes, and that for the better Economy of the World, the Men, who were to be the Law-givers, had the larger share of Reason bestow'd upon them...Your Sex wanteth our Reason for your Conduct, and our Strength for your Protection.[3]

Men were expected to demonstrate their greater share of reason by exercising self-control or 'self-mastery' over the passions, emotions and temptations which were thought so easily to sway the 'weaker' vessel.[4] Much of a man's upbringing and gender conditioning also inculcated the importance of physical strength. From the hunting of the social

---

[1] I should like to thank Keith Bartlett, Helen Berry, Anthony Fletcher and Garthine Walker for their helpful comments on this article.

[2] T. Smith, *De Republica Anglorum*, (London,1583), p.13, as cited in R.A. Houlbrooke, *The English Family 1450–1700* (1986), 103.

[3] G. Savile, 1st Marquis of Halifax, *The Lady's New Year's Gift: Or, Advice to a Daughter* (1688), as cited in *Women in the Eighteenth Century: Constructions of femininity*, ed. V. Jones (1990), 18.

[4] For the importance of self-mastery see K. Hodgkin, 'Thomas Whythorne and the Problems of Mastery', *History Workshop Journal*, XXIX, (1990), 20–41, especially 21.

elite to the football and wrestling matches of village society men learnt that honour could be earned by displaying strength and courage.[5] Once married men were expected to use this training to maintain physical control over their households. Martin Ingram and E.P. Thompson have shown us that if men lost this physical control and allowed their wives to dominate over them, then they could become victims of charivari. The husband in these rituals could be represented as a transvestite, a figure who had lost all claim to manhood because of his inability to use force to control his household. The symbols of a 'world turned upside down' reminded village audiences that without male vigour or 'lustiness' there would be no social and gender order.[6] But just as patriarchal social order was endangered when physical strength was exercised too weakly, so there was also criticism of men who applied their strength too readily and forcefully. In a literary world which thought in terms of binary opposites, conduct book writers of the early seventeenth century were aware of the dangers of men using their powers to excess, or extreme, as well as too feebly or infrequently. Both William Gouge and William Whateley warned their male readers against the dangers of excess in their relationships with their wives and servants; 'the husband must beware of extending the use of his commanding power too far' Whateley wrote.[7]

This paper demonstrates that notions of honour played an important part in the power dynamics of husband/wife relationships and had significant consequences for the married lives of many couples. Forty-four cases for separation from bed and board brought by wives on grounds of cruelty between 1660 and 1700 to the court of Arches, the appeal court for the ecclesiastical courts in the province of Canterbury, were studied.[8] They reveal that many violent husbands exhibited a deeply entrenched desire to be in control of their wives, and to gain honour by demonstrating this control to others. But this desire could lead to the excesses and extremes of which conduct book writers were

---

[5] R. Manning, *Hunters and Poachers* (Oxford,1993); R.W. Malcolmson, *Popular Recreations in English Society 1700–1850* (Cambridge,1973), 34–40,42–3.

[6] M. Ingram, 'Ridings, Rough Music and the "Reform of Popular Culture" in Early Modern England', *Past and Present*, no.105 (1984), 79–113, and M. Ingram, 'Ridings, Rough Music and Mocking Rhymes in Early Modern England', in *Popular Culture in Seventeenth Century England*, ed. B. Reay (1985), 129–97; E.P. Thompson, *Customs in Common* (1991), c. 8.

[7] W. Whateley, *A Bride Bush* (1623), 157, see also 129,159–60; W. Gouge, *Of Domesticall Duties* (3rd edn, 1634), 423, 604; for a fuller discussion of these issues see E. Foyster, 'The Concept of Male Honour in Seventeenth Century England' (Ph.D. thesis, Durham University, 1996).

[8] For the procedure of the court of Arches see M.D. Slatter, 'The Study of the Records of the Court of Arches', *Journal of the Society of Archivists*, I (1955), 29–31; and L. Stone, *Road to Divorce: England 1530–1987* (Oxford,1990), 33–41.

so afraid. There was a point at which use of physical control could threaten rather than enforce patriarchy.

In 1672 Lady Ann Boteler accused her husband, Sir Oliver, of marital cruelty. Over sixteen years of marriage, according to Ann and the twenty-two witnesses who spoke for her in the court of Arches, Oliver had repeatedly called her whore and other abusive names, beaten her and threatened to 'beat out' her brains, thrown chamber pots and a chair at her, kicked her out of the house in the middle of the night, boasted of his sexual inconstancy and infected her with the pox. He was alleged to have whipped and beaten three of their children in front of her, dangling the eight-year-old Elizabeth over three flights of stairs, threatening to drop her if anybody interfered with him. In his need to control his wife Oliver demanded from her total obedience, and he tested and inflated his sense of authority by commanding Ann to perform demeaning and nonsensical tasks. When he went to bed he commanded her to stand by his bed and watch over him all night, even though on one occasion she was pregnant and was only permitted to wear a smock. On another occasion one witness recalled how Oliver 'made her kneel down by his bedside' and 'forced her to bow and incline herself with her face to the floor', telling her 'I will have or will make you as submissive as my spaniel.' He tried to force her to drink a glass of wine when she abstained from alcohol, and made her take off his shoes and stockings even when there were servants in the room, saying that she was 'not worthy to wipe his shoes'. His insistence on obedience even extended to his attempt to force her to yield sexually to him in front of the servants, pulling her clothes off, and then beating her when she refused to oblige him. His violent anger could break out whenever he became suspicious that his wife was disobedient, and he was particularly wary of the way in which her loyalties to her family could conflict with his authority. Hence he accused her of siding with her mother in a quarrel between him and her relations, and witnesses recalled how Oliver would order his wife 'to call or say that her said father was a rogue and her said mother a whore'. In other instances his anger seems to have been triggered by his irritation at the minute details of his wife's behaviour; he became angry on one occasion in 1666 when he saw Ann wearing a hood and a handkerchief around her neck, saying that he had forbidden her to wear the same, pulling them off her and throwing them into the fire.[9]

Sir Oliver's behaviour was exceptional for this period in its scale and

<hr/>

[9] Lambeth Palace Library, Court of Arches [hereafter CA], Case 1041 [case numbers taken from J. Houston, *Index of the Cases in the Records of the Court of Arches in Lambeth Palace Library, 1660–1913* (1972)] (1672), Personal Answer [hereafter Ee], 3, fos. 738–41r; 745r–6v; Deposition [hereafter Eee], 4, fos. 613v–15v,807–8,815–18r,821v–2,850v–83r; Eee5, fos. 24v–5r.

brutality. The combined physical, sexual and mental cruelty which Lady Ann endured and Sir Oliver's abuse of both his wife and children was relatively unusual. It is impossible to accept Lawrence Stone's assertion that there is 'nothing uncommon about the cruelty' in the Boteler case.[10] However, there were some details of Sir Oliver's behaviour which were common to other violent husbands of the period. In particular, the court records show that some husbands' sensitivity about their loss of control could extend to an insistence on such strict obedience, that what might otherwise be interpreted as the smallest of wifely transgressions, could provoke the most brutal violence. Just as Sir Oliver Boteler was enraged to see his wife wearing a hood which he disliked, in the 1660s a witness for Cecily Bradley told the court of Arches how Cecily was beaten when she failed to prepare her husband's dinner on time, and another witness for Rachael Norcott told how Rachel's husband had been so dissatisfied with the butter on his pudding that he threw a stool at her with such force that she fell into a swoon.[11] In John Charnock's defence against his wife's accusations of violence in 1673, he added substance to his presentation of her as a scolding woman who would have enraged any man, by telling the court how she provoked him to anger by feeding him with poor cuts of meat, and dressing in an old waistcoat or vest 'which was not fit for her to wear'.[12] Similarly Thomas Stoddard of Eltham, Kent, defended his violence in 1684 by claiming that his wife was a poor cook who allowed 'Lamb and other good victuals' to spoil.[13] Finally, a servant of the Hubbards, who were wigmakers in St Clement Danes, London, recalled how the couple had two main arguments which led to violence. One of these had been caused when Grace Hubbard had not made her husband's shirts 'as he would have them'.[14]

Of course, a wife's duties in this period included managing a household, providing food and attending to laundry. But occasional failures to perform these tasks to a husband's satisfaction did not amount, in the eyes of those who witnessed the beatings, to serious affronts to a husband's honour; a wife who put too much butter on a pudding or did not care for her husband's shirts as he liked was not in fact questioning his control over the household. But in their paranoia about being in control some husbands, like those in the examples above, treated these minor misdemeanours as gross errors. They probably saw disobedience when there was none. Being repeatedly hit

---

[10] L. Stone, *Broken Lives* (Oxford, 1993), 37.

[11] CA, Case 1127 (1663), Eee1,fo. 83; CA, Case 6659 (1666), Eee2, fo. 101.

[12] CA, Case 1813 (1673), Ee4, fos. 118v–28; for a witness who supported John's claim that he was fed inadequately see Eee5, fo. 17r.

[13] CA, Case 8770 (1684), Ee6, fo. 11.

[14] CA, Case 4834 (1669), Eee3, fo. 299r.

on the head by a husband's fists, as Cecily Bradley experienced, or, as witnesses for Grace Hubbard recalled, being so badly beaten on the mouth and lips that the swelling meant she could not even 'get ale into her mouth', were not beatings of a kind which restored household order by reminding subordinates of the importance of obedience. Instead this marital violence destroyed order, and by consequence a husband's honour. Ironically, then, the result of these husbands' actions was often directly opposed to what their behaviour had originally been designed to bring about.

Dishonour and shame, it can be argued, was the result of this type of wife beating because as a response to perceived disobedience it was unreasonable. The husbands cited in the cases above had failed to grasp that their manhood and honour did not just rest on reason and strength, but upon the exercise of reason in the use of strength. The conduct book writer, Gouge, instructed husbands never to 'rebuke their wives when they are in passion'. For passion raised 'a dark mist before the eyes of reason; which, while it remaineth, keepeth reason from giving any good direction'.[15] The author of *The Lawes Resolution of Women's Rights* argued in 1631 that a husband could only exercise 'reasonable correction' of his wife.[16] Whateley wrote that it was wisdom and prudence, synonyms for reason, which should ensure that a man's authority was 'free from excess, and free from defect'.[17] When men become passionate with anger, Whateley warned, then they forget 'the use of thy reason'.[18] Whateley was unusual in that he believed that a husband could beat his wife, but significantly only in 'the utmost extremities of unwifelike carriage'.[19] In other words, extreme disobedience or defiance could call for extreme measures. In other circumstances wife beating was labelled as madness.[20] As in marriage a man and a woman became one flesh who, 'but a frantic, furious, desperate wretch will beat himself' asked Gouge.[21] Henry Smith had resolved that 'these mad men which beat themselves should be sent to

[15] Gouge, *Of Domesticall*, 389
[16] T.E., *The Lawes Resolution of a Woman's Rights* (1631), 128–9, as cited in S.D. Amussen, ' "Being Stirred to Much Unquietness": Violence and Domestic Violence in Early Modern England', *Journal of Women's History*, VI, no. 2 (1994), 71.
[17] Whateley, *A Bride Bush*, 128–9, see also 99–100,139.
[18] Ibid., 171.
[19] Ibid., 123; see also A. Fletcher, 'The Protestant Idea of Marriage in Early Modern England', in *Religion, Culture and Society in early modern Britain*, ed. A. Fletcher and P. Roberts (Cambridge, 1994), 172–3; in the 1540s the Augsburg Council ruled that husbands should not beat their wives 'without reason', see L. Roper, *The Holy Household : Women and Morals, in Reformation Augsburg* (Oxford,1989), 189.
[20] Whateley, *A Bride Bush*, 170–3.
[21] Gouge, *Domesticall Duties*, 395.

Bedlam till their madness be gone'.[22] The Homily on marriage, recited in many churches, also taught that a man who beat his wife was like a madman.[23] If a man did beat his wife the consequence for his honour was made clear by Dod and Cleaver, 'he which woundeth her, woundeth his own honour'.[24] 'God forbid that! For that is the greatest shame that can be, not so much to her that is beaten, but to him that doth the deed', taught another homily. Wife beating was not just condemned by church leaders; Richard Steele wrote in *The Spectator*:

> [C]an there be any thing more base, or serve to sink a Man so much below his own distinguishing Characteristic (I mean Reason)...as that of treating an helpless Creature with Unkindness, who has-...deliver[ed] her Happiness in this World to his Care and Protection?[25]

Witnesses in the court of Arches were ready to label the excessive violence of husbands as so lacking in reason that it was madness. One servant of Sir Oliver Boteler's described how his master had 'fantastic fits' which preceded his cruelty to Lady Ann. Another witness described Sir Oliver as 'like a mad man' who frightened his wife and the servants when he was in a violent rage.[26] John Payne, a witness in 1666 in the separation case brought by Rachael Norcott, the wife who claimed to have been beaten after her husband was unhappy with butter on his pudding, said that Rachael had never given him 'any occasion for such madness or distraction she being most obedient'.[27] In other cases men lose their grip on reason because of drinking. So in 1676 Edmund Clarke was described as 'distempered' with drink when he beat his wife, and the 1690 case brought against Thomas Holford described him as violent when he was 'disordered with drink'.[28] The seventeenth-century physician Richard Napier also made the connection between wife beating and irrationality when he noted of one of his patients, 'her husband [is] light-headed and beateth his wife'.[29] Similar cases have been found in the church courts of the early seventeenth century.

[22] H. Smith, *A Preparative to Marriage* (1591), 73.

[23] Church of England, *Two Books of Homilies*, 510–11, as cited in M. MacDonald, *Mystical Bedlam: Madness, Anxiety, and Healing in Seventeenth Century England* (Cambridge,1981), 102.

[24] J. Dod and R. Cleaver, *A Godly Forme of Householde Government* (1614), sig. G2.

[25] J. Addison and R. Steele, *The Spectator*, ed. D.F. Bond (Oxford,1965), II, no. 236, 417, as cited in M. Hunt, 'Wife Beating, Domesticity and Women's Independence in Eighteenth-Century London', *Gender and History*, IV, no.1 (1992), 10.

[26] CA, Case 1041 (1672), Eee4, fos. 874r,876r.

[27] CA, Case 6659 (1666), Eee2, fo. 124r.

[28] CA, Case 1888 (1676), Eee6, fo. 278v; CA, Case 4688 (1690), Eee7, fo. 120v; see for another example of a drunken husband beating his wife CA, Case 2177 (1676), Eee4, fo. 799r.

[29] MacDonald, *Mystical Bedlam*, 102.

Martin Ingram observed regarding five Wiltshire cases involving cruelty that he studied 'all the husbands involved showed signs of mental disturbance or instability'. One of these husbands was Geoffrey Benger of Fyfield who was described as someone who behaved as a 'frantic'.[30] In Essex in 1587 one William Staine was accused of 'misusing his wife with stripes contrary to all order and reason'.[31] And finally, if we look beyond the seventeenth century, Lawrence Stone has noted of court of Arches cases of the eighteenth century that marital violence often took 'extreme forms bordering on madness'.[32]

Observers did not describe these occasions of wife beating as madness to defend or excuse the husbands' actions as temporary instances of insanity, instead they employed this terminology to condemn wife beating. For such demonstrations of loss of self-control were equated with a lack of manliness. It is clear that wife beating could reach a point at which it became an act which shamed the husband. This is shown by the responses of servants and neighbours to extreme violence. The reactions of those who say husbands violently abuse their wives ranged from simply gathering around the couple to stare in 'wonderment', as happened when Mary Whiston was dragged through the street by her angry husband, to more active attempts to help or rescue the wife.[33] When Ellenor Younger's husband beat her on the belly when she was pregnant, and called her whore in the streets of Cheapside in 1670, her neighbours sent for constables.[34] In other cases witnesses were willing to openly condemn the husband. So when John Bradley of St Giles, Middlesex, who had a history of beating his wife, started to strip her of her clothes in an alehouse because he claimed she had been a whore, customers gathered around and some cried 'shame upon him', so that John was forced to 'run away as fast as he could run, and many after him, crying stop him he hath killed his wife'.[35] Others openly declared that such extreme violence jeopardised a husband's claim to manhood. Edward Trussell of St Martin-in-the-Fields appeared as a witness for Elizabeth Hooper in July 1673 and claimed that Elizabeth was 'commonly pitied by her Neighbours and persons of quality for her sufferings and the unmanly Actions wherewith...the said John [her husband] hath treated her'.[36] Humphrey Mildmay of Queen Camel,

[30] M. Ingram, *Church Courts, Sex and Marriage in England, 1570–1640* (Cambridge,1990), 183–4.
[31] F.G. Emmison, *Elizabethan Life : Morals and the Church Courts* (Chelmsford,1973), 162, as cited in MacDonald, *Mystical Bedlam*, 102.
[32] Stone, *Road to Divorce*, 199.
[33] CA, Case 9870 (1669), Eee3, fo. 555v.
[34] CA, Case 10406 (1671), Eee4, fos. 512–13.
[35] CA, Case 1127 (1663), Eee1, fo. 63v.
[36] CA, Case 4747 (1673), Eee5, fos. 250v-1r.

Somerset, defended himself in court in 1672 by denying that he had ever struck his wife, which, he said he did 'account it a very unmanly unworthy thing for any gentleman so to do'. One of Humphrey's servants supported his master by claiming that he had never seen Humphrey behave in any 'unmanly' way towards his wife.[37] Another example of how wife beating could be shameful is from a case brought by Elizabeth Spinkes in the London consistory court between the years 1711 and 1713. Elizabeth's husband had been troubled by his wife's attempts to 'scandalize [his] good name and reputation' which he claimed she had been trying to achieve by telling others of how he beat her. Clearly John Spinkes believed that his honour could be damaged if he was known as a wife beater.[38]

The most extreme expression of public disapproval against wife beating detailed in these records is that experienced by William Bullocke in Bristol during 1667. One witness stated that the cruelty of William to his wife was so notorious that it was of common report in Bristol and Bath 'and many miles about'. His treatment of Posthuma his wife was thought to be 'cruel and inhumane' so that he was 'much cried shame of'. He was so hated that he was forced to employ a constable 'to guard him from the fury of the people and especially the women who knew him to be a base fellow and his said wife to be a good and virtuous Gentlewoman'. Few dared to be seen with William, and men boasted that even if they were paid £40 they would not 'walk the streets with him'. Posthuma took up separate lodgings from her husband, no doubt for her own safety. But anger with William erupted in February 1667 when he decided to walk through Bristol to the house where his wife was living and attempt a reconciliation. A crowd of people gathered around William and followed him, calling him 'base names telling him his wife was too good for him'. They showed their disapproval by throwing dirt at him, and appeared so menacing that William was forced to take shelter in a house 'to avoid the fury of the people'.[39] William Bullocke's behaviour towards his wife led him to be socially ostracised from his community, and to become the victim of a loud mocking demonstration characteristic of charivari. E.P. Thompson found that it was not until the nineteenth century that the majority of charivaris were triggered by wife beaters rather than husband beaters, so the action against William may have been unusual in this period.[40] But exceptional behaviour called for an exceptional response. It is

[37] CA, Case 6244 (1672), Ee4, fo. 51v; Eee4, fo. 767r.

[38] GLRO DL/C/154 fo. 509, as cited in M. Hunt, 'Wife Beating, Domesticity and Women's Independence in Eighteenth-Century London', *Gender and History*, IV, no. 1 (1992), 22.

[39] CA, Case 1432 (1667), Eee2, fos. 538–40.

[40] Thompson, *Customs in Common*, especially 505.

significant that throughout the main deposition for this case it is emphasised how Posthuma's behaviour did not deserve the treatment she received, she was a 'good and virtuous Gentlewoman', he was a 'base fellow' and a 'rogue'. In other words, there was no reason for her husband's violence, and it is because of this that William's behaviour was condemned.

Hence husbands who were accused of cruelty frequently defended themselves by arguing that firstly, there was a reason for their violence, namely wife disobedience, and secondly, that they exercised reason in their use of violence by showing restraint. So, for example, Richard Goodall told the court in 1662 how when his wife kept suspicious company even after he had forbidden her to do so, he gave her 'a little light tap upon her head with his hand which as he believed would not have hurt a child of two years old'.[41] John Charnock in 1673 said that when he gave his wife a 'clap' on the mouth, he did it with 'the back of his hand without...any blood caused thereby'.[42] Thomas Stoddard emphasised in 1684 how he only gave his wife a single blow on the waist which 'did her no harm' when she threatened him with a spit from the fire. Finally, when John Hubbard in 1669 and Robert Bendish in 1673 admitted striking their wives, they made it clear that it had been in response to disobedience, and that their violence must have been controlled for no bruising resulted. Robert Bendish declared that he felt sure that if his violence had reached that level of severity his wife would have complained to others, and significantly at this stage of the proceedings, his wife produced no witnesses to prove otherwise.[43]

The threat or actual use of violence was widely accepted as a way in which men could maintain their control within marriage in late Stuart England. But the check on male power which was intended to prevent patriarchal rule becoming tyrannical was the use of the reason seen as the essence of manhood. As Susan Amussen has argued, whilst wife beating was lawful in the seventeenth century, patriarchal power was never unlimited.[44] Witnesses to marital violence frequently state how at the time of the beating they asked the husband the reason for his violence.[45] For if wife beating was a response to disobedience which was threatening to male honour, then it could be justified as a form of

[41] CA, Case 3789 (1662), Ee1, fo. 195v.

[42] CA, Case 1813 (1673), Ee4, fos. 127v-8r.

[43] CA, Case 8770 (1684), Ee6, fo. 11r; CA, Case 4834 (1669), Ee3, fo. 343; CA, Case 757 (1673), Ee3, fos. 59-60; for other examples of husbands arguing that they showed restraint when beating their wives see, CA, Case 1888 (1676), Ee4, fo. 494r, and CA, Case 6364 (1663), Ee1, fo. 258r.

[44] Amussen, "Being Stirred", 70-89.

[45] See, for example, CA, Case 1041 (1672), Eee4, fos. 856r, 868v; CA, Case 1128 (1675), Eee5, fo. 681r; CA, Case 1813 (1673), Eee5, fo. 20v; CA, Case 4747 (1673), Eee5, fo. 251v.

social control. Furthermore, if reason was exercised in the use of strength then male violence could be regarded as a necessary disciplinary tool. Otherwise wife beating could reach a level at which it was shameful, 'unmanly' and dishonourable. Women who found themselves victims of domestic violence faced the task of finding witnesses to their husband's violence who could testify to its being without reason, and used in a manner which was so excessive that it was life threatening. That many wives had to endure years of violence before they brought suits to the church courts shows the difficulty of proving that male physical strength could in some circumstances be dishonourable as well as praiseworthy.

# WOMEN, STATUS AND THE POPULAR CULTURE
# OF DISHONOUR

## By Laura Gowing

READ 25 MARCH 1995 AT THE UNIVERSITY OF CAMBRIDGE

THE history of honour in early modern English society has tended of necessity to focus on dishonour. The ways in which women and men were defamed, shamed and dishonoured have seemed to offer a vivid insight into how what we call 'honour' worked in early modern society. And yet honour and dishonour were not exactly correspondent points on the same axis of values: what was dishonouring was not necessarily the opposite of what constituted honour. This was especially true where sex was concerned; sexual conduct could be dishonouring in all sorts of ways, but rarely if ever did it confer honour. Sexual dishonour was a concept and a process with a disrupting power of its own, applied most powerfully to women.

Honour has generally been conceptualised as one of the means by which standards of behaviour and social relations between men and women were regulated. Insults to honour had their effect by shaming people into conformity. But if we focus on the dishonour that was the omnipresent threat contained in the idea of honour, the functioning of an honour rhetoric becomes more problematic. Dishonour was far more than a threat that could be pressed into service to order social relations; it could be an active, disruptive process in which shame dislocated relationships and hierarchies. This was particularly so in the case of the dishonour of women. In the cultural discourses of early modern England, the model of honourable femininity—passive, chaste, obedient—had one kind of power; the discourses of female dishonour, read very often through sexual misconduct, quite another. Indeed, the force with which women's unchastity was imagined, ridiculed and proscribed made for a culture in which the possibilities of dishonour seem almost to erase those of honour.

The literature of female advice, litigation over defamation and the language of insults of women centred on chastity.[1] Chastity was no

---

[1] On defamation see J. A. Sharpe, *Defamation and Sexual Slander in Early Modern England: The Church Courts at York*, Borthwick Papers V (York, 1980); Martin Ingram, *Church Courts, Sex and Marriage in England, 1570–1640* (Cambridge, 1987), ch. 10; I discuss the language of slander and honour in chapters 3–4 of Laura Gowing, *Domestic Dangers: Women, Words, and Sex in Early Modern London* (Oxford, 1996).

simpler a term than honour; like honour, it was negotiable and depended on appearance as well as deeds, on social as well as sexual behaviour. But in public discussions of female honour, chastity essentially meant passivity, the avoidance of sin. It was the absolute opposite of the activity, work and consequence that constituted male honour. In practice this equation of women's honour with doing nothing, and men's with doing something, was impractical and largely irrelevant, particularly for working women. Garthine Walker's work shows the range of deeds and identities that might constitute honour for working women: honour was not just what was done to them but what they did; and the readiness of working women to go to law over their reputation also suggests that honour, for them, might have an active component. For higher status women, I want to suggest here, the ideology of passivity had more purchase. Honour, for them, was likely to be neither a result of public deeds, nor a reward that could be won by battle: for the countess of Castlehaven, as Cynthia Herrup has shown, fighting for her good name would not have restored it.[2]

The meaning of women's dishonour was neither constant nor unvariable. The force with which much contemporary culture made chastity central to women's honour has tended to obscure, in particular, the difference that status made to the construction and destruction of reputation. In practice, social and economic status was central to the culture of dishonour. The rare cases in which disputes about the reputation of higher status women reached the courts can be exceptionally revealing about the specificities of dishonour and shame as applied to women in—or aspiring to—high places; and, I want to suggest, about a misogynistic language that sought both to underline and to blur the divisions of status. The cases of libel and slander discussed here come from the Jacobean court of Star Chamber. There, such complaints came very largely—in about 80 percent of cases— from plaintiffs above the rank of yeomanry, complaining very often against defendants of a lower status.[3] Status differences were not only typical of Star Chamber libel cases, but fundamental to their meaning: they record a rhetoric of dishonour which centred on the disturbing intersection of status and gender and which both undermined and buttressed the hierarchies of rank and gender.

The libels sued at Star Chamber represented a very specific genre of early modern culture that has been most powerfully described by

---

[2] See here Garthine Walker's and Cynthia Herrup's papers in this volume.

[3] Thomas G. Barnes, 'Star Chamber Litigants and their Counsel, 1596–1641', in *Legal Records and the Historian*, ed. J. H. Baker (1978), 9–10. Women suing cases as femes soles were even more often of gentry and noble status.

Martin Ingram and Adam Fox.[4] They were simultaneously part of both literate and oral culture: most of them were long rhymes or songs, read or sung aloud in streets and alehouses; occasionally plans were made to print them. Audiences responded to them, it seems, with laughter and sometimes took offence: in Dorset in 1609, a rhyme read out by John King aroused some to 'good laughing thereat', but his mother, lying in childbed, told him to 'gett out of her company ... she could not abide to heare her neighbours ... to be abused'.[5] The words that such men, and a few women, said or sung combined insults, jokes and rumours and references to popular culture, folk stories and even classical mythology. As public performances or documents, libels were designed to publicise dishonouring secrets, imagining or elaborating on complex episodes of sexual dishonour and stressing, in particular, the gaps between public status and private shame. The multiple authors of slanderous texts assumed a certain kind of speaking voice that gloried in bringing their claims to the ear of the victim or the public, opening with phrases such as this: 'Walter Robbins all health I wish unto you, I am very sorry to heare the Reporte that goeth abroade.'[6] Overlaying the force of this censorious, shaming voice, the sheer mass of words contained in most libels carried its own power. In the culture of reputation and disrepute, any words about women could be taken as dishonouring: simply to be talked about seemed to presuppose shame.

The high status of the women involved in libel suits at Star Chamber, their supposed distance from street culture, gave these slanders a special sticking power. For one thing, to be insulted in the oral culture of streets and marketplaces necessarily had a different impact on working women who laboured there, and gentlewomen who did not. As well, the potential for response and negotiation depended on status: proceedings at the more local courts which working women used to respond to slurs on their reputations may well have had considerably more purchase than those of the distant Star Chamber on the intricate negotiations of credit at a local level. And in a society in which verbal insult was becoming increasingly associated with the idea of legal, as well as informal, responses, the unwillingness or inability of higher status women to defend themselves in court gave a further weight to the invectives designed to shame them and their husbands.

While the touchstone of libels targeting female dishonour was, not surprisingly, sexual chastity, their greatest concern was a material and

---

[4] Martin Ingram, 'Ridings, Rough Music and Mocking Rhymes in Early Modern England', in *Popular Culture in Seventeenth-Century England* ed. Barry Reay (London and Sydney, 1985); Adam Fox, 'Ballads, Libels and Popular Ridicule in Jacobean England', *Past and Present*, no. 145 (1994), 47–83.

[5] *King* v. *Lawrence* (1609), Public Record Office STAC 8 190/07, m. 14,15.

[6] *Robbins* v. *Corniche* (1610), STAC 8 254/29 m. 2.

tangible issue that bore directly on the mechanics of social status: the economics of marriage. Correspondingly, most of these cases were sued by couples rather than by individual men or women. It is by no means always clear who was the most insulted by their words: attacks, however bitterly personal, on married women could always be perceived as bearing on their husbands' reputations. Libels featured story after story in which the whole process of exploits and endeavours by which women and men contract themselves in marriage was fraught with potential for dishonour, so much so that the problems women brought to the marriage contract seemed to make an honourable marriage impossible. Relatively rarely do these libels actually refer to whoredom, or frame specific accusations of women selling their honour or their bodies. Yet the exchange of women's bodies for men's money underlies much of what they say about husbands and wives: thus the framework of whoredom turns out to be at the heart of marital relations.

The dishonour of these women was effected in the context of an economic, sexual and material marketplace. In Buckinghamshire in 1607, Dorothy Poole was the protagonist and victim of a song set 'to a new tune called Pride and Lecherie' and with the chorus 'daynty Dall Lee'. Its narrator—the usual composite voice of a concerned neighbourhood—charged: 'when she came first unto the Towne ... she had but one poore thredbare gowne ... and now she hath gownes either two or three ... But how she gotte them, I cannot tell yee.' As well as the gowns, Dorothy had gained 'stockinges of watchett blewe' and 'Shee hath a hundred powndes before ... some say tys with layeinge her legges soe wyde'. Her precise, corrupt economic and sexual position was clarified: 'her maydenhead is not to sell'. It had gone already, in exchange for better clothes. Although this song was entirely about Dorothy Poole, 'daynty Dall Lee', it was not Dorothy who took it to court, but the man, 'ould baldepate', who features in it as her paying lover. It was he, William Abraham, who construed himself as the more dishonoured and sued the nine perpetrators, claiming that they had not only caused their children and servants to sing the rhyme, but had also sent it to a London printer.[7] Dishonour, here, runs deeper than the purely sexual. Women's sexuality, however neatly it seems to fit into a sexual and economic marketplace, is fundamentally a devalued commodity and a waste of money. It is so, at least, for William Abraham; but Dorothy Poole comes out rather the better from the transaction, having made some apparent progress upward with her new dresses.

It was in the light of this sexual and material economy that marriage could be read as dishonouring. The context of marriage was, of course,

[7] *Abraham v. Tyckell* (1609), STAC 8 036/06.

what defined women's sexual role; but it also defined women's status. The combination of these two processes emerged, in the words of dishonour, as a peculiarly troubling nexus of status and sexuality. Central to this vision of the sexual economy was the size and significance of a woman's marriage portion. Agnes Nightingale, formerly Bellamy, and the husband she had recently married, a Staffordshire yeoman, came to court in 1611 to complain of a rhyme that was first circulated locally and eventually printed.[8] In the familiar form of a narrative of hearsay, it ran:

> Abroade as I was walking
>  I hearde some people talking ...
> one said it greived him wonderfully
> to part with sweete An Bellamy
> tutt said the other lett her goe
> we have better marriages than her I troe
> her porton is so extreame small
> it is not to be counted on at all
> we have choice of five or six I say
> that be her betters everyway
> her better say you how can it be
> she exceeds all maydes in huswiffery
> with it they say she will reape the gane
> a man may live and take no payne

The rhyme goes on to tell the story of Ann Bellamy's marriage to Richard Nightingale, 'kinsman to a foole', expounding in precise detail the bad bargain of marriage. At the top of the list is Ann's lack of portion:

> although she is her fathers heire
> and a velvett hatt doth seeme to weare
> it is not thirty pounds of mony
> will mainteine her with the charge of her conny

Huswifery turns out to be irrelevant: instead a relationship between chastity, status and portion emerges. Ann's constant 'running abroade' at night, and a liaison—encouraged by her mother—with the miller mean a direct loss of both money and honour to her husband. A 'nice wief and a backe dore', concludes the rhyme, 'do often make a rich man poore.'[9] Women's side of the marriage bargain appears, in stories like this, to be totally unreliable; their sexual credit is easily undermined,

---

[8] Adam Fox, 'Aspects of Oral Culture and its Development in Early Modern England' (D.Phil. thesis, University of Cambridge, 1992), 233–4.
[9] *Nightingale* v. *Rotton* (1611), STAC 8 220/31, m. 15.

their wifely skills do not compensate for a lack of portion, and the money they do bring to the marriage can be tainted.

Slanderous rhymes homed in on the tensions of the intersection between class and gender. Marriage conferred status upon women, but their dishonourable characters or pasts could undermine it. So Lucy Bressy, a Warwickshire gentleman's wife, ended up in court in 1616 defending her breeding and honour against allegations of base life from her servant. Lucy's husband opened his complaint to Star Chamber by insisting she had always lived 'in the fashion and habite of a gentle-woman accordinge to her qualitye and degree', and that she had taken a place before her marriage as a 'wayteing gentlewoman' to Lady Harrington but had never undertaken any 'inferiour place of attend-ance'. Lucy had been slandered by the couple's servant, George James, described by them as a 'notorious lewd fellow and of very base swaggering and riotous and intemperate life': in her husband's absence, he had had begun to grow 'dissolute and outrageous', giving Lucy 'many opprobious rayling and revyling speches unbeseeminge any sarvante to give his maystrisse', and provoking 'by his lewd example' others of the servants to do the same. Lucy's particular fears, here, were not so much for her status as for its symbol, the livery cloak they had bought for George to wear. They had specifically insisted that he was not to be entitled to it until he had completed his service with them, and Lucy, fearing he would run away with it, had locked it up. This, the couple argued, was the spur that set George James's fury off, provoking him to attack Lucy with further abuse and reproaches and trying to 'deceave her of her honest and vertous reputation' by plotting with one Elizabeth Banckes—'a woman of very lewde behaviour'—to invent a rhyme which they wrote down, delivered to several people and sang and repeated in Lucy's hearing. The essence of their rhyme was a story of Lucy's baseness: it set out deliberately to undermine her claims to gentility, her position as a gentleman's wife, and, hence, the status that enabled her and her husband to be so high-handed with the livery cloak. If Elizabeth Banckes was as base as the Bressyes's complaint made out, the libel she helped to contrive was intended to bring Lucy—and with her her husband —to her level. It ran:

> Roysters give Roome, for here comes a Lass:
> Thoughe shee never solde Broome, nor had a good face.
> Yet is shee stoute, courageous and bolde:
> more shameles and impudent, than shee is yeres olde.
> For taking of false oathes she doth not care
> For picking of pocketts, or lockes she is rare.
> For stealing of cloakes, gold Buttons, or Bandes:
> Or cuffes for to weare to grace her false handes.

No oyster queane putteth her downe for use of Tongue:
Nor kitchin-stuffes Drabbe if she doe doe a wronge.
To sell Aqua-vitae sometyme she did use:
No labour nor travayle this Dowde did refuse...

The rhyme reveals how neatly sexual implications are woven into the language of dishonour. If Lucy is not a whore herself, she is an equal to any 'queane' or 'Drabbe': her very ability to match words betrays her honour. It is here that Lucy's pretensions to high status make their mark. For gentlewomen, the fighting over words that might vindicate lower status women could simply mark them out as further dishonoured. Aspirations to high status carry with them, it seems, the obligation to avoid 'courage' and 'boldness', those double-sided attributes that honour men, but dishonour women. In the same vein, Edward and Elizabeth Frances, a gentry couple from Melbury Osmond, Dorset, found themselves in 1623 the butts of a rhyme by a tanner and some others, accusing him of striving 'to maister all the Towne', and her, more specifically and discreditingly, of a more sexual kind of self-assertion. 'Bes the beare', it ran,

> doth swell and swer she will maister be of all the wyves for
>   hye degree
> And well she maye I tell you trues be maistres in London
>   of the stues
> for Pompe and Pride she beares the bell
> Shee is as proude as the devill of hell[10]

Countering this, the plaintiffs took care to point out in their complaint that they enjoyed 'quiet and peaceable estates' (in fact, Edward himself had been accused of seditious words against the queen in 1598: trying to persuade a woman to 'lead an incontinent life with him', he had claimed that 'the beste in England: had much desyred the plesure of the fleshe, and had allso three bastardes by nobell men of the courte'").

The credit and status of women such as Elizabeth Frances were seen to be fragile, easily damaged commodities of shifting value. Work, money and demeanour all changed women's status; not just at marriage, but continually thereafter, women's status could be subject to problematic and very visible shifts. John Eliot complained in 1609 of a series of libels insulting him, telling how he had fallen in love first with 'a propsy young mayed, a good yeoman gentlewoman as it is sayd'; but her friends 'would not suffer her' to marry him, and he moved on to 'a five hundred pound wench not farre from his brother'. He 'brought

[10] *Gordon & Frances v. Auncell* (1623), STAC 8 153/29, m. 2.
[11] PRO SP 12/269, no. 22.

her hither like a gentlewoman borne, in a hat and a feather and perhaps with a horne, with many fine guegawes and other pretty thinges, her countenenance lovely her handes with golde ringes'. The rhyme traces the changes of status of a man who, in court, styled himself gentleman; it has Eliot turning with fortune's wheel 'from a meane man to a player from a player let him reele / to a gentleman born or else a proud bragger / then to a yeoman next turne heile turne bagger'. But the main sign, and cause, of those changes is his wife, the 'five hundred pound wench' whom he eventually married. Her clothes and demeanour testify to his downward mobility. The £500 is, of course, deceptive, and her shaky claims to gentry status are undermined by the manner of their courtship: he 'wood her in seacret and spake through a truncke / as players use to deale with a puncke'. She ends up sitting 'yeomanlye in a taffata hatt / her handes doe so worke shee cannot bee fatt'.[12] The bodies, dress and behaviour of women mark their husbands' status: their changeability suitably reflects the slipperiness of women's hold on status.

Far more slippery was the female body itself. In the rhetoric of dishonour women's bodies were both the cause and register of shame; slanderous rhymes effected shame by describing the female body as grotesque. Anne, Elizabeth, Frances and Dorothy Venables, daughters of a Northamptonshire gentleman, complained in 1604 of being defamed by three men who had called them and their mother whores, jades and queanes 'trulls puncks Bitches hedge whores twelvepenny hackneys, munckeyfaces, divills faces'. A rhyme, put 'to the tune of panders come away' elaborated: 'they are like to muncks they are soe ugly shaped, I fear theyll prove puncks, they being so often japed'. They were accused of having 'sweating arses', 'their munckys fall an itchinge', and 'they hang down their chynn as thapes in Paris Garden'. The Venables daughters claimed these words were a plot to 'scandalize their parents and hinder their preferments in marriage'. Indeed, they did so in a very specific way: calling gentlemen's daughters looking for preferment 'base trulls' and 'twelvepenny hackneys' made of sexual insult a precisely economic attack.[13]

More fantastic visions provided a particularly fertile way of undermining superior bodies. The imaginings of rhymes and libels of women's bodies run on one theme: that women's bodies are in a state of incipient decay, for which the medicine of masculinity was the only salve. James Cowane, a Gloucester mercer, was accused in 1609 of defaming a gentleman's wife in a long rhyme that, amongst other stories, told how she

---

[12] *Eliot* v. *Deering* (1609), STAC 8 138/05. Both John and his accusers gave themselves the rank of gentlemen in court.

[13] *Venables* v. *Knight* (1603), STAC 8 288/12, m. 51.

chanced 'to catch a fall' and bruised herself 'agaynst a stony wall' (presumably a sexual metaphor), 'puuled' with pain, and could only be cured by 'oyle of man'.[14] The fine delineation of the wounds and decay in these libels conjures up a peculiarly dangerous sexual economy. It is sex with men that wounds these women; and yet those very wounds also call for men to mend them, often, explicitly, for more sex. These images of grotesque femininity recall the gross, lascivious alewives of stories and ballads, the incontinent tradeswomen of city comedies, and the promiscuous women of bawdy songs whose genitals are mistaken for gaping wells. They suggest, too, pornographic and medical discourses about raging nymphomania; and a much broader trope, familiar in Renaissance culture, of women as leaky vessels and unenclosed wildernesses, leaking both words and fluids.[15] Longest and grossest of these rhymes, taking the leakiness of women to its utmost limits, was a song about Mary Lawrey that was circulated in the town of St Columb in Cornwall in 1616. It describes at length a fantasy of monstrous incontinence. After a 'thrust' her 'flood hatch' was broken; she 'always doth bedue her sheats', her water bursting out in an unstemmable tide. In an attempt to 'change her lief', she 'sold away her maydenhood and is become a wief'. Her husband, a carpenter, tries to 'mend her floodgate'—with, of course, a pin (penis); 'but all his labour was in vayne he could no goode at all'. The incontinence continues, she has to hire a maid to hold her chamber pot; the only cure, the song goes on, is for her to eat skinned mice baked in pies and cover her 'what I call' with the skins. Finally, if this doesn't work, she is to 'take some heare and sue [sew] her geare and bit away the threade'—closing her dangerous orifice entirely.[16] Under the exuberant brutality of this piece, revelling as it does in both the scale of bodily crisis and its remedy, lies a predictable message about the betrayal of women's respectability by their bodies and their desires.

Tapping into established languages of misogyny and investing them with the power of local specificity, rhymes like these depend for their power on the implicit connections between all these images of femininity:

---

[14] *Taylor v. Cowane* (1609), STAC 8 285/27

[15] On which ideas see Gail Kern Paster, 'Leaky Vessels: The Incontinent Women of City Comedy', *Renaissance Drama*, n.s., XVIII (1987), 43–65; Peter Stallybrass, 'Patriarchal Territories: The Body Enclosed', in *Rewriting the Renaissance: The Discourses of Sexual Difference in Early Modern Europe*, ed. Margaret Ferguson, Maureen Quilligan and Nancy Vickers (Chicago, 1986), 123–42; Judith Bennett, 'Misogyny, Popular Culture, and Women's Work', *History Workshop Journal*, XXXI (1991), 166–88; and Margaret Miles, *Carnal Knowing: Female Nakedness and Religious Meaning in the Christian West* (Boston, 1989), ch. 5. It is perhaps worth noting here that Elizabethan popular fantasies about the highest woman in the land, the Queen, focused not on the openness of her body but its supposed closure—her alleged incapacity for sexual intercourse: Carole Levin, *The Heart and Stomach of a King: Elizabeth I and the Politics of Sex and Power* (Philadelphia, 1994), 83.

[16] *Lawrey v. Dier* (1616), STAC 8 202/30, m. 3.

the instability of sexual honour, the deceptive mobility of status and class, the fragility of the dishonoured body. As they strip away the signs of high status, these images return women to a plane in which they are defined by fantasies of total corruption and collapse. Here, women's place is never fixed: not in the marriage market, nor in the hierarchies of status; and nothing can hold the disintegrating female body together. Above all, the rhetoric of dishonour is a disruptive one. It makes nonsense of the established rules of precedence, hierarchy and dress codes by insisting that, as far as women are concerned, no evidence of status is reliable. These libels exemplify the process Peter Stallybrass has described where, through misogynistic discourse, 'the elimination of class boundaries is produced by the collapsing of women into a single undifferentiated group'.[17] Thus, the potential women carry for dishonour can destabilise the whole economy of domestic, social and marital relations. It was a powerful language for servants or middling status men and women: focusing ostensibly on sexual sins, it actually dismantled the trappings of higher status women's rank and the credit of their marriages.

If this was a disruptive language, it was also one that buttressed gender order. Misogynist fantasies of grotesque femininity forcefully exposed the tensions of the intersection of status and gender and in particular the nexus of that intersection, marriage; they also fulfilled and supported the power of patriarchal order to marginalise and undermine women. It is rarely possible to measure the material damage of words to reputations: we might more usefully appraise the power of dishonour by looking at a wider context than its immediate victims. Shaming women by describing them as these libels did not only draw on a set of established images; it created new, potent visions of femininity. It was the application of images such as these to real women that made a difference. Libels suggested that bodily and public dishonour could be pinned on the most exalted or the least important women. All women were potentially grotesque; none of them had stable bodies or lasting credit. The achievement of these libels was to transpose misogyny from the realm of jokes and songs into the everyday world.[18] The rhetoric of dishonour suggested that high status femininity and honest wifehood were incompatible with activity or 'boldness', that honourable marriage could always founder on the rocks of women's corruption, and that women's bodies could always be reduced to a state of grotesque, incapable crisis. It both presupposed and contributed to a culture in which the power of patriarchal norms drew strength from the daily application of brutal misogyny.[19]

[17] Stallybrass, 'Patriarchal Territories', 133.

[18] For an analysis of the material power of misogyny in the world of work, see Bennett, 'Misogyny'.

[19] I would like to thank Faramerz Dabhoiwala, Cynthia Herrup and Sarah Waters for their comments on this paper.

# EXPANDING THE BOUNDARIES OF FEMALE
# HONOUR IN EARLY MODERN ENGLAND

## By Garthine Walker

READ 25 MARCH 1995 AT THE UNIVERSITY OF CAMBRIDGE

WITHIN the historiography of gender and reputation in early modern Europe, female and male honour are usually presented as being incommensurable; yet they are constantly compared. Female honour has been discussed primarily in the context of sexual reputation. Male honour is commonly imagined as 'more complex', involving matters of deference, physical prowess, economic and professional competence and the avoidance of public ridicule. Thus the predominant model of gendered honour has been oppositional—female to male, private to public, passive to active, individual to collective and, by extension, chastity to deeds.[1] Such a model, however, is misconceived. Just as the honour of men could be bound up with sexuality and the body, so these constituted merely one—albeit powerful—concomitant of feminine honour.[2] Sexual probity was indeed central to the dominant discourse of early modern gender ideology, and historians have quite properly noted the significance of a social code of female honour 'which was overwhelmingly seen in sexual terms'.[3] But the potency of this discourse has itself frequently led to the selection of sources in which sexual conduct and reputation are central issues, and in which sexual constructions of female dishonour are immediately visible.[4] Because

---

[1] E.g., J.R. Ruff, *Crime, Justice and Public Order in Old Regime France. The Sénéchaussées of Libourne and Bazas, 1696–1798* (1984), 73–4, 167–9, at 73; L. Roper, *Oedipus and the Devil. Witchcraft, Sexuality and Religion in Early Modern Europe* (1994) [hereafter Roper, *Oedipus*], 65, 108–9.

[2] Roper, *Oedipus*, 108; T.V. Cohen and E.S. Cohen, *Words and Deeds in Renaissance Rome: Trials Before the Papal Magistrates* (Toronto, 1993) [hereafter Cohen and Cohen, *Words and Deeds*], 23–4.

[3] A. Fletcher, *Gender, Sex and Subordination in England 1500–1800* (New Haven and London, 1995) [hereafter Fletcher, *Gender, Sex and Subordination*], 101–5, 124, at 101. See also J. Pitt-Rivers, 'Honour and Social Status', in *Honour and Shame: The Values of Mediterranean Society*, ed. J.G. Peristiany (1965) [hereafter Pitt-Rivers, 'Honour and Social Status'], 42–6, 52–3, 62–71.

[4] E.g., S. Cavallo and S. Cerutti, 'Female Honor and the Social Control of Reproduction in Piedmont between 1600 and 1800', in *Sex and Gender in Historical Perspective*, ed. E. Muir and G. Ruggiero (1990) [hereafter *Sex and Gender*, ed. Muir and Ruggiero], 73–109; L. Ferrante, 'Honor Regained: Women in the Casa del Soccorso di San Paolo in Sixteenth-Century Bologna' [hereafter Ferrante, 'Honor Regained'], in *Sex and Gender*, ed. Muir and

235

women's honour has effectively been imagined in terms of *dishonour*, constructions of shame—especially those associated with sexuality and sexual behaviour—have been privileged over, or compounded with, those of affront. Even when it has been noted that sexual insult could be a mundane response 'in every sort of local and personal conflict', conceptualisations of women's honour have been defined over-whelmingly by the nature of such responses rather than the conflicts themselves.[5] In effect, distinctions between social and personal codes of honour for women have often been blurred, with the latter being subsumed into the former.[6] Gender ideology is thus perpetuated and alternative forms of feminine honour are overlooked.

   The manner in which female occupation has been located within its household context is also connected to this partial view of female honour, for honour is seen to be something which exists only in public terrain. Although women's contributions to their household economies are acknowledged to be not properly private, women's work is never-theless frequently characterised by an absence of the occupational and institutional identity which provides an important and highly visible locus for male honour, both individually and collectively. The corollary of this is that women's work lacked the public esteem considered so essential to honourability. The neglect of the relevance of women's work and household position to feminine codes of personal and social honour seems strange: not only did concepts of honour provide a means of 'negotiating the politics of daily life',[7] but it is widely accepted that women's contributions to their household economies gave them a subjective sense of social identity and self-worth, as well as neigh-bourhood status, all of which have a relation to honour.[8]

   A further problem has arisen from the way in which the term 'honour' is sometimes used interchangeably with certain others: 'name', 'fame', 'carriage', 'condition', 'reputation', 'credit', 'honesty', 'virtue'

Ruggiero, 46–72; Roper, *Oedipus*, 65, 107, 108, 229; L. Gowing, 'Gender and the Language of Insult in Early Modern London', *History Workshop Journal* XXXV (1993), 1–21.
   [5] L. Gowing, 'Language, Power and the Law: Women's Slander Litigation in Early Modern London', in *Women, Crime and the Courts in Early Modern England*, ed. J. Kermode and G. Walker (1994) [hereafter *Women, Crime and the Courts*, ed. Kermode and Walker], 26–47, at 30.
   [6] On social and personal codes of honour, see P. Schneider, 'Honor and Conflict in a Sicilian Town', *Anthropology Quarterly*, XLII, 3 (1969) [hereafter Schneider, 'Honor and Conflict'], 144–5.
   [7] T.V. Cohen, 'The Lay Liturgy of Affront in Sixteenth-Century Italy', *Journal of Social History*, XXV (1991–2) [hereafter Cohen, 'Lay Liturgy of Affront'], 857.
   [8] R. Cust, 'Honour and Politics in Early Stuart England: The Case of Beaumont v. Hastings', *Past & Present*, CXLIX (1995), 91; S.R. Rigby, *English Society in the Later Middle Ages: Class, Status, Gender* (1995), 280. Cf. M. Chaytor, 'Husband(ry): Narratives of Rape in the Seventeenth Century', *Gender and History* VII, 3 (1995) [hereafter Chaytor, 'Husband(ry)'], 382–4.

and 'chastity'. Each of these terms and the conditions they describe undoubtedly had a bearing on how honour was imagined and constructed, but the precise and shifting nature of those relationships begs further investigation. The definition of honour which is applied here is '[one's] estimation of [one's] own worth, [one's] *claim* to pride, ... the acknowledgement of that claim, [one's] excellence recognized by society, [one's] *right* to pride.[9] In particular, personal honour is 'the work of an individual, an ideology that [one] constructs to rationalize or enhance [one's] power in interpersonal relations'.[10] Accordingly, I shall use the terms 'honesty' and 'credit' as they are related to honour in the form of esteem, morality and dignity. The purpose of this essay is to offer a preliminary exploration of ways in which the boundaries of female honour might be expanded beyond those directly related to sexual conduct.

According to witnesses' depositions, in August 1667 Joan Williamson 'uttered many base words and curses' against her husband Henry when she found him drinking with Robert Legh in an alehouse. Ellen Peake, then present, asked, '[w]hy doe you keepe such a Stirre, for your husband hath not been here soe longe?' Joan replied by calling Ellen 'a whore' and 'my husband's whore', upon which Ellen slapped her face. When Ellen's daughter went to help her, Joan 'fell very violently upon them both'. The three women were parted by Henry and Robert; afterwards Joan and Ellen were each bound by recognisance to be of good behaviour towards the other. In this case, insult and dishonour were partially *expressed* in terms of the dominant—sexual—code of social honour for women. Yet witnesses' depositions suggest that the *construction* of honour and dishonour here were broader. Ellen Peake, after all, seemingly became a focus for spousal discontent only after she publicly entered what was essentially a personal dispute between another woman and her husband. According to Jane Holt, the alewife, Ellen's presence there was not explained by an illicit *rendezvous* with Henry Williamson, for Ellen had gone there 'to buy some graines ... and [Holt] not being ready to give [her] ... the said graines soe soone as she came', Ellen waited, 'stay[ing] in the open house' where Williamson and Legh happened to be drinking. The dishonour associated with the language of adultery and whoredom which implied the disruption of order in Joan's household was countered by an assertion of Ellen's honest undertaking of the business of hers.[11]

[9] Pitt-Rivers, 'Honour and Social Status', 21–2.
[10] Schneider, 'Honor and Conflict', 144.
[11] Cheshire Record Office, Quarter Sessions Files [hereafter QJF] 95/3, fos. 106, 103, 104.

Women's honour, and assaults upon it, could be imagined through the hierarchies and obligations of household order. Wives' tales of economic and sexual displacement by their husbands' mistresses is but one well-known manifestation of this; another is found when adulterous wives were seen to bring dishonour not only upon themselves, but upon their husbands and their entire households. More positively, women's honour resided in the fulfilment of a wife's household duties, for if honour resided in feelings of self-worth, pride and status, status was in turn 'established through the recognition of a certain social identity'.[12] A married woman's social identity was not solely defined by her marital status but also by her labours. Thus, housewifery was 'the measure by which every woman was judged', a skill admired as much as that of husbandry, an 'esteemed' role through which she could achieve respect, and one which 'afforded a gratifying means of favourable comparison with other women'.[13] Some contemporary commentators ascribed 'a certain vocational dignity' to women's work in the household. Sir Robert Filmer asserted that a wife's labour 'determines her eminence', and that housewifery defined the 'honour and Profit of a virtuous woman'; conversely, he identified idleness as one of the worst vices of the 'contintious wife'.[14] While Richard Gough's highest praise of all the inhabitants of Myddle was for good housewives, he noted that 'an idle housewife' could bring about the ruin of her family.[15]

Accordingly, the role of 'good' housewife was one through which women could assert and defend honour, whilst the term 'idle huswife' was taken to be one of insult. When, in 1624, Anne Blanchard invited her husband's cousin into her house, saying 'Cozin John, you shall come in, and welcome', John's wife Margaret retorted, 'Dost thou cozine him now ... [when previously you have said] that he was born in a stable ... thou idle huswife?' Anne replied by pulling rank: 'I scorn thy termes, I am noe huswife, I was never so base as thou to be a servant', to which Margaret responded, 'noe, I think thou never waste [a] *good* huswife'.[16] Women's depositions suggest that being insulted in this way was considered sufficient justification for verbal, physical and legal retaliation. Katherine Sponne claimed that John Frances had undermined her authority by entering her alehouse after she had barred

[12] Pitt-Rivers, 'Honour and Social Status', 22.
[13] Fletcher, *Gender, Sex and Subordination*, 223, 226; A.L. Erickson, *Women and Property in Early Modern England* (1993), 53–4; A. Vickery, 'Women and the World of Goods: A Lancashire Consumer and her Possessions, 1751–81', in *Consumption and the World of Goods*, ed. John Brewer and Roy Porter (1993), 283.
[14] Cited in M. Ezell, *The Patriarch's Wife: Literary Evidence and the History of the Family* (1987), 134, 176–7, 137, and see 36–42, 133–7.
[15] Cited in Fletcher, *Gender, Sex and Subordination*, 226, 268.
[16] Cheshire Diocesan Record Office, Consistory Court Cause Papers [hereafter EDC] 5 (1624)2, William and Anne Blanchard c. John and Margaret Blanchard. My italic.

him 'and did ... revile and call [me] by divers ill and base terms; calling [me] idle huswife, with other words to the like effect'.[17] Ellen Wright maintained that she called John Warman a 'Cuckoldy witwally foole' under provocation for, when she had asked for information about her son, Warman had 'bidden [me] go or get away like any idle huswife'.[18] This insult struck at the very core of feminine identity of women of the plebeian and middling sorts. It tells us something of the nature of affront rather than that of shame: as it was as much an assault on personal as on social honour one cannot assume that women did not *feel* this honour or its loss.

The significance of such cases is illuminated by their fragile legal status. Under canon law, defamatory words had to allege behaviour which comprised an ecclesiastical offence.[19] Inadequate housewifery clearly did not do so unless it was compounded with other forms of misconduct. Thus terms such as 'Idle sawcie huswife', 'base houswife' and 'drunken huswife' were prosecuted by women as defamatory words.[20] Witnesses deposed that they were unable to remember whether Richard Tottie had called Eleanor Waine 'durtie Queane *or* huswife': the case resting upon which of these terms was used.[21] A Chester innkeeper, Isabell Anyon, sued a man for calling her 'a brazen fac't slutt, a stinkinge Nasty durty huswife, a bold impudent Queane, a drunken slutt, a beggars bratt'.[22] The emphasis here is on dirtiness as much as it is on whoredom *per se*; in constructions of honour and dishonour a woman's body could represent her household as well as vice versa. And, of course, the words 'idle housewife' might well have been amongst those 'other vile, base and opprobrious terms' so often referred to in defamation cases. While sexual insult provided a conceptual and linguistic repertoire through which women's honour could be damaged, defended and asserted, that honour was not necessarily itself sexual. Furthermore, when women emphasised their household position in refuting sexual dishonour, they did not do so merely as a means of ascribing innocence (as opposed to knowledge) to themselves, as Miranda Chaytor has suggested.[23] They also laid claim to an honourability which was defined by what women *did* rather than what was done to them.

[17] EDC 5(1626)2, John Frances c. Katherine Sponne.
[18] EDC 5(1628)7, Sarah Warman c. Ellen Wright.
[19] T. Meldrum, 'A Woman's Court in London: Defamation at the Bishop of London's Consistory Court, 1700–1745', *London Journal*, XIX, 1 (1994), 8.
[20] E.g., EDC 5(1628)1, Margery Chambers c. Thomas Williams; EDC 5(1669)28, Mary Mainwaring c. Jane Tompson.
[21] EDC 5(1661)38, Eleaner Waine c. Richard Tottie. My italic.
[22] EDC 5(1667)47, Isabell Anyon c. Robert Moulson. See also EDC 5(1663)41, Ann Taylor c. Frances Eaton.
[23] Chaytor, 'Husband(ry)', 398–9.

Women countered labelling as idle housewives and many sorts of dishonesty with assertions of their honourable, hardworking and honest undertakings in their households. We can see this too in poor women's petitions to the bench at quarter sessions requesting licences to build cottages on commons and wastes. In these petitions, notions of honesty and credit are compounded. Women spoke of having taken 'extra-ordinarie care and paines' to maintain themselves and their children, and swore that if a licence were granted, they would 'be content to work day and night towards their maintenance'.[24] When groups of inhabitants petitioned the bench seeking to prevent the granting of licenses, they inverted the image of the good housewife: John Wilson's wife, for example, was said to be a 'verie able woman, but [who] will not work'.[25] The conceptual credit accorded to the good housewife was crucial, for poor women, by definition, lacked economic credit.[26]

Publicly undermining a woman's authority within her household and, by extension, her standing outside it, was in part an assault upon her honour. This was clearly so in the events which led Anne Lea to prosecute Anne Lewis for defamation in 1620. Lea's honour was compromised in the events which *precipitated* alleged sexual slander. As Anne Lea and her husband walked past Anne Lewis in Nantwich churchyard, Lewis 'made a Curtesy in a scornefull and deridinge manner'. Lea 'upon a soddaine, left her husband and turned back againe', demanding '[w]hoe dost thou laugh att? Dost thou laugh at mee?'. '[Yes,] I laugh at thee', replied Lewis. At this point the depositions differ, with witnesses on behalf of each woman deposing that she had been defamed by the other. But almost everyone was in agreement that, whatever Lea had said, Lewis 'did stryke ... Anne Lea upon the face with her hand or fiste in a violent and angrie manner', and 'did spitt in her face'. Lea's sensitivity to this treatment should be interpreted in the context of tainted household authority. For Lewis had formerly been one of Lea's servants, but had been 'turned forthe'; 'the occasion of her going thence ... was her late mistress Anne Lea'.[27]

Defending the honour which resided in household authority could easily assume the character of dishonesty. For example, the dishonour associated with receiving stolen goods caused Mary Janson to claim that she and her children had been 'utterly undone' by the magistrate, Edward Legh, who issued a warrant to search her house. She responded

[24] QJF 89/2, fo. 231; QJF 89/3, fo. 36.
[25] QJF 49/1, fo. 165; Cheshire Record Office, Quarter Sessions Book, QJB 1/5, fo. 69v.
[26] G. Walker, 'Crime, Gender and Social Order in Early Modern Cheshire' (Ph.D. thesis, University of Liverpool, 1994) [hereafter Walker, 'Crime, Gender and Social Order'], 253–68.
[27] EDC 5(1620)26, Anne Lea c. Anne Lewis.

to this potential damage to her reputation and social credit with an assault on that of the magistrate, for whom she cared 'no more than for a fart of her arse'. Janson was subsequently bound over by recognisance not for any part in theft, but because she 'hath lately spoken and uttered divers opprobrious and scandalous words against Edward Legh of Bagulcy'.[28] Women who protected the reputation, goods or other members of their households might well have done so in accordance with a concept of honour based on morality and 'right' behaviour, but their actions could, at the same time, conflict with alternative concepts of righteousness and order.

This is exemplified by the prominent role of women in rescues. Anne Knevis, aided by three other women, set upon the constable who attempted to apprehend her son John for fathering a bastard, 'and did beat and abuse him and rescued ... John Browne out of his hands'; occurrences of this sort were commonplace.[29] Women alone or collectively—were also particularly active, and often successful, in resisting attempts by officials to distrain goods or collect taxation.[30] In such cases, honour accrued to 'the willingness to defend one's honour from those who would steal it away'[31] in a quite literal sense. Because of the manner in which women's social worth was defined, defending household stuff, livestock, clothes, even customary rights, was at once a material and symbolic act. Moreover, given that 'men and women partook of the honour of those solidarities to which they looked for social definition',[32] women's collective action may be particularly instructive in determining the boundaries of female honourability. Women acted collectively or communally in regulating both the sexual honesty of their neighbourhoods and the dishonest behaviour of other women regarding theft and receiving stolen property.[33] The part played by women in food and enclosure riots, which was associated with and justified through women's household role, might be also reconsidered in this light.[34] In each of these spheres of activity, the theoretical equation between female domesticity and good social order permitted women in practice to define their own concepts of honesty and honour, both individually and collectively. Moreover, the collective identity of

[28] QJF 95/2, fos. 49, 85, 87.
[29] QJF 95/3, fo. 96. See also QJF 93/1, fos. 92, 93, 94, 95; QJF 95/1, fo. 61.
[30] E.g., QJF 51/3, fo. 22; QJF 95/4, fo. 35.
[31] Cohen, 'Lay Liturgy of Affront', 862.
[32] Cohen and Cohen, *Words and Deeds*, 23.
[33] Gowing, 'Language, Power and the Law', *passim*; G. Walker, 'Women, Theft and the World of Stolen Goods', in *Women, Crime and the Courts*, Kermode and Walker, *passim*.
[34] J. Bohstedt, 'Gender, Household and Community Politics: Women in English Riots 1790–1810', *Past and Present*, CXX (1988), 88–122. See also R.M. Dekker, 'Women in Revolt: Popular Protest and its Social Basis in Holland in the Seventeenth and Eighteenth Centuries', *Theory and Society*, XVI (1987), 337–62.

the household meant that household honour could be defended by women and men together when their economic and social credit was undermined.[35] Household honour was not simply the preserve of the head of each household; it concerned both women and men. Issues of personal or neighbourhood morality, both sexual and non-sexual, mediated through household authority, thus constituted a range of sites in which female honour can be located.

If female honour is in large part related to their place within the household, we might expect women who were displaced in household order to have little access to honourable language and concepts. For instance, according to the tenets of the social code of (sexual) feminine honour, the dishonour attached to women who bore bastards should have made it very difficult for such women to adopt honest, honourable personae before magistrates. Mothers of bastards nevertheless found ways of doing just that. Whereas in cases of sexual insult women publicly gauged their honesty by comparison with other women, in bastardy cases they often measured their own honesty against the dishonesty of the men whom they held responsible for their pregnancy. The stories they told presented sexual dishonour as the result of a dishonourable act done *to* them: Anne Williams described Thomas Prince's breach of his promise to marry her as 'this so great awronge committed against me, which unto my shame and utter overthrow I have, and am, to sustaine at his handes'.[36] Yet the tone and content of such narratives implies that feelings of shame and social dishonour did not preclude a sense of personal honour which was manifest in feelings of affront and which was not so easily destroyed.[37]

A broken promise of marriage was perhaps the most common claim which women made in tales about bastardy, referring to contractual promises, the bans being read in church, or having arranged wedding dates with ministers.[38] But they almost always used a language of justice, equity and righteousness on their own parts and accorded the opposites of these to their erstwhile lovers. These men were said to have acted 'contrarie to [their] promise and to equitie and conscience', 'contrary to all equity and right', or, as Katherine Lockett said, against 'both ... the law and honesty'.[39] Lockett, like many other women, asserted her own honesty by emphasising the non-sexual implications of dishonest acts on the part of the man by whom she was pregnant. Not only had

[35] E.g., QJF 89/2, fo. 56.
[36] QJF 51/3, fo. 112.
[37] Walker, 'Crime, Gender and Social Order', 243–53.
[38] E.g., QJF 49/1, fo. 139; QJF 49/2, fo. 104; QJF 49/2, fos. 106, 107; QJF 51/3, fo. 112; QJF 89/2, fos. 191, 192; QJF 89/3, fo. 76; QJF 89/4, fos. 75, 76; QJF 95/4, fo. 55; QJF 97/1, fos. 57, 93.
[39] QJF 49/2, fos. 67, 176; QJF 51/2, fo. 119.

Thomas Torkington broken his promise to marry her, but he denied all responsibility for her condition. When Lockett 'in ende was forced to flee to the consistorie ... for releif' and arranged to affiliate the child 'with the handes of seven honest women', Torkington acted dishonourably again: he 'did solicit the greatest part of the women for the filiacon not to be present att that tyme'. According to Katherine Lockett, she had acted honourably within the law; Torkington dishonourably attempted to pervert it.[40]

By aligning themselves with the legal process—in common or canon law—women accessed concepts of honour which could eclipse the shadow of dishonour that their sexual activity might otherwise have cast upon their testimonies. In such cases, women's honour simply could not be mediated through their sexuality if their words were to have any force. Non-sexual morality was a crucial component of female honour. Law provided women with a public voice with which to consolidate their claims and reinforce their own dignity; it provided, therefore, a means of through which personal and, ultimately, social honour could be reinscribed.

Another feature of these narratives was the contiguity of different notions of credit. But men, with their economic, social and sexual advantage, appear to have used the language of credit in social and economic terms to a greater extent than women did. Undermining women's reputations by accusing them of lewd behaviour was a common means whereby men attempted to elevate, in contrast, their own credit in order to give weight to their denials of fatherhood. Arthur Blackemoore, for example, claimed to be a gentleman with an inheritance worth forty marks per annum. His accuser, Jane Briscoe, was in comparison 'a woman of very ill behaviour' who 'hath had divers bastards', and who formerly 'alleged another to be father'.[41] However, the concept of credit could be further manipulated. Robert Bertles alias Pedley reported that Mary Ryle was 'a moste lewde woman for she hath had three basse children since the death of her husband'. His own credit in the community was little: he had only recently arrived in Mobberley parish, and he was a poor man. It was this very lack of financial and social credit which, Bertles claimed, had led Ryley to father her child upon him. Such a man did not have the means, in any sense of the word, to counter such accusations.[42] In another case, John Turner said that the mother of his bastard child refused to marry him although he 'did earnestly solicit' her to do so. Instead, she landed

[40] QJF 51/3, fo. 112; QJF 51/4, fos. 113, 163.
[41] QJF 49.2, fos. 156, 163; QJF 49/3, fo. 58. See also QJF 49/3, fo. 88; QJF 51/1, fo. 117; QJF 51/3, fo. 99.
[42] QJF 55/1, fo. 47. See also QJF 55/3, fo. 95; QJF 95/4, fo. 68.

herself employment as wetnurse to a 'Noble Family ... where she lives in great plenty'. Moreover, 'she has a £20 portion left her by her friends, besides her great wages and gifts, and refuses to pay anything at all towards the maintenance of the child'. In contrast, Turner was worth only £5 a year, and was likely to suffer 'great want and misery and the child to starve'.[43] Cases of this sort suggest the difficulties in using 'credit' as a simple gauge of honesty or honour for women. Sexual virtue and scolding speech might have been 'unique' definers of women's credit,[44] but they were not the only ones.

The loss of one sort of credit could easily lead to the loss of others. Margaret Sharples was prosecuted for stealing cloth, 'which she had converted into a petticoat for her own wearinge', from Richard Bennett's shop. Her defence was that she had bargained with Bennett's servant for the cloth, 'but haveinge not moneye sufficient in her purse to pay for it, took it away with purpose to paye for it so soone as she Could: and that she afterwards agreed with Mr Bennett of a price for it'. Bennett confirmed that this was so: after agreeing to pay him 22s, Margaret 'delivered a hamper with goods in it as a pawne for securyty of the money, And 4s 9d in money'. But 'soon after he disliked upon better consideration to hold agreement with her: and delivered the hamper and goods back', and commenced formal legal proceedings against her. For Margaret Sharples, loss of credit had the most extreme repercussions: she was convicted and condemned to hang.[45] This case serves as a reminder that honour, honesty, credit and reputation were not merely concepts, abstractions and linguistic terms. They also had a material basis, and one upon which the fate of an individual might rest.

The value of an individual, 'like any material good, could be socially damaged, destroyed, or reconstructed'.[46] One of the most convenient ways in which a woman's social value might be damaged or destroyed was undoubtedly through the idiom of sexual insult. Nevertheless, even in cases of sexual slander sued at church courts, many witnesses implied that the defamed women on whose behalf they testified were not less esteemed by them as a result of the alleged defamation.[47] Moreover,

[43] QJF 89/2, fo. 213.
[44] L. Gowing, 'Women, Sex and Honour: The London Church Courts, 1572–1640' (Ph.D. thesis, University of London, 1993), 82.
[45] Cheshire City Record Office, Quarter Sessions Files, QSF 67, fos. 4, 10, 11.
[46] Ferrante, 'Honor Regained', 57.
[47] E.g., EDC 5 (1620)23, Jane Leadbetter c. Elizabeth Sutton; EDC 5(1622)36, Elizabeth Billinge alias Billington c. Alice Rogerson; EDC 5(1626)32, Richard Wood and Mary Wood his daughter c. Randle Kirkham; EDC 5(1626)3, Jane Cattarall c. William and Elizabeth Cattarall; EDC 5(1626)81, Alice Ratcliffe c. Alice Collinge.

when a woman such as Mary Carter requested that she be released from her bond to appear before the Cheshire bench for a non-sexual offence in 1650, she was able to do so on the grounds that she had 'ever lived in good esteeme and credit without being blemished or taxed with *any* manner of dishonesty'.[48] A woman's honesty, credit and reputation—constituents of her honour—were not solely defined and located according to the prescriptive sexual honour codes which under-pinned the gender system of early modern England. The honour of women was also situated in the authority invested in their daily labours and household position.

Women's work within the household—as diligent and honest house-wives—was central to the construction of a code of feminine honour. This concept could be applied competitively between women, or as a way for both women and men to discredit women. It was also a means of asserting female honesty. Many disputes between women where honour was undermined or asserted were those in which their household concerns were in direct opposition. When those concerns came into conflict with those of others, such as constables or baliffs, female honour was likewise undermined and asserted. When displaced from the household and positive positions within it, as in the case of female bastard bearers, certain forms of honour were beyond reach, but not all. Future research into female collectivities might prove to be particularly illuminating regarding alternative constructions of female honour. Motherhood, associated with both female collectivity and with com-petition between women, might constitute another fruitful area of inquiry.[49] I would like to suggest, then, that the oppositional model of honour with which I began this essay underestimates the extent to which women's honour was public, collective, active and connected to women's *deeds*. Ascriptions of authority—whether individual, communal, or mediated through the household or the law—constituted a cor-nerstone of honour, for women as for men.[50]

[48] QJF 79/1, fo. 116. My italic.

[49] J.A. Sharpe, 'Witchcraft and Women in Seventeenth-Century England: Some North-ern Evidence', *Continuity and Change*, VI (1991), 179–99; Roper, *Oedipus*, 199–225.

[50] I am grateful to Andy Wood for commenting upon a draft of this essay.

# SUMMARY OF CLOSING PLENARY DISCUSSION ON 'HONOUR AND REPUTATION IN EARLY MODERN ENGLAND'

Complied by Ingrid Tague and Helen Berry

RICHARD Cust connected honour to his work on political culture and the gentry. He introduced the work of Mervyn James on honour as a framework for thinking about behavioural change over time. He suggested that the new historical approach is a multi-layered rather than a teleological one. Certain speakers had emphasised change rather than continuity over time, while others challenged such an approach. Important new themes had been introduced by the conference speakers, such as the importance of lineage, the impact of the companionate marriage, the relationship between public and private notions of honour and the acceptability of violence as a means of defending or challenging honour. He suggested two related ways of thinking about honour that had not been touched on by any of the speakers: the notion of 'honesty' to refer to a godly magistrate following his conscience, and the importance of godliness generally, a pious reputation as key means of establishing one's honour.

Clive Holmes approached the issue of honour from the point of view of a legal historian, using an anecdote about a conflict over a fraudulent funeral monument to encapsulate some of the themes of the conference. He pointed out that the law of defamation failed to provide adequately for people's attempts to regain their honour. The law embodied two contradictory principles: first, 'words are but wind' (the idea that these are simply trivial quarrels); second, 'words incite to revenge' (the idea that they could lead to violence and breaches of the peace). There was a tension between the need for moderate revenge and the desire not to overwhelm the courts with trivial cases. He also emphasised that reliance on legal records leads historians to selective impressions of the nature of disputes over honour because of the limited concerns of the specialist courts involved; for example, ecclesiastical courts dealt only with sexual offences. The failure of the law was caused by the inability of lawyers to define precisely what honour meant, by the very flexibility and multivalency of the concept.

There followed a discussion between the panel and the floor, chaired by Anthony Fletcher. The value of considering honour as an historical concept was debated. It was agreed that the difficulty of defining the concept, both in the past and for historians today, made its use problematic. Attention was drawn to the potential breadth of honour and its different meanings depending upon, for example, gender, class, occupation, religion and geographical location. The question of focusing on the individual or on communities of honour was also raised. The subtleties of the chronology of honour, and even the difficulty of creating any such chronology, were emphasised because of the above. Discussion dealt particularly with the issue of gender: it was suggested that historians have focused too much on the assumption that male honour is self-evident, whilst female dishonour has received more attention than female honour, with undue attention to chastity and sexual transgression. It was suggested that this focus on issues of sexuality detracted attention from other potentially important indexes of change over time, such as the acceptability of violence. One major concern of the discussion was that a focus on the codes of honour amongst the gentry and aristocracy ought to be balanced by consideration of the meanings of the concept of honour to lower social orders. Again, this concern emphasised the multiplicity of different and competing honour codes among different groups.

# THE ROYAL HISTORICAL SOCIETY
## REPORT OF COUNCIL, SESSION 1995–1996

THE Council of the Royal Historical Society has the honour to present the following report to the Anniversary Meeting.

1. Developments within the Society during the year
    a) A new Editorial Board for *Studies in History* was appointed composed of Professor Martin Daunton (chairman), Dr. Steven Gunn, Professor Colin Jones, Dr. Peter Mandler, Dr. Simon Walker and the Society's Treasurer and one of the Literary Directors. The chairman of the Board is *ex officio* a member of the Publications Committee, to which the Board reports. The Board has drawn up plans for a new series of *Studies in History* and is actively considering several proposals.
    b) The Library of the late Sir Geoffrey Elton was transferred on permanent loan to the Borthwick Institute of the University of York. A ceremony to mark the bequest is to be held at the Borthwick Institute in September 1996. The Society saluted the memory of Sir Geoffrey Elton by holding a conference, arranged by Dr. George Bernard and Dr. Felicity Heal, on 'The Eltonian Legacy' in March 1996.
    c) The Society continues to support the activities of young research historians, notably through its Postgraduate Research Support grants for research visits and attendance at conferences. The Society devotes up to 14 per cent of its annual income to these purposes. It believes that in so doing it makes a small, but significant, contribution to historical research at a time of exceptional pressure on public funds for such purposes. During the year it awarded a total sum of £13,321 to 60 students, 10 to attend short-term training courses, 18 for research visits within the United Kingdom, 18 for research visits outside the United Kingdom, 10 to assist the financing of small specialized conferences, and 4 to students already in receipt of an Overseas Research Scheme award.
    d) Cambridge University Press is now the publisher for most of the Society's publications, other than *Studies in History*. While sales figures to date have not met expectations, Council believes that it has now established a sound working relationship with the Press. A rolling programme of future publications – *Transactions, Camden Series* and *Guides and Handbooks* – shows that the Society's publication plans are in good heart. While the Society continues to adhere to its policy of publishing texts and guides of enduring value to historians, it is also mindful of the need to be alert to the general and commercial interest of its publications. Council welcomed the attractive appearance and high quality of two recent reprints of

much-used volumes in the *Camden Series*, viz. 'Political Songs' (new ed. P.R. Coss) and 'Stonor Letters' (new ed. Christine Carpenter).

e) The Society's Library is being consolidated and upgraded in conformity with the decisions regarding its future taken by Council in 1993–1994. Much of the Library's expenditure at present is earmarked for the conservation and preservation of the pre-1850 books.

f) The Society has continued to promote and defend the interests of historical study in Britain.

  – In January 1996 it held a successful one-day conference in the Institute of Historical Research to discuss taught postgraduate courses in British universities.

  – Council has been considering with History at the Universities Defence Group the issues raised by the recent sharp increase in postgraduate courses in history and by the Harris Report on the broader issues of postgraduate standards.

  – Representations have been made to various public bodies about issues of concern to historians, notably to the Economic and Social Research Council on Thematic Priorities.

g) The Society has renewed its funding for a Research Fellowship at the Institute of Historical Research. It has also continued to contribute to the Young Historian Scheme of the Historical Association and has provided prizes for outstanding A-level students.

2. Bibliographies

The Society has an exceptional record in the services it has provided for historical bibliographies in and of Britain for over seventy years. Even by this high standard 1995–1996 was an *annus mirabilis*.

a) During the year Professor Keith Robbins's massive *Bibliography of British History, 1914–1989* was published. The volume completes the remarkable series of one-volume bibliographies of British history published under the auspices of the Society since 1975.

b) The Bibliography of British and Irish History project under the general editorship of Dr. John Morrill drew to a conclusion this year. The Society wishes to place on record its deep indebtedness to Dr. Morrill, the members of the Editorial Board, the period editors, and the team of 120 scholars who have contributed to the completion of this venture. It also gives special thanks to the two full-time project assistants, Margaret Lantry and Peter Salt, who have undertaken the day-to-day work at Cambridge, and to the University of Cambridge for providing working space and equipment for the project.

It is hoped that the CD-Rom version of the Bibliography will be made available by Oxford University Press during 1997. Decisions regarding other formats of publication are under active consideration.

c) Work on the *Annual Bibliography of British History 1995* has been undertaken by Dr. Austin Gee under the general direction of Professor R.A. Griffiths and the Honorary Librarian. This project is funded directly by the

Society. The Institute of Historical Research provides invaluable assistance for the project.

d) The Society has decided to launch a new bibliographical project for the next five years. Its overall purpose will be to update and upgrade the Bibliography of British and Irish History (see b) above). The material currently published in the *Annual Bibliography* (see c) above) will henceforth be subsumed into this new project. An Editorial Board has been appointed by Council for this new project and it is hoped that the project will be fully operational from 1 January 1997.

e) The Society is very pleased to receive a munificent grant of $100,000 over five years from the Andrew W. Mellon Foundation, New York, towards the funding of this new bibliographical project.

3. Meetings of the Society

The Society held Council meetings, paper readings and receptions at the Universities of Edinburgh, Swansea and Leeds. All were well attended and as in previous years their success owed much to the excellent hospitality provided by the Universities' History Departments and local Fellows. The Society has arranged to meet at York during the 1996–1997 session.

Two two-day conferences, 'Britain and Europe since 1789' and 'The Eltonian Legacy' were held at the Institute of Historical Research, London, in September 1995 and March 1996. Arrangements are in hand to hold a further two-day conference at the University of York in September 1996.

A well-attended Annual Reception was held for members and guests in the Upper Hall at University College London on Wednesday 28 June 1995.

4. Prizes

a) The Whitfield Prize for 1995 was awarded to Dr. Kathleen Wilson for her book, *The Sense of the People: Politics, Culture and Imperialism in England, 1715–1785*, (Cambridge University Press). The judges commented on the high quality of the entries received.

b) The Alexander Prize for 1996 was not awarded.

5. Publications

Transactions, Sixth Series, Volume 5, was published during the session, and *Transactions, Sixth Series*, Volume 6, went to press, to be published in 1996.

*The Diaries of Edward Henry Stanley, 15th Earl of Derby, 1826–1893*, ed. John Vincent (Camden, Fifth Series Volume 4), *The Austen Chamberlain Diary Letters*, ed. Robert C. Self (Camden, Fifth Series, Volume 5) and *Household Accounts and Disbursement Books of Robert Dudley, Earl of Leicester, 1558–1561, 1584–1586*, ed. Simon Adams, (Camden, Fifth Series, Volume 6) were published during the session. *Seventeenth-Century Political and Financial Papers Miscellany XXXIII*, (Camden, Fifth Series, Volume 7) went to press during the session, to be published in 1996.

The Society's *Annual Bibliography of British and Irish History, Publications of 1994*, was published by Oxford University Press during the session, and the *Annual Bibliography of British and Irish History, Publications of 1995* went to press, to be published in 1996.

In the *Studies in History* series, Vivienne Larminie, *Wealth, Kinship and Culture: the Newdigates of Arbury* (Volume 72) and Richard Stewart, *The English Ordnance Office, 1585–1615: a case study in bureaucracy* (Volume 73) were published during the session. Lorna Lloyd, *Peace through Law* (Volume 74) went to press and is due to be published in the next session. A further four volumes went to press during the session, for publication to launch a new series in 1997.

6. Papers Read

At the ordinary meetings of the Society the following papers were read:

'An Airier Aristocracy: the Saints at War', by Professor Christopher Holdsworth (28 June 1995, Prothero lecture).
'William Cobbett: Patriot or Briton?' by Dr. John Stevenson (20 October 1995 at the University of Edinburgh).
'The Limits of Totalitarianism: God, State and Society in the GDR' by Professor Mary Fulbrook (26 January 1996).
'British Politeness and the Progress of Western Manners: An Eighteenth-Century Enigma' by Dr. Paul Langford (23 February 1996 at the University of Wales Swansea).
'History as Destiny: Gobineau, H.S. Chamberlain and Spengler' by Professor Michael Biddiss (26 April 1996).
'Constructing the Past in the Early Middle Ages' by Dr. Rosamond McKitterick (24 May 1996 at the University of Leeds).

At the Anniversary meeting on 24 November 1995, the President, Professor R.R. Davies, delivered an address on 'The Peoples of Britain and Ireland, 1100- 1400: III. Laws and Customs'.

At the two-day conference entitled 'Britain and Europe since 1789' held at the Institute of Historical Research, London, on 22–23 September 1995, the following papers were read:

'Britain as a European State – 1789–1815' by Professor J. Black.
'Britain as a European Ally, 1789–1815' by Professor M. Duffy.
'The British Industrial Revolution and the Industrialisation of Europe, 1763–1914' by Professor P.K. O'Brien.
'The British Sonderweg: the Peculiarities of British Free Trade, 1845–1880' by Dr. J. Davis.
'Variations in Liberalism: Britain and Europe in the mid-Nineteenth Century' by Professor J. Breuilly.
'Variations in Socialism: Britain and Europe in mid-Nineteenth Century' by Dr. C. Eisenberg.
'Reluctant Engagement: Britain and Continental Europe, 1890–1939' by Dr. P. Salmon.

'The Foreign Office and Europe in the First Half of the Twentieth Century' by Dr. E. Goldstein.
'Why Britain Rejected the Schuman Plan' by the Right Hon E. Dell.
'Britain and Europe, 1945–1957: the View from the Continent' by Professor C. Wurm.
'Above the glass ceiling: politics, personalities and the first British Application to the EEC, 1961–1963' by Dr. A. Deighton.
'Britain and Europe and the wider world, 1960–1963' by Professor A.S. Milward.
'Styles and Strategies of British MEPs' by Dr. C. Jackson.

At the two-day conference entitled 'The Eltonian Legacy' held at the Institute of Historical Research, London, on 27 and 28 March 1996, the following papers were read:

'The Eltonian State' by Mr. C.S.L. Davies.
'Public Finance', by Dr. R.W. Hoyle.
'The Parliament of England' by Dr. P. Croft.
'Cromwell's Doctrine of Parliamentary Sovereignty' by Professor the Earl Russell.
'Discussion of "The English"' by Professor J. Gillingham, Professor C. Richmond and Mr. P. Wormald.
'Politics' by Dr. S.L. Adams.
'The Law' by Dr. C.A. Holmes.
'Religion' by Dr. C.A. Haigh.
'The Practice of History' by Professor Q.R.D. Skinner.

7. Finance

The Review of the Society's activities held in 1993–4 made certain recommendations relating to the Society's finances. The principal of these were:

a) Cambridge University Press to take over our publications and to handle institutional subscriptions. This arrangements has been in place since early 1995. It has worked reasonably satisfactorily in the first year. It has not yet increased our profits from publications, but this was not to be expected in the first year

b) The Fellowship subscriptions to be raised to £28 per annum, with the option of opting out of receiving publications other than *Transactions*, for a subscription of £20 per annum plus the opportunity to buy publications at a reduced price. The great majority of Fellows have opted to continue to receive all publications.

c) The new category of Membership to be introduced, primarily for junior scholars. 45 new Members have been elected.

d) Provision of a rolling budget over 3–4 years. This will be attempted when our income from publications can be estimated more precisely. Due to the recent transfer to our publications to CUP and since we do not yet have clear estimates of costs for the coming year, this is not yet possible.

e) A Research Endowment Fund to be established. Council has now agreed terms of reference.

Income from investments, subscriptions and royalties continues to be satisfactory. The small overall deficit this year arose from the fact that we published one more *Camden* volume than in recent years. Publications continue to form the bulk of our expenditure.

## 8. Membership

Council records with regret the deaths of 17 Fellows, 1 Corresponding Fellow and 3 Associates. They included Professor H. Hearder and Professor J.P. Kenyon.

The resignations of 5 Fellows and 1 Associate were received. 99 Fellows, 30 Members and 12 Corresponding Fellows were elected. 21 Fellows transferred to the category of Retired Fellow. The membership of the Society on 30 June 1996 numbered 2259 (including 35 Life, 355 Retired, 49 Corresponding Fellows, and 131 Associates). It is interesting to note that the membership of the Society in 30 June 1990 stood at 1811.

The Society exchanged publications with 15 Societies, British and Foreign.

## 9. Officers and Council

At the Anniversary Meeting on 24 November 1995, the Officers of the Society were re-elected.

The Vice-Presidents retiring under By-law XVII were Professor O. Anderson and Professor H.T. Dickinson. Professor M.D. Biddiss and Dr. A.M.S. Prochaska were elected to replace them.

The members of Council retiring under By-law XX were Professor J.M. Black, Professor P.A. Clark, Professor D.M. Palliser and Dr. A.M.S. Prochaska. Following a ballot of Fellows, Professor D. Bates, Dr. A.E. Curry, Professor J.A. Guy and Professor R.I. Moore were elected in their place.

MacIntyre and Company were appointed auditors for the year 1995–1996 under By-law XXXIX.

## 10. Representatives of the Society

The representation of the Society upon various bodies was as follows:
Mr. M. Roper, Professor P.H. Sawyer and Mr. C.P. Wormald on the Joint Committee of the Society and the British Academy established to prepare an edition of Anglo-Saxon charters;
Professor H.R. Loyn on a committee to promote the publication of photographic records of the more significant collections of British Coins;
Professor G.H. Martin on the Council of the British Records Association;
Emeritus Professor M.R.D. Foot on the Committee to advise the publishers of *The Annual Register*;
Dr. G.W. Bernard on the History at the Universities Defence Group;
Professor C.J. Holdsworth on the Court of the University of Exeter;

Professor A.G. Watson on the Anthony Panizzi Foundation;

Professor M.C. Cross on the Council of the British Association for Local History; and on the British Sub-Commission of the Commission International d'Histoire Ecclesiastique Comparee;

Professor J. Sayers on the National Council on Archives;

Miss V. Cromwell on the Advisory Board of the Computers in Teaching Initiative Centre for History; and on the Advisory Committee of the TLTP History Courseware Consortium;

Dr. A.M.S. Prochaska on the Advisory Council of the reviewing committee on the Export of Works of Art;

Professor R.A. Griffiths on the Court of Governors of the University of Wales Swansea;

Professor A.L. Brown on the University of Stirling Conference;

Professor W. Davies on the Court of the University of Birmingham;

Dr. R.D. McKitterick on a committee to regulate British co-operation in the preparation of a new repertory of medieval sources to replace Potthast's *Bibliotheca Historica Medii Aevi*; and

Professor P.K. O'Brien on the ESRC Working Group on *Quality and Data Collection*.

Council received reports from its representatives.

During the year, Professor J. Breuilly agreed to represent the Society on the steering committee of the proposed British Centre for Historical Research in Germany; Dr. A.M.S. Prochaska agreed to succeed Professor J. Sayers on the National Council on Archives; and Dr. S.R.B. Smith agreed to succeed Professor P.K. O'Brien on the ESRC Working Group on *Quality and Data Collection*.

26 September 1996

# THE ROYAL HISTORICAL SOCIETY

Trustees' Report for the Year Ended 30 June 1996

## STATEMENT OF TRUSTEES' RESPONSIBILITIES

The Council is required to prepare financial statements for each financial year which give a true and fair view of the state of affairs of the Society and of the surplus or deficit of the Society for that period. In preparing those financial statements, the trustees are required to:

- select suitable accounting policies and then apply them consistently;
- make judgements and estimates that are reasonable and prudent;
- state whether applicable accounting standards have been followed, subject to any material departures disclosed and explained in the financial statements;
- prepare the financial statements on the going concern basis unless it is inappropriate to presume that the society will continue in business.

The Council is responsible for keeping proper accounting records which disclose with reasonable accuracy at any time the financial position of the society. They are also responsible for safeguarding the assets of the society and hence for taking reasonable steps for the prevention and detection of fraud and other irregularities.

By Order of the Council
Honorary Secretary

## AUDITORS REPORT

## TO THE MEMBERS OF ROYAL HISTORICAL SOCIETY

We have audited the financial statements on pages 257 to 262 which have been prepared under the historical cost convention and the accounting policies set out on page 260.

### RESPECTIVE RESPONSIBILITIES OF THE COUNCIL AND AUDITORS
As described on page 8 the company's trustees are responsible for the preparation of financial statements. It is our responsibility to form an independent opinion, based on our audit, on those statements and to report our opinion to you.

### BASIS OF OPINION
We conducted our audit in accordance with Auditing Standards issued by the Auditing Practices Board. An audit includes examination, on a test basis, of evidence relevant to the amounts and disclosures in the financial statements. It also includes an assessment of the significant estimates and judgements made by the council in the preparation of the financial statements, and of whether the accounting policies are appropriate to the society's circumstances, consistently applied and adequately disclosed.

We planned and performed our audit so as to obtain all the information and explanations which we considered necessary in order to provide us with sufficient evidence to give reasonable assurance that the financial statements are free from material misstatement, whether caused by fraud or other irregularity or error. In forming our opinion we also evaluated the overall adequacy of the presentation of information in the financial statements.

### OPINION
In our opinion the financial statements give a true and fair view of the state of the Society's affairs as at 30 June 1996 and of its result for the year then ended.

MacIntyre & Co
Chartered Accountants
Registered Auditors

London

# THE ROYAL HISTORICAL SOCIETY

## BALANCE SHEET AS AT 30TH JUNE 1996

| | Note | 1996 £ | 1996 £ | 1995 £ | 1995 £ |
|---|---|---|---|---|---|
| **FIXED ASSETS** | | | | | |
| Tangible assets | 2 | | 504 | | *1,628* |
| Investments | 3 | | 1,884,318 | | *1,753,227* |
| | | | 1,884,822 | | *1,754,855* |
| **CURRENT ASSETS** | | | | | |
| Stocks | 1(c) | 5,264 | | *6,619* | |
| Debtors | 4 | 11,519 | | *12,626* | |
| Cash at bank and in hand | 5 | 12,814 | | *16,377* | |
| | | 29,597 | | *35,622* | |
| **LESS: CREDITORS** | | | | | |
| Amount due within one year | 6 | (42,072) | | *(37,164)* | |
| NET CURRENT (LIABILITIES) | | | (12,475) | | *(1,542)* |
| NET ASSETS | | | 1,872,347 | | *1,753,313* |
| **REPRESENTED BY:** | | | | | |
| General Fund | | | 1,767,543 | | *1,654,586* |
| E.M. Robinson Bequest | | | 73,250 | | *66,107* |
| A.S. Whitfield Prize Fund | | | 36,446 | | *34,790* |
| *Studies in History* | | | (4,892) | | *(2,170)* |
| | | | 1,872,347 | | *1,753,313* |

President: R.R. DAVIES
Honorary Treasurer: P.M. THANE

The attached notes form an integral part of these financial statements.

## INCOME AND EXPENDITURE ACCOUNT FOR THE YEAR ENDED 30TH JUNE 1996

### GENERAL FUND

| | Note | 1996 £ | 1996 £ | 1995 £ | 1995 £ |
|---|---|---|---|---|---|
| **INCOME** | | | | | |
| Subscription | 7 | | 61,373 | | *57,942* |
| Investment income | | | 76,386 | | *80,698* |
| Royalties and reproduction fees | | 14,782 | | *7,160* | |
| Commission | | (4,787) | | *—* | |
| | | | 9,995 | | *7,160* |
| Donations and sundry income | | | 3,878 | | *2,594* |
| G.R. Elton Bequest | | | 4,111 | | *4,718* |
| Sales of library volumes | | | — | | *20,575* |
| | | | 155,743 | | *173,687* |

257

# GENERAL FUND

| EXPENDITURE | Note | 1996 £ | £ | 1995 £ | £ |
|---|---|---|---|---|---|
| SECRETARIAL AND ADMINISTRATIVE | | | | | |
| Salaries, pensions and social security | | 26,541 | | 25,213 | |
| Computer consumables, printing and stationery | | 6,172 | | 5,901 | |
| Postage and telephone | | 1,635 | | 1,906 | |
| Bank charges | | 1,190 | | 2,006 | |
| Audit and accountancy | | 3,126 | | 2,681 | |
| Insurance | | 933 | | 773 | |
| Meetings and travel | | 10,744 | | 13,148 | |
| Conference net costs | | 2,043 | | 1,910 | |
| Repairs and renewals | | 875 | | 320 | |
| Depreciation | 1(b) | 1,124 | | 1,389 | |
| Circulation costs | | 4,257 | | — | |
| | | | 58,640 | | 55,247 |
| PUBLICATIONS | | | | | |
| Publishing costs | 8(a) | 79,837 | | 9,448 | |
| Provision for publications in progress | 8(b) | 3,000 | | 20,350 | |
| Other publications | 8(c) | 9,191 | | 11,411 | |
| | | | 92,028 | | 41,209 |
| LIBRARY AND ARCHIVES | 1(d) | | | | |
| Purchase of books and publications | | 2,349 | | 2,363 | |
| Binding | | 5,288 | | 5,822 | |
| | | | 7,637 | | 8,185 |
| OTHER CHARGES | | | | | |
| Centenary fellowship | | 4,908 | | 5,775 | |
| Alexander prize and expenses | | 163 | | 340 | |
| Prothero lecture | | 274 | | 250 | |
| Grants | | 114 | | 900 | |
| Research support grants | | 13,321 | | 13,605 | |
| Donations and sundry expenses | | 768 | | 263 | |
| A-level prizes | | 900 | | 900 | |
| Young Historian Scheme | | 2,500 | | 2,000 | |
| | | | 22,948 | | 24,033 |
| | | | 181,253 | | 128,674 |
| (Deficit)/Surplus for the year | | | (25,510) | | 45,013 |
| Realised (deficit)/surplus on sale of investments | | | (11,238) | | 76,679 |
| Transfer to revaluation reserve | | | 149,705 | | 30,988 |
| Retained surplus for the year | | | 112,957 | | 152,680 |
| Balance brought forward at 1.7.95 | | | 1,654,586 | | 1,501,906 |
| Balance carried forward at 30.6.96 | | | 1,767,543 | | 1,654,586 |

## NOTE OF HISTORICAL COST SURPLUS AND DEFICIT

| | 1996 £ |
|---|---|
| Reported surplus for the year | 112,957 |
| Difference between reported deficit on disposal of fixed asset investments and surplus calculated on a historical cost basis | 24,983 |
| Historical cost surplus for the year | 137,940 |

# THE ROYAL HISTORICAL SOCIETY

## INCOME AND EXPENDITURE ACCOUNT FOR THE YEAR ENDED 30TH JUNE 1996

### SPECIAL FUNDS

|  | 1996 £ | 1996 £ | 1995 £ | 1995 £ |
|---|---|---|---|---|
| **E.M. ROBINSON BEQUEST** | | | | |
| INCOME | | | | |
| Investment income . . . . . . . | | 2,976 | | 2,743 |
| EXPENDITURE | | | | |
| Grant to Dulwich Picture Gallery . . . . | — | | 2,000 | |
| | | — | | (2,000) |
| Surplus for the year . . . . . . . | | 2,976 | | 743 |
| Realised surplus on disposal of investments . . | | — | | 6,111 |
| Transfer from/(to) revaluation reserve . . | | 4,167 | | (1,305) |
| | | 7,143 | | 5,549 |
| Balance brought forward at 1 July 1995 . . . | | 66,107 | | 60,558 |
| Balance carried forward at 30 June 1996 . . . | | 73,250 | | 66,107 |

The fund has no recognised gains or losses apart from the results for the above financial periods.

| | | | | |
|---|---|---|---|---|
| **A.S. WHITFIELD PRIZE FUND** | | | | |
| INCOME | | | | |
| Investment income . . . . . . . | | 1,247 | | 1,383 |
| EXPENDITURE | | | | |
| Prize awarded . . . . . . . . | 1,000 | | 1,000 | |
| Other expenses . . . . . . . . | 164 | | 20 | |
| | | 1,164 | | 1,020 |
| Surplus for the year . . . . . . . | | 83 | | 363 |
| Realised surplus on disposal of investments . . | | — | | 3,634 |
| Transfer from/(to) revaluation reserve . . | | 1,573 | | (1,142) |
| | | 1,656 | | 2,855 |
| Balance brought forward at 1 July 1995 . . . | | 34,790 | | 31,935 |
| Balance carried forward at 30 June 1996 . . . | | 36,446 | | 34,790 |

The fund has no recognised gains or losses apart from the above financial periods.

| | | | | |
|---|---|---|---|---|
| **STUDIES IN HISTORY** | | | | |
| INCOME | | | | |
| Royalties . . . . . . . . | | 1,694 | | 1,125 |
| Investment income . . . . . . | | 516 | | 426 |
| | | 2,210 | | 1,551 |
| EXPENDITURE | | | | |
| Executive editor's honorarium . . . . . | 3,500 | | 3,500 | |
| Executive editor's expenses . . . . . | 1,031 | | 960 | |
| Sundry expenses . . . . . . . | 401 | | 38 | |
| | | (4,932) | | (4,498) |
| (Deficit) for the year . . . . . . | | (2,722) | | (2,947) |
| Balance brought forward . . . . . | | (2,170) | | 777 |
| Balance carried forward . . . . . | | (4,892) | | (2,170) |

The fund has no recognised gains or losses apart from the results for the above financial periods.

# THE ROYAL HISTORICAL SOCIETY

## Notes to the Accounts for the Year Ended 30th June 1996

1. ACCOUNTING POLICIES

   (a) *Basis of accounting*

   The accounts have been prepared under the historical cost convention as modified by the revaluation of quoted investments to market value.

   (b) *Depreciation*

   Depreciation is calculated by reference to the cost of fixed assets using a straight line basis at rates considered appropriate having regard to the expected lives of the fixed assets.
   The annual rates of depreciation in use are:

   | | |
   |---|---|
   | Furniture and equipment | 10% |
   | Computer equipment | 25% |

   Prior to 1st July 1987 the full cost of fixed assets was written off to General Fund in the year of purchase.

   (c) *Stocks*

   Stock is valued at the lower of cost and net realisable value.

   (d) *Library and archives*

   The cost of additions to the library and archives is written off in the year of purchase.

   (e) Income is recognised on a received basis except for subscriptions received in advance.

2. TANGIBLE FIXED ASSETS

| | Computer Equipment | Furniture and Equipment | Total |
|---|---|---|---|
| | £ | £ | £ |
| *Cost* | | | |
| At 1st July 1995 and 30 June 1996 . . | 10,215 | 1,173 | 11,388 |
| *Depreciation* | | | |
| At 1st July 1995 . . . . . | 9,208 | 552 | 9,760 |
| Charge for the year . . . . | 1,007 | 117 | 1,124 |
| At 30th June 1996 . . . . . | 10,215 | 669 | 10,884 |
| *Net book value* | | | |
| At 30th June 1996 . . . . . | — | 504 | 504 |
| At 30th June 1995 . . . . . | 1,007 | 621 | 1,628 |

Prior to 1st July 1987 the cost of furniture and equipment was written off in the year of purchase. Items acquired before that date are not reflected in the above figures.

3. INVESTMENTS

| | 1996 | 1995 |
|---|---|---|
| | £ | £ |
| Quoted Securities, at cost . . . . . . . . . | 978,859 | 1,027,035 |
| Surplus on revaluation . . . . . . . . . . | 793,310 | 661,358 |
| Quoted Securities at market value . . . . . . . | 1,722,169 | 1,688,393 |
| Money invested at call . . . . . . . . . . | 112,149 | 64,834 |
| | 1,884,318 | 1,753,227 |

Quoted Investments are stated at market value in the Balance Sheet as at 30th June 1996.
The surplus arising on re-valuation plus profits (less losses) realised on disposals of investments is credited to Income and Expenditure Account in the case of investments held on General Fund and to the relevant fund accounts where investments are held for specific funds.
Movements in quoted investments during year were:

| | £ |
|---|---|
| Cost at beginning of year . . . . . . . . . . . . . | 1,027,035 |
| Additions during year . . . . . . . . . . . . . | 165,337 |
| Disposals during year . . . . . . . . . . . . . | (213,513) |
| Cost at end of year . . . . . . . . . . . . . | 978,859 |

| Investment by fund at market value were: | 1996 | 1995 |
|---|---|---|
| | £ | £ |
| General Fund | 1,760,206 | 1,638,099 |
| A.S. Whitfield Fund | 37,098 | 34,681 |
| E.M. Robinson Bequest Fund | 78,514 | 71,947 |
| *Studies in History* | 8,500 | 8,500 |
| | 1,884,318 | 1,753,227 |

## 4. DEBTORS

| | 1996 | 1995 |
|---|---|---|
| | £ | £ |
| Sundry debtors | 8,300 | 9,407 |
| Prepayments | 3,219 | 3,219 |
| | 11,519 | 12,626 |

## 5. CASH AT BANK AND IN HAND

| | 1996 | 1995 |
|---|---|---|
| | £ | £ |
| Deposit accounts | 12,507 | 10,158 |
| Current accounts | 307 | 6,219 |
| | 12,814 | 16,377 |

## 6. CREDITORS

| | 1996 | 1995 |
|---|---|---|
| | £ | £ |
| Sundry creditors | 1,000 | 1,000 |
| Subscriptions received in advance | 1,758 | 2,396 |
| Accruals | 6,692 | 13,418 |
| Provision for publications in progress | 3,000 | 20,350 |
| Cambridge University Press | 29,622 | — |
| | 42,072 | 37,164 |

## 7. SUBSCRIPTIONS

| | 1996 | 1995 |
|---|---|---|
| | £ | £ |
| Subscriptions | 46,632 | 55,690 |
| Income tax on covenants | 2,456 | 2,252 |
| Library subscriptions | 17,550 | |
| Less: Commission paid to Cambridge University Press | (5,265) | |
| | 61,373 | 57,942 |

## 8A. PUBLICATIONS

| | Transactions Sixth Series Volume 5 | Camden Fifth Series Volume 4 | Camden Fifth Series Volume 5 | Camden Fifth Series Volume 6 | Guides and Handbooks Reprint Costs | Total |
|---|---|---|---|---|---|---|
| Cambridge University Press. Costs | £ | £ | £ | £ | £ | £ |
| Printing | 10,418 | — | 15,889 | 20,225 | — | 46,532 |
| Off prints | 1,023 | — | — | — | — | 1,023 |
| Reprints | — | — | — | — | 7,191 | 7,191 |
| Carriage | 382 | — | 635 | 768 | — | 1,785 |
| Airfreight | 66 | — | 139 | 91 | — | 296 |
| Society's costs | 3,114 | 24,411 | 3,058 | 3,017 | — | 33,600 |
| | 15,003 | 24,411 | 19,721 | 24,101 | 7,191 | 90,427 |
| Closing stock | (830) | — | (2,292) | (2,142) | — | (5,264) |
| Less: Provision brought forward | | | | | | (20,350) |
| Paper | | | | | | 15,024 |
| | | | | | | 79,837 |

|  |  | 1996 £ | 1995 £ |
|---|---|---|---|
| B. | Provisions for publications in progress | | |
| | *Camden, Fifth Series, Vol. 4* | — | *16,850* |
| | *List of Fellows* | 3,000 | *3,500* |
| | | 3,000 | *20,350* |
| C. | Other publication costs | | |
| | *Annual Bibliography* | 10,543 | *12,444* |
| | Less: royalties received | (1,352) | *(1,033)* |
| | | 9,191 | *11,411* |

|  |  | 1996 £ | 1995 £ |
|---|---|---|---|
| 9. | OPERATING LEASE COMMITMENTS | | |
| | On leases due to expire between one and five years | 3,523 | *3,523* |

|  |  | 1996 £ | 1995 £ |
|---|---|---|---|
| 10. | MOVEMENTS IN TRUSTEES FUNDS | | |
| | Retained surplus for the year | 112,957 | *152,680* |
| | Opening Trustees funds | 1,654,586 | *1,501,906* |
| | Closing Trustees funds | 1,767,543 | *1,654,586* |

# ROYAL HISTORICAL SOCIETY
# THE DAVID BERRY ESSAY TRUST

## BALANCE SHEET AS AT 30TH JUNE 1996

|  | 1996 £ | 1996 £ | 1995 £ | 1995 £ |
|---|---|---|---|---|
| **FIXED ASSETS** | | | | |
| 1117.63 units in the Charities Official Investment Fund | | | | |
| (Market Value £7,483.1994 £7,298) . . . . | | 1,530 | | 1,530 |
| **CURRENT ASSETS** | | | | |
| Bank Deposit Account . . . . . | 11,186 | | 10,500 | |
| **LESS: CREDITORS** | | | | |
| Amounts falling due within one year . . . . | 4,126 | | 4,126 | |
| NET CURRENT ASSETS . . . . . . . | | 7,060 | | 6,374 |
| TOTAL ASSETS LESS LIABILITIES . . . . . . | | 8,590 | | 7,904 |
| | | | | |
| Represented by: | | | | |
| Capital Fund . . . . . . . . | | 1,000 | | 1,000 |
| Income and expenditure reserve . . . . | | 7,590 | | 6,904 |
| | | 8,590 | | 7,904 |

## INCOME AND EXPENDITURE ACCOUNT FOR THE YEAR ENDED 30TH JUNE 1996

|  | 1996 £ | 1996 £ | 1995 £ | 1995 £ |
|---|---|---|---|---|
| **INCOME** | | | | |
| Dividends . . . . . . . . | | 366 | | 263 |
| Bank Interest Receivable . . . . . | | 320 | | 280 |
| | | 686 | | 543 |
| **EXPENDITURE** . . . . . . . . | | | | |
| Adjudicator's Fee . . . . . . . | | — | | 50 |
| Excess of income over expenditure for the year . | | 686 | | 493 |
| Balance brought forward . . . . . | | 6,904 | | 6,411 |
| Balance carried forward . . . . . | | 7,590 | | 6,904 |

The fund has no recognised gains or losses apart from the results for the above financial periods.

1. ACCOUNTING POLICIES
Basis of accounting. The accounts have been prepared under the historical cost convention.
The late David Berry, by his Will dated 23rd April 1926, left £1,000 to provide in every three years a gold medal and prize money for the best essay on the Earl of Bothwell or, at the discretion of the Trustees, on Scottish History of the James Stuarts I to VI, in memory of his father the late Rev. David Berry.
The Trust is regulated by a scheme sanctioned by the Chancery Division of the High Court of Justice dated 23rd January 1930, and made in action 1927 A 1233 David Anderson Berry deceased, Hunter and Another v. Robertson and Another and since modified by an order of the Charity Commissioners made on 11 January 1978 removing the necessity to provide a medal.
The Royal Historical Society is now the Trustee. The investment consists of 1117.63 Charities Official Investment Fund Income units. The Trustee will in every second year of the three year period advertise inviting essays.

REPORT OF THE AUDITORS TO THE TRUSTEES OF THE DAVID BERRY ESSAY TRUST

We have audited the accounts on page 263 which have been prepared under the historical cost convention and the accounting policies set out (above).

*Respective responsibilities of the Council and Auditors*
The Trustees are required to prepare accounts for each financial year which give a true and fair view of the state of affairs of the Trust and of the profit or loss for that period.
In preparing those accounts, the Trustees are required to:
—select suitable accounting policies and then apply them consistently;
—make judgements and estimates that are reasonable and prudent;
—prepare the accounts on the going concern basis unless it is inappropriate to presume that the Trust will continue in business.
The Trustees are responsible for keeping proper accounting records which disclose with reasonable accuracy at any time the financial position of the Trust. They are also responsible for safeguarding the assets of the Trust and hence for taking reasonable steps for the prevention and detection of fraud and other irregularities.
As described above the Trustees are responsible for the preparation of accounts. It is our responsibility to form an independent opinion, based on our audit, on those accounts and to report our opinion to you.

*Basis of opinion*
We conducted our audit in accordance with Auditing Standards issued by the Auditing Practices Board. An audit includes examination, on a test basis, of evidence relevant to the amounts and disclosures in the accounts. It also includes an assessment of the significant estimates and judgements made by the Trustees in the preparation of the accounts, and of whether the accounting policies are appropriate to the Trust's circumstances, consistently applied and adequately disclosed.
We planned and performed our audit so as to obtain all the information and explanations which we considered necessary in order to provide us with sufficient evidence to give reasonable assurance that the accounts are free from material misstatement, whether caused by fraud or other irregularity or error. In forming our opinion we also evaluated the overall adequacy of the presentation of information in the accounts.

*Opinion*
In our opinion the accounts give a true and fair view of the state of the Trust's affairs as at 30th June 1996 and of its surplus for the year then ended.

MACINTYRE & CO
*Chartered Accountants*
*Registered Auditors*
London

264

# ALEXANDER PRIZE

The Alexander Prize was established in 1897 by L.C. Alexander, F.R.Hist.S. The Alexander Prize is offered annually for a paper based on original historical research. The winner of the prize is awarded £250. The prize provides an opportunity for historians to gain both national recognition and guaranteed publication of their work. Candidates must *either* be under the age of 35 *or* be registered for a higher degree *or* have been registered for such a degree within the last three years. The paper will be read to a meeting of the Royal Historical Society and will then be published in the Society's *Transactions*. The paper—which must not exceed 8,000 words including footnotes—can relate to any historical subject approved by a Literary Director of the Society. The paper may be derived from a doctoral thesis (either in progress or completed), but it should be self-contained and suitable for reading as a lecture. The closing date for submission is 1st November. Entry forms are available from the Executive Secretary.

## 1996 PRIZE

No award was made this year.

## DAVID BERRY PRIZE

The David Berry Prize was established in 1929 by David Anderson-Berry in memory of his father, the Reverend David Berry. The prize is awarded every three years for an essay on Scottish history, within the reigns of James I to James VI inclusive. The subject of each essay must be submitted in advance and approved by the Council of The Royal Historical Society. The essay must be a genuine work of research based on original material. The essay should be between 6,000 and 10,000 words excluding footnotes and appendices. The next competition will be held in 1997. Further details may be obtained from the Executive Secretary.

# WHITFIELD PRIZE

The Whitfield Prize was established by Council in 1976 out of the bequest of the late Professor Archibald Stenton Whitfield. The prize is currently awarded to the best work on a subject of British history published in the United Kingdom during the calendar year. It must be the first solely authored history book published by the candidate and an original and scholarly work of research. Authors or publishers should send three copies (non-returnable) of a book eligible for the competition to the Executive Secretary before the end of the year in which the book is published. The award will be made by Council and announced at the Society's annual reception in the following July. The current value of the prize is £1,000.

## 1995 PRIZE WINNER

Associate Professor Kathleen Wilson, BA, MA, MPhil, PhD
'The Sense of the People:
Politics, Culture and Imperialism in England, 1715–1785'

This study examines how constructions of 'the people,' the empire and the political subject became central, if contentious, issues in the politics and culture of eighteenth-century English cities between the Hanoverian Succession and the American war. Drawing upon a rich range of sources and both literary and historical perspectives, it argues that the ideologies and practices of extra-parliamentary politics in provincial towns and London attuned ordinary men and women to the implications of state power and imperial expansion, enabling a variety of groups to claim a stake in national affairs. They also defined relations between the state and the citizen in terms of gender, class and racial difference. The 'sense of the people' thus constructed both a rational, libertarian political public to which the state was held to be accountable, and exclusionary conceptions of political subjectivity that would shape notions of the national identity into the next century.

# THE ROYAL HISTORICAL SOCIETY

(INCORPORATED BY ROYAL CHARTER)

*Patron*
HER MAJESTY THE QUEEN

## OFFICERS AND COUNCIL

DECEMBER 1995–NOVEMBER 1996

*President*
Professor R.R. DAVIES, CBE, DPhil, FBA

*President elect*
Professor P.J. Marshall, MA, DPhil, FBA

*Honorary Secretary*
R.E. Quinault, MA, DPhil

*Literary Directors*
Professor M.C.E. Jones, MA, DPhil, DLitt, FSA
Professor D.S. Eastwood, MA, DPhil

*Honorary Treasurer*
Professor P.M. Thane, MA, PhD

*Honorary Librarian*
D.A.L. Morgan, MA, FSA

*Vice-Presidents*
Professor R.A. Griffiths, PhD, DLitt
J.S. Morrill, MA, DPhil, FBA
V. Cromwell, MA
Professor H.C.G. Matthew, MA, DPhil, FBA
Professor P. Collinson, MA, PhD, DLitt, DUniv, FBA, FAHA
R.D. McKitterick, MA, PhD, LittD
Professor M.D. Biddiss, MA, PhD
A.M.S. Prochaska, MA, DPhil

268    TRANSACTIONS OF THE ROYAL HISTORICAL SOCIETY

*Council*

G.W. Bernard, MA, DPhil
Professor K. Burk, MA, DPhil
Professor A.J. Fletcher, MA
F. Heal, MA, PhD
Professor P.R. Coss, PhD, FSA
Professor L.J. Jordanova, MA, PhD
Professor F. O'Gorman, PhD
J.R. Studd, PhD
Professor R.C. Bridges, PhD
Professor P.J. Corfield, MA, PhD
Professor J.L. Nelson, PhD
Professor P.A. Stafford, DPhil
Professor D. Bates, PhD
A.E. Curry, MA, PhD
Professor J.A. Guy, MA, PhD
Professor R.I. Moore, MA

*Honorary Vice-Presidents*

G.E. Aylmer, MA, DPhil, FBA
Professor J.H. Burns, MA, PhD, FBA
Professor A.G. Dickens, CMG, MA, DLit, DLitt, LittD, FBA, FSA
Professor P. Grierson, MA, LittD, FBA, FSA
Sir John Habakkuk, MA DLitt, FBA
Sir James Holt, MA, DPhil, DLitt, DLitt, FBA, FSA
Professor R.A. Humphreys, OBE, MA, PhD, DLitt, LittD, DLitt, DUniv
Miss K. Major, MA, BLitt, LittD, FBA, FSA
Professor D.B. Quinn, MA, PhD, DLit, DLitt, DLitt, DLitt, LLD, MRIA,
    DHL, Hon FBA
The Hon. Sir Steven Runciman, CH, MA, DPhil, LLD, LittD, DLitt, LitD,
    DD, DHL, FBA, FSA
Sir Richard Southern, MA, DLitt, LittD, DLitt, FBA
Professor F.M.L. Thompson, CBA, MA, DPhil, FBA

*Honorary Legal Adviser*
Professor D. Sugarman, LlB, LlM, LlM, SJD

*Executive Secretary*
Mrs J.N. McCarthy

*Library and Offices*
University College London, Gower Street,
London WCiE 6BT

*Bankers*
Barclays Bank PLC

STANDING COMMITTEES 1996

*Finance Committee*

PROFESSOR K. BURK
P.J.C. FIRTH, MA
PROFESSOR R.A. GRIFFITHS
PROFESSOR L. JORDANOVA
PROFESSOR P. MATHIAS, CBE, MA, DLitt, FBA
PROFESSOR R.I. MOORE
DR. A.M.S. PROCHASKA
And the Officers

*Publications Committee*

PROFESSOR D. BATES
DR. F. HEAL
PROFESSOR H.C.G. MATTHEW
DR. J.S. MORRILL
PROFESSOR P.A. STAFFORD
*Studies in History* Board Convenor
And the Officers

*Research Support Committee*

MISS V. CROMWELL (CHAIRMAN)
DR. G.W. BERNARD
PROFESSOR K. BURK
PROFESSOR P.J. CORFIELD
DR. A.E. CURRY
DR. J.R. STUDD
And the Officers

*Membership Committee*

PROFESSOR M.D. BIDDISS
PROFESSOR R.C. BRIDGES
MISS V. CROMWELL
PROFESSOR A.J. FLETCHER
PROFESSOR J.L. NELSON
PROFESSOR F. O'GORMAN
And the Officers

*General Purposes Committee*

PROFESSOR M.D. BIDDISS
PROFESSOR P. COSS
PROFESSOR P. COLLINSON
PROFESSOR J.A. GUY
DR. R.D. McKITTERICK
And the Officers

*Studies in History Editorial Board*

PROFESSOR M.J. DAUNTON, PhD (Convenor)
S.J. GUNN, MA, DPhil
PROFESSOR C.D.H. JONES, DPhil
P. MANDLER, MA, PhD
S.K. WALKER, MA, DPhil
A Literary Director
The Honorary Treasurer